Comprehensive Literacy for All

Comprehensive Literacy for All

Teaching Students With Significant Disabilities to Read and Write

by

Karen A. Erickson, Ph.D.
Center for Literacy and Disability Studies
Department of Allied Health Sciences
University of North Carolina at Chapel Hill

and

David A. Koppenhaver, Ph.D.
Department of Reading Education and Special Education
Appalachian State University
Boone, North Carolina

·P·A·U·L·H·
BROOKES
PUBLISHING CO. ®

Baltimore • London • Sydney

Paul H. Brookes Publishing Co.
Post Office Box 10624
Baltimore, Maryland 21285-0624
USA
www.brookespublishing.com

Typeset by Absolute Service, Inc., Baltimore, Maryland.
Manufactured in the United States of America by Sheridan Books, Inc., Chelsea, Michigan.

The individuals described in this book are composites or real people whose situations are masked and are based on the authors' experiences. In all instances, names and identifying details have been changed to protect confidentiality.

Library of Congress Cataloging-in-Publication Data

Names: Erickson, Karen A., author. | Koppenhaver, David, 1956- author.
Title: Comprehensive literacy for all : teaching students with significant
  disabilities to read and write / by Karen Erickson, Ph.D., Department of
  Allied Health Sciences, University of North Carolina at Chapel Hill and
  David A. Koppenhaver, Ph.D., Department of Reading Education and Special
  Education, Appalachian State University, Boone, North Carolina.
Description: Baltimore, Maryland : Paul H. Brookes Publishing Co., [2019] |
  Includes bibliographical references and index.
Identifiers: LCCN 2019026326 (print) | LCCN 2019026327 (ebook) | ISBN
  9781598576573 (paperback) | ISBN 9781681253732 (epub) | ISBN
  9781681253749 (pdf)
Subjects: LCSH: Learning disabled children—Education. | Reading—Remedial
  teaching. | English language—Composition and exercises—Study and
  teaching (Elementary) | Literacy—Study and teaching.
Classification: LCC LC4704 .E75 2020 (print) | LCC LC4704 (ebook) | DDC
  371.91/44—dc23
LC record available at https://lccn.loc.gov/2019026326
LC ebook record available at https://lccn.loc.gov/2019026327

British Library Cataloguing in Publication data are available from the British Library.

2023   2022   2021

10   9   8   7   6   5   4

Table of Contents

About the Downloads vii
About the Authors ix
Foreword   *David E. Yoder* xi
Acknowledgments xiii
Introduction xv

Section I   **Core Understandings**
Chapter 1   All Children Can Learn to Read and Write:
                A Theoretical Rationale 3
Chapter 2   Establishing the Environment for
                Successful Literacy Learning 15

Section II   **Building a Foundation for Literacy**
Chapter 3   Alphabet Knowledge and
                Phonological Awareness 33
Chapter 4   Emergent Reading 49
Chapter 5   Emergent Writing 63

Section III   **Learning to Read and Write**
Chapter 6   Comprehensive Literacy Instruction:
                A Research-Based Framework 87
Chapter 7   Reading Comprehension and
                Vocabulary Instruction 99
Chapter 8   Self-Directed Reading:
                Supporting Motivation and Fluency 119
Chapter 9   Writing 141
Chapter 10   Decoding, Word Identification,
                and Spelling 163

Section IV   **Implementation**
Chapter 11   Using Assistive Technology
                Effectively to Support Literacy 185
Chapter 12   Organizing and Delivering
                Effective Instruction 199

References 213
Index 237

About the Downloads

Purchasers of this book may download, print, and/or photocopy sample lesson outlines for educational use. These materials appear in the print book and are also available at http://downloads.brookespublishing.com for both print and e-book buyers. To access the materials that come with the book

1. Go to the Brookes Publishing Download Hub: http://downloads.brookespublishing .com

2. Register to create an account (or log in with an existing account)

3. Filter or search for your book title

About the Authors

Karen A. Erickson, Ph.D., David E. and Dolores J. "Dee" Yoder Distinguished Professor of Literacy and Disabilities and Director, Center for Literacy and Disability Studies, Department of Allied Health Sciences, University of North Carolina at Chapel Hill

Karen Erickson is Director of the Center for Literacy and Disability Studies, Professor in the Division of Speech and Hearing Sciences, and the Yoder Distinguished Professor in the Department of Allied Health Sciences at the University of North Carolina at Chapel Hill. She is a former classroom teacher whose research addresses literacy and communication intervention and assessment for students with significant disabilities.

David A. Koppenhaver, Ph.D., Professor, Department of Reading Education and Special Education, Appalachian State University, Boone, North Carolina

David Koppenhaver is a professor in the Department of Reading Education and Special Education at Appalachian State University and the cofounder with David Yoder of the Center for Literacy and Disability Studies at the University of North Carolina at Chapel Hill. He is a former language arts teacher whose research addresses literacy learning and instruction of individuals with significant disabilities.

Foreword

Thirty years ago, I would ask graduate students and workshop participants consisting of speech-language clinicians and teachers of children with significant disabilities (primarily children for whom speech was not a major means of communication), "How many of you believe the persons for whom you are providing services can learn to read and write?" Reluctantly, about 20%–30% would raise their hands, and I had the feeling the majority of the others were unable to commit themselves. When I pursued why the attendees thought nonspeaking children with significant disabilities could not learn to read, they would usually respond with, "Speech is a prerequisite to reading." Pushing the issue further for evidence of their belief, it appeared to hinge mostly on little more than a hunch or something they had heard someone say or read in an outdated textbook that learning to read could not happen without speech. How is it, I would ask, that children who are deaf, without oral language and communicate primarily with sign language, learn to read? Have we forgotten that there is evidence of language comprehension that allows us to formulate a means of communicating, including reading and writing? "Yes, but and but and but," would be the usual responses.

How then does one break this faulty thinking and practice? One has to look for the evidence that people with significant disabilities can learn to read and write; they can become literate. Therein was the challenge that was put before some of us who believed that no one is too anything to learn to read and write—not too intellectually, emotionally, neurologically, or physically challenged to learn to read and write; to become literate (Yoder, 2001). Or those of us who agree with the writer Pat Conroy (1995), who said, "One can do anything, anything at all, if provided with a passionate and gifted teacher" (p. 380).

In 1989, David Koppenhaver and I began "dreaming things that never were, and said 'why not?'" (Shaw, 1921, Part 1, Act 1). We established a literacy center that initially focused on teaching children for whom speech was not a primary means of communication to read and write. From the initial grant from the Kate B. Reynolds Foundation, the center has evolved, providing evidence-based research on effective ways to teach people with significant disabilities to read and write. This book you are about to read will challenge you to provide a reading and writing program for all people with significant disabilities, and we believe, when you finish studying the information the book provides, you will raise your hand in belief that people with significant disabilities can learn to read and write, and you will endorse our collective belief statement:

> It is our collective belief and practice that all individuals regardless of ability or disability have the right to an opportunity to learn to read and write in order to increase and enhance their communicative competence, their educational opportunities for vocational success, self-empowerment capabilities, and independence.
> (Yoder, Erickson, & Koppenhaver [as cited in Yoder, 2001])

David E. Yoder, Ph.D.
Director Emeritus, Center for Literacy and Disability Studies
University of North Carolina at Chapel Hill

REFERENCES

Conroy, P. (1995). *Beach music*. New York, NY: Nan A Talese/Doubleday.

Shaw, G. B. (1921). *Back to Methuselah: A metabiological Pentateuch*. New York, NY: Brentano's.

Yoder, D. E. (2001). Having my say. *Augmentative and Alternative Communication, 17,* 2–10. https://doi.org/10.1080/aac.17.1.2.10

Acknowledgments

Writing a book is sometimes a labor of love and always a labor. This book would not have been written and published without the love and labor of many. Foremost among those to whom we are indebted are our mentors Jim Cunningham and David Yoder. You continue to teach, mentor, and collaborate with us, and, most important, believe, like us, that all students can learn to read, write, and communicate when they are taught well.

The principles, strategies, examples, and insights in this book are the result of several decades spent observing and interacting with students of all ages with significant disabilities, their families, educators, paraprofessionals, and related services professionals in classrooms, summer camps, homes, and community settings. It has been a true privilege to learn from and with all of you.

Many thanks to colleagues past and present at the Center for Literacy and Disability Studies who coauthored many of the studies referenced in this work, asked important questions, sought practical solutions, and continue to generate new understandings, new practices, and new directions.

Several colleagues in particular gave generously of their time and talents in reading and responding to early drafts of each chapter. We owe a debt of gratitude for honest feedback and steady encouragement from Sally Clendon, Jane Farrall, Kathy Howery, Tina Moreno, and Toby Scott. Your insights about children, families, teachers, clinicians, classrooms, schools, augmentative and alternative communication, assistive technology, reading, writing, and other topics too numerous to remember were and are invaluable.

This book would still be unfinished if not for the persistence of a series of editors and staff at Brookes Publishing over the past several years. Special thanks especially to Jolynn Gower for her gentle and persistent inquiries, and ultimately for scaring us with a specific deadline, and to Tess Hoffman for her exceptional developmental editing skills.

Dave thanks his wife, Janice, for her love and for sharing the journey before, during, and since this endeavor.

Karen thanks all of her family and friends for understanding when there is just one more deadline to meet before she is ready to enjoy her time with them.

Finally, for all of you who have been asking us for years whether we were done, let us say in the immortal words of Lane Smith, "It's a book!"

Introduction

More than 25 years ago, we (Dave and Karen) sat down for the first time to talk about our mutual interest in teaching students with significant disabilities to read and write. We worked with colleagues to first build and then continue to inform a field that was very new. Today, it is common for parents, educators, clinicians, and researchers to talk regularly about literacy for students with significant disabilities, but that was not the case when we met in 1991. We both feel lucky to have found another colleague who is willing to grapple with difficult questions while working to find solutions for today and even better solutions for tomorrow. This book is our collaborative effort to record today's solutions.

WHAT THIS BOOK IS AND IS NOT

We have been fortunate in our careers to have learned from and worked with some remarkably talented students, families, educators, clinicians, and professors. The two people who have influenced our careers and our views of literacy the most have been David Yoder and Jim Cunningham, each a professor emeritus at the University of North Carolina at Chapel Hill. David once told us that his interest in literacy in individuals with significant disabilities began in the mid-1980s, when a young man with cerebral palsy indicated by pointing to symbols on a communication board that he desperately wished to be taught how to read and write. Jim used to keep us grounded in the practical as graduate students by separating the theoretical from the practical, and when potential solutions became too complex or unrealistic for classroom practice, he reminded us, "Even Horace Mann and John Dewey team teaching couldn't make that work in a classroom."

These key ideas from our mentors are what ground our thinking in writing this book. We are trying to help families, educators, and clinicians teach children with significant disabilities to read and write, and we are attempting to keep the ideas as practical as possible. We are sharing what has worked for us; what has worked for families, educators, and clinicians; and most important, what has worked for children with significant disabilities we have observed or worked with over the years.

We have had to make important decisions as authors when addressing these two ideas. Throughout the book, we have referenced others' ideas when appropriate. For example, we begin each chapter with a review of the literature we find most relevant in guiding our thinking. We have made no attempt, however, to provide a comprehensive review of the literature. That would be more useful to researchers than to our target audiences of educators, clinicians (speech-language pathologists [SLPs], occupational therapists, and other related services providers), people studying to become educators and clinicians, and families.

Rather than attempt to provide comprehensive access to all of the possible ways of teaching various reading and writing skills, we have focused on what has worked best in our experience. We recognize that there are other effective methods of instruction, but we have not yet found the need to draw on them in helping students with significant disabilities learn to read and write. We have focused on neither inclusive nor self-contained settings but rather on instructional strategies and resources that apply across settings. We think that students with disabilities, wherever they are placed, need to learn to read and write better and deserve to receive high-quality literacy instruction. In fact, if we successfully help them learn to read and write, perhaps they can advocate more effectively for education in the settings that best fit their own needs.

Finally, this is a book about literacy instruction, not technology-supported literacy instruction or methods of accommodation that theoretically alleviate the need to learn to read and write. Our goal is to help all students learn to read and write. Furthermore, the reality of today's schools is that some children and teachers are very well supported with every possible resource, and some are provided very little that is instructionally meaningful. We hope that whatever level of support and resources you may have, you will find that you can take advantage of the ideas, strategies, and resources found in this book and teach your students to read and write better.

WHAT LITERACY IS AND IS NOT

There are multiple literacies in wide currency these days. Digital literacy, computer literacy, media literacy, information literacy, cultural literacy, and political literacy are just a few that are studied and taught. We value these literacies, but in this book, we refer to and attempt to teach just one kind of literacy to students with significant disabilities—print literacy, which is reading and writing traditional orthography, or alphabet letters, for meaningful purposes.

We acknowledge that this is a narrow view of literacy, but we also see it as essential to the successful instruction of students with significant disabilities. This is the kind of literacy that will enable children who cannot talk to say exactly what is on their minds to anyone who can either read or hear. This is the kind of literacy that convinces school systems to move students into inclusive classrooms and puts teeth into transition programs. This is the kind of literacy that increases employment options, makes social media tools accessible, and enables individuals with significant disabilities to have greater choices over medical procedures, therapies, and other important life decisions.

We find that other literacies distract us from assisting children with significant disabilities to read and write with increasing independence and meaning for wider purposes. For example, it is common practice to symbolate texts for many students with significant disabilities. Various technologies make these symbols easy to create and reproduce. We think, and research supports the idea, symbols are wonderfully supportive in face-to-face communication, but if you want to teach children to read and write, then you must use traditional orthography (Erickson, Hatch, & Clendon, 2010). We have met many individuals with complex communication needs who are highly skilled in the use of low- and high-tech augmentative and alternative communication systems but are not very skilled in reading or writing print. For example, Alan McGregor expressed his frustration insightfully by telling us years ago that he just hoped to be literate enough to read his own gravestone when he died.

This narrow focus on literacy as print-based reading and writing is not intended to exclude students. Rather, it is intended to ensure that all students are provided with an opportunity to learn to read and contribute to the print that surrounds us each and every day. When definitions of literacy include idiosyncratic, nonconventional, and graphic-symbol-related behaviors, students with significant disabilities are in danger of being denied meaningful, intensive, ongoing opportunities to develop skills in print-based reading and writing because the skills and behaviors they are already demonstrating are viewed as sufficient.

WHO CAN LEARN TO READ AND WRITE?

We believe that all children can learn to read and write. Not just children in inclusive classrooms and not just those in schools with healthy finances. Not just those who can see or hear or walk or talk or who have intelligence perceived to be at an acceptable level for learning. As such, we are not excluding any students with significant disabilities from the focus of this book.

The students we have taught, include, and encourage you to teach throughout this book are students with severe developmental disabilities, including students with intellectual disabilities, physical disabilities, language impairments, communication impairments, sensory impairments, and the most complex combinations of these things. It includes students who are not yet communicating in ways that others understand. It includes those who have learned to read or write some but could benefit from learning to read and write better. In this book, we share specific approaches that have worked with students with autism spectrum disorder (ASD), Down syndrome, Rett syndrome, cerebral palsy, fragile X syndrome, Angelman syndrome, Williams syndrome, deafblindness, behavior disorders, traumatic brain injury, and myriad other (dis)abilities. We refer to all of these students as students with significant disabilities throughout this book.

This book is intended for any adult who works with these students. We use the term *teacher* throughout, but we acknowledge the crucial role therapists, school staff, parents, and others play in comprehensive literacy instruction. For example, SLPs have a responsibility to play a role in the literacy programs of the students they serve (see the ASHA position statement available at https://www.asha.org/policy/ps2001 -00104.htm). Teaching assistants, paraprofessionals, and other school staff are often assigned to work with children with significant disabilities during the school day. Parents and other caregivers are often the primary teacher for their children with significant disabilities or must supplement what their child receives at school because there simply is not enough time during the school day to meet all of their child's needs. Literacy instruction opportunities are not confined to the classroom, and the audience for this book extends beyond the classroom teacher as well.

We believe that students learn what they are taught, and we often have not taught them in ways that effectively result in successful reading and writing because of the complexities of their disabilities or our lack of understanding. We have visited many classrooms where students with significant disabilities are read to but where those same students are not provided opportunities to read and write print themselves. We have seen other classrooms where students are taught to recognize words in isolation but not how to use them in meaningful ways. We have met older teenagers and adults who know all of the letters of the alphabet, both upper- and lowercase, but do not know that uppercase A or B is the same letter as lowercase a or b or any other upper- and lowercase pairings. We have worked with adolescents who have been taught letter–sound relationships in isolation and can produce a /t/ sound when shown the letter *T,* or can find the letter *D* when someone says a /d/ sound, but they cannot spell or write words in order to communicate their thoughts. We have been told that some students cannot learn phonics because they are visual learners, they are deaf, or they are too intellectually impaired.

We do not know how to teach all children with significant disabilities to read and write at a third-grade level by the end of third grade, as is required in many places in the United States. Yet, we know that individuals with dysarthric speech can communicate more clearly and quickly if they point to the first letter of each word they are trying to say (Hustad & Beukelman, 2002). We have watched individuals who can spell phonetically use spelling prediction systems to write more clearly. We have met young adults with ASD who could not read, write, or communicate independently as teenagers. We have seen them become adults who are employed in offices because they can read, follow written and verbal directions, and manage documents flawlessly. We have seen children with significant disabilities and their parents connect in new ways when they read and discuss books together. We have seen students who are deafblind change posture and affect, acquire voice output communication devices, and engage more joyfully in their interactions with their families, teachers, and peers when literacy activities were incorporated into their instructional days. We may not know how to teach all students with significant disabilities to read and write at a third-grade level, but we do know that any efforts to assist all students in learning to read and write better have led to important outcomes that have contributed positively to the quality of their lives.

We choose not to pretend that we can predetermine who can and cannot learn to read and write. We have learned that it is never too late to learn. Our mentor David Yoder did not learn to read until his aunt taught him in third grade, and one of us (Karen) struggled with reading throughout elementary school. Andrew Sheehan could not write coherent text until he was a young teenager but coauthored an article in a peer-reviewed journal a few years later (Sheehan & Sheehan, 2000). Don Johnston, whose company creates assistive technologies to support literacy learning, did not learn to read until his ninth-grade English teacher, Mrs. Tedesco, helped him (Johnston, 2009). They, and countless other individuals, learned because someone believed they were capable of learning despite their difficulties and provided them excellent instruction.

We believe that students with significant disabilities must receive highly effective instruction in order to learn to read and write. We have done our very best to describe how this might be achieved in practical ways. We hope this book helps you provide your children or students with the excellent literacy instruction they deserve and need.

A COMPREHENSIVE APPROACH

Throughout this text, we will refer to an approach to literacy instruction that we call *comprehensive* because it addresses each of the elements that is required for a student to learn to read with comprehension and to write to convey thinking (Erickson, 2017). This comprehensive approach stands in contrast to the reductionist or functional approaches to literacy that have dominated education for students with significant disabilities for decades. Whether students are just emerging in their understandings of reading, writing, and communication or working to further develop conventional skills, comprehensive instruction takes time—2 or more hours per day—and a focus on the application and use of skills.

Comprehensive literacy instruction addresses emergent and conventional literacy skills. In the first part of this text, we present a comprehensive approach to emergent literacy instruction, which focuses on students who are developing the skills and understanding they will eventually use to read and write. In the second part, we describe the components of comprehensive, conventional reading and writing instruction for students who know the letters of the alphabet, understand that print carries meaning, and are interested and engaged when we read with them.

THE OVERALL STRUCTURE OF THE BOOK

This book is structured in four sections. Section I, Core Understandings (Chapters 1–2), emphasizes emergent literacy. We begin by arguing that all children can learn to read and write and introducing our instructional model in depth. Next, we describe the conditions that must be established for successful literacy learning. In Section II, Building a Foundation for Literacy (Chapters 3–5), we discuss specific emphases that must be combined to offer comprehensive emergent literacy instruction via shared and independent reading, writing, and alphabetic and phonological awareness. Section III, Learning to Read and Write (Chapters 6–10), emphasizes conventional reading and writing instruction. We first present a framework to organize instruction and then describe specific strategies to teach reading comprehension, self-directed reading, writing, and word identification (including decoding and spelling). Finally, Section IV, Implementation (Chapters 11–12), addresses a range of topics that must be considered when planning and delivering comprehensive emergent or conventional literacy instruction to children with significant disabilities. These topics include the effective use of assistive technology (AT), as well as how to organize and deliver instruction in various settings. In organizing this text, we made the decision to address topics such as word identification (Chapter 10) and AT (Chapter 11) at the end of the book because we find they are often overemphasized in the planning and delivery of instruction for students with significant disabilities. Certainly, reading requires the ability to decode and identify words, and writing requires the ability to spell words, but teaching students to read and spell words is pointless if it is not done as part of a comprehensive approach to instruction, one that recognizes that reading with comprehension and writing to convey meaning are the ultimate reasons for teaching decoding and spelling. Similarly, AT is important, if not critical, for many students with significant disabilities, but the best AT in the world is useless in the absence of meaningful reasons to use it. We believe that we must first have a clear set of instructional goals before considering which technologies might support students in achieving those goals.

Our intent in planning this text was to make sure that educators, families, and clinicians could find a starting place, whether they were trying to figure out how to get started with a student with the most complex multiple disabilities, move forward with a student who has acquired dozens of sight words but lacks comprehension, or expand the skill set of a student who can read text with comprehension but cannot write to express thoughts to others. We intentionally planned this text so that no student with significant disabilities is excluded from instruction that has the potential to build core skills in reading and writing over time. We leave it to those who attempt to implement the ideas in this book to determine whether we have fulfilled our intent.

REFERENCES

Erickson, K. A. (2017). Comprehensive literacy instruction, interprofessional collaborative practice, and students with severe disabilities. *American Journal of Speech Language Pathology, 26,* 193–205. doi:10.1044/2017_AJSLP-15-0067

Erickson, K. A., Hatch, P., & Clendon, S. A. (2010). Literacy, assistive technology, and students with significant disabilities. *Focus on Exceptional Children, 42,* 1–16. doi:10.17161/foec.v42i5.6904

Hustad, K. C., & Beukelman, D. (2002) Listener comprehension of severely dysarthric speech: Effects of linguistic cues and stimulus cohesion. *Journal of Speech, Language, and Hearing Research, 45,* 545–558. doi:10.1044/1092-4388(2002/043)

Johnston, D. (2009). *Building wings: How I made it through school.* Volo, IL: Author.

Sheehan, A. D., & Sheehan, C. M. (2000). Lost in a sea of ink: How I survived the storm. *Journal of Adolescent and Adult Literacy, 44,* 20–32.

To the Moreno, Cunningham, and Nance families, who get it

Core Understandings

CHAPTER 1

All Children Can Learn to Read and Write

A Theoretical Rationale

Chloe's mother is trying to read *Green Eggs and Ham* (Seuss, 1960) to her. Chloe is screeching, wriggling, and crying, which is something she often does during storybook reading. Her mother sits on the floor to read because Chloe struggles with such ferocity that she occasionally slips out of her mother's grasp, and her mother does not want her to fall. Chloe has been diagnosed with Rett syndrome. She can neither talk nor walk, her tiny fists are always in motion to and from her mouth, and professionals in several fields have told her parents that she has significant intellectual disabilities.

Only 3 months later, Chloe stares intently at the book as her mother reads and sings *The Wheels on the Bus* (Zelinsky, 1990). Her mother pauses after singing, "The driver on the bus says, 'Move on back . . .'" Chloe looks up at her mother, then to a large, single-message voice output device; she eventually reaches forward with her left hand because her right is in a splint and completes the line, "All through the town." Her mother wraps Chloe in a warm embrace, and they both smile. The splint, voice output device, and additional communication symbols have increased Chloe's ability to participate on more equal terms during storybook reading. She no longer resists storybook reading because she can communicate during the experience. She has become a learner.

Miss Becky, a special educator in a rural school system who teaches children with the most significant intellectual disabilities, is trying to engage Katy, a 5-year-old with severe physical impairments and complex communication needs. She has just introduced Katy in the past month to core vocabulary as a means of augmentative and alternative communication (AAC) (i.e., communication approaches that supplement or replace speech). Katy has not previously received any early intervention services and has had no prior access to AAC. As Miss Becky reads aloud, she pauses and points to symbols representing core vocabulary words in a communication book (i.e., a collection of pages joined by a pair of ring binders that have four symbols displayed on each page). She points to the symbols and says the words HE LIKE. Then she elaborates, "He likes playing in the snow. Do you like playing in the snow?" Katy pushes her communication book onto the floor and screeches. Miss Becky retrieves the communication book and continues reading and pointing to the symbols representing core vocabulary when they match her speech. Katy repeatedly flips through the nine pages of her communication book, peers through the pocket protector sheets as if they were windows, mouths the corners of the pages and book, and pushes or drops the book to the ground many times a day. And so it continues, day after day.

Augmentative and Alternative Communication and Core Vocabulary

AAC is a term that describes a range of communication approaches that can supplement or replace speech. AAC can be unaided (e.g., facial expressions, gestures, sign language) or aided (e.g., graphic symbols, tactile symbols, photographs, devices, and special apps). Until students can spell, they depend on others to decide which words to provide them in aided AAC. In Chapter 11, more information is provided about AAC and selecting vocabulary, but throughout the book we refer to *core vocabulary,* which comprises the words used most frequently in oral and written English (Banajee, Dicarlo, & Stricklin, 2003; Dennis, Erickson, & Hatch, 2013). Core vocabulary words are mostly pronouns, verbs, prepositions, and adjectives. These words are conceptual and flexible and can be used across contexts, purposes, and partners. For more on core vocabulary, see the web site for Project Core, directed by the Center for Literacy and Disability Studies at the University of North Carolina at Chapel Hill, at http://project-core.com.

A year and a half later, Katy loses her balance while using a makeshift walker and falls face first in the hallway. After Miss Becky helps her up and gets her seated, Katy turns pages of a more sophisticated version of her early communication book, one that now includes both high-frequency core vocabulary and other, more specific vocabulary (e.g., body parts, feelings). Katy points to symbols through her tears: NOT GOOD. NOSE. HURT. Miss Becky gives her a hug. Over the course of the school year, Katy will go on to demonstrate accurate recognition of the entire upper- and lowercase alphabet, regularly participate in shared reading, initiate conversations throughout the school day, and use phonetic spelling to begin to write words using initial letter sounds. When one of her classmates seems unhappy, Katy turns to a page in her communication book and points to SAD.

Miss Becky replies, "She does seem sad. I wonder why."

Katy turns to her classmate, flips to her alphabet page, and points to *Y.*

Unlike Chloe, Katy's learning difficulties went beyond access challenges. These difficulties may have been due to her disabilities or associated health conditions or to the fact that the adults in her home spoke a different language than the adults at school. Whatever the reason, Katy, just like Chloe, became a learner when she was given time, repeated experience, demonstrations of how to point to symbols to communicate, daily participation in the kinds of emergent literacy activities described in this chapter and book, and a patient and persistent teacher. Both girls began to demonstrate emergent literacy skills.

THEORETICAL MODELS OF EMERGENT LITERACY

Emergent literacy explains how individuals with even the most significant disabilities begin to make progress toward becoming independent readers, writers, and symbolic communicators when given appropriate support and experience over time. *Emergent literacy* is defined quite simply as all of the reading and writing behaviors and understandings that precede and develop into conventional reading and writing (Sulzby, Branz, & Buhle, 1993). Table 1.1 defines some of the most common terms used to refer

Table 1.1. Key literacy terms defined

Term	Definition
Alphabet knowledge	The ability to name, distinguish and produce the shapes, and identify the sounds of alphabet letters.
Alphabetic principle	The understanding that written letters represent speech sounds.
Alternate pencils	Nonconventional writing tools and techniques that provide students with access to all 26 letters of the alphabet when they are unable to hold a pencil or type on a keyboard.
Concept of word	The awareness that spoken words match to printed words in the reading of text.
Core vocabulary	Refers to the small number of most frequently occurring words that make up a large percentage of our face-to-face communication (e.g., *go, more, like, not*).
Inside-out literacy processes and skills	Knowledge of the rules and procedures for translating print into spoken words or spoken words into print.
Language comprehension	The ability to process and understand words, phrases, sentences, and discourse in written or spoken language.
Metalinguistic awareness	The ability to think about and discuss language as an object (e.g., to talk about words or sentences as entities) or discuss language as a system (e.g., understanding that changing word order changes meaning).
Oral language comprehension	The ability to process and understand words, phrases, sentences, and discourse in spoken language.
Outside-in literacy processes and skills	Knowledge of the world and oral language that children bring to the particular printed words they are trying to read (e.g., word or sentence meaning, background knowledge).
Partner-assisted pencils	A collection of writing tools and techniques (i.e., alternate pencils) designed as low-tech solutions to alphabet access for students with significant physical impairments who cannot hold pencils or type on keyboards. The partner presents the alphabet to the learner one letter at a time, the student indicates when the partner presents a desired letter, and the partner writes down the choices of the learner.
Phonemic awareness	Awareness of and ability to cognitively manipulate the individual sounds in spoken words; a *phoneme* is the smallest possible unit of speech sound.
Phonics	Instructional methods focused on teaching the use of letter–sound relationships to figure out the pronunciation of words.
Phonological awareness	A set of skills that includes recognizing and cognitively manipulating units of oral language such as words, syllables, onsets, and rimes. It does not involve print awareness.
Print concepts	Knowledge of how print works in reading and writing (e.g., letters and words convey the message, we read from left to right and top to bottom on a page).
Print functions	The range of uses for written language. Some functions of print include memory support, problem solving, acquiring knowledge, or maintaining social relationships.
Reading comprehension	The ability to process text and understand its meaning.
Syntactic awareness	The ability to evaluate and manipulate word order in a sentence.
Word knowledge	Also called *vocabulary,* word knowledge is defined as those words known and used by a person.

to these behaviors and understandings, along with additional terms relating to literacy instruction. (A downloadable and photocopiable version of Table 1.1 is available with the downloadable materials for this book.) Three theoretical models of emergent literacy are widely accepted in the literature today as descriptions of its components (see, e.g., Neumann, Finger, & Neumann, 2017; Piasta, Groom, Khan, Skibbe, & Bowles, 2018), each overlapping with the others:

1. One proposes that emergent literacy consists of four areas of interacting knowledge—print concepts and functions; writing; letter, sound, and word knowledge; and language comprehension (Mason & Stewart, 1990).

2. Another divides a comparable set of skills and understandings into interdependent outside-in and inside-out processes (*outside-in* refers to what children understand about the contexts of reading and writing, and *inside-out* refers to what children understand about translating print into sound or sound into print) (Whitehurst & Lonigan, 1998).

3. The final model represents a third organization, making four categories of knowledge separate and distinct—conceptual knowledge about the functions of print and self-perceptions of learning; procedural knowledge related to letters, sounds, and words; oral language knowledge and comprehension; and metalinguistic skills related to phonological and syntactic awareness (Sénéchal, LeFevre, Smith-Chant, & Colton, 2001).

Several features of all three models are particularly relevant. First, although reading, writing, speaking, and listening can be categorized in various ways, ultimately they are language skills and understandings that influence emergent literacy learning concurrently, interactively, and recursively. For example, we have worked with preschoolers with autism spectrum disorder (ASD) who did not speak before they could read and write a few words. We have taught children who could not talk but who learned to use phonetic spelling to communicate messages. We have interacted with children with dual sensory impairments who acquired increasingly sophisticated written language skills over a period of years through alternative means of input and expression. The fact that no one area of skill or knowledge must precede any others, or is more important than any of the others, makes emergent literacy a particularly resilient learning model for children with significant disabilities.

A second feature of emergent literacy, particularly relevant to individuals with significant disabilities, is that it exists on a continuum that appears to begin just before birth as infants in utero gain various forms of language awareness (Moon, 2017). That means there are no prerequisites beyond life. There are no candidacy questions beyond being a human being. That also means that emergent literacy never ceases to be relevant. When 61-year-old Danny, who has significant multiple disabilities, lives in a residential facility, and has never received formal literacy instruction, demonstrates some alphabet awareness and an interest in looking at magazines, it is important to provide opportunities and experiences that will enable him to relate that knowledge to reading, writing, and communicating. Progress begins when learning opportunity begins.

A third aspect of all three models is that they suggest that the functions of literacy are just as important as the forms. That is, students with significant disabilities must be engaged in exploring and using reading and writing in real-world contexts from the beginning. They must have opportunities to observe how others integrate reading and writing into their daily lives. Students must be given opportunities to make lists, write invitations and thank-you notes, muddle around in texts that represent their experiences and interests, and interact with others who are also learning. Teachers must demonstrate how these forms of print work and reduce hesitance, reluctance, and confusion by making print experience more accessible.

Finally, the models suggest that students develop increasingly more sophisticated understandings of emergent literacy through active and interactive engagement with the world. It is not only the trip to the zoo that is informative, but also the collection of photographs to prompt memory of the event later, the conversations with others about that experience, and the reading, writing, drawing, and thinking associated with the initial learning opportunity. Emergent literacy understandings and skills progress when students have opportunities to 1) engage directly with the world; 2) explore related print in order to develop understandings of its forms, functions, and uses; and 3) interact with others who are literate in order to gradually refine those understandings in school and beyond (National Early Literacy Panel, 2008).

Emergent literacy is highly dependent on the nature, frequency, accessibility, and interpretability of experiences with print. For this reason, many older students and even adults with significant disabilities are still emerging in their understandings of literacy because of limited learning opportunities earlier in their lives (Erickson, Koppenhaver, & Yoder, 2002). For example, Zach is a 27-year-old young man with ASD who lives with his mother. Zach missed out on many early learning opportunities because of his extreme dysregulation and challenging behaviors. He knows little more about literacy than what he observes in his home and community. The particular challenge for Zach, and for other individuals who no longer attend school, is gaining sufficient quantity, quality, frequency, and variety of emergent literacy experience in homes or community settings that generally are not designed to provide instruction.

> Emergent literacy consists of all reading and writing behaviors and understandings that precede and develop into conventional reading and writing.

WHEN IS COMPREHENSIVE EMERGENT LITERACY INSTRUCTION APPROPRIATE?

Comprehensive emergent literacy instruction is required to address the diverse needs, understandings, and backgrounds of individuals with significant disabilities. Before we describe what comprehensive emergent literacy instruction is, however, it is important to consider when it is most appropriately provided to students with significant disabilities. Some aspects of emergent literacy are called for as soon as a child is born, and reading aloud or similarly rich oral language experiences are called for even before birth. For example, studies have found that in the third trimester, fetuses begin to distinguish language from other auditory stimuli, detect when their mother is talking, and may be able to distinguish their mothers' language from foreign languages (May, Byers-Heinlein, Gervain, & Werker, 2011; Moon, 2017; Moon, Lagercrantz, & Kuhl, 2013).

In school (or beyond), we determine whether comprehensive emergent or conventional literacy instruction is more appropriate by answering four very simple yes/no questions. We want to know whether the student

1. Identifies most of the letters of the alphabet, most of the time

2. Is interested and engaged during shared reading

3. Has a means of communication and interaction

4. Understands that print has meaning (Erickson, Koppenhaver, & Cunningham, 2017)

Four "yes" responses indicate that the student is likely to be successful with the introduction of comprehensive conventional literacy instruction (see Chapter 6). One or more negative answers indicates the need for comprehensive emergent literacy instruction. A comprehensive approach is called for because of the enormous variety in learners with significant disabilities and because emergent literacy knowledge and understandings have such foundational importance to later conventional literacy learning. That is, emergent literacy represents a set of vital beginnings that, with further experience and instruction, will lead to the more important ends of independent communication, reading, and writing capabilities and to the choices, opportunities, and increased control those skills represent for people with significant disabilities (Koppenhaver, 2000).

WHAT IS COMPREHENSIVE EMERGENT LITERACY INSTRUCTION?

Comprehensive emergent literacy instruction consists of a set of experiences designed to enable the development of print knowledge through a variety of meaningful interactions with literate others and texts (Koppenhaver, Coleman, Kalman, & Yoder, 1991). Such instruction includes a mix of skill development, integrated communication and literacy activities, use of print in meaningful contexts, and purposeful and independent exploration of reading and writing tools, materials, and experiences. Done well, this instruction will lead students with significant disabilities to develop the print concepts, alphabet knowledge, phonological awareness, language comprehension, and communication skills that will enable them ultimately to benefit from conventional literacy experiences and instruction. Equally important, it will help students develop identities as readers and writers, understand the personal value and power of symbolic communication and literacy, and recognize a wide variety of purposes for reading and writing, and it will motivate continued learning. The central activities of comprehensive emergent literacy instruction are implemented daily and include shared reading and writing, instruction in alphabet knowledge and phonological awareness, and independent reading and writing. Each is described next.

Shared Reading

Shared reading is defined as the interactions that occur between an adult and a student as they look at and read a book together (Ezell & Justice, 2005). The goals of shared reading are to increase student engagement and interactions during the shared reading experience and encourage students to take the lead in these interactions as they gain competence and confidence. Shared reading outcomes largely depend on the degree to which adults are responsive to the learner(s) with whom they are reading.

Effective adult language responses should be oriented to the student, promote interaction, or model language (Girolametto & Weitzman, 2002). Student-oriented responses require following the student's lead and providing sufficient wait time for student contributions. An adult might observe a student looking intently at an illustration and comment, "I see you looking at that bear. That's a scary bear!" The adult would then wait in order to provide opportunity for further student contributions. Interaction-promoting responses require the adult to use open-ended questions or comments and monitor student attention, engagement, and participation. For example, instead of asking for a correct response pertaining to the name of a character or element in an illustration, the adult might comment, "I wonder what is going to happen next." Finally, language modeling requires adults to acknowledge and expand or extend students' communication attempts. For example, a student might comment on a dog in the story, pointing to the word *good*. The adult might then respond, "He is a good dog. He's helping." Such interactions over time, accompanied by sufficient time for students to think and consider their own comments, provide repeated language learning opportunities, value the student's contributions, and lead to increased student participation (Ezell & Justice, 2005).

A few studies have attempted to incorporate such strategies in working with individuals with significant disabilities and demonstrated success with a wide variety of students and communication partners. When an educational assistant was taught the previous strategies while modeling AAC use with a 3-year-old boy with ASD, he increased his turn-taking, use of gestures and speech, and proficiency with an AAC device (Sennott & Mason, 2016). In another study, parents were taught similar strategies in introducing story-specific vocabulary to young girls with Rett syndrome and complex communication needs during storybook reading (Skotko, Koppenhaver, & Erickson, 2004). The girls increased their attention to books and parents, responding, and commenting. Finally, a teacher was taught these three responsive adult language types as she engaged in shared storybook reading with three children with significant intellectual disabilities and complex communication needs, two of whom lived in homes where English was spoken as a second language (Cheek, Harris, & Koppenhaver, 2019). All three students increased their engagement with text, interactive communication, and use of shared reading strategies as measured by an adapted form of the Adult/Child Interactive Reading Inventory (DeBruin-Parecki, 1999). Studies such as these suggest that adults can learn to provide responsive shared reading experiences, and students will benefit if they do. (More information about shared reading is provided in Chapter 4.)

Shared Writing

Shared writing is a common practice in primary classrooms serving typically developing students and students who struggle in learning to read, but it can have wider use. In shared writing, adults regularly scribe messages that students dictate about the day's events, activity preferences, and a variety of other student experiences in and out of school. This language experience approach to literacy learning, first detailed in Allen's (1976) book of lesson variations, requires students to be able to orally dictate ideas that teachers scribe. Such a process presents problems for many students with significant disabilities who may have a variety of speech, language, or communication challenges (Erickson & Geist, 2016).

Predictable chart writing is a variation on the approach that uses repeated sentence frames and offers greater structure and predictability while reducing the expressive language demands of the original activity (Hall & Williams, 2001). Every aspect of the lesson requires repeated student attention to highly predictable text structures addressing their personal interests. The lesson structure across the week enables teachers to adapt instructional conversations throughout the activities in order to target student attention to letters and sounds, concept of word, sight words, and print conventions or to address their communication needs. More specific detail about predictable charts is found in Chapter 5.

Alphabet Knowledge and Phonological Awareness

Knowledge of alphabet letter names, sounds, and graphic shapes is vitally important in the context of learning to read and write. In fact, alphabet knowledge becomes the single strongest predictor of learning to read when taught in the context of wide-ranging and meaningful text-based literacy experiences (National Early Literacy Panel, 2008). Letter names help children map print onto speech and begin to identify letter–sound relationships (Foulin, 2005) because nearly every letter represents its sound at the beginning or end of its name (e.g., the name of the letter *s, ess,* ends in /s/, the name of the letter *b, bee,* starts with /b/) (Jones, Clark, & Reutzel, 2013). Furthermore, the recognition of letters and the association between their names and sounds helps emergent readers come to recognize concept of word in text by observing the white space next to the initial letters they recognize (Morris, Bloodgood, Lomax, & Perney, 2003). Letter name and shape recognition, along with growing concept of word knowledge, lead emerging readers to attend to additional letters and sounds in words and ultimately support learning to decode, spell, and read words (Morris et al., 2003). Letter names and their associated sounds and shapes are not equal in the learning challenges they present to students. For example, students with significant intellectual disabilities are 10% more likely to recognize letters in their own name than other letters of the alphabet (Greer & Erickson, 2018).

Four tasks are particularly helpful in contextualizing alphabet instruction from the beginning—letter name identification, letter sound identification, identifying the letter in texts, and producing the letter form (Jones et al., 2013). There is additional evidence to suggest that pairing letters with personally meaningful pictures can support remembering what is taught (Shmidman & Ehri, 2010). In addition, the prevalent letter-of-the-week instruction is inefficient, based more in tradition than research evidence (Huang, Tortorelli, & Invernizzi, 2014; Justice, Pence, Bowles, & Wiggins, 2006), and should be replaced with more distributed practice that a letter-of-the-day approach offers, particularly for students who are at risk for literacy learning difficulties (Earle & Sayeski, 2017; Piasta & Wagner, 2010b).

Students must have repeated daily opportunities to engage in reading and writing experiences involving purposeful use of text, regardless of the methods used to introduce letter names, shapes, and sounds. We have met adolescents and adults who have learned all of the letter names, upper- and lowercase, and sometimes even their associated sounds, but who can neither read text nor spell words. This outcome is an artifact of instruction, not learner capability. Writing with talking word processors, listening to others read texts aloud, engaging in guided experiences with repeated line texts, writing predictable charts, and participating in shared reading are all opportunities for contextualized experience in recognizing and using alphabet knowledge to accomplish wider and more meaningful purposes.

Phonological awareness describes the recognition of different units of sounds in spoken language within words, phrases, or sentences. It can be acquired by individuals with significant disabilities through experience, even in the absence of explicit instruction (Erickson, Clendon, Abraham, Roy, & Van de Carr, 2005). For example, while visiting a preschool classroom, we observed Matthias, a young boy with ASD and complex communication needs, clapping along to a children's song. Matthias initially clapped in rhythm, but then he shifted unconsciously in midverse to clapping each syllable, clearly demonstrating his phonological awareness. Phonological awareness can also be acquired through instruction,

> Every day, give students opportunities to engage in reading and writing experiences involving purposeful use of text. Alphabet knowledge and phonological awareness are important but should not be the sole focus of instruction.

particularly instruction that links letter names and shapes with the sounds they represent and is delivered in small groups in brief lessons a few times a week (Browder, Ahlgrim-Delzell, Courtade, Gibbs, & Flowers, 2008; National Reading Panel, 2000). A wide range of activities incorporate opportunities to develop and begin to apply phonological awareness skills in the course of engaging activities, including choral reading of nursery rhymes or poetry, singing songs (particularly when accompanied by the lyrics), using text-to-speech writing apps or software, and reading alphabet books (Erickson, 2017; Murray, Stahl, & Ivey, 1996). (More information about alphabet knowledge and phonological awareness can be found in Chapter 3.)

Independent Reading

Children with significant disabilities will engage in independent reading in ways that mirror their understanding of book handling and reading when they are given access to texts such as predictable charts, models such as shared reading, and the wide-ranging experiences of a comprehensive emergent literacy program. Some children will browse through books, flipping the pages quickly from front to back or in reverse (Katims, 1991; Koppenhaver & Erickson, 2003). One older gentleman with significant intellectual disabilities whom we knew in a group home always looked at magazines from back to front with the pages upside down. Other students will silently study pages, particularly illustrations, move their hands over the print, or point to particular letters, often the ones in their names (Koppenhaver, Milosh, & Cheek, 2019). Katy, whom we introduced earlier in this chapter, would silently study each page, examine the illustrations, and vocalize to no one in particular. When she reached a page of particular interest—for instance, one with illustrations of frogs, which were a long-term fascination—she would slap the page and pull on the hand of any adult within reach, indicating that she wanted someone to read that page aloud. Rich, a second grader with significant disabilities, loved to look at picture books, often labeling the picture or relating it to his own experience. We watched him read a board book. When he saw the picture of a pig, he read aloud, "peee"; when he saw a picture of a pie, he read, "puhpuhpuhpie"; and when he saw a cake, something he loved for his mother to bake, he read, "mamamamahh." Still other students may ignore books; mouth, throw, or tear them; or engage in a variety of other behaviors indicating that they need more opportunity to learn how books are used.

Time for independent reading is an important component of comprehensive emergent literacy instruction because it provides students with opportunities to apply what they are learning about printed words, illustrations, book handling, and the world while developing the dispositions that can lead to lifelong reading with continued support and instruction (Owocki & Goodman, 2002). These explorations and readings of books at levels commensurate with student experience and understanding lead to measurable gains in emergent literacy (Hatch & Erickson, 2018).

Independent reading is also valuable for the assessment information it provides. Brenda, a child with significant intellectual disabilities, ignored books or rubbed her hands along the edges during independent reading time. The latter behavior led her instructional team to place a basket of books near her during morning setup, snack time, and other breaks. By observing her persistent tactile explorations and engaging in shared reading, the team ultimately found an oversized book with bright, colorful illustrations that led Brenda to begin turning pages herself to examine the illustrations. Our recent explorations using eye-tracking technologies have shown us how important print-referencing strategies can be in directing young girls with Rett syndrome to attend to print in digital texts. Simply pointing to print while reading, highlighting similarities or differences in letters or words, or identifying print conventions while engaging in shared reading can shift children's focus from the illustrations to also including print.

A father of a 2-year-old boy with severe physical impairments and complex communication needs who loved to look at books himself or be read with taught us a key strategy to use when children resist reading. When his son pushed books away or screamed, his father would find a single illustration in the book that connected with his son's experiences, show it to his son, talk about it, and then put the book away as soon as fussing began. He gradually increased the number of pages they could read and discuss together. By observing his son closely in this way over a period of several months, he helped his son find personal interest in books and gradually come to love them.

Independent reading for many individuals with significant disabilities will need to be supported with adapted or digital texts. The Tar Heel Reader web site (http://tarheelreader.org) is one of the easiest, most accessible free libraries for emergent and beginning readers. This collection can be read online, read on tablets or smart phones, or downloaded in a variety of formats depending on student needs. The capability of creating books personalized to the learner's unique interests is a particularly important feature for parents and professionals trying to assist resistant emergent readers. However texts are accessed, it is critical for adults to closely observe students and gradually provide experiences that will lead them to independent exploration and gradually more complex engagement with reading. (Detailed information about independent reading is provided in Chapter 4.)

> Regular opportunities for independent reading and writing help students apply what they are learning and develop the habits and dispositions to become lifelong readers and writers.

Independent Writing

Independent writing is structured to give students maximum control over every aspect of the writing process so that they can apply their emerging understandings of alphabet knowledge, phonological awareness, and print concepts. With the use of partner-assisted writing tools, even students with the most significant disabilities can engage in relatively independent writing by dictating what they want their partner to write for them (Hanser, 2006). All emergent writers are provided with access to all 26 letters, with no expectation that they know any of them initially and with no requirements of copying or tracing. Instead, independent emergent writing emphasizes communicating messages with whatever degree of understanding students may have.

Students may initially fail to use a writing tool or string together what appear to be random letters lacking conventions of spelling, print, or even message intent. Continued encouragement, teacher and peer demonstrations, shared reading interactions, predictable chart lessons, and alphabet and phonological awareness instruction gradually enable student creation of increasingly more conventional and readable texts. Adults must be vigilant kid watchers (Owocki & Goodman, 2002) who observe everything, refrain from correcting or criticizing, and always encourage students to write more. When adults provide a model of conventional writing, it is in response to the student's chosen topic and nonconventional text, and it is consistently a simple demonstration of convention that is never followed by demands for child adherence. For example, a child with complex communication needs who does not yet initiate conversation might choose a picture of lions at the circus and write XPQZASDFGHJKLLL. The teacher could respond helpfully, "I love what you wrote about lions at the circus! I'm going to write *lion*, L-I-O-N. That lion is scary! Write some more about lions at the circus." Simple responses such as this help students develop their own identity as writers, convey that their writing is valued, and begin to develop the useful habit of elaborating their ideas. Such responses do not require a teacher to pretend to read the message, only to value it. A particularly observant teacher might notice that the previous student selected letters on the home row of his keyboard to generate the message, indicating a careful and systematic, though nonconventional, approach to writing. This teacher might slowly and deliberately model using a single finger to type while making sure the student was attending to the keyboard, demonstrating for the student how a keyboard works. (Detailed information about independent writing is provided in Chapter 5.)

A FINAL NOTE: THE BEGINNINGS OF LITERACY

Emergent literacy understandings and behaviors represent important initial steps in learning to communicate symbolically and read and write independently (Koppenhaver, 2000). When 6-year-old Katy, who has severe physical disabilities, significant intellectual disabilities, and complex communication needs, spells *Y* to ask a question, it is no small accomplishment. The day that 3-year-old Jason, who has ASD and was thought to have complex communication needs, began to speak after learning to write his name was astonishing to his mother. When 18-year-old Winston, who has severe physical impairments, complex communication needs, and dual sensory impairments, began to spell phonetically after 2 years of emergent literacy instruction, it was cause for a major celebration. As life changing as these emergent literacy acts were, however, they were all just individual steps, critically important individual steps, along an even more important journey toward convention:

- The symbolic communication capabilities to communicate sophisticated messages that are widely understood

- The spelling abilities that enable specific composing beyond the limits of AAC systems with graphic symbols

- The conventional reading abilities that allow independent learning and research about the world or escape into fiction

- The conventional writing abilities that support memory, complex problem solving, processing of experience, recording of history, and wide communication through an endless and continually evolving set of technologies

The world is a richer place because conventional literacy and communication skills enabled people such as William Rush (Rush, 1986), Ruth Sienkiewicz-Mercer (Sienkiewicz-Mercer & Kaplan, 1989), and Temple Grandin (Grandin, 1995) to write from their own perspectives about their personal histories, interactions, and perspectives on life. All three began with nonconventional forms of communication and literacy as children and were supported in moving beyond those hesitant beginnings.

In the remainder of this book we describe how to help individuals with significant disabilities get started with emergent communication and literacy, gradually gain understanding and skill through instruction and experience, and ultimately communicate conventionally face to face and in writing. They may or may not choose to write poems, autobiographies, or journals, but they will experience increased autonomy, self-advocacy, and human connection. They and we will be the richer for it.

RECOMMENDED READINGS AND RESOURCES

The following readings and resources will deepen readers' understanding of emergent literacy in students with significant disabilities.

Butler, D. (1979). *Cushla and her books.* Boston, MA: The Horn Book.

Center for Literacy and Disabilities Studies. (2019). *Project Core.* Retrieved from http://project-core.com

Erickson, K. A. (2017). Comprehensive literacy instruction, interprofessional collaborative practice, and students with severe disabilities. *American Journal of Speech-Language Pathology, 26,* 193–205. doi:10.1044/2017_AJSLP-15-0067

CHAPTER 2

Establishing the Environment for Successful Literacy Learning

It is not easy to learn to read and write for most students with significant disabilities. Students with disabilities are 2.5 times more likely to read below basic levels of achievement, three times less likely to read at proficient levels, and five times less likely to read at advanced levels than same-age peers without disabilities (U.S. Department of Education, 2015a). By Grade 4, they are unlikely to be able to make basic inferences, identify main ideas or the central problem in a work of fiction, or gather new information from nonfiction texts (U.S. Department of Education, 2015b). Only one in 10 individuals with severe communication and physical disabilities is able to read at the same levels as same-age peers without disabilities (Koppenhaver & Yoder, 1992), and it is even more difficult for students with significant intellectual disabilities. Only 14% can read even short passages with basic, literal understanding, whereas a mere 2% can read fluently with critical understanding in print or braille (e.g., differentiate fact from opinion, identify point of view) (Towles-Reeves, Kearns, Kleinert, & Kleinert, 2009). More than 80% can read only basic sight words or are emergent in their understanding of print (Towles-Reeves et al., 2009).

CONDITIONS FOR LEARNING

Statistics such as these illustrate how significant disabilities may affect literacy learning. Nonetheless, Bob Williams, who has severe communication and physical impairments, is a high-ranking official in the Administration on Disabilities and the Administration for Community Living with the U.S. government (https://acl.gov/news-and-events/announcements/bob-williams-join-acl-deputy-commissioner-administration-disabilities). Haben Girma is a deafblind graduate of Harvard Law School, a public speaker, and storyteller (https://habengirma.com). Don Johnston, who had significant learning disabilities and could not read until he was in high school, founded his own assistive technology (AT) company and authored an autobiography, *Building Wings* (http://donjohnston.com/building-wings). Andrew Sheehan has dysgraphia, Raynaud's syndrome, severe attention-deficit/hyperactivity disorder (ADHD), a hearing impairment, and a successful career in technology, and he coauthored a journal article when he was 15 years old to help teachers learn how to teach students with complex needs (Sheehan & Sheehan, 2000).

How did these individuals and others with significant disabilities learn to read and write so well? Over the years, we have seen 10 elements at work when individuals with significant disabilities are successfully learning to read and write:

1. Knowledgeable others

2. Means of communication and interaction

3. Repetition with variety

4. Cognitive engagement

5. Cognitive clarity

6. Personal connection to the curriculum

7. Encouragement of risk taking

8. Comprehensive instruction

9. Significant time allocation

10. High expectations

We describe these elements in depth in the following sections.

Knowledgeable Others

Teachers matter. In fact, they are the single greatest influence on student learning in educational environments (Cochran-Smith & Zeichner, 2005; Darling-Hammond, 2000). Teacher experience and skill contribute measurable differences to student reading achievement and vocabulary growth (Palacios, 2017; Rockoff, 2004). Effective teachers know their students as individuals, care about their learning and progress, and involve them as active participants in their own learning (Park, Brownell, Benedict, & Bettini, 2019; Skinner & Belmont, 1993). These personal relationships contribute not only to students' skill development but also to their belief systems and values (Wentzel, 2009). As a result, personal relationships have an effect beyond immediate classroom success. Students internalize some beliefs and values about their own capabilities, the value of learning to read and write, and their own abilities to contribute to the world, and they carry them to new classrooms and learning environments (Ryan & Deci, 2009; Wigfield et al., 2015). All children should regularly hear that they are smart, capable, and important. Every child should feel loved and valued.

Although studies almost exclusively focus on licensed teachers, it is abundantly clear in the lives of students with significant disabilities that many different people take on teaching roles. Joy Nance did that formally when she studied and obtained both a teaching and an AT degree and worked with teams to teach her son, Jordan, who as a third grader with multiple disabilities evidenced little communication or literacy capability and was perceived as having significant intellectual disabilities. The result of her and others' efforts (Erickson, Koppenhaver, Yoder, & Nance, 1997) was that Jordan was capable of interviewing more than 40 people and directing a documentary film, *Broadcast: A Man and His Dream* (Broadcast the Dream, 2014), by the time he was a young man. Parents, grandparents, siblings, other relatives, librarians, speech-language pathologists (SLPs), and many others have contributed to the literacy learning success of individuals with significant disabilities (Brown, 1991; Butler, 1980; Koppenhaver, Evans, & Yoder, 1991; Sheehan & Sheehan, 2000).

To become literate, students with significant disabilities need teachers who understand that learning is not dependent on perfectly functioning bodies, learning occurs at different rates and in fits and starts, and students benefit from different kinds of print experiences. They need families who coordinate with teachers and other service providers, who read with them, involve them in family print use, and build their self-confidence and resilience. They need SLPs to implement language and communication interventions. They need occupational therapists to assist in making books and writing tools accessible. They need AT specialists who coordinate with families and other professionals in making their world more accessible. They need teams who believe in their capabilities, appreciate that difficulties are inevitable, understand that learning failures are more productively identified as teaching failures, and are willing to problem-solve and experiment as long as it takes to achieve success.

Means of Communication and Interaction

Individuals with significant disabilities need some means of communication and interaction. The International Communication Project (2014; https://international communicationproject.com/) labels *communication* "the most fundamental of human capacities" whereas the organizing principle of the U.S. Society for Augmentative and Alternative Communication (USSAAC; 2016) reads, "Communication is the essence of human life" (p. 1). Ruth Sienkiewicz-Mercer, a woman with severe communication and physical impairments, explained:

> Communication is the starting point for self-determination. Without it, there can be no understanding between people. Every person needs to communicate in order to establish his or her own ideas, to let others know how he or she feels, to choose what he or she wants and when he or she wants it, to assert his or her opinion, to establish relationships, and to achieve everything that has to do with being an individual. (n.d., para. 12)

Spelling ability is a critical component of communication, particularly when students have difficulties speaking. Spelling is a flexible and versatile skill that ultimately enables individuals with communication disabilities to communicate the widest array of the most precise messages to the greatest range of audiences. Jamil was a young man with severe cerebral palsy who communicated via an elaborate eye-pointing system with whole words and phrases but struggled mightily with spelling. When we asked his favorite book, he replied by pointing to four symbols, BROWN, FOOD, BIG, HOUSE. After many minutes of unsuccessful guessing, we had to ask his teacher for clarification and discovered the book was *Charlie and the Chocolate Factory* (Dahl, 1998). AAC in the absence of conventional spelling ability is frequently subject to approximations of intended messages, miscommunications, and breakdowns.

Symbolic communication can be learned in the process of acquiring increasingly sophisticated emergent literacy understandings, but it is essential to conventional literacy. Students

> Spelling is a flexible and versatile skill that ultimately enables individuals with communication disabilities to communicate the widest array of the most precise messages to the greatest range of audiences.

have to make predictions, summarize main ideas, ask questions, and make comments in conventional literacy lessons. They need to be able to suggest revision and editing ideas in peer writing conferences. They need to talk to family members, classmates, and teachers about what they like or do not like to read and why and what they hope to read in the future. Precise communication enables educators and families to support the growing independence of students with significant disabilities and adjust and adapt experiences to enhance their continued success. Communication with classmates, educators, and families paves the path to becoming active members of the literacy learning community.

Repetition With Variety

A few years ago, a classroom consultant told us about being called in to help with an unusual problem involving a class of elementary school-age students with autism. It seems that the students would rise from their chairs, go to various places in the room behind bookshelves and dividers, and start to take their clothes off. You probably can guess where the behavior originated. The previous year their teacher had wanted to work on independent dressing skills, and she would task them with disrobing for the sole purpose of getting dressed again. Because the students were already dressed when they arrived at school, they needed to take their clothes off before the lessons could begin. The students had learned exactly what they had been taught. They had never learned to generalize that learning to appropriate, real-world contexts because they had engaged in rote repetition of the learning activity in a single context.

Repetition with variety keeps learning interesting and prevents learning opportunities from being reduced to rote repetition. Repetition with variety was at work when Madalyn was taught the form of a riddle and then wrote example after example based on her summer camping experience—riddles about the lake, the cabin, the fire, and dozens of other camping interests. The text structure was repeated over and over, but the content changed with each riddle. Repetition with variety has been seen in guided reading for multiple purposes when teachers introduce a text such as *Itsy Bitsy Spider* on Monday and ask students to read it in order to generate a title, reread it on Tuesday to summarize what happened, read again on Wednesday to sequence events from the text, reread on Thursday to infer whether the spider is climbing up the inside or the outside of the spout, and reread on Friday to make up a new verse. The variety of reading purposes sustains beginning readers' interest while providing the rereading practice (i.e., repetition) necessary to increase interaction, vocabulary knowledge, sight word automaticity, reading fluency, and text comprehension.

Repetition with variety is applied when teachers work with students to revise a text for publication, revisiting the text to consider whether it conveys what the author intended and whether the intended audience will understand. Repetition with variety is in the structure of word wall lessons in which teachers introduce a new set of words each week and then engage the class in dozens of different daily activities with all of the words to help increase students' sight word knowledge. Repetition with variety is at work in predictable charts when the beginning sentence stems are the same, but the conclusion of each sentence is based on individual students' interests. It is seen in shared reading in which teachers model and interact with beginning communicators using core vocabulary but use it differently on each page and in each text to build generative and flexible communication. It is what leisure reading is all about, as students engage in the same act of processing words, relating them to what they know about the world and anticipating what might happen or what they might learn in text after text after text.

Repetition with variety prevents students from tuning out during instruction. It increases their independence and flexibility in using reading and writing strategies and communicating their thoughts. It helps them learn vocabulary from context and gain self-confidence as readers and writers. Repetition with variety couches new learning in familiar experience, increases the quantity and quality of learning opportunities in the classroom or community, and enables students to grow as readers and writers.

Cognitive Engagement

Cognitive engagement refers to the act of putting persistent effort into mental processes such as thinking, reasoning, and judgment in order to understand and learn. Cognitive engagement leads to greater time on task, more positive affective responses to reading and writing, greater depth of comprehension and learning, greater interaction and participation in reading lessons, and greater amounts of reading both in and out of school (Ben-Eliyahu, Moore, Dorph, & Schunn, 2018; Guthrie, Wigfield, & You, 2012). Cognitive engagement leads to increased persistence in the face of challenging tasks and is a powerful predictor of achievement (Guthrie, 2004).

A number of instructional practices are known to contribute to cognitive engagement—help in gaining reading independence, instruction in reading strategies, selection of reading topics connected to students' lives, collaboration with classmates, provision of large numbers of interesting texts, and high levels of teacher involvement (Guthrie & Davis, 2003; Guthrie & Klauda, 2014; Kim et al., 2016). Student perception that classwork is worthwhile, relevant, and instrumental to future success is an additional factor contributing to cognitive engagement (Flowerday & Shell, 2015; Greene, Miller, Crowson, Duke, & Akey, 2004; Lau, 2009). Cognitive engagement tends to result when teachers take advantage of intrinsic motivation by incorporating student choice and self-direction while reducing external rewards and consequences (Ryan & Deci, 2009). Above all, cognitive engagement rests on a foundation of successful learning experiences (Morgan & Fuchs, 2007).

Abbey is benefitting from evidence-based practices in cognitive engagement when her teacher provides her choice in what she wants to write about, teaches her how to use spelling prediction, and provides time for her to share her writing with classmates. Ervin's one-to-one aide is providing him choice and opportunity for self-direction that can increase his cognitive engagement when she does not specifically tell him what to revise but instead encourages him to write more. Kinsey's SLP is supporting her autonomy and self-direction as a more independent reader when she models how to make predictions about story events based on illustrations and then sets a purpose of reading to check the accuracy of Kinsey's predictions. Cognitive engagement grows when classrooms look less like worksheets and assessments and more like places of personalized reading and writing with large, in-class libraries, regular student publication, and high levels of student interaction.

> Cognitive engagement grows when classrooms look less like worksheets and assessments and more like places of personalized reading and writing with large, in-class libraries, regular student publication, and high levels of student interaction.

Cognitive Clarity

Cognitive clarity has been defined as a lucid understanding that can lead to learning (Downing, 1979). It answers the question, "What is in it for me?" and results when students understand the reasons for particular instructional activities, view those instructional activities as both significant and worthwhile, and consequently are willing to commit to learning something new (Goodwin, 2018). Developing readers often lack the experience and understanding to achieve cognitive clarity without teachers' assistance, and their resulting cognitive confusion impedes learning. The confusions range from the most fundamental questions ("What is the purpose of written language?") to more specific ideas ("What is the purpose of this task?") to the language of print (e.g., "What is a letter? Word? Paragraph?") (Downing, 1971). Cognitive clarity is required for students to determine what they should attend to in learning and instructional activities, which strategies to consider, what background knowledge to draw on or consider, or how to self-monitor their progress and success (Cunningham, Koppenhaver, Erickson, & Spadorcia, 2004). Cognitive clarity enables learners to identify what is worth remembering and, equally important, what is worth forgetting. In this way, the learner's brain is not overloaded with trivia, it is more efficient in reducing the influence of outdated information, and it is better able to generalize what is learned (Richards & Frankland, 2017). Cognitive clarity is most likely to result in students when their teachers have cognitive clarity about what they are teaching, how, and why.

Logan, a teenager with significant language learning disabilities, attended several of our literacy camps in Minnesota. One year he came to us with a complaint. The educator working with him had asked him to read repeatedly books that had been written for first graders in an attempt to improve his reading fluency. He was frustrated, insulted, and approaching a breaking point. The educator had identified his reading abilities accurately (i.e., approximately first-grade level). She had identified one of his significant challenges (i.e., reading fluency). She had selected an evidence-based practice—repeated reading (see Institute of Education Sciences, n.d.). The problem, however, was that she had not considered the importance of cognitive clarity in Logan's success with the task. He did not see how reading what he considered "baby books" might improve his reading, and he found the texts not only boring but also embarrassing to have to read in front of his peers. Logan became a more willing participant when we talked to him about the role of reading fluency in comprehension, discussed the value of being able to read text without difficulty so that he could focus on the meaning, and, most important, replaced the first-grade texts with lyrics from his favorite rock band.

Teachers need to engage students in meaningful and interesting texts and tasks to build their cognitive clarity. When a letter is introduced, teachers can not only help students name and form the letter, but also assist them in writing words that begin with that letter and composing texts for real audiences requiring use of that letter. When students are reading for meaning, teachers can set a purpose to guide their comprehension and help them make connections between what they already know and the text to be read. When students are writing first drafts, teachers can remind them to read aloud what they have written to see whether it sounds like what they meant to write. Teachers can help students clearly understand why they are being asked to engage in particular activities (e.g., a making words lesson to learn to compare and contrast letters and sounds so they can spell and decode words they need to read and write). When students have cognitive clarity, then cognitive engagement follows, as does the possibility of generalized learning and future application of skills practiced.

Personal Connection to the Curriculum

One author of this book, Karen A. Erickson, often says in workshops, "It is not our job to make students do anything. It is our job to make them want to." One easy way to do that is to provide students with personal connections to the curriculum. Here is how one teacher accomplished that goal with Dillon, a 14-year-old with intellectual disabilities who was having a rough day. On the morning in question, Dillon kept putting his head down and closing his eyes no matter how much his teacher encouraged, explained, or cajoled him. It was not clear why, and he did not explain. Finally, his teacher asked her aide to take a series of photographs of Dillon and her at the table. She inserted the pictures into a slide program and entered a simple, patterned text (*Ms. A read, and Dillon snored. Ms. A wrote, and Dillon snored. Ms. A typed, and Dillon snored. Finally, Ms. A and Dillon snored.*). She roused Dillon and showed him the personalized book. He looked confused, but intrigued, and he kept his head up, listening carefully as she read the text. He chuckled at each page. Knowing that one of his special talents was burping alphabet letter names, she made the transition to a shared reading with the first few chapters of *The Burp Book: Burp It, Belch It, Speak It, Squeak It!* (Davis, 2013), and Dillon was back on track. Personalizing the curriculum provided Dillon with a needed bridge to learning.

Teachers provide their students with personal connections to the curriculum in many ways. In writing activities, teachers facilitate student topic choice and publish student writing. In guided reading lessons, teachers regularly choose texts that build on students' existing understanding and experience. In self-directed reading, teachers continually seek out texts for student reading or listening that represent individual or collective student interests. Teachers also seek out inclusive children's literature (Pennell, Wollak, & Koppenhaver, 2017), review the International Literacy Association's annual Children's Choices (available at https://literacyworldwide.org /get-resources/reading-lists/childrens-choices-reading-list), track topics and texts their students read at Tar Heel Reader (https://tarheelreader.org), and talk with students, families, and previous years' teachers about reading interests. They gradually acquire hundreds of books in their classroom libraries to increase the possibility of students making personal connections between what they are reading and their own lives and interests.

Teachers seek to make personal connections for students at every opportunity by creating a welcoming classroom environment not only because they care about their students, but also because they know that students with disabilities learn better when they feel a sense of belonging and connection (Edmonds & Spradlin, 2010). Students who feel a sense of belonging are more likely to develop positive feelings—both about themselves, in the form of self-esteem and self-worth (Martin & Dowson, 2009), and about others, leading to the development of emotional attachments to classmates and the teacher. Positive feelings and relationships contribute to an increased willingness to interact with others and participate in classroom activities as well as increased internalization of the teacher's and

> Students learn better when they have reasons to put persistent effort into learning and can answer the question, "What is in it for me?" They learn better when teachers help them make personal connections to the curriculum.

classroom community's values (e.g., persistence, achievement motivation) (Meyer & Turner, 2002). These increased feelings of belonging contribute to an overall sense of emotional security, leading to increased student engagement and learning opportunity (Pianta, 1998). In essence, personal connections invite students into learning by building their trust in their own abilities and their confidence that they can rely on the people surrounding them at home and in the classroom to help as needed.

Encouragement of Risk Taking

Students who are self-aware about their learning struggles become reluctant to take advantage of learning opportunities. The fear of failure looms large in their minds. For example, Mitchell was an 8-year-old with severe language learning disabilities who had been placed in the bottom reading group of his classes for 3 years and referred for testing on multiple occasions. His feelings about reading were so negative that the only way his mother could get him to read anything was to promise him he could either burn the text or shred it when he was finished.

Frank was a high school student with ASD. He found it extremely difficult to generate ideas and language around the topics that teachers set for his class. He revealed a strong interest in pirate books when he arrived at literacy camp. He confirmed that pirates were a source of fascination during a topic generation exercise (i.e., "List five things you love to read about"). Yet, given opportunity to write about pirates at literacy camp, he tried everything he could think of to avoid the writing task. First he claimed, "My ears are deaf." When his literacy counselor asked if they were plugged, he covered them with both hands, and screamed, "Oww, oww!" The literacy counselor patted him on the back and asked if he could begin writing. He picked up the pencil and whined, "I wanna go home." She reassured him that he was fine, pointed to his paper, and asked him to begin. He said, "The pirates were still . . ." then paused and asked, "Is this the end of the story?" She told him no, that he was just beginning. "When is the end?" he asked. She told him at the end of the week because he would be going home on Friday. She told him he had great ideas and encouraged him again to get started, to which he replied, "I need headphones."

At this point, she pointed to his paper, and said, "Go ahead. I'm going to do my writing. You do your writing." Then she began writing beside him. After she had written almost half a page, he began to write the first line of text.

Frank participated in a community of readers and writers all week. All of the campers and counselors were reading, writing, and sharing their experiences and texts with one another. Surrounded by multiple models of expected behavior, receptive audiences, and a remarkably persistent and patient educator, he finally wrote and illustrated a 16-page pirate story by the end of the third day of camp and then wrote another nine-page story during the final 2 days of camp.

Like many of the other conditions for learning already described, a willingness to take risks comes from a student's sense of safety and belonging in the classroom. Here is a simple way a student teacher developed this willingness in a spelling activity in her inclusive first-grade class. She had observed her mentor teacher leading a lesson in which children were generating words that rhymed with either *hat* or *car*. Child after child called out *cat, fat, far, tar* and told the teacher which word they rhymed with, and he wrote them in the correct column on the board. A boy with Down syndrome tried for several minutes to get the teacher's attention so he could suggest a word, but the teacher was reluctant to call on him because he did not think the boy understood the concept of rhyme. When raising a hand did not work, the boy waved his arm, and when that failed, he was standing in his desk, waving and calling the teacher's name. Having no choice, the teacher called on him, and the boy said proudly, with a large smile on his face, *"Man!"*

"Nope," said the teacher, "that doesn't rhyme with *hat* or *car*." Then he called on another student. The student teacher watched the young boy wilt into his seat, his head on his hands for the rest of the morning.

The next week, the student teacher conducted a parallel activity using *in* and *it*, but she was wise enough to create a third column on the board titled "other words." When she called on the boy with Down syndrome, he tentatively said, *"Not?"*

She responded, "What a great word! That goes right here in our 'other words' category." Throughout the lesson, she was able to guide the entire class in comparing and contrasting the words in each column to help build the concept of rhyme in those who did not yet understand it. There were no errors or failures, just words that went into one column or another. Every child's response was accepted and used as an opportunity to teach.

We observed a vocabulary lesson conducted by a fifth-grade teacher who asked the class the meaning of *piety*. A girl with severe language learning disabilities who rarely spoke raised her hand, and the teacher called on her. The girl said she thought that *piety* meant little pioneers. Rather than reject this incorrect response, the teacher wisely asked the girl to explain her reasoning. "Well, *piety* sounds like *pioneer* at the beginning," she said, "so I thought they must be related. And *piety* ends like *kitty* or *doggie*, and those are little cats and dogs. So *piety* must mean little pioneers." The teacher praised the girl's strategic thinking, telling the whole class that it was important to apply such strategies when they were unsure of a word. Then she made the transition to the idea of cross-checking for meaning in the sentence and passage context. After she had read aloud the relevant passage, the girl was able to come up with the correct definition, and the teacher was able to praise her use of not only morphemic decoding but also cross-checking.

In addition to structuring lessons for inclusion and teaching, and praising strategy use regardless of outcome, risk-encouraging teachers welcome all of their students in other ways. Teachers who employ the use of core vocabulary (see http://www.project-core.com) or partner-assisted pencils convey to students that their ideas matter by getting them started communicating from their first day in the classroom and attributing meaning to all student attempts. Teachers who accept and shape nonconventional communication attempts are telling students it is safe to try to communicate. Teachers who do not restrict reading choices to narrow achievement bands and encourage discussion about reading rather than assessing student understanding convey to students that their ideas matter more than their test scores. Publishing all students' work, using mixed ability groups, thinking aloud and modeling potential ways of communicating ideas, and helping students find interesting materials they can read successfully all encourage risk taking. They are also examples of Noddings' (2013) concept of caring. That is, such actions demonstrate that teachers are attempting to understand the classroom experience from their students' perspective and act in ways that promote students' learning success and sense of belonging. As students become aware of the safety and security of the classroom, they become more willing risk takers; new learning then transforms from possibility to probability.

Comprehensive Instruction

All teaching is a compromise. Every instructional choice has associated opportunity costs. A choice of one curriculum is a choice not to use a different curriculum. A choice to tutor an individual is a choice not to teach in a group. Two central ideas underlie the implementation of comprehensive instruction. First, students learn to read and write in different ways. Second, teachers must teach everything about reading and writing, from letter–sound relationships to reading fluency to independent text comprehension, in order to meet students' different needs. It is clearly impossible to teach everything about reading and writing in a finite school day, so teachers must have a way to organize the instructional day to accommodate the widest possible array of learning opportunities and make compromises systematically.

Multiple models of comprehensive instruction have been proposed, the most complex of which is the current federal definition found in the Every Student Succeeds Act of 2015 (PL 114-95), which incorporates 12 multifaceted criteria, including literacy instruction in content areas, vocabulary and language development, differentiated instruction, and principles of universal design. Comprehensive literacy instruction definitions and descriptions in special education are usually based on the National Reading Panel report's (2000) identification of instruction in the components of literacy—the alphabetic principle (i.e., letters represent sounds), phonemic awareness (i.e., awareness of individual sounds in spoken words), phonics (i.e., instructional methods of learning to use letter–sound relationships to figure out words), vocabulary, and reading comprehension—as evidence-based practices (see, e.g., Allor, Mathes, Roberts, Cheatham, & Champlin, 2010; Browder, Wakeman, Spooner, Ahlgrim-Delzell, & Algozzine, 2006; Light & McNaughton, 2009).

The model of comprehensive instruction we have implemented since the mid-1990s and describe in this book is based on the work of Patricia Cunningham and her colleagues in mainstream classrooms (Cunningham, Hall, & Defee, 1991, 1998; Erickson, Koppenhaver, & Cunningham, 2017) and built on widely accepted literacy instructional principles (Pressley & Allington, 2014). This model is particularly appropriate for students with significant disabilities for three reasons:

1. It balances skill and meaning emphases from the beginning so that students engage in reading for meaning, communicating in writing, and learning simultaneously how to decode and spell. Skill mastery is not treated artificially as a prerequisite to engaging in meaningful literacy activity.

2. It does not rely on separating students into ability groups for instruction, a practice that historically has had, at best, mixed results in achievement and negative effects on the self-efficacy of students in lower reading ability groups (Good & Brophy, 2008).

3. It balances student direction of writing and independent reading, which is important for developing motivation and engagement, with direct instruction in reading comprehension and word identification. That is, students receive a wide variety of learning experiences for a portion of every day, some of which provide a great deal of choice and control and some of which teachers guide. For example, students involved in writing choose topics and are taught independent strategies for revision, whereas teachers targeting word study select the specific materials and strategies and then teach them directly.

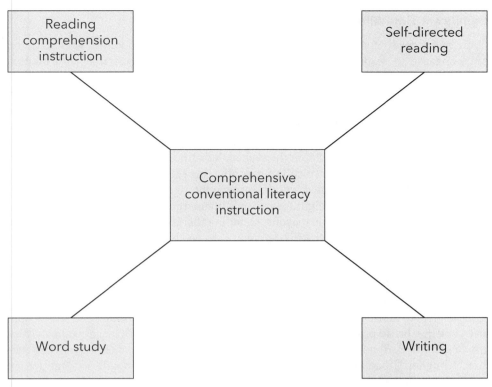

Figure 2.1. Activities that form the basis of comprehensive conventional literacy instruction.

Comprehensive conventional literacy in this model consists of equal attention to reading comprehension instruction, self-directed reading, word study, and writing (see Figure 2.1). The research basis of comprehensive instruction is elaborated in Chapter 6, and each of the four components receives specific attention in Chapters 7–10. The primary goals of comprehensive conventional literacy are to teach students to read texts silently with comprehension, compose meaningful texts that can be read and understood by others, and learn to decode and spell words in order to support comprehension and composition, as well as face-to-face communication by students with complex communication needs. An additional goal is to provide students with engaging and successful experiences with print so that they come to value independent reading and engage in it beyond the classroom.

Comprehensive emergent literacy, however, is focused on developing students' abilities to engage with text, communicate effectively during reading and writing activities, and recognize and use letters and words so that, ultimately, they can benefit from conventional literacy instruction. Emergent literacy instructional methods are elaborated on in Chapters 3–5 and include shared reading and writing, independent reading and writing, and alphabetic knowledge and phonological awareness. Early studies suggest that this comprehensive emergent literacy promotes student communication (Geist, Erickson, Hatch, Erwin-Davidson, & Dorney, 2017), enhances instructional quality (Koppenhaver, Milosh, & Cheek, 2019), and is relatively easily implemented (see http://project-core.com).

Significant Time Allocation

Time spent reading and engaged in reading instruction in school is important, and time engaged in reading in and out of school is positively associated with reading comprehension performance (Guthrie, Wigfield, Metsala, & Cox, 1999). Time engaged in self-selected reading benefits readers of all ability levels (Cunningham & Stanovich, 1997), including poor readers (Mol & Bus, 2011) and students with significant disabilities (Hatch & Erickson, 2018). Research does not clarify how much literacy instruction is enough, particularly for students with significant disabilities, but a large-scale survey of school administrators found that they scheduled almost 2 hours a day of reading and language arts instruction for typically developing third graders (Hoyer & Sparks, 2017). Logically, students with significant disabilities ought to receive at least that much time, if not more. Yet, students with significant disabilities actually may receive very little time for literacy learning for various reasons, including therapy schedules, provision of special education services, and meeting personal care needs (see, e.g., Mike, 1995). Implementing comprehensive literacy instruction requires that teachers carefully consider not only the total instructional time allocated but also exactly how that time is spent. For example, special educators report a strong preference for allocating more time to explicit instruction in basic reading skills and less time to independent reading for beginning readers (Cunningham, Zibulsky, Stanovich, & Stanovich, 2009). Teachers seldom use evidence-based practices in classrooms serving students with learning disabilities (Swanson, 2008). Teachers devote little time to reading comprehension strategy instruction (Klingner, Urbach, Golos, Brownell, & Menon, 2010) or evidence-based practices in general (Ciullo et al., 2016) in response to intervention (RTI) settings serving struggling readers, and substantial time is devoted to comprehension assessment and nonacademic activities (Swanson, Solis, Ciullo, & McKenna, 2012). The situation is little different in classrooms serving students with significant disabilities in which considerable time is lost to noninstructional activities (e.g., classroom management, personal care, technology repair or setup), students are passively engaged in reading activities, and substantial time is devoted to completion of worksheets and decontextualized study of words or sentences in isolation (Koppenhaver & Yoder, 1993; Ruppar, 2015). Other studies suggest that neither the textbooks nor the instruction provided in teacher preparation programs are likely to prepare teachers to offer a broader array of instruction to their students (Al Otaiba, Lake, Greulich, Folsom, & Guidry, 2012; Joshi et al., 2009a, 2009b).

Comprehensive instruction frameworks take on even greater importance given the impact of beliefs on teachers' use of allocated instructional time and the suggestion that neither teacher preparation experiences nor readings may sufficiently prepare teachers to provide best practices in their classroom. Frameworks can specify the broad emphasis of a period of instruction and the amount of time to be allocated without micromanaging teacher decision making. In the conventional literacy framework described by Erickson (2017) and Cunningham et al. (1991, 1998), teachers are to provide 30 minutes of guided reading instruction, but they also are given wide latitude in selecting texts and strategies to emphasize within that time frame.

High Expectations

We believe that universal literacy is not only an ideal but also a potential reality that has not yet been achieved. Students with significant disabilities can learn to read and write, just like any other children and young adults, but they require more time and supports. As a young adult, Alan McGregor (cited in Koppenhaver, 2000), who has significant communication and physical impairments, once explained,

> When I was seven, I started learning to read, and I have not stopped yet. I find reading very difficult. A complete pain. Only now am I beginning to feel that I am improving. At this present rate, I should be a pretty good reader by the time I reach 80. Just in time to read the words on my gravestone! (p. 274)

When we first began collaborating with David Yoder in the late 1980s, he often shared a story with practitioners. It seems that his son, Eric, at age 5, had asked, "Can I go out and play? It's not too anything." His mother replied, "What do you mean, it's not too anything?" Eric explained, "It's not too windy. It's not too rainy. It's not too hot. It's not too cold. It's not too anything." David would then explain to audiences that the same reasoning should be applied to literacy in people with significant disabilities—no one is too anything to learn to read and write. They are not too physically, emotionally, communicatively, or cognitively challenged. Their hearing, vision, and behavior are not too impaired. They are not too disadvantaged or too old. No one is too anything to learn to read and write.

That important idea underlies the Literacy Bill of Rights (Yoder, 2000), which begins, "All persons, regardless of the extent or severity of their disabilities, have a basic right to use print. Beyond this general right, there are certain literacy rights that should be assured for all persons." The eighth, and final, right in the list reads, "The right to live and learn in environments that maintain the expectations and attitudes that all individuals are literacy learners." See Figure 2.2 for the entire Literacy Bill of Rights.

Ann Donnellan (1984) proposed the criterion of the least dangerous assumption, which contended that in the absence of conclusive evidence, education teams should proceed with curricula and strategies that, if they were poor choices, would have the least dangerous impact on student learning and growth. The least dangerous assumption about human beings is to assume that they are capable of emergent literacy and communication, regardless of the severity or complexity of their disabilities. That assumption sets into motion

- Daily reading aloud with the individual
- Writing or partner-assisted writing activities
- Interactions and modeling with symbolic communication
- Shared reading interactions
- Predictable chart writing
- Exploration of independent student access to books

Here is what implementation of that assumption led to in the case of one child with complex needs. Matthew was a member of a preschool class of 12 children, six of whom had a range of disabilities and six of whom were typically developing. He was medically fragile, received nutrition through a feeding tube, required breathing support from an oxygen tank, and spent much of the school day in a cot with his eyes closed. His team wanted to implement an emergent literacy program with the entire class but were uncertain of how to incorporate Matthew. With the aid of a creative consultant, they ultimately decided to begin by engaging in shared reading with the entire class

---

Literacy Bill of Rights

All persons, regardless of the extent or severity of their disabilities, have a basic right to use print. Beyond this general right, there are certain literacy rights that should be assured for all persons. These basic rights are:

1. The right to *an opportunity to learn* to read and write. *Opportunity* involves engagement in active participation in tasks performed with high success.

2. The right to have *accessible*, clear, meaningful, culturally and linguistically appropriate *texts* at all times. Texts, broadly defined, range from picture books to newspapers to novels, cereal boxes, and electronic documents.

3. The right to *interact with others* while reading, writing, or listening to a text. *Interaction* involves questions, comments, discussions, and other communications about or related to the text.

4. The right to life *choices* made available through reading and writing competencies. *Life choices* include, but are not limited to, employment and employment changes, independence, community participation, and self-advocacy.

5. The right to *lifelong educational opportunities* incorporating literacy instruction and use. Literacy *educational opportunities*, regardless of when they are provided, have potential to provide power that cannot be taken away.

6. The right to *have teachers and other service providers who are knowledgeable* about literacy instruction methods and principles. *Methods* include but are not limited to instruction, assessment, and the technologies required to make literacy accessible to individuals with disabilities. *Principles* include, but are not limited to, the beliefs that literacy is learned across places and time, and no person is too disabled to benefit from literacy learning opportunities.

7. The right to live and learn in *environments* that provide *varied models of print use*. *Models* are demonstrations of purposeful print use such as reading a recipe, paying bills, sharing a joke, or writing a letter.

8. The right to live and learn in environments that maintain the *expectations and attitudes* that all *individuals are literacy learners*.

Figure 2.2.   Literacy Bill of Rights. (From Yoder, D. E., Erickson, K. A., and Koppenhaver, D.A. [1997]. *A literacy bill of rights*. Chapel Hill: University of North Carolina at Chapel Hill, Center for Literacy and Disability Studies.)

and to do so a few times a day because the attention span of young children is only a few minutes at a time. They began with *How About a Hug* (Carlson, 2003), which includes seven iterations of the question, "What is it?" The answer follows each time on the next page, "A (good morning, have a great day . . .) hug." They gathered the children near Matthew's cot each time they read, and they would give Matthew a hug on the repeated line, causing an audible exhalation from Matthew because he lacked full control of his breathing. They would read the book several times a day, so Matthew was hugged 14–28 times a day. Because the class enjoyed the book and reading with their friend, Matthew, the teachers continued reading it the next week. On Tuesday morning, on the first reading of the day, when the teacher read the repeated line, "What is it?" Matthew exhaled voluntarily before he was hugged. He had demonstrated his first voluntary, albeit nonconventional, form of communication.

Students with significant disabilities require and deserve the best instruction and learning experiences that schools and homes have to offer in order to learn to read, write, and communicate. The very least we can do, as teachers and families, is to maintain "literacy optimism" (Katims, 2000, p. 12), a belief in their ability to learn. The value of this belief in students is that it leads to productive problem solving if and when learning does not proceed as planned. If an instructional attempt fails, then instead of attributing the failure to students' disabilities, we might make personalized books, find more time to incorporate read-alouds, teach typically developing peers how to use the core vocabulary system interactively, assess students' hearing or vision, or explore new assistive technologies. We would keep trying.

Successful teachers of students with significant disabilities do not ignore their difficulties. They simply recognize that although disabilities affect literacy learning, they need not impair it. As Stephen Jay Gould wrote,

> **Effective teachers provide comprehensive literacy instruction to students with significant disabilities and understand that this instruction requires a significant time investment. They have high expectations of their students and encourage students to take risks in the classroom.**

> We pass through this world but once. Few tragedies can be more extensive than the stunting of life, few injustices deeper than the denial of an opportunity to strive or even to hope, by a limit imposed from without, but falsely identified as lying within. (1996, pp. 60–61)

BUILDING ON THE CONDITIONS FOR LEARNING

The attitudes, beliefs, and actions of adults in the learners' environment, whether in classrooms, homes, or elsewhere in the community, play a significant role in the learning success of students with significant disabilities. You already must have high expectations for your students' literacy learning success or you would not be interested in a book like this, and you are increasing your capabilities as a knowledgeable other because you have read this chapter. You have been introduced to the related concepts of cognitive engagement, which will result in more concentrated and sustained efforts to learn by your students, and cognitive clarity, which will reduce their confusion and increase their ability to generalize what they learn. By varying the ways that you approach texts, you will provide the repetition with variety that your students require to augment their prior experience with new learning. If you seek out and assist students in making personal connections to the curriculum, then you will be inviting their engagement and making them feel welcome and safe in your classroom, thereby providing an encouragement of risk taking so that they try new activities and revisit previous areas of struggle in new ways. You must all the while support development and growth in their means of communication and interaction so that they will take on increasingly active and more independent roles in the classroom and their own learning. All of these ways of structuring activities will require a significant time allocation of approximately 2 or more hours per day if your students are to learn to read, write, and communicate and advance those skills over time. In the remainder of this text, we discuss in detail the ways that you can implement comprehensive instruction in emergent and conventional literacy to take advantage of these conditions and maximize your students' learning opportunities.

A FINAL NOTE: THE ENVIRONMENT FOR LITERACY LEARNING

Students with the most significant disabilities can and do learn to read, write, and communicate, and their lives are qualitatively different as a result. Jaylen, who has severe cerebral palsy, can help his family make an important decision, explaining clearly through symbols and spelling on his communication aid that he wants a potentially life-threatening surgery because rewards outweigh the risks. Sally, who has ASD and has never spoken, can share her thoughts and feelings with her mother through a shared dialogue journal. Brandon, who has significant behavioral and psychological disorders, can write a letter to a camp director explaining clearly what is bothering him. Maggie, who has intellectual disabilities, can write her own chapter in a book about individuals with Down syndrome and their lives. Egan can create his own written schedules, Eron can communicate his love for his family, and Kirsty can gain employment as a secretary.

Disabilities affect learning because they impair abilities to see text, hear instruction, process language, hold pencils, understand experience, and otherwise gain access to the world. These difficulties have been resolved again and again by talented and committed educators, families, related services personnel, librarians, administrators, and others who believe in the abilities of all students to learn. They understand ultimately that a learning failure is a singular instance best characterized as a teaching failure. It can be studied and improved on by thoughtful and caring individuals who seek to maximize learning opportunities for students who seldom find the path to literacy and communication smooth. These individuals make literacy engaging and personal. They help children and young adults learn to communicate and understand why they are engaged in various activities. They provide repeated learning opportunities and make it safe for students to try something new or something that they previously found difficult. They allocate significant time for instruction and provide a wide range of different kinds of literacy instruction and experience during that time. They provide the conditions for learning described in this chapter and employ the kinds of methods, processes, materials, and technologies described in the rest of this book.

> Ultimately, a learning failure is a singular instance best characterized as a teaching failure.

RECOMMENDED READINGS AND RESOURCES

The following readings and resources will deepen readers' understanding of how to establish the conditions needed for successful literacy instruction to take place.

Erickson, K. A. (2017). Comprehensive literacy instruction, interprofessional collaborative practice, and students with severe disabilities. *American Journal of Speech-Language Pathology, 26*, 193–205.

Erickson, K., Koppenhaver, D., & Yoder, D. (2002). *Waves of words: Augmented communicators read and write.* Toronto, Ontario, Canada: International Society for Augmentative and Alternative Communication.

The web site of Camp ALEC (http://campalec.com), a summer camp focused on literacy in a fun environment for students with physical disabilities, ages 7–21, who rely on AAC.

Building a
Foundation for Literacy

Alphabet Knowledge
and Phonological Awareness

Kevin, a 9-year-old with ASD who does not use speech to communicate, works quietly to match the small, laminated red letters of the alphabet with the blue letters on the laminated file folder in front of him. He moves quickly through the task, taking the small letters one at a time out of a big envelope, quickly scanning the file folder, and placing each letter on top of its match. When he finishes, he closes the folder, sets it aside, and moves on to the next task. The next day, he will do the same routine again, perhaps with different colored letters or letters in different fonts, but each day he dutifully matches the letters, closes the folder, and moves on, only to find the folder waiting for him again the next day.

Kevin's experience is not unlike the experience of many students with significant disabilities we have encountered through the years. His teacher understands that she must help Kevin develop alphabet knowledge, but the approach taken does little to develop deep levels of awareness of letters, the sounds they represent, and the purpose they serve in reading and writing. Furthermore, the emphasis on independent mastery of skills fails to provide students like Kevin with the level of language-based interaction they need to develop *phonological awareness*—that is, an awareness of, and ability to manipulate, the sounds in oral language.

RESEARCH BRIEF: ALPHABET AND PHONOLOGICAL AWARENESS

Alphabet knowledge (Adams, 1990; Chiappe, Siegel, & Gottardo, 2002; Foulin, 2005) and phonological awareness (Ehri et al., 2001; Hulme, Bowyer-Crane, Carroll, Duff, & Snowling, 2012; Lonigan, Burgess, & Anthony, 2000; Melby-Lervåg, Lyster, & Hulme, 2012) are fundamental to literacy learning. Both are strong predictors of later reading success in young children (Hammill, 2004; National Institute for Literacy [NIFL], 2008; Piasta, Petscher, & Justice, 2012; Piasta & Wagner, 2010a). Alphabet knowledge is likely important because letter names help children link print to speech (Bowman & Treiman, 2004; Foulin, 2005; Treiman & Rodriguez, 1999) and directly contribute to letter–sound knowledge (Piasta & Wagner, 2010b; Roberts, Vadasy, & Sanders, 2018; Treiman, Pennington, Shriberg, & Boada, 2008). Phonological awareness is important because it allows children to reflect on and manipulate the sound structure of words, which is critical to successful word reading at beginning levels (Anthony & Francis, 2005). The connection between phonological and phonemic awareness is explained next.

Phonological and Phonemic Awareness: Different but Related

Phonological awareness refers to the ability to identify and manipulate sounds in spoken language. Early developing phonological awareness skills include the ability to hear the number of words in a sentence or syllables in a word. Later developing skills include the ability to recognize rhyme and words that begin with the same sound.

Phonemic awareness is a form of phonological awareness that is later developing. *Phonemic awareness* refers to the ability to manipulate the smallest units of sound (i.e., phonemes) within words.

See Gillon (2017) for more information.

It comes as no surprise that students with significant disabilities struggle with literacy skills such as alphabet knowledge (Erickson & Geist, 2016; Towles-Reeves et al., 2009, 2012) and phonological awareness (Channell, Loveall, & Conners, 2013; Dessemontet, de Chambrier, Martinet, Moser, & Bayer, 2017; Sun & Kemp, 2006; Verucci, Menghini, & Vicari, 2006). Increasing evidence indicates, however, that students with significant disabilities can learn letters, letter sounds, and the skills required to use that knowledge to decode words (e.g., Allor, Mathes, Roberts, Cheatham, & Al Otaiba, 2014; Browder et al., 2008; Finnegan, 2012). The challenge is ensuring that these skills are taught in ways that help students with significant disabilities learn them and learn to apply them in generalized ways in reading and writing.

We regularly encounter students with significant disabilities who can identify all of the upper- and lowercase letters of the alphabet and many who can identify the printed letter that represents each letter sound, but who cannot apply those skills in reading and spelling words. Jared, a young man we assessed at the request of his mother, was highly motivated by reading and writing. Given a printed display of 26 uppercase and then 26 lowercase letters, Jared could identify every letter when asked, "Show me . . ." Yet, Jared did not know that there was a relationship between the upper- and lowercase letters. Jared could also identify the letters that represented the sounds we produced when he was asked to, "Write /t/." He could even write words when we stretched them out, pronouncing each letter sound independently. Unfortunately, Jared could not use these skills to read or spell words. Jared mastered important emergent literacy skills, but he had not received instruction that helped him learn to use those skills to read and write.

Alphabet Knowledge

Alphabet knowledge is fundamental to literacy learning (Chiappe et al., 2002; Foulin, 2005) and includes the ability to distinguish letter shapes, name them, write them, and identify the sounds they represent. It is a strong predictor of later reading success in young children without disabilities (Hammill, 2004; National Early Literacy Panel [NIFL], 2008; Piasta et al., 2012; Piasta & Wagner, 2010a). It is also strongly related to word and nonword reading as well as later reading comprehension for students with significant disabilities (Dessemontet & de Chambrier, 2015). The impact of alphabet knowledge grows stronger over the first 2 years of reading development in students with significant disabilities because they learn to apply their knowledge to word reading (Dessemontet & de Chambrier, 2015). In contrast, the importance of alphabet knowledge decreases after the first year for students without disabilities because they quickly learn to apply that knowledge to word reading and move on to more complex reading processes (NIFL, 2008). This is an important indicator that students with significant disabilities may need more time to learn to apply knowledge of letter sounds to decoding words and reading texts than their peers without significant disabilities (e.g., Allor et al., 2014).

In some ways, development of alphabet knowledge is similar for students with and without significant disabilities. For example, students with significant disabilities are most likely to learn the letters of their own names before other letters of the alphabet (Greer & Erickson, 2018), like children without disabilities (Justice et al., 2006). Young children without disabilities, however, are influenced by the order that letters appear in the alphabet string (Justice et al., 2006) and the frequency of letters in written English (Turnbull, Bowles, Skibbe, Justice, & Wiggins, 2010). The same has not been found for students with significant disabilities, but this is likely due to differences in instruction and learning opportunity rather than student characteristics (Greer & Erickson, 2018).

There is clear evidence that successfully developing alphabet knowledge and applying that knowledge in later reading is related to instructional opportunity rather than severity of disability. For example, the relationship between alphabet knowledge and later reading is strongest for students with significant disabilities included in general education settings where much more time is focused on reading instruction when compared with separate special education classes (Dessemontet & de Chambrier, 2015). Furthermore, many students with significant disabilities, such as Jared, struggle to learn or generalize alphabet knowledge when it is taught in isolation using direct instruction techniques (e.g., Bailey, Angell, & Stoner, 2011; Flores, Shippen, Alberto & Crowe, 2004). In contrast, students with significant disabilities can develop alphabet knowledge and apply it meaningfully to reading and spelling when it is taught and immediately applied in the context of comprehensive instruction that extends over a period of months and years (e.g., Allor et al., 2010; Fallon, Light, McNaughton, Drager, & Hammer, 2004; Johnston, Buchanan, & Davenport, 2009; Koppenhaver & Erickson, 2003). Students with significant disabilities need to be taught alphabet knowledge, but the instruction must offer regular and sustained opportunities to apply what they are taught during comprehensive emergent literacy instruction.

Phonological Awareness

Phonological awareness refers to an individual's knowledge of and ability to manipulate the sound structure of oral language (Anthony & Francis, 2005; Scarborough & Brady, 2002). The relationship between phonological awareness and reading is strong for typically developing students (Hulme et al., 2012) and similarly strong among students with significant disabilities (Adlof et al., 2018; Dessemontet & de Chambrier, 2015; Sun & Kemp, 2006). Students with significant disabilities, however, have much less developed phonological awareness skills than peers without disabilities (Dessemontet et al., 2017; Sun & Kemp, 2006; Verucci et al., 2006). Phonological awareness instruction among students with significant disabilities supports letter sound knowledge, first-letter identification, and word reading when it is explicitly taught as part of a phonics-based program (Lemons et al., 2015; Lemons, Mrachko, Kostewicz,

& Paterra, 2012). Phonological awareness explicitly taught as part of comprehensive literacy instruction supports a variety of foundational reading skills, including letter name and sound identification (Colozzo, McKeil, Petersen, & Szabo, 2016), word identification (Colozzo et al., 2016; Lemons et al., 2012), print concepts (Colozzo et al., 2016), and passage comprehension (Adlof et al., 2018).

Students with significant disabilities appear to have more difficulty developing phonological awareness than their peers without disabilities, but they can develop it. Furthermore, when phonological awareness instruction is part of comprehensive literacy instruction, students with significant disabilities develop phonological awareness skills, word decoding, and word identification skills (Ahlgrim-Delzell et al., 2016; Ahlgrim-Delzell, Browder, & Wood, 2014; Hansen, Wadsworth, Roberts, & Poole, 2014) that they can generalize to reading new words (Waugh, Fredrick, & Alberto, 2009).

> Teaching literacy skills in isolation makes it harder for students to learn to generalize these skills. Instruction in alphabet knowledge and phonological awareness should be integrated within comprehensive literacy instruction.

DEVELOPING ALPHABET AND PHONOLOGICAL AWARENESS

All shared and independent reading and writing instruction provides an opportunity to teach alphabet and phonological awareness. For example, during shared reading, adults can talk about letters and the sounds they represent and help students develop an awareness of rhyme, alliteration, and other features of oral language. Similarly, during independent or shared writing, adults can provide feedback that focuses student attention on the meaningful use of letters and their relationships to letter sounds in words. These activities can be considered intentional yet embedded instruction in alphabet knowledge and phonological awareness. Combining this instruction with brief periods of explicit instruction helps students learn the skills required for later success in reading and writing while increasing the likelihood that they will be able to apply the skills to meaningful reading and writing (Waugh et al., 2009). This combination of explicit and embedded instruction has been formally described by Justice and Kaderavek (2004) as instruction that systematically integrates explicit skill-based instruction in natural learning opportunities throughout the school day.

Explicit, Targeted Instruction

Explicit, systematic instruction designed to help students master targeted skills is the norm for students with significant disabilities. Textbooks on teaching students with significant disabilities consistently recommend explicit, systematic instruction as a primary approach to teaching most skills, including literacy skills (see, e.g., Browder & Spooner, 2011, 2014; Collins, 2012). As we describe in this chapter, some explicit instruction is important to help students learn skills that are required for reading and writing; however, that explicit instruction has to help students develop the thinking and problem-solving skills that are required for literacy learning and use. It cannot simply focus on mastery of the target skills. As such, the approaches to explicit instruction described next do not employ the elements of systematic instruction (e.g., time delay, errorless learning) that are often recommended for students with significant disabilities.

Explicit Alphabet Instruction   As part of a comprehensive approach to emergent literacy instruction, teachers should devote some targeted instructional time each day to helping students learn letter names, shapes, and the sounds they represent. This explicit instruction will provide teachers with a way to monitor student progress in alphabet knowledge, but it should be paired with efforts to help students develop alphabet knowledge during reading and writing interactions across the day.

Enhanced Alphabet Instruction   Many teachers organize their alphabet instruction around a letter-of-the-week or letter-of-the-month approach (Bowman & Treiman, 2004). The practice seems to have its roots in tradition rather than evidence of its success (Justice et al., 2006). In fact, there is no evidence to suggest that a week or a month is the appropriate amount of time needed to teach a letter. To the contrary, letters vary greatly in terms of difficulty and therefore require different amounts of instructional time and learning effort (Treiman, Levin, & Kessler, 2007). As a result, focusing on one letter each week is counterproductive and actually disadvantages the students who are most in need of alphabet instruction (Piasta & Wagner, 2010a). Among the many problems identified with a letter-of-the-week approach, the one that seems most relevant to students with significant disabilities is that learning takes repetition and practice, but it must be distributed over time (Jones et al., 2013). Teaching just one letter a week would require 26 weeks before a letter was revisited as the focus of instruction. We all know students who seem to lose knowledge and skills over a holiday break or even just a weekend. How do we expect them to retain a skill we do not revisit for 26 weeks?

Jones and colleagues (2013) proposed an explicit approach to alphabet instruction that addresses the challenges inherent in a letter-of-a-week approach. In their enhanced alphabet instruction routine, about 10 minutes each day are devoted to teaching an individual letter. Each day a new letter is targeted. All of the letters have been introduced by day 26, and each letter can be targeted again over the next 26 days. This rapid cycling through the letters can occur at least seven times during the school year, and each letter is targeted again at least once every 26 days. More important, the rapid cycling allows for distributed rather than massed practice, which supports deeper learning and use (Jones & Reutzel, 2012). The other advantage of this approach is that letters can be taken out of the cycle as they are learned, providing more time to focus on the letters that students are struggling to learn. Finally, the approach helps teachers think about varying the order of letters in each cycle based on features that make them relatively easier (e.g., they occur in the first half of the alphabet) or more difficult (e.g., they represent more than one sound) to learn (Justice et al., 2006).

The orders that Jones and colleagues (2013) recommended for each cycle of 26 letters draw on a variety of areas of research regarding alphabet knowledge. They recommended a sequence of six instructional cycles during which one letter of the alphabet is targeted each day:

1. During the first 26 days of the school year, the letters are taught one per day, beginning with the letters that appear most frequently in the names of students in the classroom.

2. During the next 26 days, the letters are taught in alphabetic order.

3. In the third 26-day cycle, the letters are taught beginning with those that represent sounds that are in the letter name (i.e., *b, p, f, m*) and moving to letters that represent sounds that are not in the name (i.e., *h, q, w, y*) or represent more than one sound (e.g., a possible order might be *b, f, m, p, j, d, k, t, v, z, l, n, r, s, h, q, w, y, c, g, x, i, a, e, o, u*).

4. In the fourth cycle, the letters are taught based on the frequency of use of the letters in written English. Teachers begin with the letters that appear least frequently and focus on one letter each day (e.g., a possible order might be *y, q, j, z, x, w, k, h, g, v, f, b, m, p, d, c, l, s, n, t, r, u, o, e, a, i*).

5. In the fifth cycle, the sequence is based on the order in which typically developing children learn to say sounds in spoken English. Teachers begin with letters that children without disabilities are able to articulate earliest and move through to the sounds for which articulation develops latest (e.g., a possible order might be *n, m, p, h, t, k, y, f, b, d, g, w, s, l, r, v, z, j, c, i, a, e, o, u, x, q*).

6. Finally, in the sixth cycle, the order is based on the visual features that make letters relatively easier or more difficult to distinguish from one another. Clusters of letters that are visually similar (i.e., *C* and *G*; *b, d, p, q*; *M, N, W*) are taught across several adjacent days (e.g., a possible order might be *c, g, o, b, p, d, q, a, m, n, w, r, h, t, l, f, i, j, g, y, v, u, e, z, s, k*).

Beyond recommending that teachers address one letter each day with different cycles that emphasize different aspects of alphabet knowledge, Jones and colleagues (2013) also recommended a specific instructional routine to follow each day. Although not all students with significant disabilities will be able to actively participate in each step, teachers should lead students through as many steps as possible. The routine is described in the "Explicit Alphabet Knowledge Instructional Routine" textbox, with specific recommendations for making it accessible to students who cannot use speech to say the letter names and sounds, as well as students whose physical disabilities prevent them from pointing to individual letters in text or writing them with a standard pen or pencil. (A printable and photocopiable version of this routine is available with the downloadable materials for this book.) Notice that each day the routine emphasizes the letter name, the upper- and lowercase forms, the sound the letter represents, its use in naturally occurring text, and the way it is written or selected from a keyboard or alternate pencil. This integrated approach increases the likelihood that students will come to develop deep alphabet awareness rather than disconnected mastery of each of the elements of alphabet knowledge.

Other important things to notice about the routine recommended by Jones et al. (2013) include the simultaneous emphasis on upper- and lowercase forms as well as letter names and sounds. When we separate these two, we end up with students such as Jared who fail to learn the relationships. The other thing to notice about the routine is the fact that students are taught that letters represent particular sounds rather than make sounds. It is true that letters do not make sounds no matter how hard you poke, prod, or squeeze them. Using the common language to suggest that letters make sounds may be especially confusing for students with significant disabilities who are struggling to make sense of abstract letter shapes, names, and sounds. *Represent* is a much more challenging word, but using it may reduce possible confusion for at least some students.

Explicit Alphabet Knowledge Instructional Routine

Steps 1 and 2: Letter Identification

1. This is the letter (<u>letter name</u>). This is the uppercase letter (<u>letter name</u>). This is the lowercase letter (<u>letter name</u>). (*Show and/or write the uppercase and then the lowercase letter.*)

2. Let's practice naming this letter. What is this letter? (*Point to upper- and lowercase letters in different orders at least three times, asking students to say the letter name.*)

If students do not use speech to communicate, then say, "Let's practice naming this letter. You say it to yourself while I will say it aloud."

Steps 3 and 4: Letter Sound Identification

3. This letter (<u>letter name</u>) represents the sound (/<u>letter sound</u>/). (*Provide stories, mnemonics, and key words to help students remember the sound.*)

4. Let's practice saying the sound this letter represents. The letter (<u>letter name</u>) represents the sound (/<u>letter sound</u>/). Say (/<u>letter sound</u>/) with me. (*Point to upper- and lowercase letters in different orders at least three times, asking students to say the letter sound.*)

If students do not use speech to communicate, then say, "Let's practice saying this letter. The letter (<u>letter name</u>) represents the sound (/<u>letter sound</u>/). You say the sound (/<u>letter sound</u>/) to yourself while I say it aloud."

Hint: For vowels, teach the short vowel sound. As you begin conventional instruction, you can explain that the letter can represent its name or its sound in reading and writing.

Step 5: Recognizing the Letter in Text

5. Now, let's look for the letter (<u>letter name</u>). (*Help students look for the upper- and lowercase letter in naturally occurring print, such as books, charts, signs, and other places in the environment that include print. Each time they locate the letter, students should state the letter name and the sound it represents.*)

If students have physical disabilities that prevent them from pointing to the letters in print, then use partner-assisted scanning (see Chapter 11) or other ways to vary the presentation so that the student is not restricted to identifying the letter from an array of individual letters.

Steps 6 and 7: Producing the Letter Form

6. Let me show you how to write the letter (<u>letter name</u>). This is (<u>letter name</u>), and this is (<u>letter name</u>). (*Describe how to write the upper- and lowercase forms of the letter as you write them.*)

If students write with alternate pencils (see Chapter 11), then demonstrate how to write or select the letter using the student's alternate pencil.

7. Let's practice writing the letter (<u>letter name</u>) together. (*Practice both the upper- and lowercase forms.*)

If students write with alternate pencils (see Chapter 11), then ask the students to write the letter using their alternate pencils.

Source: Jones et al., 2013

Mnemonics   Step 3 of the enhanced alphabet instruction routine previously described suggests that teachers provide stories, mnemonics, and key words to help students remember the sound. When students are struggling to learn particular letters, pairing those letters with mnemonics (e.g., pictures of objects that begin with the target letter—*b*, bike—or actions with names that begin with the target letter—*j*, jump) can support learning (see Dilorenzo, Carlotta, Bucholz, & Brady, 2011; Ehri, Deffner, & Wilce, 1984). The idea is to build a strong association that helps students remember the letter names and associate them with particular pictures, words, actions, or sounds. There are commercially available programs that use mnemonics to teach alphabetic awareness (e.g., *Letterland*; Wendon & Carter, 2014), but these programs use the same mnemonics with every student. Mnemonics are more effective when they are personally relevant (Shmidman & Ehri, 2010). This means that mnemonics will be most effective if teachers consider the interests and experiences of their own students when pairing letters with pictures, words, actions, sounds, or foods that are meaningful to their students.

> Our recommended approach to explicit alphabet instruction is based on the work of Jones et al. (2013) and involves six 26-day cycles that each emphasize different aspects of alphabet knowledge. During each cycle, teachers address one letter per day, following a specific instructional routine.

Summary   Explicit approaches to alphabet instruction must be multifaceted and address all elements of alphabet knowledge. They also have to go beyond matching and sorting tasks that focus only on the letter shape or name and systematically integrate knowledge of upper- and lowercase, letter names, and letter sounds. Finally, explicit approaches should apply principles of distributed learning while attending to the fact that some letters are more challenging to learn than others. As a result, instruction should be flexible enough to provide more repetition with variety for the more challenging letters.

Explicit Phonological Awareness Instruction   For most children, developing phonological awareness requires at least some explicit instruction (Justice, Chow, Capellini, Flanigan, & Colton, 2003; Petursdottir et al., 2009; Phillips, Clancy-Manchetti, & Lonigan, 2008). For students with significant disabilities, this explicit instruction must provide repetition with variety (Gardner, 1999; Perkins & Unger, 1999), combined with careful modeling and scaffolding (Archer & Hughes, 2011; Johnson, 1998). These instructional features are consistent with the conditions of learning we described in Chapter 2 and are elements of phonological awareness interventions involving students with significant disabilities that result in student application and use of skills taught (e.g., Allor et al., 2014). As with explicit alphabet instruction, time spent on explicit instruction in phonological awareness should be focused and brief.

One challenge in providing explicit phonological awareness instruction to students with significant disabilities is that many instructional activities require speech production. The underlying skill is most often altered when those activities are adapted to make them accessible to students with poor speech intelligibility or no speech at all, and what starts as an interactive learning activity turns into a test (Barker, Saunders, & Brady, 2012). In their tutorial on phonological awareness instruction, Schuele and Boudreau (2008) warned against testing rather than teaching phonological awareness. They stated that an effective teacher does not just ask, but

> explains, models, highlights critical concepts, carefully sequences teaching, provides sufficient practice, and scaffolds, contingent on the child's current level of performance ... The adult controls the learning situation, provides ample input, and shows the child how to move from question to answer. (p. 10)

This focus is on helping students figure out how to determine an answer rather than systematically teaching them the answer. This focus is a distinguishing feature between the explicit instruction described here and the systematic instruction that is often the focus with students with significant disabilities (e.g., Browder & Spooner, 2011, 2014; Collins, 2012).

Schuele and Boudreau's (2008) explicit approach to phonological awareness instruction begins by addressing shallow phonological awareness skills (Hindson et al., 2005), such as recognizing rhyme and alliteration (i.e., the initial sounds are the same in words). After students have developed awareness of these shallow skills, the focus shifts to deep skills, such as blending and segmenting sounds in words. As we work with students who are emergent readers and writers, we are most interested in developing shallow phonological awareness skills and will describe that instruction here. (Approaches to developing deep phonological awareness skills, often called *phonemic awareness skills,* are described in Chapter 10, where decoding and spelling are the focus.) As you work to help students develop awareness of syllables in words, rhyme, and alliteration, remember that the goal is not mastery of a specific set of items in a prescribed order. In general, children develop an awareness of words in spoken language before syllables, then rhyme and then alliteration, but they do not necessarily demonstrate mastery of one before beginning to develop awareness of the next. The goal is increased independence in demonstrating awareness of these important phonological awareness skills. Therefore, try introducing some rhyming as soon as students begin to show some success with segmenting syllables, and introduce alliteration as soon as students begin to show some success with rhyming. Moving on to another skill often helps students consolidate and learn to apply the skills they have been working to develop. Specific information about teaching awareness of syllables in words, rhyme, and alliteration is described in the following sections.

Segmenting Words Into Syllables   After students begin recognizing and responding to individual words in spoken language, they begin to become aware of the words within spoken sentences and ultimately the syllables within words. These early forms of phonological awareness can be explicitly taught in very brief segments of time throughout the day. For students who are learning to communicate using AAC, you can help build an awareness of words in sentences by demonstrating communication using the student's AAC system, using symbols that represent single words and combining them to make short phrases and sentences. For all students, you can clap out the words in sentences while talking, reading, and singing. For example, many years ago, we watched in delight as a media specialist in an elementary school read a book with a small group of young children with ASD. Only one of the students used speech to communicate, and most of his speech was in the form of delayed echolalia. This group was often quite difficult to engage in any group task, yet this media specialist regularly captured their attention with the books she selected and the way she read them. On this particular occasion she was reading the book *Over in the Meadow* (Langstaff & Rojankovsky, 1973) and sang rather than read the text to the children while she showed them the pictures. We watched as the classroom teacher and paraprofessionals began to clap along with the rhythm of the music: *Over* (clap) *in the meadow* (clap) *in a dam* (clap) *built of sticks* (clap). One little boy then demonstrated an awareness of more than just the rhythm of the music. First, he demonstrated that he heard the individual words in the song when he clapped once for each word in the phrase—*build* (clap) *said* (clap) *the* (clap) *mother* (clap) *beaver* (clap), *build* (clap) *said* (clap) *the* (clap) *six* (clap). Then, much to our delight, he clapped the syllables in the words in the next refrain—*old* (clap) *mo* (clap) *ther* (clap) *frog* (clap) *gy* (clap) *and* (clap) *her* (clap) *sev* (clap) *en* (clap) *pol* (clap) *ly* (clap) *wogs* (clap).

Seeing this demonstration of awareness, which most people did not know the boy possessed, gave the teacher the information she needed to continue to support the awareness of words in sentences by clapping as she announced, "*Clean* (clap) *up* (clap), *clean* (clap) *up* (clap), *everybody* (clap) *clean* (clap) *up* (clap)," when she sang about the days of the week, "*Today* (clap) *is* (clap) *Monday* (clap)," and whenever she sang or chanted in the class. Having had the experience with the first boy, she knew to watch closely for others to demonstrate the same understanding. As she watched, she noted that not all of the children were clapping. One girl was rocking to the left, then the right, with each word. Another boy was flicking his hand. Only two used clapping to demonstrate their understanding, but before long, each demonstrated an awareness of words in a sentence, and the teacher shifted her clapping to match the syllables. It did not take long for each of the children to begin doing the same.

Students with physical disabilities present a challenge as we look for evidence of their awareness of words in sentences and syllables in words. Their inability to clap, rock, flick, or otherwise show us what they know often leads to modifications, such as asking the student to identify the number of words in the sentence. Unfortunately, this introduces a math skill that increases the complexity of the task. Instead of adding complexity, look for other ways to have them demonstrate their phonological awareness. Several students we know can smack their lips, tap, grunt, and otherwise demonstrate a growing awareness of words in sentences and syllables in words. In the end, for some students, you have to move on to more complex phonological awareness tasks that offer more diverse means of demonstrating awareness rather than sticking with this level until you have established a reliable means of demonstrating understanding.

Teaching Rhyme Awareness   When teaching rhymes, start with rhyming words that have sounds at the end that are made with distinct mouth movements that the student can see (e.g., *tap, map*). This provides an additional clue to students as they work toward developing an awareness of rhyme. Over time, move to other rhymes that end in consonants but are less visible when spoken (e.g., *tan, man*) and eventually to rhyming words that end with vowels rather than consonants (e.g., *way, may*). Working in this way, explicit instruction in rhymes moves from rhymes that are most salient (visually and auditorily) to those that are least salient.

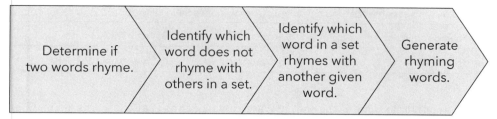

Figure 3.1.   Increasing complexity of rhyme awareness tasks.

At the same time, the tasks students are asked to do with these rhyming words should become increasingly complex over time. Start with deciding whether two words rhyme (e.g., "Do *tap* and *map* rhyme?"), then move to determining which word in a set of words does not rhyme (e.g., *tap, map, bat*). Next, work on identifying a word in a set that rhymes with another given word (e.g., "Which word rhymes with *man? Hat, ball, can*"), eventually generating rhyming words (e.g., "Tell me a word that rhymes with *map*"). Figure 3.1 shows this progression. Note the overlap among the tasks; students do not need to master one before beginning another.

The instructional activities you use to teach these skills should vary from lesson to lesson. Rather than practicing with a single set of words until they are mastered, use different words and rotate through as needed. Rather than always providing response arrays with two, three, or four options, get creative with your lessons to avoid turning lessons into tests. You can use pictures to illustrate words or say the words, but variety is key. For example, use games such as Memory when teaching students to determine whether two words are rhymes. Make your own game cards with a small set of rhyming word pairs represented with pictures. Take turns revealing two cards and deciding whether the words represented by the pictures rhyme. When they do, keep the pair. If students can say the words, then ask them to say the words aloud that are represented by the pictures, and then explain whether they sound the same at the end, or rhyme. If the student labels the pictures differently than expected, then say the intended words, ask the student to repeat the word pair, and determine whether they rhyme. If students cannot use speech to communicate, then give them time to think about the words in their heads before labeling the pictures for them and asking whether the pair rhymes.

There are many other games you might play to explicitly teach rhyming. For example, use the set of cards from the Memory game and deal five or six cards to the student and yourself. Place one card face up, in the middle of the game area, and take turns selecting cards from your hand that rhyme with that card. If you can make a rhyming pair, then keep the pair and turn over a new card from the deck. If not, then draw a new card and have the next player go. The complexity of this game can be increased by putting down two cards and working to make a pair with one or the other. You can create similar games using interactive white boards, and numerous apps and online games address similar skills.

Interacting directly with students to provide informative feedback regarding the answers they give is the key during explicit instruction focused on rhymes. Avoid simple praise (e.g., "Good job!") when students give correct responses; instead, point out the thinking the student might have done to get to the right answer (e.g., "I saw you looking at my mouth. Did you see it look the same?"). When students make errors, teach them how to determine the right answer (e.g., "Let's say the words again.

Table 3.1.   Increasingly challenging sounds to use when teaching alliteration

Continuing sounds	Stop sounds	Tricky sounds
/m/, /s/, /f/, /l/, /r/, /n/, /v/, /z/	/b/, /d/, /g/, /p/, /t/, /k/, /j/	/h/, /w/, /y/, /x/, /q/

Do they sound the same at the end?" "Watch my mouth as I say the words again. Does my mouth look the same at the end?"). Do something different with the next step to help the student succeed, such as offering an easier task (e.g., selecting rhymes that are easier to emphasize and distinguish).

Teaching Alliteration   Use continuing sounds that can be drawn out and emphasized as you begin working on alliteration (e.g., /m/, /s/, /f/, /l/, /r/, /n/, /v/, /z/). As students grow increasingly successful with these sounds, begin using letters that represent stop sounds that are difficult to say without adding the schwa sound /uh/ to the end (e.g., /b/, /d/, /g/, /p/, /t/, /k/ represented by *c* or *k*, /j/). Save the tricky sounds (e.g., /h/, /w/, /y/, /x/, /q/) for later, after students have developed deeper levels of phonological awareness. Table 3.1 shows this progression; however, note that it is not necessary for students to master one set of sounds before continuing to the more challenging sets.

You can use the same cards you created for the rhyming games to have students identify pairs that begin with the same sound and figure out which word in a set of three has a different beginning sound. Similarly, if you deal one card face-up in the middle of the game area, then students can look at the cards in their hand to identify one that represents a word that begins with the same sound as the card in the middle. Alternatively, you can play Go Fish and ask students, "Do you have one that starts like ___?"

There are many possibilities, and, as with the explicit instruction in rhyming, the adult should interact with the student and provide informative feedback regarding both correct and incorrect responses. When students are correct, you might say, "Did you stretch out those sounds? They are the same." When they are incorrect, stretch out the sounds for the student (e.g., /m-m-m/) or, in the case of a stop sound, emphasize and repeat the sound while enunciating the whole word (e.g., /b/-/ee/) to help the student hear the similarity or difference. You can ask students to say the word themselves and pay attention to where the sound is produced in their own mouths; however, take care not to teach students to depend on watching your mouth for visual cues because they will not be able to apply this strategy in their own reading and writing.

> Explicit phonological awareness instruction should focus on helping students figure out how to determine an answer rather than systematically teaching them the answer.

Embedded Approaches to Instruction

In addition to teaching students the skills of alphabet and phonological awareness, we have to work to ensure that they understand how to apply the skills in reading and writing. Taking advantage of naturally occurring opportunities to point out and teach students about the alphabet and make them aware of the sounds in language will help move them toward the kind of applied use required for reading and writing.

Embedded Alphabet Instruction   Alphabet instruction can be embedded throughout the school day in many ways. The one thing you want to avoid is doing the same activity over and over again. Students can learn alphabet skills by repeating the same activity over and over, but they will not learn what to do with letters if we teach in this way. It is not enough for students to be able to identify or name the letters or the sounds associated with them. Students must understand that letters represent sounds and are useful in reading and spelling. (Recall from Chapter 2 that this understanding, known as the *alphabetic principle,* is essential to literacy.) You can embed alphabet instruction in many engaging ways throughout the day. We describe a few in the following sections.

Alphabet Books   One way to teach the alphabet is to use alphabet books during shared and independent reading. Focus on letter names and sounds while reading alphabet books. Read the page and highlight the target letter and the word that is intended to represent the letter. If the letter appears on the page in both upper- and lowercase forms, then point them out, talk about them, and help students understand the relationship between the two forms of the letter and the sound(s) they represent. Alphabet books are especially useful because they highlight individual letters, and they use letters in meaningful contexts. Alphabet books also tend to use clear pictures and simple language. Many alphabet books can be found in your school or public library. Hundreds of alphabet books are also available on http://tarheelreader.org, including books about Peppa Pig, NASCAR races, the American Revolution, and just about any other topic you can imagine. You can read the books on the site without registering, or you can register and create books yourself that align with your curriculum and your students' interests.

You can focus on individual letters or small groups of letters as you select or create alphabet books. For example, you might select or create a book that features a letter you know a student is struggling to learn or one that features two or more letters that can be confusing (e.g., *b, d, p*). One teacher discovered that some of her students thought *l, m, n,* and *o* were actually a single letter named *elemeno.* After several shared readings (see Chapter 4) of some books she made featuring *l, m, n,* and *o,* the students started to look for them and understand that they were actually four different letters that had individual names and represented different sounds.

Alphabet Puzzles and Games   Young children are often immersed in play that involves letters. Toy stores have entire aisles devoted to alphabet toys and games—as simple as wooden letter blocks or puzzles and as complex as handheld electronic games. All of these toys and games provide opportunities for adults to teach young children about letters and sounds while playing. As with other learning, the key is interacting with the child and introducing variety to ensure that students are attending to the letter shapes, names, and sounds.

It can be a little more challenging to find age-respectful alphabet games as students get older, but a little creativity can make the games work for students of any age. One high school teacher we know used a marker to write the letters of the alphabet on Jenga blocks, which are designed to be stacked in a tower, from which players then took turns removing and reading blocks. He added rules as he and his students played. For example, they had to name the letter before removing the block, or they had to name the letters on each of the blocks they secured before being able to try for a new one. Another teacher created decks of playing cards that featured letters rather than standard suits. Some decks had only uppercase letters. Some had only lowercase, and some had both. Students used the cards to play classic card games such as Go Fish and Slap Jack. In Go Fish, students asked for or showed others the letter they were looking for and collected pairs. In Slap Jack, the students negotiated which letter they would slap (e.g., slap *M*) before starting. These games may have to be modified to make them accessible, but playing with letters in this way is one more way to help students learn the alphabet.

Student Names   Names can be used to introduce and teach many emergent literacy skills (Kirk & Clark, 2005). Dozens of opportunities to read or write student names occur across a school day. Students often have cubbies or lockers with name tags, attendance is taken, lunch is ordered, names are placed on work, students are assigned to groups, and so forth. Each of these provides an opportunity to teach students about the letters in their names. As you encounter student names or reasons to write them, say the letter names and sounds and encourage students to say or identify them. Names have such importance and appear with enough regularity in a child's life that young children without disabilities are seven times more likely to know the letters in their name than any other letters of the alphabet (Justice et al., 2006). Similarly, students with significant disabilities are 10 times more likely to recognize the first letter of their first name than they are other letters in the alphabet (Greer & Erickson, 2018). Certainly, other words appear more frequently in the environment, but there is no other single word that is more personally relevant to individual students. Chapter 5 provides more information about helping students learn to write their names.

Environmental Print   The letters of the alphabet are everywhere. Letters are on the signs inside, outside, and around your school; the lunch menu; the labels on food that students eat; schedules; and in books and other materials. We read and write letters as we use these items every day. This naturally occurring print provides ongoing, embedded opportunities to teach the letters of the alphabet, and it does so in a way that clearly communicates that these letters have a purpose. Take a moment to stop and ask students to name or point to a few letters on a sign. Alternatively, go on scavenger hunts that require students to find specific letters throughout the school. Students might write the letter each time they find it, take a photograph of it, or type it one more time on their communication device, tablet, or other portable technology.

Computers and Apps   Computers and keyboards clearly provide students with opportunities to develop alphabet knowledge. Students can explore keyboards with talking word processor software that speaks each letter as it is selected. Students using word prediction software might also explore the relationship among letters and the words that begin with those letters; long before they can spell any words, students can select a letter from a keyword and explore the words that result in a word prediction list. In addition, there are literally thousands of apps intended to teach the alphabet. The most useful apps focus on letters in the context of meaningful words or link them to pictures and actions. Avoid apps that only focus on matching and sorting letters; instead, seek variety. Students who use only one app are often paying attention to the wrong thing and finding success with the specific program while not actually developing alphabet knowledge in ways that can be generalized to meaningful reading and writing.

Summary   These ideas for embedded alphabet instruction are just that, ideas. There are an endless number of ways you can point out, talk about, and teach the alphabet and build student understanding about letters, the sounds they represent, and their purpose in reading and writing. Regardless of which activities you choose, the goal is to help students begin to attend to and think about the print in their environment as a means of helping them apply the alphabet knowledge they are gaining through your explicit efforts to teach them.

> Different forms of print in students' environment provide endless opportunities to embed alphabetic instruction throughout the school day.

Embedded Phonological Awareness Instruction   It can be challenging to explicitly teach phonological awareness without the instruction feeling more like testing than teaching. Many of the strategies we use to shift the balance toward teaching come from embedding the instruction throughout the day. Although the existing research has not involved students with significant disabilities, it is clear that most students require at least some explicit instruction to develop phonological awareness (Justice et al., 2003; Petursdottir et al., 2009; Phillips et al., 2008); however, if we only provide explicit instruction, students with significant disabilities often fail to learn to use the skills they develop to improve their reading and writing (Coleman-Martin, Heller, Cihak, & Irvine, 2005; Fallon et al., 2004). As a result, we recommend combining your explicit efforts to help students develop an awareness of words, syllables, rhyme, and alliteration in oral language with embedded instruction in meaningful language and literacy interactions.

Nursery Rhymes, Raps, and Poetry   Reading nursery rhymes to young children, raps to older students, and poetry to all students can help develop phonological awareness. Writing each in large print on the board, chart paper, or an interactive white board provides a meaningful, visual representation of language that you can read, reread, and explore in order to help students develop awareness of words, rhymes, syllables, and alliteration. It is obvious that nursery rhymes and raps intentionally include words that rhyme. We can emphasize and draw student attention to the rhymes as we read texts and sing these lyrics. Students can provide the rhyming words or other words you intentionally delete or cover as the texts become more familiar. These texts often use short sentences that allow us to draw students' attention to the words in sentences and the syllables in words. We are not expecting the students to read or even understand how to distinguish one word from another in text, but having the printed words allows us to pull out the trusty pointer, point to each word as we read it, and otherwise help students develop an awareness of the individual words in the sentences and then the syllables within words.

Shared Reading   Shared reading is discussed in detail in Chapter 4. Here we focus on the fact that shared reading is intended to maximize interactions page by page while reading with students. You can select or create books for shared reading from Tar Heel Reader that have repeated sentence patterns (e.g., I like red trucks. I like blue trucks.) to help students develop an awareness of the slight differences in the words from one page to the next. When you select books for shared reading that have many rhyming words or a lot of alliteration, you can encourage the students to indicate whenever they hear words that rhyme (i.e., sound the same at the end) or have the same beginning sounds. You can stop and comment on these aspects yourself or draw students' attention to one word and ask them to listen for the other that rhymes or starts the same. If you support phonological awareness only during shared reading, then your students are unlikely to make a great deal of progress (see Justice et al., 2003). Using shared reading as an opportunity to embed phonological awareness instruction in naturally occurring language interactions, however, will support students in applying the skills they acquire during explicit instruction.

> Combine explicit phonological awareness activities—which help students develop an awareness of words, syllables, rhyme, and alliteration in oral language—with embedded instruction in meaningful language and literacy interactions.

A FINAL NOTE: LANGUAGE, LETTERS, AND SOUNDS

Alphabet knowledge and phonological awareness are critical foundational skills that directly contribute to later success in reading and writing, but only when they are taught in ways that help students understand their application and use. As part of a comprehensive approach to emergent literacy instruction, a combination of explicit and embedded instruction can help students learn letter names, upper- and lowercase forms, and the sounds they represent. As part of a comprehensive approach to emergent literacy instruction, a combination of explicit and embedded instruction can help students learn letter names, upper- and lowercase forms, and the sounds they represent. It also helps students develop the ability to attend to and manipulate the sounds in oral language.

RECOMMENDED READING AND RESOURCES

The following readings and resources will deepen readers' understanding of how to teach alphabet knowledge and phonological awareness.

Jones, C. D., Clark, S. K., & Reutzel, D. R. (2013). Enhancing alphabet knowledge instruction: Research implications and practical strategies for early childhood educators. *Early Childhood Education Journal, 41,* 81–89. doi:10.1007/s10643 -012-0534-9. https://digitalcommons.usu.edu/teal_facpub/404/

Project Core professional development modules on alphabet and phonological awareness instruction for beginning communicators. Available at http://project-core.com /professional-development-modules/

Schuele, M., & Boudreau, D. (2008). Phonological awareness intervention: Beyond the basics. *Language Speech and Hearing Services in Schools, 39,* 3–20. doi:10.1044 /0161-1461(2008/002)

CHAPTER 4

Emergent Reading

During a workshop on emergent literacy, the authors of this book showed a video of a teenager who had attended one of our literacy camps. He was successfully reading about water with the help of a highly predictable text and pictures that provided clues to new words on each page. After reading each page, he turned and grinned at the camera. He was so proud. At the end, a member of the audience raised her hand and said, "But he wasn't really reading." We replied that he was really reading: he was just really reading like an emergent reader.

Emergent reading is defined as all of the behaviors and understandings of learners of any age that precede and develop into conventional reading (Koppenhaver, Coleman, Kalman, & Yoder, 1991; Sulzby, 1985). Emergent readers cannot identify words out of context, but they often can successfully tell the story of a familiar book and interact with other reading materials that they find interesting when they are given the right kinds of supports and experiences. Although they may not meet everyone's definition of "really reading," they are inching closer to conventional reading each time they interact with print. In fact, learning to read is a process that begins at birth (Sulzby, 1991) and develops with opportunity and experience. All very young children are emergent readers because they have not had the opportunity and experience required to be conventional readers.

Older students with significant disabilities may also be emergent readers because of a lack of access, experience, or opportunity. Emergent reading experiences for most children begin in the home and then extend to other environments where they see and use print materials and tools, observe others reading and writing, and engage in interactions about reading and writing (Teale & Sulzby, 1986). Parents who read to their children at bedtime, preschool teachers who encourage children to interact with a variety of reading materials, bus drivers who point out the stop or exit signs, and friends who share notes with one another are all promoting growth in children's emergent reading abilities.

RESEARCH BRIEF: ABOUT EMERGENT READERS

Decades ago we began to understand that many students with significant disabilities missed out on literacy learning opportunities because they had fewer (Marvin & Mirenda, 1993) and different (Light & Smith, 1993) home literacy experiences than their peers without disabilities. More recent research suggests that the parents of children with disabilities give literacy a high priority (Al Otaiba, Lewis, Whalon, Drylund, & McKenzie, 2009), but their children may be less interested in print-based experiences than children without disabilities (Justice, Logan, Isitan, & Sackes, 2016). The emergent reading interventions described in this chapter are one set of ways that we can increase interest in print and engagement during print-based experiences.

This chapter focuses on emergent reading for students with significant disabilities. Unlike conventional reading, which requires close attention to and interpretation of print, emergent reading may be entirely picture based or memory based, as was the case with the boy in the video we showed at that workshop. Emergent readers are working to understand the functions of print and print conventions, phonological awareness, alphabet knowledge, and important receptive and expressive language skills such as vocabulary, syntax, and narrative skills. As these skills and understandings develop, emergent readers can engage more actively with text and move toward identifying words and constructing understandings while reading.

The vast majority of students with significant disabilities are emerging in their understandings and use of print. Fewer than one third can read fluently with basic, literal understanding (Erickson & Geist, 2016; Towles-Reeves et al., 2012). Although many more can read some words, they are still emerging in their understandings of print because their reading instruction is likely to focus on pictures, worksheets, responding to questions (Ruppar, 2015), or reading words in isolation in the absence of the kind of integrated, comprehensive instruction that is required to read conventionally with comprehension (Browder et al., 2006).

It takes a broad range of opportunity and experience to learn everything that emergent readers must learn. At a minimum, emergent readers must

- Learn why we read

- Build background knowledge and concepts

- Develop understandings of concepts about print

- Develop phonemic awareness

- Learn to identify some concrete words

- Learn to identify some letter names and sounds

- Develop a desire to learn to read

Each of these is supported when we work to engage emergent readers in shared and independent reading. Both provide emergent readers with an opportunity to engage with text in a way that helps them construct their understandings and apply new skills over time.

Shared reading for students with and without significant disabilities is an activity supported by research (D'Agostino, Dueñas, & Plavnick, 2018; Muchetti, 2013; National Early Literacy Panel, 2008; Skotko et al., 2004). Shared reading focuses on the interactions that occur between an adult and student while reading a book together (Ezell & Justice, 2005) and supports a range of emergent language and literacy skills and understandings, including oral language, phonological awareness, and print awareness (e.g., Justice, Kaderavek, Fan, Sofka, & Hunt, 2009). At the same time, independent reading helps students develop an understanding of why we read and a desire to learn how to read while independently applying other emerging skills and understandings.

Independent reading is taken for granted in the lives of most children without disabilities. In fact, most typically developing children have more than 1,000 hours of meaningful experiences with print by the time they reach kindergarten (Heath, 1983), including hundreds of hours spent independently interacting with reading materials. In contrast, students with significant disabilities often have far more limited opportunities to engage in independent reading because of difficulty interacting with books and other reading materials or difficulty sustaining attention to or interest in reading materials when looking at them independently. All students should be provided with regular opportunities to engage in shared and independent reading as part of a comprehensive approach to emergent literacy instruction (Erickson, 2017).

> More than two thirds of students with significant disabilities are emerging in their understandings and use of print. They need integrated, comprehensive instruction that includes both shared and independent reading to learn how to read conventionally with comprehension.

ENGAGING IN SHARED READING

Shared reading is defined as the interaction that occurs between an adult and student as they read a book together (Ezell & Justice, 2005) with the intention of enhancing the student's language and literacy skills (U.S. Department of Education, 2015c). The Commission on Reading called shared reading "the single most important activity for developing the knowledge required for eventual success in reading" (National Academy of Education & Anderson, 1985, p. 23). Since that time, shared reading has become increasingly prominent in the research literature as a key context for language and literacy intervention for children with and without disabilities (e.g., Bellon-Harn & Harn, 2008; Justice, McGinty, Piasta, Kaderavek, & Fan, 2010; Skotko et al., 2004). The research on shared reading with students with disabilities consistently suggests that it supports the development of the same emergent literacy and language skills that are developed in children without disabilities (e.g., Swanson et al., 2012). For example, highly structured versions of shared reading helped students with ASD improve their ability to initiate and respond (D'Agostino et al., 2018; Muchetti, 2013) and listen with comprehension (Mims, Browder, Baker, Lee, & Spooner, 2009). A less structured approach to shared reading with children with Rett syndrome helped them improve their symbolic communication (Skotko et al., 2004).

The language and literacy skills that are acquired during shared reading are the result of the ways that adults communicate with students while reading (Bellon-Harn & Harn, 2008). For example, Justice et al. (2009) noted that adults can build language and literacy skills in several ways during shared book reading:

- Labeling objects in the illustrations (e.g., "I see a dog.")

- Talking about what is going on in the book (e.g., "That dog is making a big mess.")

- Referring to real-life connections to the story (e.g., "Sometimes we make messes too!")

- Referencing the print (e.g., "There is a *b* like the *b* in your name.")

In addition, adults can increase student attention and engagement by commenting and responding to the student's initiations and interests rather than reading every page from start to finish (Bellon & Ogletree, 2000).

One teacher we observed demonstrated this as she read with a group of three teenage boys. The boys sat around her as she began to read a picture book about the Hall of Fame for various sports. As soon as he saw the first page, one of the boys, Damien, started naming the sports in the pictures. The teacher responded to his interests and tried to engage the other boys as follows.

Teacher: What sports do you play, Chad?

Chad: Basketball.

Teacher: Basketball. They have snowboarding too, and you told me you snowboard, right, Chad?

Damien: That's what I just said, basketball!

Teacher: *[To Damien]* Awesome. That's cool. Two people can have the same idea.

Damien: They shoot like this *[demonstrating a basketball shooting motion]*. I don't know why they shoot like that.

Teacher: It's just a good form, I guess.

Damien: *[Pointing to a picture in the book]* Do you know that is the Olympic flame?

Teacher: Yes! Do you want to tell us about it?

Damien: The Olympic flame represents your heart.

Teacher: Okay *[Nodding]*.

Damien: It goes into your heart so you never forget about it.

Teacher: Yeah, and it never stops. The fire never goes out. Different athletes, the people who do sports, carry the Olympic flame across the country where the Olympics are happening.

Teacher: *[Reading the text]* It says, "Jim Thorpe, he was good at everything." *[Then pointing to a picture]* So he played?

Damien: Baseball!

Teacher: Okay, we also see that he ran. He is like you guys. He does a lot of different sports.

[Chad and the third boy, DJ, nod their heads and smile in agreement.]

DJ: Did you know that I used to do the Olympics?

Teacher: Really, oh, cool!

DJ: I do swimming. I got a first place.

Damien: I was wondering where he got that shirt from.

Teacher: *[Pointing at DJ]* This shirt?

Damien: No, the other shirt.

Teacher: Wow, that is a good connection that you remember DJ's shirt. Did it say Olympics on it?

Damien: Yes! *[Pointing at a picture.]* Is that guy Jim Thorpe also?

Teacher: I don't know. Let's read and find out. *[Turns the page.]* It is him! "He is in the football Hall of Fame."

Damien: *[Talking over the teacher]* "I knew it!"

This teacher was experienced in reading books with students of all ages, and the three boys all had the ability to talk with her during their shared reading interaction. This made it relatively easy for her to follow the boys' lead when they made comments and asked questions, but she had to work to keep Damien from monopolizing the interaction and encourage DJ and Chad to participate. Although shared reading might look a little different with students who have more complex needs, the goal is always to maximize interactions page by page while enjoying a book together.

Getting Started: Unstructured and Structured Approaches

Teachers and other adults can choose among a number of structured and unstructured approaches that support shared reading. Unstructured approaches, like the approach the teacher took with Damien, DJ, and Chad, have been used successfully with students with significant disabilities. For example, mothers successfully used an unstructured approach to shared reading in promoting the communication skills of their children with Rett syndrome (Skotko et al., 2004). The mothers read storybooks while using single-message voice output devices and picture communication symbols to label pictures and make comments about the book. Rather than following a particular structure, the mothers learned to 1) attribute meaning to all communication attempts, 2) provide sufficient wait time, 3) ensure that the girls looked when they pointed to communication symbols, and 4) make use of the voice output communication device and symbols provided through questions and comments rather than directing the child to "hit your switch." As a result of their mothers' efforts, the girls increased their engagement, made more comments, and responded more frequently.

More structured approaches to shared reading have also been used successfully with students with significant disabilities. For example, teachers were taught to follow a structured book-reading protocol while using picture symbols, three-dimensional objects, and simplified text to teach students to answer questions after listening (Browder, Mims, Spooner, Ahlgrim-Delzell, & Lee, 2008). The elementary school-age students with multiple disabilities answered more questions correctly as a result of the intervention. Using the same basic approach, young children with ASD and little speech increased engagement and the average number of correct responses (Mucchetti, 2013).

The decision to take a more or less structured approach to shared reading will depend on the adult's comfort in understanding or interpreting a student's efforts to communicate, as well as the adult's skill in recruiting and maintaining a student's interest and engagement during shared reading. Several ways to structure shared reading are described in the following sections.

> **Both structured and unstructured approaches to reading have been used successfully with students with significant disabilities.**

Follow the CAR   CAR is an acronym for the following three steps:

1. **C**omment and wait.

2. **A**sk for participation and wait.

3. **R**espond by adding a little more.

Adults have to pause and wait quietly between each step to give the student an opportunity to respond or make a new comment. This approach to shared reading stems from work focused on building early language skills that promote literacy learning (Cole, Maddox, Lim, & Notari-Syverson, 2002). CAR was created for use across interactions with young children to facilitate interaction and language development. We apply it specifically to shared reading in which the ultimate goal is for the student to lead the shared reading interaction, and Following the CAR is one way to help them learn to do that.

To Follow the CAR, the adult begins by reading one short segment of a selected text. For example, he or she might read "On Friday, a big wind blew Milky the cow into a tree" from *Chickens to the Rescue* (Himmelman, 2006). Then the adult makes a simple comment about something that might capture the student's attention (e.g., "Milky goes up!") and waits quietly. Commenting and waiting quietly is one way to elicit communication, but we need to wait or pause for a long time for many emergent readers with significant disabilities. For example, many students with significant cognitive disabilities need 15, 20, or even 30 or more seconds of silence after adults comment in order to think and coordinate a reply or a comment of their own (e.g., Koppenhaver, Erickson, & Skotko, 2001).

If the student communicates something during the expectant pause (e.g., "Cow tree."), then the adult repeats the communication act, adds a little more (e.g., "Cow tree. Cow is in the tree."), and moves on. If the student does not communicate during the expectant pause, then the adult asks or encourages the student to participate.

The adult was taught to ask questions and wait in the original version of the CAR; however, we do not jump right to asking questions. Instead, we ask for the student's participation with requests such as "tell me" and repetitions of our original comment. Once again, if the student communicates something during the expectant pause (e.g., "go"), then the adult repeats the communication act, adds a little more (e.g., "Go get. They go get it."), and moves on, as in the example that follows. If not, then the adult continues to the next segment of text and repeats the cycle. (See Figure 4.1 for a flowchart showing the process; a version of this flowchart is available with the downloadable materials for this book.)

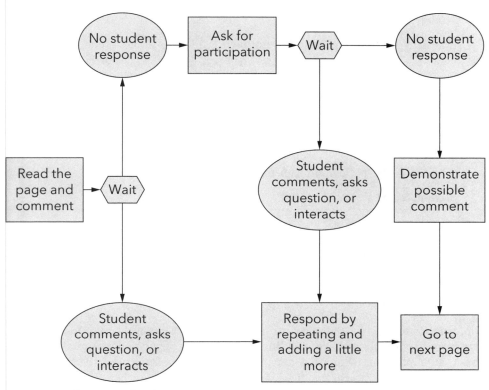

Figure 4.1.   Follow the CAR flowchart.

Follow the CAR in Action

While she was learning to Follow the CAR during shared reading, Ms. Amy decided to preplan the comments she would make. She knew that she often reverted to questions, and she was determined to avoid them to see whether she could increase her students' engagement and interaction when she read with them. As she previewed each page, Ms. Amy thought about her students and identified one comment she could make. She wrote the comment on a small sticky note and attached it to the page.

Her students gathered on the carpet when it came time to read. Several used AAC to communicate and brought their devices with them. Ms. Amy sat in her low chair so that all of the students could see the book. The position also allowed her to see all of the students and reach the AAC display that was hanging on the wall behind her. She started reading:

Ms. Amy: "Chickens to the rescue."

Student 1:   *[unintelligible vocalization]*

Ms. Amy: Yeah, chickens to the rescue. *[Points to the stop sign on the front cover of the book while reading the preplanned comment.]* I see a stop sign. *[Points to the graphic symbol for* STOP *on the AAC display that was hanging on the wall behind her.]*

Student 2:	Stop sign
Ms. Amy:	Stop sign. There is a stop sign. "Chickens to the rescue." *[Reading the preplanned comment.]* They help. *[Points to the graphic symbol for THEY and HELP on the AAC display hanging on the wall behind her.]*
Student 3:	*[Using AAC device]* COW CHICKEN
Ms. Amy:	*[Repeating student's comment]* Cow chicken. Tell me more.
Student 3:	HELP
Ms. Amy:	Help. Cow, chicken, help. Oh, the chickens help the cow. Yes or no?
Student 3:	YES

Ms. Amy, like many other teachers, found that it was easier to engage her students with significant disabilities when she started by avoiding questions and led with comments instead. Although not as structured as some approaches, the CAR gave her guidance to follow as she worked to shift her practice.

Dialogic Reading   Dialogic reading (Lonigan & Whitehurst, 1998) is a specific, structured approach to shared reading. The adult uses specified prompts and a process that emphasizes evaluating, expanding on, and repeating what the student contributes during the interaction. Dialogic reading is effective when the adult reading partner is a parent (e.g., Gettinger & Stoiber, 2014; Leech & Rowe, 2014) or a teacher (e.g., Liboiron & Soto, 2006). It is also effective with students who have developmental disabilities (e.g., Davie & Kemp, 2002) and language impairments (e.g., Justice & Kaderavek, 2003).

An adult applies a reading technique called PEER, which is quite similar to the CAR, during dialogic reading:

- **P**rompt the student to communicate.

- **E**valuate the student's accuracy of response.

- **E**xpand on the student's utterances.

- **R**epeat the student's response.

Much like the CAR, the purpose of PEER is to stimulate increased student communication and interaction during shared reading. The specific ways that adults prompt students to communicate are described by the acronym CROWD:

- **C**ompletion

- **R**ecall

- **O**pen-ended

- **W**h-

- **D**istancing

Combining PEER and CROWD provides adults with a structure to apply during shared reading that enhances the student's language development (U.S. Department of Education, 2010).

Adults work to rotate through the different types of prompts in the CROWD during dialogic reading. For example, they use completion prompts to get students to provide a word or phrase that completes a sentence (e.g., "He huffed and he puffed and he ____"). They use recall prompts to ask about things that have already been read (e.g., "What happened to the car?"). They generally use open-ended prompts (e.g., "Tell me what you see here.") and *wh-* prompts (i.e., traditional questions that begin with who, what, where, why, when, or how) to focus on the pictures (e.g., "What's happening here?") and vocabulary (e.g., "Where is the tarantula?"). Finally, adults use distancing prompts to relate the text to the student's personal experiences. One mom we know frequently uses distancing prompts while reading with her daughter. For example, she used a distancing prompt when she read a line of text from a book, "I have to eat the bird's seed," and then said, "Oh my goodness! That is like Mr. Will. He is always putting out bird seed." She has the advantage of knowing her daughter very well, and she uses that knowledge to help connect books to her life experiences as often as possible, which helps her daughter learn that reading involves constructing meaning and making connections.

Put the CROWD in the CAR   As students start commenting and leading the interaction during shared reading, we often combine CAR (Cole et al., 2002) and CROWD from dialogic reading (Lonigan & Whitehurst, 1998) by using the CROWD prompts during the Ask step of CAR. Given the similarities between PEER and CAR, we could use dialogic reading in its entirety. Yet, we wanted to have a way to help adults understand how to use CAR to get students engaged and interacting during shared reading before adding the specific prompts featured in CROWD.

Some time ago, we used this CROWD in the CAR structure for all shared reading, but our more recent work in classrooms with students with the most complex disabilities who do not have a formal means of communication led us to rethink our starting point. Now, we take the CROWD out of the CAR and focus on interaction and engagement with the CAR until students are actively initiating and responding during shared reading. For some students, this means focusing on building a comprehensive approach to communication. (See Chapter 11 for information about core vocabulary as a starting place.) After students begin successfully engaging and interacting during shared reading, using the same communication system they use throughout their day (e.g., speech, signs, symbols), we put the CROWD back in the CAR and worked on refining and expanding the ways that students interact with us.

With CROWD in the CAR, we are systematically using the CROWD prompts during the Ask step of CAR. We start the CAR by reading the text and then making a comment about the page. If the student responds or otherwise initiates with a book-directed question or comment, then the adult responds by repeating what the student offered and adding a little more. If the student does not interact, then the adult asks for participation using one of the CROWD prompts. (See Figure 4.2 for a flowchart showing the process; a version of this flowchart is available with the downloadable materials for this book.) Teachers of students with significant disabilities have found success using the CROWD in the CAR during

> The structured approaches described in this chapter will help to build students' language skills and increase their engagement and interaction during shared reading.

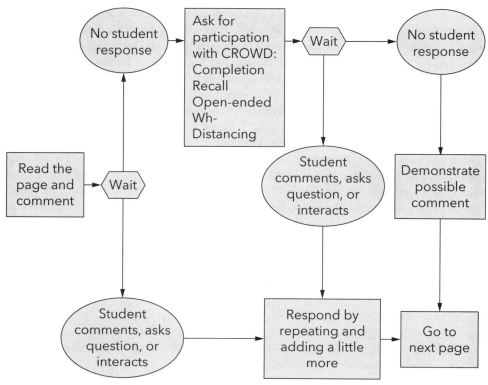

Figure 4.2.   Put the CROWD in the CAR flowchart.

shared reading to increase the number of questions their students answer correctly during shared reading (Cheek, 2016).

Print Referencing   Print referencing is not really an approach to shared reading; rather, it describes a set of techniques used to draw the student's attention to print during shared reading (Justice, Kaderavek, Bowles, & Grimm, 2005). The goal is to increase emergent readers' knowledge regarding the forms and features of print (Justice & Ezell, 2004). The adult uses verbal and nonverbal techniques during print referencing to increase the student's attention to and interaction with the reading materials by providing explicit information about the print (or braille). Verbal references can include comments (e.g., "Here is a *B*, and here is a *b*."), questions (e.g., "What do you think this says?"), or requests (e.g., "Find the *B*."). The references can also be nonverbal as adults point to the words, letters, or other features of the print. Print referencing improves outcomes in oral language (Gettinger & Stoiber, 2014) and print concepts (Justice et al., 2005) without interfering with the other meaning-based comments adults make during shared reading (Dennis, 2018).

Selecting Reading Materials

Beyond deciding whether to follow a structured or unstructured approach to shared reading, adults must choose the reading materials they will use. Notice, we use the term *reading materials* or *texts,* not *books.* Books can be perfect for shared reading, but many other types of reading materials might also interest students. This topic is addressed in detail in Chapter 8, but it is worth mentioning here that shared reading can be successful with reading materials that include books, magazines, newspapers, articles on the web, e-books, peer compositions, letters and e-mails from friends, and much more.

Familiar and Unfamiliar Texts   Familiarity of text is one issue to consider when planning for a shared reading interaction. The nature of adult–student interactions when texts are familiar differs from adult–student interactions when texts are unfamiliar. For example, adults sharing unfamiliar texts tend to read the text and focus on the content by explaining new vocabulary and labeling pictures (Hammett-Price, van Kleeck, & Huberty, 2009). As texts become more familiar, adults focus more on complex questions and connections while interactions with students extend to more diverse topics, compared with the topics these interactions focus on when texts are unfamiliar (e.g., McArthur, Adamson, & Deckner, 2005).

Repeated reading is one way to increase the familiarity of a text. Several studies employed repeated reading with students with significant disabilities and reported positive effects of increased familiarity with the texts. For example, repeated reading and the subsequent increased familiarity increases turn-taking for young children who use AAC (Edmister, 2007) and children with ASD (Bellon, Ogletree, & Harn, 2000). It also increases active engagement among children with ASD (Fleury & Hugh, 2018). Repeated reading has also been associated with increased success responding to questions and an increased frequency of communication behaviors in general among students who use AAC (Edmister, 2007).

Electronic Books   Most studies of shared reading have employed traditional print books, but there is increasing support for the use of e-books during shared reading (e.g., Korat, Shamir, & Heibal, 2013). In some cases, very positive effects have been reported for oral language (Korat, 2009; Korat & Shamir, 2007, 2008; Shamir, 2009) and literacy (Korat & Shamir, 2008; Shamir & Korat, 2007) as a result of shared reading with e-books versus traditional books (Verhallen, Bus, & de Jong, 2006). Other studies, however, indicate that e-books negatively affect the way adults communicate with students during shared reading by increasing attention to the mechanics of reading the book (e.g., using the mouse, clicking the arrow to turn the page) and decreasing the number of text-related comments and connections to personal experiences (Cheng & Tsai, 2014). Furthermore, Cheng and Tsai revealed decreases in the quality of student communication when reading e-books versus traditional print books. These differences between print and e-books are magnified when e-books are enhanced with animations and games, which detract from rather than add to the interactions between adults and students during shared reading (Chiong, Ree, Tekeuchi, & Erickson, 2012).

More important, adults report that they prefer to use print books when interacting with students during shared reading (Strouse & Ganea, 2017). Parents in the United States (Scholastic, 2015a) and other countries (Scholastic, 2015b, 2015c) reported that they prefer that their children read print books rather than e-books. In one study, only 9% of respondents ($n = 2{,}986$) reported that they believed e-books were better than print books when reading to children (Pew Research Center, 2012). Regardless of these impressions, e-books are increasingly available to students with significant disabilities who cannot access traditional print books. In addition, e-books offer educators, clinicians, and parents an increasing selection of reading materials on topics of interest to older, emergent readers, written at a level that is cognitively and linguistically accessible.

Given the importance of e-books for many students with significant disabilities, it is critical to consider the features that make them more or less successful. For example, as mentioned previously, enhanced features such as animations can detract from the value of shared reading (Chiong et al., 2012). Other research (Skibbe, Thompson, & Plavnick, 2018) suggests that e-books that highlight words while reading them aloud might increase student attention to print and illustrations. The authors pointed out, however, that this is only an advantage when e-books are used for independent rather than shared reading. Finally, research suggests that having adults engaged in shared reading of e-books with students leads to improved performance on measures of concepts about print and phonological awareness, relative to shared reading of print books (Segal-Drori, Korat, Shamir, & Klein, 2010), especially for students who have poor letter recognition knowledge (Rvachew, Rees, Carolan, & Nadig, 2017).

SUPPORTING INDEPENDENT READING

In addition to shared reading, comprehensive emergent literacy intervention must include opportunities for independent reading. These interactions with reading materials help any emergent reader to independently apply emerging print knowledge while developing the dispositions required for lifelong reading (Owocki & Goodman, 2002). Even before students with significant disabilities can read or understand printed words, opportunities to choose from and read a large collection of interesting, age- and ability-appropriate materials lead to measurable gains in as few as 6 weeks (Hatch & Erickson, 2018).

Independent reading for many students with significant disabilities will require accommodations or electronic reading materials. Physical impairments can make it very difficult to independently explore reading materials, sensory impairments may make books inaccessible, and communication impairments can make it challenging for students to indicate choice. It is encouraging to note that new and emerging technologies make independent exploration of reading increasingly possible. For example, Tar Heel Reader (http://tarheelreader.org) is an open-source library of accessible books for beginning readers of all ages. Parents, teachers, therapists, friends, and others write these books about topics they choose. Thousands of books are available about typical academic topics, current events, popular culture, and other topics likely to address the interests of most emergent readers. Whether students access texts through Tar Heel Reader; another online source; a school, classroom, or home library; or a magazine rack, opportunities for independent exploration and use are an important part of comprehensive emergent literacy instruction. Chapter 8 provides extended detail about supporting student choice and motivating independent reading. Here, the focus is on some ways to engage students with significant disabilities in independent reading before they can read.

Looking at (Wordless) Picture Books

Students who cannot read words can engage in independent reading using picture books. We often think about picture books for young children, but there is an increasing selection of picture books with and without text that are appealing to students of all ages. We have laughed along as a 10-year-old giggled his way through a *Dumb Bunnies* book by Dav Pilkey (1994). The boy pointed at, talked about, and laughed at picture after picture in the book. We have looked on as a small group of teenagers worked their way through *Dirty Bertie* (Roberts, 2002) and swapped stories about the gross things they do every day. We have been delighted by a group of students with significant disabilities in a postsecondary transition program who related the emotions displayed on characters' faces in *Famous* (Musselwhite, 2006) to their own mixed emotions about school. None of these students could read, but all of them engaged purposefully and meaningfully in their interactions with these picture books that were traditionally written for much younger readers.

Viewing or Reading Online Books

Many picture books are available in online formats. These may be more accessible to some students with significant disabilities, but take care to avoid versions that use music and animation to engage the student. These features take student's attention away from the print we are working to get them to understand. Selecting texts and sites that read aloud to students, especially when they offer word-by-word highlighting, attracts student attention to print (Skibbe et al., 2017), but animations and embedded actions and games do not (Chiong et al., 2012).

Following Along as a Partner Reads

Students with significant disabilities who cannot read can follow along as their peers and other partners read to them. The key is to encourage the student to attend to the text and follow along rather than listen passively. The goal is increased access to a wide range of reading materials and success interacting with these materials in a way that includes attention to print.

Following Along With Text Read Aloud by a Computer Program

Common word processing programs such as Google Docs, Microsoft Word, and Apple Pages all include text-to-speech options. There are also many other screen reading tools that will read aloud the text on web sites, in pdf files, and in other formats beyond those that can be read in word processing programs. These enable a student who cannot read to listen to the text being read and follow along with it on the computer. Students are often motivated to use this feature to read the texts their peers have written. They can also use it to read the school newspaper, the television guide, and any other text that might be interesting and engaging.

Due to physical, sensory, or communication impairments, many students with significant disabilities require accommodations or electronic reading materials to engage in independent reading. New and emerging technologies make independent exploration of reading increasingly possible.

Reading Captioned Movies and Video Clips

If a student is not motivated by reading materials, but is motivated by television, movies, and video clips, then turn on the closed captions. Adding closed captions to movies and videos can improve literacy skills ranging from comprehension and word recognition to alphabet and letter–sound knowledge (Linebarger, Piotrowski, & Greenwood, 2010). In fact, this research suggests that the students who benefit the most from closed captions are those who are not yet reading fluently with comprehension.

A FINAL NOTE: ENCOURAGING EMERGENT READING

In our work with at-risk preschool children who did not have identified disabilities, we tried to make sure every child participated in three or more shared reading interactions every day. Whether these occurred with a group or one to one, all were focused on maximizing interaction and engagement for the purpose of building language and literacy skills. In addition, books were strategically placed in every learning center, and a basket full of books made its way out to the playground every time the class headed outside to play. It was not unusual to see an adult sitting next to a child in a sandbox reading a book about the diggers and dump trucks the children were using. This group of at-risk children arrived at preschool with very limited experiences with print, and their teachers responded by maximizing the experiences they encountered at school. We must provide the same kinds of daily opportunities for shared and independent reading opportunities for students with significant disabilities if we want to help them inch toward conventional literacy. We must also focus these opportunities on interaction and engagement until we have students who eagerly initiate and respond when we read with them and they read to themselves.

RECOMMENDED READINGS AND RESOURCES

The following readings and resources will deepen readers' understanding of how best to support emergent readers.

Dynamic Learning Maps Professional Development web site (http://dlmpd.com). See the module on shared reading.

Ezell, H. K., & Justice, L. M. (2005). *Shared storybook reading: Building young children's language and emergent literacy skills.* Baltimore, MD: Paul H. Brookes Publishing Co.

Project Core web site (http://project-core). See the modules on shared reading and independent reading.

CHAPTER 5

Emergent Writing

Matthew, a 10-year-old with significant multiple disabilities, is seated on his mother's lap. They are being introduced to a large adapted keyboard that an AT consultant hopes will achieve at least two goals. First, she hopes it will enable Matthew to begin to write despite his fine motor difficulties, and second, she wants him to be able to see what he has written on a large computer monitor despite his significant visual impairments.

Matthew begins banging on the keyboard as if it were a conga drum. Tap-tap, tap-tap-tap, bang-bang-bang, tip-tip, bang-bang-bang, bang-bang-bang, slam-bang! As he engages in his fierce, rhythmic exploration, his mother speaks gently, but directly, in his ear, "You made an M. You made another M."

She presses the Speak button on the keyboard, and Matthew pauses as a male, synthetic voice speaks aloud the letter names his drumming has produced, "M, M, B, J, B, J, B, J, B, A."

Matthew looks up at the computer screen. Slam! Slam! Ker-slam! Ka-bam! He hits the keyboard with two hands simultaneously. His mother gently takes hold of both of his elbows and says quietly in his ear, "Need you to stop." He looks at the computer monitor. "Yeah," Mom reassures him. She types his name. Matthew leans in toward the computer, staring intently at the letters he has banged out, and that she is typing. "Let's hear what it says," she tells him.

"Mabj, isejj, J, igbee. Matthew," says the computer.

Matthew looks from the keys to the computer monitor to the keys and back at the monitor. "Did you hear that?" asks his mother. He continues exploring. Sometimes he bangs, sometimes he taps, sometimes he rests his chin on the keyboard and bangs with both hands. His mother periodically comments on his writing, directs him to "listen to what the computer says," and praises his "wonderful writing." Finally, the consultant prints out Matthew's first writing, and his mother says, "That's pretty cool, isn't it? Let's look at it. Momma's so proud of you."

Matthew was not engaged in writing as we describe in Chapter 9. He was not composing texts in traditional orthography that could be read by others. Instead, he was engaged in emergent writing that was fully supported by his mother, a consultant, and technology. Emergent writing can be thought of as the explorations, experiments, and inventions of learners who do not yet fully understand all of the conventions that make written communication possible because of their inexperience with print generally, and writing tools specifically, as well as their individual differences. Matthew bangs on the keyboard because he has not yet had the opportunity to learn to type.

The computer's resilient keyboard, large visual display of high-contrast letters, talking word processor, printer, the consultant, and his mother reward his explorations. He has been introduced to ideas such as the following:

- When I bang my hands, squiggles (letters of the alphabet) appear on the computer screen.

- Sometimes the squiggles go together, and sometimes there are spaces between them.

- The squiggles have names that are spoken aloud by the computer or my mother.

- Some combinations of squiggles produce things I know, such as my name.

- My mother is very happy when I make these squiggles.

> Emergent writing can be thought of as the explorations, experiments, and inventions of learners who do not yet fully understand all of the conventions that make written communication possible because of their inexperience with print generally, and writing tools specifically, as well as their individual differences.

RESEARCH BRIEF: ABOUT EMERGENT WRITERS

Emergent writing, like emergent reading (see Chapter 4), represents a paradigm shift in our understanding of children's learning and how best to support it. Emergent writing emphasizes written language use even before children know what writing looks like, how to produce it, or the purposes it serves. Children are encouraged to engage in frequent and regular writing experiences while teachers and families demonstrate conventional print use. Emergent writing progresses through fairly predictable stages when children have such experiences. Initial writings are best characterized as large, continuous, whole-page scribbling or drawing. These scribbles become smaller, separate, and more distinct with experience and time. Scribbling will often branch into handwriting-like, continuous, wavy, horizontal lines. Distinct scribbles then become more letter-like and eventually are mixed with actual letters, often not quite matching conventional print (e.g., *M*'s with 4 humps or *F*'s that look like upside down *L*'s). Letters become more and more conventional in appearance and are grouped in horizontal strings that gradually become more word-like as spacing is added between letter strings. Soon children's letter strings become more phonetic and readable (e.g., *I lk u*), and writing conventions become more and more prominent across time. Byington and Kim (2017) provided a very readable overview of emergent writing stages and supportive instruction.

   Emergent writing, then, is defined as all of the writing behaviors and understandings of learners of any age that precede and develop into conventional writing (Koppenhaver, Coleman et al., 1991; Sulzby, 1985). Long ago, research confirmed that intelligence explains a relatively small portion of early conventional literacy success (see, e.g., Gates & Bond, 1936) or progress in learning to read and write in school (see, e.g., Gray, 1969). Instead it seems to be the case that four processes contribute to the acquisition of literacy skills and understanding—observation, collaboration, independent practice, and performance (Holdaway, 1984).

When adults think aloud as they use an assistive writing tool, individuals with significant disabilities get to observe the mechanics or underlying cognitive and communicative aspects of writing. When adults engage in dialogic writing experiences or respond with enthusiasm to nonconventional writing attempts, learners become increasingly motivated to communicate their thoughts with others. When adults provide opportunities, encouragement, and support for independent writing, individuals with significant disabilities have a chance to explore writing forms, self-evaluate written products, and demonstrate current understandings. When adults assist in publishing emergent writings, learners share what they can do and gain the approval of peers, family members, and teachers. The more frequently students engage in these experiences, the richer the interactions with adults within and surrounding those experiences, and the more engaging and understandable these writing events, the more efficiently students advance toward conventional literacy.

Although emergent writing is important, students with the most significant disabilities often have few opportunities to learn to write (Erickson, Koppenhaver, & Cunningham, 2017). The complexity and severity of their disabilities appear to contribute to these diminished early writing opportunities in homes as parents struggle to address their children's health care needs and individual differences (Craig, 1996; Fallon, Cappa, & Day, 2008; Light & Kelford Smith, 1993; Light & McNaughton, 1993). Reduced opportunity to engage in emergent writing experiences has been found in the homes of children with ASD (Lanter, Watson, Erickson, & Freeman, 2012), intellectual disabilities (Trenholm & Mirenda, 2006; van der Schuit, Peeters, Segers, Van Balkom, & Verhoeven, 2009), and multiple disabilities (Craig, 1996; Marvin, 1994). Although fewer studies have examined emergent writing in preschool environments, those that have suggest few learning opportunities for children with disabilities, including complex communication needs, multiple disabilities, and deafblindness (Coleman, 1991; Marvin & Mirenda, 1993; McKenzie, 2009; Peeters, de Moor, & Verhoeven, 2011).

Although typical home and preschool environments may not ideally support emergent writing growth, children with significant disabilities do benefit when provided with the range of learning opportunities reported in preschools serving typically developing children. This includes children with a wide range of moderate to severe disabilities (Katims, 1994; Kliewer, 2008; Kliewer et al., 2004; Lieber, Horn, Palmer, & Fleming, 2008), ASD (Koppenhaver & Erickson, 2003; Travers et al., 2011), significant intellectual disabilities (Erickson et al., 2005), and deafblindness (McKenzie, 2009). Preschool teachers in inclusive environments seem particularly open to the learning potential of students with disabilities, with more than 90% believing that children with disabilities benefit from emergent literacy instruction (McDonnell et al., 2014).

WHAT DOES EMERGENT WRITING LOOK LIKE OVER TIME?

Emergent writing progresses along a fairly predictable path toward increasingly conventional writing as learners engage in interactive experiences with print. Children may initially draw when given writing tools and materials and invited to write. They are familiar with drawing activities from homes and preschool and may be uncertain about the meaning of an invitation to write. They may also consider drawing and writing to be synonymous. Children's perceptions and misperceptions are more easily interpreted by observant educators and family members when they can speak or communicate effectively. They will either read the picture if they view it as text or talk about it if they see it as a drawing. Eric, a child with ASD, read his drawing, shown

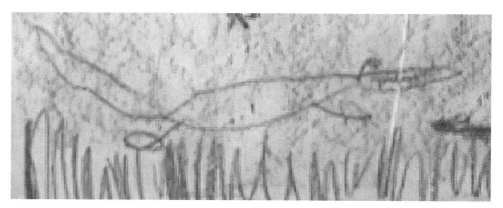

Figure 5.1   Eric's drawing, as read aloud to his aide: "Crocodiles have big tails."

in Figure 5.1, to his one-to-one aide: "Crocodiles have big tails." Aaron, a young adult with ASD, read aloud his journal entry drawing, shown in Figure 5.2: "Big snake."

Children's drawings and scribbling become increasingly letter-like with time and experience. Children become more familiar with the distinction between writing and drawing and have experiences seeing print as it is read aloud or written for them. This growth in understanding is dependent more on experience than age. Jimmy, a middle-aged man with cerebral palsy, wrote the alphabet in response to our query about his ability to write (see Figure 5.3). He wrote from left to right with a carriage sweep from the end of the first line to the left-hand side on the second line. When asked who

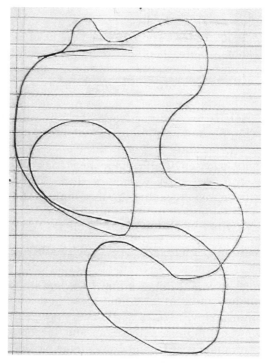

Figure 5.2.   Aaron's journal entry drawing, as read aloud: "Big snake."

Figure 5.3. The alphabet Jimmy wrote when asked about his ability to write.

taught him to write, he explained, "They didn't teach people like me when I was a kid. I learned from watching TV." Matthew's banging on the keyboard, described earlier, is an example of scribbling with a keyboard.

Dustin, a teenager with Landau-Kleffner syndrome, demonstrates how individuals who are able to draw often mix writing forms. A sample of his writing combines drawing, conventional spelling of his name, and nonphonetic letter strings and numbers (see Figure 5.4).

Figure 5.4. Dustin's writing, which combines drawing, conventional spelling of his name, and nonphonetic letter strings and numbers.

Derrick, an 8-year-old with multiple disabilities, typed the following message letter-by-letter for a classmate and read it aloud to his teacher, "To Taz, I fell on my head."

ST kn mn I lc
S amd

This message shows how he is intentional in his letter use and has begun to demonstrate understanding of two other writing conventions—the use of capitalization and the use of white space as a boundary between words in text. He does not yet understand that letters represent sounds in text.

It is common practice to provide students with disabilities a limited set of words, often accompanied by picture symbols, for writing activities. We do not recommend this practice. To illustrate why, let's examine one example of the writing that may result. Using a limited set of words, Ian, a third grader with multiple disabilities, composed the following message, essentially controlled scribbling with whole words:

Ten Dad is no came Lachlan Pendrick Pizza.

Ian then read it aloud: "Drink dad in the car and eat too." Although each word is readable, Ian has no idea what the words are, and, like a child who scribbles, he assigns his own arbitrary meaning to the resulting text. Unfortunately, in the process, he has no chance to learn how letters of the alphabet are the elements of written composition.

Letter use becomes more fully representative of the sound system over time as students hear letters, words, and texts read aloud by others or technologies. Callie, a teenager with ASD, wrote the following using invented spelling, which she read aloud as, "We opened the door."

weoepndoop

Her concept of word has not yet developed, but she demonstrates growing awareness of letter–sound relationships. The example in Figure 5.5 illustrates how students' phonetic representations of letters and words increase as they develop concept of

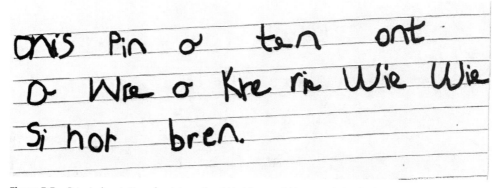

Figure 5.5.   Brian's description of a picture of a girl holding a rabbit, as read aloud: "Once upon a time there was a girl. She had a bunny."

He wrse a sadl.

Figure 5.6. Scott's writing, as typed, to describe a horse he loved: "He wears a saddle."

word. Brian, a third grader with significant language learning disabilities, wrote this description of a picture of a girl holding a rabbit and read it aloud: "Once upon a time there was a girl. She had a bunny."

Scott, a 10-year-old boy with Down syndrome, typed, "He wears a saddle," while describing the horse he loved (see Figure 5.6).

Once children develop a concept of word, understand the alphabetic principle (i.e., that letters represent sounds in spoken language that can be combined to form words), and acquire a few sight words, their writing takes on more and more convention and becomes increasingly readable by others. Eric, who as a young boy wrote by drawing about crocodiles, later composed letter by letter using an office label maker. He produced many texts like the one shown in Figure 5.7. He needs to learn a good deal about many aspects of conventional writing, but his concept of word, understanding of letter–sound correspondences, and increasing knowledge of sight words enable him to compose more readable texts.

GETTING OFF TO A GOOD START

Although emergent literacy rests on a foundational understanding that there are no prerequisites, that is not the case with emergent writing. There are two prerequisites—something to write with and something to write on. Chapter 11 provides more specific detail on using AT to support emergent and conventional reading, writing, and communication. We discuss a few of these ideas in emergent writing contexts next.

Explore Writing Tools and Surfaces

It is important to explore a wide variety of writing tools and media and keep an open mind about what might work with individual students. It is equally important, however, that students' writing not be put on hold while exploration proceeds. Partner-assisted writing enables all students to begin writing immediately and continue daily while you and other members of the interdisciplinary team explore independent writing possibilities. Various low-tech tools and techniques (e.g., alternate pencils) are used in partner-assisted writing to provide alphabet access for students with significant physical

BIRD DINNER EATING BOY
BIRDS EATING WERMS

Figure 5.7. A text Eric composed using an office label maker.

impairments who cannot hold pencils or type on keyboards. The partner presents the alphabet to the learner one letter at a time, the student indicates when the partner presents a desired letter, and the partner writes down the choices of the learner. This approach allows students to begin interacting with and using the alphabet for writing while they are learning the alphabet and learning to use it to spell and write words.

Explorations should not be conducted hastily. Students require time to learn how different writing tools work, see what they can do with the tool, and even at times show us their own solutions to difficulties they may experience. As they explore writing tools, you can observe how they use a particular tool, what they produce with it, what difficulties they encounter, and whether they sustain their engagement in exploring writing with it. The pace at which technology changes means that some tools disappear and new tools are introduced each year, but there are organizations such as Closing the Gap (https://closingthegap.com), Web Accessibility in Mind (https://webaim.org/articles/motor/assistive), and the Assistive Technology Industry Association (https://atia.org) that offer resource listings, conferences, and training opportunities that allow you to explore and get to know current alternatives.

Students' motivation to use various writing tools can sometimes mitigate fatigue or access challenges and sometimes surprise us. Kyle, a 5-year-old with ASD, produced mostly illegible writing with little sustained attention until he was provided a writing surface angled at 45 degrees. Almost immediately, his teachers could recognize that he was writing the letters of his name and exploring print purposefully. AT specialists recommended that Jordan, a 9-year-old with multiple disabilities, use a headstick to point to symbols or type, but he insisted on using his hand. An occupational therapist fashioned a grip for his hand and attached a piece of hard plastic to it. He could initially gain access to only two very large keys. He persisted, however, and, with experience over many years and the patient support of his teachers, parents, and instructional aides, he gradually improved to his current keyboard that has all 26 letters, punctuation, navigation arrows, and keys that support the kind of word prediction that is now integrated into most smart phones. Eric, a boy with ASD, initially wrote with a pencil, then only with an office label maker, then with a pencil and keyboard, and today he primarily writes with handheld smart technologies.

Students like those previously mentioned have taught us many different possibilities for initiating increasingly independent emergent writing. Low-tech writing tools can be fashioned from a wide variety of freely available materials found in most schools. Alphabet letter sets, blocks, or alphabet letter stamp sets enable students to write with or without assistance. Use of pens, pencils, crayons, and chalk can be assisted with grips of all sorts. Felt-tip markers can be hot glued to LEGO Duplo cars or punched through tennis balls to decrease some students' fine motor difficulties. Erasable surfaces such as white boards, chalkboards, and write-on wipe-off boards provide a wide variety of reusable and personal writing surfaces. Take photographs of students' written products and periodic videos as they write with these tools in order to document performance and growth and explore student needs and interests. Table 5.1 presents a menu of options to explore with emergent writers.

Table 5.1.   Options that might be explored with emergent writers

Writing tools	Writing surfaces
Hand-held light tech (e.g., pencils, pens, markers, crayons, paintbrushes) with adapted or supportive grips as needed	Paper of various sizes at tables, on easels, on walls
Dry-erase markers, chalk	Dry-erase and chalkboards, both personal and wall mounted; SiDiKi writing tables, which are transparent, portable, and adjustable
Alphabet sets in various sizes and types such as magnetic letters, letter stamp kits (with handles if needed), foam letter sets, Mason Pegz Clickable letter stamp sets, LEGO Duplo letter sets, 3D printer alphabet sets (braille), alphabet tiles and blocks	Magnetic surfaces, tables, trays, floor
Alphabet technologies such as label makers, manual and electric typewriters, older computers with word processing programs	Label maker tape, paper
Writing and drawing toys such as Fisher Price Doodle Pro, Cra-Z-Art Magna Doodle, V Tech Write and Learn Creative Center, LeapFrog Scribble and Write	Writing surfaces integrated with the writing tool
Computers with (talking) word processors and assistive keyboards, such as Big Keys, or flexible and waterproof silicone keys, tablets and iPads with or without external keyboards, other handheld technologies, SMART interactive white boards	Writing surfaces integrated with the writing tool; various digital writing environments observed on the screens of computers or transferred to paper by computer printer
Partner assistance with alternate pencils	Notebooks, paper, chart paper

Create a Welcoming Emergent Writing Community

An approach called *Big Paper* provides one wonderfully supportive emergent writing environment (Staples & Edmister, 2012). Emergent writers, teachers, and aides gather around a large table covered with newsprint or bulletin board paper and a variety of writing utensils. Students can see what others are doing in this shared social environment and try out new forms, topics, and tools based on those observations. Teachers can easily comment on student writing, encourage individuals or the whole group, participate as group members, provide demonstrations of writing forms, or support students in need of assistance.

Such a structure may require thoughtful planning for students who have severe physical or visual impairments or students using writing with partner assistance. Similar principles apply, however.

Celebrate All Student Writing   First, and foremost, a welcoming community requires not only a tolerance of all forms of writing but also a celebration. Older students in particular may have been made aware that their writing is incorrect through peer, family, or teacher responses over the years; difficult instructional exercises; or the dreaded red pen mark-up. Understandably, they may be reluctant to engage in further writing, thereby reducing the possibility of learning and growth.

We observed a 5-year-old whose father was emptying the boy's backpack when he arrived at home. Seeing a piece of construction paper filled with a drawing, some letters, and letter-like shapes, his father said, "This is really great. Read what you wrote to me."

The young boy replied, "Oh, that's kindergarten writing. It's not real writing."

Kindergarten writing was how his teacher described nonconventional, emergent writing to the boy's class. By doing so, she also conveyed the message that kindergarten writing was inferior. Teachers must welcome writing in all its forms and avoid describing nonconventional writing as kindergarten writing, scribble, letter shapes, marks on the paper, or any other terminology indicating that the student's writing is something different from, or less than, conventional writing. All students need to be praised for their efforts and, when they have the expressive communication skills, be asked to read aloud what they write. Thoughtful teachers record these student read-alouds on the backs of their papers, on sticky notes, or after page breaks in digital writing environments. By doing so, they keep a record of the student's intended meaning without disturbing the student's product or reducing feelings of ownership. These written records can be compared with the student's nonconventional writing attempts over time in order to interpret changes in the writing and recognize growing convention in form.

Parents, teaching assistants, colleagues, volunteers, administrators, and classroom visitors may need to be coached about how to respond positively to emergent writing. Think in terms of three pluses:

1. Listen with interest to students who read aloud what they have written.

2. Tell them it is wonderful; the more specific and content focused your comments are, the better.

3. Encourage students to write more about the topic.

One teacher we know was more ambitious and hung a poster on her classroom door. When visitors arrived, she would ask if they had read the poster and if they had any questions. Only then would she invite them to interact with her students. If students cannot talk, then visitors can still engage in a modeled writing interaction like that described in items 2 and 3 on the "Welcome to Our Classroom" poster, which is shown in the textbox.

Welcome to Our Classroom

We are learning to write. You may see a lot of what you think are errors and want to help us fix them. Don't! These mistakes help our teacher learn what to teach us next.

Here Are Some Ways You Can Help Us

1. Ask us to read to you what we have written. Write down what we say on a sticky note, and stick it on the back of our papers. Tell us how much you like what we are writing and say, "Write some more about that!"

2. Tell us your first name and show us how you write it. Say each letter aloud as you write it. Make sure we can see what you are writing. Then point to your name and say it. If any letters in your name are the same in ours, then help us find them.

> Thoughtful teachers keep a record of a student's intended meaning without disturbing the student's product or feelings of ownership.

3. Sit down next to us, draw a picture, and write no more than three words about it. Show us your picture, point to the words, and read them aloud to us.

Thanks for visiting today!

Publish Student Writing Even though emergent writers are not writing conventional texts, it is important to help them understand that we write in order to communicate with others. Nothing is more motivating to student writers than response to their publications from peers and family members. Teachers support this in many creative ways because emergent writing can be challenging or impossible for others to read. One teacher wrote a form letter to accompany student writing she sent home for families (see textbox). She kept it on the computer and printed one version for the boys and one for the girls in her class.

Dear Families,

Here are our class writings about _____. We hope you enjoy them.

PLEASE: Ask your child to show you his or her page and read it aloud to you. Tell him or her how proud you are of his or her writing. Encourage him or her to keep writing about all the things that interest him or her. Hang your child's writing on the fridge or on the wall. Share his or her writing with other family and friends.

DON'T: Tell your child about mistakes you find or require your child to correct his or her mistakes.

We are learning to write this year, and these differences between adult writing and what your child is doing (emergent writing) help me know what I need to focus on next to teach him or her better. If you have any questions, please call me or stop by my classroom after school to chat.

Thanks,
Ms. B

Expect Variability in Student Readings of Text Over Time   Emergent writing by definition lacks convention. Students' read-alouds shift from one reading to the next based on what they are thinking about or experiencing at the time. One day they read their text under the picture of a rabbit as, "Want bunny." Another day they read, "Bunny sleep." A third time they read, "Warm;" a fourth, "Pet bunny." And on and on. These readings vary even more widely without an accompanying picture.

Emergent reading and writing are constructive processes in which meaning remains fluid until the written products contain sufficient degrees of convention to constrain student reading. As student writings become more phonetically regular and incorporate more sight words over time, students will begin to read the actual words on the page and the text will become more "fixed." Any reading by the student allows you to examine student writing for evidence of letter–sound spelling strategies, growing awareness of concept of word, and other use of writing conventions that may be more difficult to identify without the student's reading.

In sum, texts produced by emergent writers are unconventional and, as a result, the meaning assigned to these texts by the writer may vary. This may present challenges for adults who want to respond meaningfully to these texts or elicit meaningful responses from other readers. Two strategies teachers can use are to pair emergent writing either with pictures or with student read-alouds.

Pair With Pictures   Pairing writing with pictures either drawn or selected by students is one way that teachers can provide a context for meaningful response to readers of emergent writing. This is especially true for students with complex communication needs who may be unable to read aloud their emergent writing for interested listeners. Teachers can find themselves at a loss for meaningful responses in the absence of a conventional text or an intelligible read-aloud. With a picture, teachers and other adults can always respond helpfully by

- Linking the picture to the emergent writing ("You wrote about cats. I like cats, too.")

- Linking the emergent writing to a classmate's interests ("You wrote about cats. Jamilla was writing about dogs yesterday. You two should share what you wrote with each other.")

- Encouraging more writing ("I love that you wrote about cats. Tell us more.")

A wide variety of technology is available to insert pictures into a document for students to write about. Various wikis, blogs, and online word documents enable insertion of scanned student work as an image file. Each of these technologies enables readers to provide feedback through written or spoken comments. These comments are motivating for emergent writers and help them understand that publication means other people read and respond to your writing. Many text creation apps enable users to insert pictures or photographs and add accompanying texts (e.g., Book Creator, StoryBuddy 2, Story Creator, My Story Book Creator, Storyteller Deluxe). Many apps enable users to caption photographs, but, in some cases, the application places the text over the photograph. That limits the amount of writing a student can do while making the picture and writing more difficult for emergent readers to see or interpret.

Pair With Student Read-Alouds of the Text   When students are able to speak, teachers can easily pair their read-aloud with their emergent writing, making it much easier for adults to respond thoughtfully to the student's text. There are many simple ways to do this electronically. All begin with creating an electronic copy of the student's writing. First, take a picture of the writing or scan it along with any accompanying pictures. Next, send the photograph to the appropriate folder or program on the computer you are using (e.g., photograph app on a smart phone or tablet, the pictures folder or software program on a desktop or laptop computer).

Multiple students' written compositions can be stored in the same place. You can use a free web site such as Little Bird Tales (https://littlebirdtales.com) and create a new book and upload each of your students' pictures and texts to a page in the book. Next, record all of the students reading aloud their individual pages. Save the resulting talking book at Little Bird Tales web site and share the URL with families.

Another alternative might be to use a web-based tool such as Screencast-o-matic (http://screencast-o-matic.com) to easily record students as they read their texts aloud. For example, you might share the recordings in a variety of video formats and upload them to a wiki or blog for publication. Or, you might share the file directly to YouTube, using the privacy settings so that only people you share the link with can see the video. (This reduces the possibility of receiving less than encouraging comments.) To save work and time, many teachers record all of the students reading their individual writings in a single file before saving or uploading the combined class file. A major advantage of using any of these sites as publishing resources is the easy opportunity for viewers to add comments. Blog sites and YouTube are especially useful because the comments are placed directly below or beside the video publication.

Many apps (e.g., Explain Everything, Book Creator, My Story, Evernote) make it easy to upload images of the students' writing, create individual pages, pair audio recordings with student writing, and share students' work in many different formats. Many teachers like to share projects created with apps to a central online location (e.g., Google Drive, Dropbox folder) that has already been shared with families or other desired audience members (e.g., another classroom). Anyone with the link can then view and comment on writings left in the folder across the school year. When teachers get in the habit of publishing each Friday or every other Friday, respondents can get in the habit of checking the digital folder and commenting in timely fashion on the new writings they find.

> Emergent writing by definition lacks convention.

SUPPORTING GROWTH TOWARD CONVENTIONAL WRITING

As you create environments that support and encourage student writing in school and at home, you must also teach in ways that enable students to increase their understanding of print conventions, letters, sounds, and words. Learning letter names, reading predictable books, engaging in shared reading experiences, and other strategies shared in Chapters 3 and 4 draw students' attention increasingly and repeatedly to print. In addition to the independent writing experiences previously described, emergent writing instruction represents a mix of guided and observed experiences that enable students to gain increasing control of writing tools, forms, content, and purposes. This section presents two forms of writing instruction that support growth toward conventional writing:

1. Day-to-day writing demonstrations that take advantage of naturally occurring opportunities to write throughout the school day

2. Predictable chart writing—a structured, systematic form of writing instruction

Day-to-Day Writing Demonstrations

Emergent writers do not know how to write without being shown. When you talk and write a text, you demonstrate the process of translating experience and ideas into print. You show students that talk and thought can be written down. You demonstrate the conventions of writing by starting at the top of the page and writing from left to right. You show students some potential uses of writing, such as planning the day, recording events, making requests, writing invitations, or telling jokes. You show students the many forms their writing might take, such as poems, journal entries, lists, descriptions, stories, text messages, and more. You demonstrate how tools are used to transfer ideas to various writing surfaces. When you provide demonstrations, you reduce some of the mystery of what to write, how, where, and why. You increase student understanding that leads to a growing desire to write and communicate clearly with others.

Each school day includes numerous opportunities to demonstrate writing (e.g., in the morning, at any time when students are expected to sign their names, other incidental opportunities throughout the day). The following sections present some specific ideas for when and how to demonstrate writing.

Morning Message   Teachers of young children often create a daily morning message on a chart tablet, white board, or chalkboard that reads something such as the following:

Good morning,
Today is Monday. Our helper is Austin.

Depending on the time of year and what students need to learn, teachers take this opportunity to model sounding out words for spelling, point out capital letters at the beginning of sentences, or put their finger on the page to create white space between words as they write. They always read aloud each word as they write and then lead the students in reading aloud the finished message as they point to each word. They know that the children cannot read text independently, but this guided practice helps students experience what reading feels like, increases their awareness of concept of word, and helps them begin to acquire some sight words through meaningful use.

Teachers of older emergent writers replicate the process in age-appropriate ways, sharing the schedule, assigning tasks, or highlighting important events.

Guess what? Tomorrow is the weekend!

or

Bella's mom brought us snickerdoodles for snack today.

The goals remain the same. Model conventional writing with short, simple messages. Think aloud as you write. Discuss a convention or strategy. Increasingly encourage students to guide you so that you can informally check their growing understanding. Reread the text together when it is finished. Help the students gain an increasingly more sophisticated understanding of writing process, form, content, and use.

Sign In, Up, or Out   Students' names represent an ideal resource for teaching students about writing. Names are also useful in assessing and documenting student growth, especially in students with complex communication needs who are unable to read aloud what they are writing. Names represent familiar language that students have heard repeatedly throughout their lives. Names contain the letters with which students are most likely to be familiar. Names provide a meaningful entry into conventional literacy learning.

Sign in, up, or out has three important steps no matter what its purpose, where it is conducted, or when. First, students are asked to write their names for a purpose. Second, students write their names. Third, only after students have finished writing does an adult demonstrate conventional writing of the name using the student's writing tool (with a hand-under-hand procedure to encourage visual attention to the written name, if relevant). At no point are students ever asked or required to correct, rewrite, or copy their names, and at no point should adults use a hand-over-hand procedure to move student hands through the process of writing their names. Here is what a sign-in procedure looked like in an after-school transition experience.

Teacher: Ezra, you need to clock in before we start. *[She holds up a pen and pencil and points to the sign-in sheet on the wall by the door.]*

Ezra: *[Choosing the pen, he grips it with his fist and makes a series of downward strokes one after another, left to right on the sheet. He stops only when he reaches the right-hand side of the sheet.]*

Teacher: Done signing in? Let me have the pen. Hop on my hand. Let me show you how I do it. E-z-r-a. *[She speaks each letter as she writes it. Ezra's right hand rests on top of hers the whole time as he watches and listens. She points first to his writing and then to hers.]* That says Ezra, and that says Ezra. Go over to your work station and Miss Tonya will help you get started. Dana, you are next.

Sign in, up, or out has replaced the once common, but decontextualized and ineffective, practices previously used to teach letters and name writing in many classrooms—copying, tracing, or drill-and-practice routines. Students learn to write their names increasingly independently and conventionally by writing their names many times a day for real reasons and by having a model provided each time when they finish. Their name writing samples provide documentation of their growing understanding of letters and writing conventions in the process.

There are many real, naturally occurring reasons for students to write their names. A few examples are provided in Table 5.2.

Table 5.2.   Reasons students sign their names

Sign	School papers, artwork, locker spaces, personal supply baskets, desks, coat hooks, lunchboxes, or backpacks
Sign in	Arriving in the classroom, at a center, in the gym, or at group activities
Sign up	Choosing items for lunch or a snack, indicating preference for free choice or centers, or selecting classroom chores
Sign out	Leaving the room during the day, completing in-class activities, going on field trips, or going home at the end of the day

Some students' writing tools are complex, but the process remains the same. Jake, a teenager with severe physical disabilities who wore eyeglasses, had complex communication needs, and was deaf, experienced writing for the first time as a 14-year-old. He used a partner-assisted pencil that presented the alphabet in groups of four to six letters, each starting with a vowel:

A, B, C, D

E, F, G, H

I, J, K, L, M, N

O, P, Q, R, S, T

U, V, W, X, Y, Z

He had two switches, one at his left elbow, which lit a green light on his lap tray, and one at his right knee, which lit a red light on his lap tray. Jake knew from prior explanation that he should use the green light to tell his partner to go to the next letter and the red light to indicate that he wanted the letter being pointed to, and his partner should write it down for him.

On this day, Jake was asked through sign language to sign in before writing about a picture of his brother that he had chosen. His teacher served as his partner in this instance. Jake watched his teacher point to *A*, and he activated the red light. She wrote *A*. She pointed to *A* again and he activated the red light. The process continued, and Jake wrote AAAABBC. His teacher signed to ask him if he was done writing his name and he smiled a *yes*. His teacher then signed, LET ME SHOW YOU HOW I DO IT. She stood behind him and reached around to the two lights, pushing the red light or green light as the aide took her role as the partner. The teacher worked through the process moving through groups of letters to spell JAKE. She pointed to his writing and hers as she signed and finger-spelled, YOU WROTE JAKE. I WROTE JAKE. Then she sat back down in front of him and signed, NOW WHAT DO YOU WANT TO WRITE ABOUT YOUR BROTHER?

Other Opportunities to Demonstrate Writing   Teachers can create or take advantage of many opportunities to demonstrate various aspects of writing throughout the day. Making lists is one easy, useful, and repeated opportunity to model writing. Teachers work with students to create the daily or weekly schedule, to-do lists, lists of ideas for writing, lists of books to look for in the library, or a list of the day's activities to share with families at home. Although these lists cannot be read independently by emergent writers, teachers may periodically refer to them through the school day as appropriate:

- "Before you begin writing today, boys and girls, let's read our list of writing interests. You might want to choose one of these today."

- "Okay, class, before you head out the door, let's read aloud the homework list you are taking with you."

- "Alyssa, let's read our list of behavior reminders before we walk to the lunchroom."

Teachers of emergent writers with complex communication needs seek opportunities to have students write known texts. They have students write labels or signs for the garden ("Mason, you write *carrots* on this sign. Kirsten, you write *cucumbers* on this sign with the cucumber picture."). They ask students to make signs for centers ("Gus, will you write *library* on this sign for our book collection? Katie, will you write *reading area* on this sign for us?"). As students create these signs, teachers closely observe and gain a better sense of whether the students are demonstrating letter–sound correspondence, learning that print progresses left to right, developing concept of word in their own writing, and so forth. Periodically, these classroom signs may get lost or mysteriously damaged so as to create additional writing opportunities. Teachers often put a picture with the emergent writing to help staff and students know what the sign says, particularly if its physical placement does not provide sufficient context.

Predictable Chart Writing

Predictable chart writing is one of the most structured and systematic ways to demonstrate writing and provide engaging instruction in print conventions to students who are emergent. Students contribute personal information to a teacher, who scribes their ideas in a repeated sentence frame. Students engage more readily in the learning process because the content is personalized to their interests and experiences, and they stay engaged because every day they are doing something different with the text. Writing becomes understood as a means of representing interests and ideas.

Students begin to develop concepts about print (e.g., text goes left to right and top to bottom on the page, there are periods at the end of sentences, or there are spaces between words) as they observe teachers scribing their thoughts and engage in a variety of text activities. As they engage in teacher-directed activities, they begin to learn letter names and print jargon as their teachers use jargon in context (e.g., I need to put a period at the end of the sentence). Teachers use high-frequency, or core, vocabulary to enable students to begin to develop a base of words that they can read, write, and communicate more easily.

The sequence of predictable chart writing is carried out daily through the week. It has five steps:

1. Write the chart.

2. Reread the chart.

3. Work with sentence strips.

4. Be the sentence.

5. Make and publish the book.

These steps are explained in detail in the following sections.

Step 1: Write the Chart On Monday, teachers lead students in writing the chart. They might begin by brainstorming and listing things to include on the chart (e.g., swing, play computer games, watch tv). Generating such a list prepares students to contribute more readily when the chart is created because they have thought about and discussed the topic. Having the list for reference also enables teachers to support the participation of students with complex communication needs. When a student with a 36-word core vocabulary board says, "Like," the teacher can ask, "What do you like?" and point to items one by one until the student indicates "yes."

Some teachers of students with significant intellectual disabilities and/or complex communication needs send home the predictable chart topic for families to discuss over the weekend. This provides the students with additional opportunity to think about and discuss the ideas they will be encountering on Monday. It provides families of students with complex communication needs a chance to gather ideas and words that the student might need as fringe, or activity-specific, vocabulary.

As sentences are written by teachers, they speak aloud each word they are spelling (*I – like – bowling*) and then guide students to read the entire sentence chorally when it is done (*I like bowling*). When the text is finished, teachers lead the group in reading the entire text chorally. Students who cannot speak follow along as others read aloud, vocalizing as they are able. Some teachers add additional layers of support for emergent learners, writing each line with a different color marker or writing each student's name after the line he or she contributes. In this way, as activities progress through the week, students have three cues (order, color, and name) to help them remember some or all of the texts that they cannot remember yet or read independently. If students have severe visual impairments or are blind, then teachers use braille labelers or other braille technology to provide a personal copy of the text, long before the students have developed skills that would allow them to read the braille independently. For example,

> I like bowling. (Debbie)
> I like basketball. (Luke)
> I like trucks. (Rashon)
> I like puppets. (Felicia)

Step 2: Reread the Chart   On Tuesday, the class begins by rereading the entire text chorally with the teacher as he or she points to each word. Teachers remind students who have complex communication needs to listen to and read the words in their heads. Teachers give individual students opportunities to point to words in the sentences as the group reads aloud, which increases student engagement and provides a check on the students' growing concept of word. Brailled text is provided as necessary for students. Once the chart has been read several times, teachers then focus student attention on one aspect of writing convention, perhaps a letter of the alphabet, a sight word, use of a punctuation mark, or capital letters, as illustrated in the following example.

Teacher: *[Pointing]* See this letter? This is a *b*. It represents the /b/ sound in *bowling*. Let's see if we can find a *b* in this next sentence.

Debbie: *[Excitedly pointing to herself and the chart.]*

Teacher: Oh, I think Debbie may have an idea.

Debbie: *[Squealing.]*

Teacher: *[Scanning her finger slowly across the words.]* Debbie, stop me when you see a *b*.

Debbie: *[Rocks and squeals and then screeches in excitement.]*

Teacher: Oh, you found it. Look everyone *[pointing]*. Debbie found a *b* in her name.

Callie: *[Points and taps repeatedly on her light tech board.]* More. More. More.

Teacher: More? More *b*'s? Oh, look everyone *[pointing]*. Callie found another *b* in Debbie's name. There are two *b*'s. One, two. *B, b.* D-e-*b*-*b*-i-e.

When the group is done with Tuesday's instructional focus, they reread the entire text a final time.

Step 3: Work With Sentence Strips

On Wednesday, the class again begins by rereading the entire text chorally as the teacher models fluent oral reading and points to each word. She passes out each student's personal contribution on individual sentence strips. Sometimes she prepares these ahead of time. Other times, she and the teacher assistants speak each word aloud and write each word on the sentence strips in front of each student.

Early in the year, and until students understand the task, teachers then demonstrate cutting a sentence into words, reading each word in isolation, and reading the remainder of the sentence each time until all the words have been cut apart. They then point to the sentence on the predictable chart, put the words back in sentence order, and read the reconstruction aloud. Later in the school year, they intentionally make mistakes and have the students help them reorder the sentence correctly. For example, they might construct the sentence as *read a Debbie book* and then ask, "Does that make sense? No, that's silly. What word does Debbie's sentence need to begin with?" Right or wrong, each time a sentence is constructed, it is read aloud by the teachers and students.

Having demonstrated the process, they then have the students cut their own sentence strips apart to the best of their ability and as independently as possible. Students who cannot physically manage scissors or present a risk to themselves or others engage in partner-assisted cutting in which the teachers hold and move the scissors along the sentence strip until students indicate they should cut. They allow students to make mistakes, always providing feedback by reading the word or partial word and asking the students whether they think it makes sense. In this way, students come to understand concept of word by repeatedly seeking meaningful sentence structures.

Martin, a 10-year-old with intellectual disabilities and ASD, cut the sentence strip shown in Figure 5.8 entirely independently after several months of weekly predictable chart writing. He began with partner-assisted cutting for safety reasons but then demonstrated through his focus in the activity that he might be trusted with a pair of safety scissors. You can see his developing understanding and self-corrections. For example, twice he made a cut in the middle of *built* before cutting *built* and *a* apart. You can see also how he cut three times in the space to the left of *a* before cutting apart *a* and *snowman*. These behaviors can be interpreted as Martin's growing concept of word because 1) he controlled the activity cognitively and, ultimately, physically, 2) his teachers read aloud his errors and helped him self-correct each week, and 3) the focus was always on the cognitive and linguistic act of reading the sentence, not the visual task of seeking space between words.

Step 4: Be the Sentence

As on previous days, the class begins by rereading the entire text chorally as the teacher models fluent oral reading and points to each word. The activity went as follows with a group of adolescent emergent writers at camp. The literacy counselor took a copy of the first sentence and wrote it on a long sheet of paper, thinking and spelling aloud as she wrote each word and placed a period at the end, "At, *a-t*, At . . . camp, *c-a-m-p*, I . . . like, *l-i-k-e*, food, *f-o-o-d*. Let's all read it together,

Figure 5.8. The sentence strip Martin cut into pieces as part of Step 3 in predictable chart writing.

'At camp I like food.'" The group of teenagers counted the words in the sentence following the teacher's lead, and then the teacher modeled cutting the sentence into individual words, "At camp I like bowling. At … camp. That is two words, *At … camp.* I'm going to cut them apart right here, camp … I. That's two words, *camp … I.* I'm going to cut them apart right here." She continued until all the words were separate and then handed a word card to each of the five teenagers, explaining that they were going to "be the sentence." They were to arrange themselves with their word cards in order matching the sentence on the predictable chart.

The young ladies moved to the front of the room and negotiated with one another, eventually holding up their cards and reading them aloud with the literacy counselor as she pointed to each teenager's word card, "I camp food at like." The literacy counselor questioned in mock surprise, "Is that what our chart said?" The girls laughed hysterically and read the sentence on the chart together with the literacy counselor. "Okay, who needs to move?" asked the literacy counselor. With further discussion among themselves, the girls rearranged themselves into the correct order. They all read the resulting sentence, "At camp I like food," and asked if they could do another.

This process may take 10–15 minutes or more early in the year. Students often can complete two or even three sentences in the same amount of time as they gain familiarity with the expectations, learn a few sight words, and pay increasing attention to the original text. Teachers usually begin with three- to four-word sentences and do not progress to longer examples until students demonstrate regular success. The day's lesson is completed with a final choral reading of the entire predictable chart.

Figure 5.9.   Final book pages students created as part of Step 5 in predictable chart writing.

Step 5: Make and Publish the Book   On Friday, the group chorally reads the entire predictable chart with the teacher. The teacher then hands all members of the group their individual sentences. Each student works with the teacher and paraprofessionals, using partner assistance as needed, and cuts the sentence into individual words. Students are guided to self-correct by comparing their attempts with the pocket chart sentences. When they have gotten it right, often after taping mistaken efforts back together a few times, they are guided to glue their words in order on a page and add illustrations and their names. Examples are shown in Figure 5.9.

Many teachers create the books using paper and file folders, and then they add the now-familiar book to the classroom library. Teachers find students reading and rereading these books during independent reading times because many of the words are known and the content is personally meaningful. Some teachers will import these books into apps such as Book Creator (https://bookcreator.com) or web sites such as Tar Heel Reader (http://tarheelreader.org). Such resources allow students to listen to the texts being read aloud and may provide accessibility options.

A FINAL NOTE: FOSTERING EMERGENT WRITING

Emergent writing opportunities that are designed and implemented as described in this chapter enable individuals of any age with severe disabilities to demonstrate their current understandings of and skill in using print. Learners eagerly engage in further learning experiences when teachers and families respond to these nonconventional texts with enthusiasm and praise. When teachers and families respond to these efforts with corrections, they misdirect the learner's attention away from learning to communicate and risk diminishing the individual's interest and engagement in writing. Our primary emergent writing goals are to

- Get students writing daily

- Keep them focused on communicating about their interests to real and valued audiences

- Provide environments and experiences that sustain interest in writing

- Observe and interpret student writing efforts to determine what might be taught or demonstrated

Doing so will improve students' use of writing conventions over time.

RECOMMENDED READINGS AND RESOURCES

The following readings and resources will deepen readers' understanding of how best to support emergent writers.

Center for Literacy and Disability Studies web site (https://med.unc.edu/ahs/clds /projects/deaf-blind-model-classroom/jakes-story/)

Dynamic Learning Maps Professional Development web site (http://dlmpd.com/all -modules-in-alphabetical-order) provides self-directed modules that are intended for individual educators and facilitated modules for schools wishing to facilitate professional development for educators of students with significant disabilities. The following modules are of particular relevance to emergent writing: Emergent Writing, Predictable Chart Writing, and Writing With Alternative Pencils.

Project Core Professional Development Modules web site (http://project-core.com /professional-development-modules). The following modules are of particular relevance: Predictable Chart Writing: Predictable Chart Writing and Independent Writing.

Alternative Pencils web site (http://alternativepencils.weebly.com)

Learning to Read and Write

CHAPTER 6

Comprehensive Literacy Instruction

A Research-Based Framework

Each summer the authors of this book hold a week-long literacy camp for students with complex communication needs (see the Camp ALEC web site at http://www.campalec.com/home). We teach classroom teachers, special educators, SLPs, and other professionals to administer diagnostic reading assessments. During the rest of the week, under our guidance, they explore and experiment with motivating reading and writing activities for the campers to expand their repertoires and contribute to a report detailing assessment results and instructional recommendations to families and the campers' home schools.

Here are the diagnostic reading profiles of three recent campers, each a male adolescent with cerebral palsy, physical impairments, and complex communication needs (see Table 6.1). Jerrold can decode and read high school–level words and read seventh-grade texts with understanding, but he struggles to comprehend text above a fifth-grade difficulty level that is read aloud to him. He needs to strengthen his written language comprehension skills to grow as a reader. Marco can decode and read words at a ninth-grade level and understand texts at a third-grade level that are read aloud to him, but he struggles to read texts to himself with understanding if they are above a first-grade difficulty level. He needs to strengthen his print processing skills to grow as a reader. Jorge can understand texts up to an eighth-grade difficulty level that are read aloud to him, but he can read neither words nor texts above a first-grade level. He needs to strengthen his sight word and decoding skills to grow as a reader.

These are three adolescents with similar disabilities who use high-end speech-generating devices (SGDs) for their face-to-face interactions, and they each have very different needs as readers. It is a small wonder that teachers at every grade level and in every classroom find individual student differences challenging. In this chapter, we describe the theoretical foundation of a comprehensive literacy instruction framework you can use to more systematically organize instruction to address diverse student profiles such as these.

ORIGINS OF OUR APPROACH

Research focused on literacy in students with significant disabilities began in earnest in the 1990s with the creation of the Center for Literacy and Disability Studies at the University of North Carolina at Chapel Hill (https://med.unc.edu/ahs/clds); the authors of this book were involved in this work, each serving as director of the Center at different times. The Center's research initially focused on the learning needs of

Table 6.1.   Reading profiles of three students with complex communication needs

Student	Word identification	Silent reading comprehension	Listening comprehension
Jerrold	12th grade	Seventh grade	Fifth grade
Marco	Ninth grade	First grade	Third grade
Jorge	First grade	First grade	Eighth grade

individuals with severe physical impairments and complex communication needs and expanded over time to include students with ASD, intellectual disabilities, deafblindness, Rett syndrome, Williams syndrome, and other developmental disabilities. The Center's earliest work primarily addressed emergent literacy, seeking to implement strategies and programs that enacted David Yoder's (2001) argument that "no one is 'too anything' to learn to read" (p. 6).

We recognized from the start, however, that emergent literacy was necessary but not sufficient to address the literacy needs of individuals with significant disabilities. Both of us had the good fortune to study advanced reading methods with Jim Cunningham—David in the 1980s and Karen in the early 1990s. Jim was a wealth of knowledge and practice who told our classes, "In the absence of truth, you must have diversity." He meant there is no foolproof method of identifying a singular approach that will teach all children to read (i.e., basal reading series, commercial reading program, software, other curricular guide), and even the needs of individual children are not stable as they respond or fail to respond to instruction and intervention. He also pointed out to us that reading is a complex cognitive, linguistic, social, and cultural act. His conclusion was that what teachers needed to do, in the absence of such a "reading truth," was to teach in diverse ways, but systematically rather than eclectically. Jim was advocating for *comprehensive instruction* long before the term gained popularity. We now discuss the theoretical foundation of comprehensive reading instruction, why comprehensive literacy is necessary for students with significant disabilities, and what it looks like.

THEORETICAL FOUNDATION: THE WHOLE-TO-PART MODEL

The whole-to-part (WTP) model of silent reading comprehension is the theoretical framework underlying our approach to reading instruction (Cunningham, 1993; Erickson, Koppenhaver, & Cunningham, 2017). The WTP model assumes that coordinated effort is required of three abilities, or whole parts—word identification, language comprehension, and print processing—in order to achieve the goal of reading silently with comprehension at every level of text difficulty (see Figure 6.1).

The model assumes that teaching students to read silently, not orally, and doing so with understanding, or comprehension, is the primary goal of literacy instruction in school. It is the ability to read silently with comprehension that changes lives. Over time, it enables students to read text of increasing length and difficulty more efficiently and with greater understanding (Morris et al., 2017). Silent reading with comprehension is the ability that can lead to lifelong learning; rich opportunities accompany this ability. We explain the components of the WTP model in more detail next.

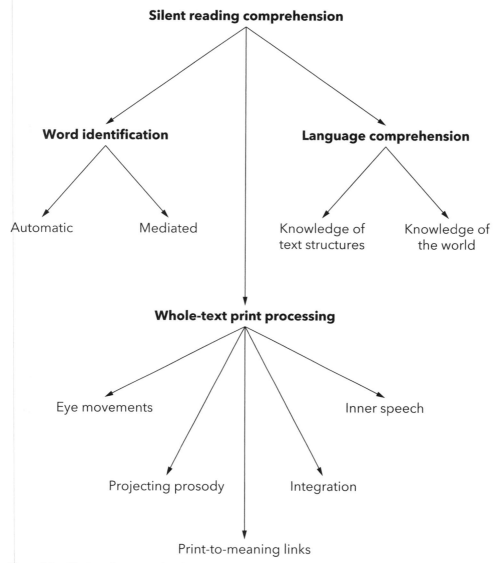

Figure 6.1. Silent reading comprehension.

Word Identification

Word identification is the cognitive process of making print-to-sound links in order to translate printed words into their speech equivalents (Cunningham et al., 2004). For young, typically developing readers, word identification begins with spoken word identification; however, the process itself does not require speech and is achieved subvocally or even neurologically during silent reading (Erickson, Koppenhaver, & Cunningham, 2017). Word identification supports working memory, which enables readers to remember words and word order, assign prosody, and support comprehension (De Jong, Bitter, Van Setten, & Marinus, 2009; Eiter & Inhoff, 2010; Rayner & Pollatsek, 1989). Word identification can be achieved either automatically or consciously with decoding strategies (i.e., mediated word identification). Automatic word identification occurs when the reader gains access to a phonological representation of a word effortlessly from memory; this supports understanding, or reading comprehension, because it frees cognitive resources to be directed toward language comprehension (Samuels, Ediger, Willcutt, & Palumbo, 2005). Mediated word identification involves the conscious decoding of those words not automatically recognized. Decoding requires gaining access to letter–sound knowledge, or spelling pattern–sound correspondences, in order to form a phonological representation for the target printed word. It also supports reading comprehension because it leads to automaticity over time (Share, 1999). This is one explanation for why beginning readers may struggle in comprehending text—they are devoting extensive cognitive resources to mediating nearly every word they encounter. In presenting predictable texts to beginning readers, we attempt to decrease the burden of extensive mediated word identification and provide sufficient repetition with variety to increase automatic word identification.

Language Comprehension

Language comprehension comprises two components—knowledge of the world and knowledge of text structures. It represents an individual's ability to comprehend written language, either while listening to a text read aloud or while reading silently. Knowledge of the world is language-based knowledge or experiences related to the topics and situations represented in any given text. Readers must not only possess relevant language-based knowledge but must also be able to gain access to that knowledge at the appropriate time in order for language comprehension to occur successfully while listening or reading. In addition, language comprehension requires knowledge of text structures, including syntax, cohesion, genre, and length (Mesmer, Cunningham, & Hiebert, 2012). (*Syntax* refers to the part of grammar dealing with the way sentences are constructed. *Cohesion* refers to the ways that ideas in a text are systematically linked to one another.) Without experience and familiarity with a variety of text structures, readers or listeners may be unable to process written language even if their knowledge of the world is such that one would anticipate success. In fact, text structure knowledge is what distinguishes written language comprehension from more general oral language comprehension. Language comprehension explains why some readers may struggle to read with comprehension despite excellent word identification skills.

Whole-Text Print Processing

Whole-text print processing is everything that silent reading with comprehension requires beyond word identification and language comprehension. This component makes the WTP model particularly appropriate as the theoretical basis for interventions with students with significant disabilities, especially those who have complex communication needs. Other models of silent reading comprehension omit it (e.g., Hoover & Gough, 1990) and, consequently, provide insufficient explanation for the reading difficulties of many of these individuals. For example, consider Marco, described at the beginning of this chapter. Although he could understand text read aloud to him at a third-grade level and identify words at an even higher level, he was only able to read with comprehension at a first-grade level. Why was his silent reading comprehension ability lower than his word identification ability and his language comprehension ability? Neither his word identification nor his language comprehension explains the discrepancy. Whole-text print processing does. Marco is unable to process connected text efficiently, although he can identify the individual words in the text and understand their meanings. Such a profile is not unusual in individuals with complex communication needs, individuals with some forms of visual impairment, or students with disabilities in classrooms where significant time is devoted to word identification and vocabulary instruction exercises, but little time is devoted to reading text of sufficient ease.

Whole-text print processing comprises five components:

1. Inner speech use

2. Projecting prosody

3. Making print-to-meaning links

4. Eye movements in reading

5. The integration of these four components

Inner speech use facilitates decoding words, interpreting sentences, and monitoring comprehension. It allows the reader to hold ideas in memory and integrate them across connected text (Acheson & MacDonald, 2011). There is evidence that although students with complex communication needs often have difficulty using inner speech initially, they can and do learn with instruction and experience (Gillon, 2003). Reading orally with expression, or projecting prosody, facilitates comprehension because it enhances interpretation of syntax (Benjamin et al., 2013). It has been demonstrated that readers also project prosody during silent reading (Kentner, 2012). Skilled readers make direct print-to-meaning links for word spellings, morpheme spellings, capital letters, and punctuation. This occurs prior to, or in tandem with, making print-to-sound associations during oral and silent reading. Making print-to-meaning links helps the reader to hold words, phrases, and clauses in working memory while the sentence being read can be interpreted and eventually integrated into understanding of the rest of the text. The eye movements required for processing connected text consist of rapid, intermittent movements (i.e., saccades) accompanied by split-second fixations and metacognitively controlled regressions that support rereading (Booth & Weger, 2013). These eye movements during the reading of text are cognitively controlled, not merely motoric or behavioral as in visual tracking, and are distinct from those involved in word identification (Luke & Henderson, 2013). Integration is simply the cognitive juggling of the four print processing components required to achieve fluent silent reading with comprehension. Print processing skills develop most efficiently when readers engage in wide reading in relatively easy texts.

The ability to read silently with comprehension changes lives by opening rich opportunities for lifelong learning. Therefore, the primary goal of literacy instruction is to teach students to read silently, not orally, and to do so with understanding, or comprehension.

WHY IS COMPREHENSIVE LITERACY INSTRUCTION NEEDED?

Beyond a theoretical attempt to explain the complexities of reading, comprehensive literacy instruction is a pragmatic and evidence-based response to the complexities of the classroom environments where a central goal should always be to teach all students to read more successfully across their years in school.

The Practical Necessity

From a pragmatic stance, comprehensive literacy instruction is based on several assumptions and understandings. First, it is based on the assumption that all children can learn to read and write, but they all have varying strengths and needs as literacy learners. Second, it is based on the recognition that we must teach everything about literacy if all students are to succeed as readers because we teach individual children whose needs are diverse and vary across time and circumstance, as well as groups of such children in a wide range of classrooms (Cunningham & Allington, 2016). Third, it rests on an understanding that all students need to learn every aspect of reading from phonemic and phonological awareness to decoding, reading fluency, and comprehension, as well as learning the coherent, cohesive, and strategic application of all of these components (Gambrell, Malloy, Marinak, & Mazzoni, 2014; Stanovich, 1980). They also need to learn how and why they might want to apply those skills to escape into fan fiction, share secrets, remember homework tasks, or ultimately engage as full participants in society (McGraw & Mason, 2017; O'Brien & Rogers, 2016). Finally, comprehensive instruction recognizes that the vast majority of students with significant disabilities experience great difficulties in learning to read, and their specific learning challenges vary widely, as the previous examples attest (Koppenhaver & Yoder, 1992; U.S. Department of Education, 2017).

The Evidence Base

Substantial evidence exists for the benefits of comprehensive instruction in beginning reading for all students (e.g., Cunningham et al., 1998; Pressley & Allington, 2014), which means that instruction must address word reading, written language comprehension, and fluency as well as increase students' independence and motivation as readers. An increasing range of research evidence also suggests that students with significant disabilities must have access to comprehensive literacy instruction (Erickson et al., 2009), and such instruction should be delivered in the same integrated, engaging, and interactive ways it is delivered to typically developing students in general education settings (Koppenhaver, Evans, & Yoder, 1991; McSheehan, Sonnenmeier, Jorgensen, & Turner, 2006; Ruppar, Fisher, Olson, & Orlando, 2018; Ryndak, Morrison, & Sommerstein, 1999).

Three studies have described positive outcomes while detailing how the researchers integrated substantial portions of comprehensive instruction and best practice for students with significant disabilities within general education settings. Tefft Cousin, Weekley, and Gerard (1993) described a team-teaching model in which two special educators worked with interdisciplinary teams in Grades 1–2 and 4–5. The curriculum was inclusive and organized thematically. Key components of instruction included reading aloud to students, discussing books, collaborative reading and writing demonstrations and activities, making connections by students identifying personal experience related to texts read in class, and supporting the needs of the students with significant disabilities within the mainstream curriculum. Blischak (1995) documented the language and literacy growth of a child in second grade with complex communication needs, severe physical impairments, and visual impairments. Key instructional components included listening to read-alouds, engaging in language experiences, engaging in writing activities, observing models of writing, and integrating use of a communication device across literacy activities. Erickson et al. (1997) is the only study to explicitly reference the WTP model in documenting the language and literacy growth of a child with complex communication needs, severe physical impairments, and visual impairments in a general education fourth- and fifth-grade classroom. Key interventions addressed self-directed reading, reading comprehension, word study, and writing while integrating use of the student's communication device across instructional activities.

A pair of studies have explored implementation of comprehensive literacy interventions consistent with the National Reading Panel's (2000) criteria in self-contained classrooms serving students with intellectual disabilities. Students in both studies demonstrated positive outcomes on a variety of literacy measures, but two in particular were most encouraging—growth in reading comprehension (Allor, Mathes, Roberts, Jones, & Champlin, 2010) and improvement of listening comprehension (Beecher & Childre, 2012). That is, those outcome measures demonstrate the growth we seek in silent reading comprehension and whole parts contributing to silent reading comprehension such as language comprehension.

Finally, given that comprehensive instruction has tended to be directed toward younger students in elementary grades, a particularly encouraging set of case studies document success in systematically combining elements of comprehensive instruction in teaching high school students with significant disabilities (Hogan & Wolf, 2002; Wershing & Hughes, 2002) and even an adult (Gipe, Duffy, & Richards, 1993).

WHAT IS COMPREHENSIVE LITERACY INSTRUCTION?

Specific definitions of comprehensive instruction vary widely. Some researchers rely on the flawed and narrowly focused lens (see Cunningham, 2001, for a discussion) of the National Reading Panel Report (2000), which included five evidence-based areas of instruction—phonemic awareness, phonics, fluency, vocabulary, and text comprehension. Interventions relying on this narrow view of what constitutes comprehensive literacy abound in special education. Typically, researchers or teachers holding this view rely on published curricula, implement instruction for less than an hour per day, and supplement the curricula of choice in modest ways for students who are emergent in their literacy understandings and skills (see, e.g., Allor, Mathes, Roberts, Jones, & Champlin, 2010; Beecher & Childre, 2012; Taub et al., 2019). At the other extreme is the federal government, which includes everything except the kitchen sink in its definition of comprehensive literacy (i.e., Every Student Succeeds Act of 2015). Its exhaustive (and exhausting) list consists of 12 items, each comprising multiple features (Sec. 2221), including:

- Literacy-specific elements (e.g., phonological awareness, phonics, vocabulary, reading fluency, reading comprehension, writing)

- Types of instruction (e.g., age appropriate, explicit, systematic, developmentally appropriate, incorporating principles of universal design)

- Types of materials (e.g., diverse, high-quality print materials reflecting the students' developmental levels and interests)

- Applications of literacy (e.g., reading and writing across the content areas, engaging in self-directed learning, navigating and understanding complex print and digital subject matter)

- Types of assessments (e.g., age appropriate, screening, diagnostic, formative, summative, progress monitoring)

- Teacher lesson planning (e.g., collaboration in planning, continuous professional learning)

We have opted for an approach to comprehensive instruction that lies somewhere between these two extremes, neither overly simplistic nor excessively complex. The approach is not prescriptive. Rather, it is an organizing framework derived initially from close attention to real school children in first and second grade and their teachers (Cunningham et al., 1991, 1998) and later adapted for beginning readers of any age with significant disabilities (Erickson, Koppenhaver, Yoder, & Nance, 1997; Erickson & Koppenhaver, 2007; Erickson, Koppenhaver, & Cunningham, 2006). It addresses all aspects of the WTP theoretical framework as well as reading independence and motivation.

The instructional framework consists of equal parts instruction in reading comprehension, self-directed reading, word study, and writing. Each of the four components receives equal instructional time in the ideal instructional setting (e.g., 30–40 minutes for reading comprehension, 30–40 minutes for self-directed reading, and so forth). There is no specified order to the four areas of focus, and there is flexibility within each to use different instructional approaches and break up the 30- to 40-minute segments as needed. It is critical, however, that every student receives daily literacy instruction that includes all four components. We describe each component of this model in brief next. Subsequent chapters of this book treat each component in greater detail.

> It is critical that every student receives daily comprehensive instruction addressing all four components of literacy— reading comprehension, self-directed reading, word study, and writing.

Reading Comprehension

Comprehensive conventional literacy instruction includes instruction in comprehension from the very beginning. This is very different than most approaches to teaching literacy to students with significant disabilities (e.g., Edmark Reading Program, 2011; Haugen-McLane, Hohlt, & Haney, 2007; Light & McNaughton, 2009). We do this because it is important for students to understand that text carries meaning, and other skills are important only to the extent that they enable students to read with greater understanding more independently. We also do this because we have met so many students with significant disabilities who have learned exactly what they have been taught and no more. They are able to identify alphabet letters, match letters and sounds, or read lists of sight words, but they are unable to read even basic texts with understanding. We are willing to bet you know many such students if you have taught children with significant disabilities for very long.

To address reading comprehension, we introduce a wide variety of text types and teach students a range of strategies such as prediction, summarization, and questioning. Our typical lesson structure follows an Anchor-Read-Apply structure.

Anchor   We engage students' thinking in two ways during the Anchor step. First, we guide them in making connections between what they know about the world and the text they are about to read. Second, we set a purpose for student reading that is related to the connection-making step. For example, we might guide students to consider the attributes of characters from a familiar story before they read to identify similarities with a new character.

Read   Students read to accomplish the designated purpose during the Reading step. The success of this step, and the degree of student independence, depend heavily on teachers' selection of texts of appropriate difficulty relative to students' current abilities. Our selection is guided by the knowledge that texts cannot be too easy but can easily be too hard. Students cannot learn the strategies we are teaching, engage in meaningful connection-making, or gain independence as readers when the texts are too difficult for them, so we prefer to err on the side of relative ease. When students are early beginning readers, we may read texts aloud to them, seek texts with predictable patterns or repeated lines, read the same text on subsequent days for new purposes to increase familiarity, or support the reading with story maps and other strategies.

Apply   Following the reading, we ask the students to apply what they have read to achieve the purpose. So, if the purpose was to compare the attributes of a new character with a familiar character, then that comparison is the immediate follow-up to reading. We might do that with a Venn diagram, a series of illustrations, a list of attributes, or an open discussion, depending on student reading and communication abilities. The lesson concludes by providing instructional, not behavioral, feedback. For example, we might ask a student who achieved the purpose to explain his or her reasoning. Nearly always, we return to the text to compare and contrast student responses with the text sources.

> Texts cannot be too easy, but can easily be too hard, for students learning to read with comprehension.

Self-Directed Reading

Self-directed reading is rarely found in lists of evidence-based reading interventions. Its absence reflects the narrow views of the lists' compilers more than it reflects the importance of self-direction in reading. Reading for comprehension for self-determined purposes is the point of learning to read. Any long-term goal that falls short of this is a waste of student (and teacher) time. As we have argued in the Literacy Bill of Rights (see Chapter 2), individuals with significant disabilities who identify what they need or want to read and why become lifelong learners who can make informed choices or gain further educational opportunities. Ervin, an older gentleman with lifelong anxieties and ASD, would have found life in a residential facility dramatically diminished had he not been a devout newspaper reader and train book enthusiast. Reading enabled him to learn about the world and converse with a wide range of visitors and staff. Molly, a young woman with Down syndrome, would have found evenings and weekends with her mother far less interactive were they not both romance novel enthusiasts. Jaylen, a gentleman with multiple disabilities, would have led a far more isolated existence in rural North Carolina without the rich variety of communications with friends and relatives on his social media accounts. Jake, a teenager with severe physical impairments and complex communication needs, would lack the escape and information his massive digital library provides, not to mention the language background he needs to compete academically in college.

Self-directed reading should not be an afterthought, nor should it be ignored because of the myopic vision of some adherents to evidence-based practices. Instructional time allotted for self-directed reading always includes teacher read-alouds from a wide range of literature and text types. The intent is to make students more aware of the breadth of possible reading topics, types, and authors so they can determine over time what reading has to offer them personally. Self-directed reading also includes substantial time for students to read materials they choose, which requires an awareness that books can be read in a variety of ways, depending on their difficulty, structure, predictability, and inclusion of illustrations. It also requires the presence of accepting teachers who understand that self-directed means *self*-directed, not selected from a list of texts at a certain grade level, an approved difficulty level, or any other teacher- or school-guided system. The success of this activity depends on the availability of a large, diverse, and ever-growing collection of reading materials from which to choose in the classroom, school, and community. It also requires a variety of supports and encouragement (e.g., comfortable seating, headphones, snacks, other features that make reading less school-like and more real).

While students read, teachers conference one to one to find out what they are reading, how it fits, what they are thinking about reading next, and so forth. After students finish reading, time is allotted for sharing with classmates about the reading, discussing whether they like it and who else they think might like it, and engaging in other real conversations that build a community of readers. A final component is a mini-lesson addressing important skills such as how to ask a librarian for help, how to search for books by a favorite author, how to choose books, how to write your own books, where to find interesting online reading sites, and so forth.

Every minute of self-directed reading is aimed at helping students figure out what they like to read, expand on that interest, find books they like, and share their thinking about reading with others to build lifelong habits of self-directed reading. The side benefits are improved reading fluency, increased vocabulary, increased knowledge of the world, and improved comprehension for all readers, not just the best readers (Allington, 2011; Cunningham & Stanovich, 1998).

> It is essential that students with significant disabilities have daily opportunities for self-directed reading, with the teacher providing a variety of supports and encouragement. The point of learning to read is to be able to read for comprehension for one's own chosen purposes.

Word Study

Word study is designed to help students learn to read and spell high-frequency words and learn patterns that will increase their ability to decode and spell words they do not immediately recognize. These approaches enable developing readers to increase their word reading skills while becoming more efficient in figuring out new words, both of which enable them to devote greater attention to comprehension when reading texts. Students with significant disabilities tend to have limitations in both receptive vocabulary and expressive communication skills. For this reason, word reading instruction focuses on learning words through use and repetition with variety rather than through rote memorization. For the same reasons, analogic approaches are emphasized in decoding and spelling instruction (i.e., students are taught to systematically analyze words they know in order to read and spell words sharing similar patterns). The goal in word instruction is always to build on what students know in order to expand their abilities to read and spell words as effortlessly as possible.

Writing

Writing instruction is an important part of this approach to comprehensive literacy not only because writing is a powerful form of communication for individuals with significant disabilities, but also because it helps many students learn to read better. Writing enables students to look within and across words as they compose their thoughts. Writing follows the writers' workshop format popularized by Donald Graves (1995) and colleagues but places an even greater emphasis on certain practices that address the needs and characteristics of students with significant disabilities. The basic components of writing instruction in this comprehensive approach include

- Mini-lessons on aspects of writing

- Sustained time for daily writing without teacher attention to what has been done incompletely, inadequately, or incorrectly

- Sharing of writing, whether in process or finished, with classmates

The heart of writing instruction is daily experience in writing to communicate thoughts, rather than writing to compose grammatically and syntactically correct sentences. Students are taught a variety of strategies for selecting their own topics (e.g., brainstorming, reviewing photographs of experiences) and audiences (e.g., interactive writing experiences, sharing texts with classmates). They are taught basic revision strategies from the beginning by being encouraged to add more detail to whatever they compose. They are provided daily opportunities to share what they have been writing with one or more classmates, and they publish their imperfect pieces regularly to motivate the entire process. Audiences—including the students' families— are educated to respond to content and ideas, rather than perceived shortcomings because they have been taught by their child's teacher that whatever they view as shortfalls ultimately becomes the next mini-lesson, without ever diminishing their child's self-confidence or interest in writing.

> The heart of writing instruction is daily experience in writing to communicate one's thoughts.

A FINAL NOTE: ADDRESSING SKILLS, COMPREHENSION, AND COMPOSITION

What makes this approach comprehensive? Literacy instruction in the way we described is comprehensive in important ways. First, it provides instruction and experience not only in reading but also in writing. It allocates instructional time to reading and writing, recognizing that writing is not only an important component of literacy but also centrally important to social-communication and self-advocacy for students with significant disabilities, particularly those with complex communication needs. Second, it encompasses four different but complementary approaches that provide students with multiple and varied opportunities to learn. Third, it provides students some degree of control and choice while at the same time respecting teachers' central importance in the learning enterprise. Students have greater control and choice over topics and materials during self-directed reading and writing, whereas teachers have greater control over skill and strategy emphases and materials during word study and comprehension instruction. Finally, it is comprehensive not only in addressing skills such as phonemic awareness and phonics (during word study), reading fluency, vocabulary, and comprehension (during guided reading), but also in addressing motivation, social, and cultural aspects of reading and writing (during self-directed reading and writing). This better prepares students for real-world reading, writing, and communicating.

Beginning reading instruction in the United States has been dominated by a stage-based model since the publication of the Eunice Kennedy Shriver National Institute of Child Health and Human Development (2000) and the passing of the No Child Left Behind Act of 2001 (PL 107-110). This model suggests that learning to read requires mastery of a sequence of skills in phonemic awareness, then phonics, then fluency before any emphasis is placed on reading comprehension. Yet, large-scale evaluations of instruction following a stage-based model revealed little positive impact on reading comprehension when this approach was implemented in schools, even for students without disabilities (Allington, 2013; Gamse, Jacob, Horst, Boulay, & Unlu, 2008; Herlihy, Kemple, Bloom, Zhu, & Berlin, 2009). In contrast to a stage-based model, the WTP model and instructional framework advocated in this chapter reflect a comprehensive approach that balances skill and meaning emphases while addressing all components of reading and writing each day in engaging ways that help students develop interest and motivation to pursue literacy for their own purposes beyond the classroom walls (Pressley & Allington, 2014).

RECOMMENDED READINGS AND RESOURCES

The following readings and resources will deepen readers' understanding of how to plan comprehensive conventional literacy instruction for students with significant disabilities.

Allington, R. L. (2013). What really matters when working with struggling readers. *The Reading Teacher, 66*, 520-530. doi:10.1002/TRTR.1154

Erickson, K. A. (2017). Comprehensive literacy instruction, interprofessional collaborative practice and students with severe disabilities. *American Journal of Speech-Language Pathology, 26,* 193–205. doi:10.1044/2017_AJSLP-15-0067

Erickson, K. A., Koppenhaver, D. A., & Cunningham, J. W. (2017). Comprehensive reading intervention in augmentative communication. In R. J. McCauley, M. E. Fey, & R. B. Gillam (Eds.), *Treatment of language disorders in children* (2nd ed., pp. 275–308). Baltimore, MD: Paul H. Brookes Publishing Co.

CHAPTER 7

Reading Comprehension and Vocabulary Instruction

Maddie was curled up in the corner of the sofa proudly reading a chapter book. She read page after page, whispering the words along the way. I (Karen) eventually sat down next to her and asked, "What are you reading?" She turned the cover of the book toward me and told me the title. I asked, "What's it about?" Maddie shrugged and went back to reading. I sat for a few minutes before trying once again, unsuccessfully, to get Maddie to talk with me about the meaning of the words, sentences, and paragraphs she was reading. It wasn't long before I realized that Maddie was reading the words without understanding the meaning of the text.

Reading with comprehension, specifically, concurrently extracting and constructing meaning from text, is the ultimate purpose of learning to read (Adams, 1990). For too long, it was assumed that comprehension automatically followed successful word recognition (Lipson & Wixson, 2013), but we know far too many students like Maddie who can read words quite successfully without understanding them or grasping the overall meaning of the text. Word reading is certainly important (see Chapters 6 and 10), but reading with comprehension involves much more than successfully reading the words.

RESEARCH BRIEF: COMPREHENSION AND VOCABULARY

Few students with significant disabilities read text with comprehension above the first-grade level (Erickson & Geist, 2016). Those students with significant disabilities who have learned to decode words can often remember explicit details in beginning level text, but they find it more difficult to make inferences or otherwise understand text written at a higher level (van Wingerden, Segers, van Balkom, & Verhoeven, 2014). Unfortunately, research on teaching students with significant disabilities to comprehend text often focuses primarily on key ideas and details or explicit-level understandings of the text (Mims et al., 2009; Mims, Hudson, & Browder, 2012). Reading with comprehension is much more than just remembering the literal, explicit-level information in a text. In fact, literal memory of text can often get in the way of grasping the intended meaning. For example, consider the lines in the picture book *Tar Beach* (Ringgold, 1996) when the protagonist describes her relationship with the George Washington Bridge. The lines are, "All I had to do was fly over it for it to be mine forever. I can wear it like a giant diamond necklace, or just fly above it and marvel at its sparkling beauty" (pp. 9–10). A literal understanding of these sentences would leave a reader confused when finally learning that being able to fly means, "I am free to go where I want for the rest of my life" (p. 10).

Reading comprehension requires readers to understand the literal information in a text and make a number of different types of inferences while integrating that information with their existing knowledge. As mentioned, students with significant disabilities typically find it more difficult to understand text in these more complex ways (van Wingerden et al., 2014), but that may be an artifact of instruction (Mims et al., 2009, 2012; Stanovich, West, Cunningham, Cipielewski, & Siddiqui, 1996) and the historically ubiquitous focus on sight words in reading instruction for students with significant disabilities (Browder et al., 2006; Roberts, Leko, & Wilkerson, 2013). Yet, it is possible for students with significant disabilities to learn to read with comprehension in more complex ways when provided with effective instruction (Reichenberg, 2014).

At least part of the challenge students with significant disabilities face with comprehending text can be explained by their global delays in receptive vocabulary (Haebig & Sterling, 2017; Loveall, Channell, Phillips, Abbeduto, & Conners, 2016) and slow rate of receptive vocabulary acquisition as they age (Cuskelly, Povey, & Jobling, 2016). As with other areas of literacy, instruction focused on vocabulary has traditionally employed massed trials (Browder et al., 2006), which demonstrated that students with significant disabilities can acquire new vocabulary but cannot then use the vocabulary to improve their comprehension in other contexts. There is, however, emerging evidence that students with significant disabilities can acquire vocabulary in ways that support conceptual development (Jimenez, Browder, & Courtade, 2009; Smith, Spooner, Jimenez, & Browder, 2013), which will contribute to improved comprehension over time.

In summary, the research regarding comprehension and vocabulary for students with significant disabilities is limited. Current evidence suggests that students with significant disabilities struggle to read with comprehension (Erickson & Geist, 2016), especially when asked to make inferences (van Wingerden et al., 2014). Similarly, students with significant disabilities generally have delayed vocabulary knowledge (Haebig & Sterling, 2017; Loveall et al., 2016) and slow rates of vocabulary acquisition (Cuskelly et al., 2016). Efforts to address comprehension and vocabulary have traditionally focused on isolated, concrete skills (Browder et al., 2006; Mims et al., 2009, 2012; Roberts et al., 2013), but students with significant disabilities can acquire conceptual vocabulary knowledge (Jimenez et al., 2009; Smith et al., 2013) and more complex text comprehension skills (Reichenberg, 2014) with effective instruction.

WHAT IS COMPREHENSION?

Many component skills are necessary for successful reading with comprehension. Whether you adhere to the Simple View of Reading that suggests that successful comprehension is a combination of decoding and language comprehension (Gough & Tunmer, 1986) or the more nuanced WTP described in Chapter 6 (Cunningham, 1993; Erickson, Koppenhaver, & Cunningham, 2017), comprehension requires more than identifying and understanding the meaning of individual words (Nation & Norbury, 2005). At a minimum, it requires the active integration of existing language-based knowledge of the world with individual perceptions of the text to construct understandings of what the text means (Kintsch, 1998, 2004). As those understandings are built, they are integrated with existing language-based knowledge of the world to further improve that knowledge and improve comprehension ability for the future (Duke, Pearson, Strachan, & Billman, 2011).

The ability to make inferences that go beyond what is explicitly stated in the text is an important facet of comprehension. Most texts require readers to make some inferences. Authors assume that the reader can rather effortlessly use the information provided in the text to think and make inferences about information that is not provided. There is no single way to categorize or describe the inferences readers must make. Yet, Cain and Oakhill (1999) made a useful distinction between text-connecting or inter-sentence inferences and gap-filling inferences. Text-connecting or inter-sentence inferences help readers connect ideas from one sentence to the next, which is required when readers face pronouns. For example, consider the sentences: "Dave likes to read. He reads whenever he can." The reader must use inferencing to determine that *he* is *Dave.* Similarly, the reader might have to make an inference to connect a noun or noun phrase with its referent. For example, suppose the text reads, "Sarah, Deon, and Jake all finished their books. Then the students traded and started reading again." The reader must determine that *the students* refers to *Sarah, Deon,* and *Jake.* These text-connecting inferences become increasingly challenging when the referent(s) is not in close proximity to the pronoun, noun, or noun phrase. Gap-filling inferences require the reader to use information that is not in the text. These inferences require the reader to draw on existing knowledge of the world. Examples of various types of gap-filling inferences are provided in Table 7.1.

Decoding and language comprehension, including the language-based knowledge of the world previously described, typically develop together, but sometimes they develop in

> The reader must understand more than just the words on the page in order to comprehend a text. Reading comprehension also involves integrating one's knowledge of the world with one's perceptions of the text to construct understandings of its meaning—and it usually involves making inferences too.

Table 7.1.   Types of gap-filling inferences

Type of inference	Example in text	Inference to make
Emotional	Bill smacked the table and sent the chair flying before storming out.	Bill is angry.
Time	We ran to get home before the streetlights came on.	It is evening or night time.
Location	After we landed, it seemed like it took forever to get to the gate.	They are on an airplane.
Cause and effect	Thunder boomed, rain poured down, and suddenly the house went dark.	A storm caused a power outage.

an uneven pattern, resulting in reading comprehension difficulties (Hoover & Gough, 1990; Nation & Norbury, 2005). This is especially the case when students have impaired or delayed receptive language skills (Nation, 2005) or other developmental disabilities (Davidson, Kaushanskaya, & Weismer, 2018; Snowling & Hulme, 2005). For example, research with students with Down syndrome and Williams syndrome (Snowling & Hulme, 2005) as well as ASD (Davidson et al., 2018) reveals that these students' reading comprehension abilities vary greatly but are highly related to their receptive language abilities. In other words, any efforts to address reading comprehension among students with significant disabilities requires attending directly to their language comprehension challenges (Beukelman, Yorkston, Poblete, & Naranjo, 1984; Cameto et al., 2010) and their limited language-based knowledge of the world (Justice & Redle, 2014).

WHAT IS VOCABULARY?

Vocabulary is one important aspect of language comprehension that is particularly important in reading comprehension. As defined by Neuman and Dwyer (2009), "Vocabulary refers to the words we must know to communicate effectively: words in speaking (expressive vocabulary) and words in listening (receptive vocabulary)" (p. 385). Students use their receptive vocabulary understanding to make sense of the words they encounter in reading and listening. Instruction designed to support vocabulary learning must go beyond learning a simple definition or matching words and pictures. It must help students build deep understandings of word meanings and the concepts and ideas represented by the words. Learning about words and their connections to each other, to concepts, and to facts helps students develop important understandings that support text comprehension (Neuman & Dwyer, 2009).

Most of the words that students are asked to read in the early stages of reading are words they already know receptively (Kamil, 2004). This helps beginning readers translate printed words into pronunciations that match known words. This knowledge of the printed form, integrated with knowledge of letter–sound relationships in the word, results in a pronunciation that matches a word that the student has heard before (Adams, 2011; see Chapter 10 for a more detailed discussion). This critical connection between print and the meaning of known words is just one of many arguments urging the use of real words rather than nonsense words in early reading instruction and assessment (Fuchs, Fuchs, & Compton, 2004).

As readers become more skilled, increased vocabulary knowledge is required for successful comprehension of connected text. Although the specific causal relationship between vocabulary and reading ability is unclear (Stanovich, 2000), the number of words that a student understands is directly related to his or her ability to understand text, whether the student has disabilities (e.g., Davidson et al., 2018) or not (e.g., Stanovich, Cunningham, & Freeman, 1984). This relationship between vocabulary and comprehension seems to be influenced by a reader's depth of word knowledge (Neuman & Dwyer, 2009). Knowing the definition of individual words is insufficient. Instead, vocabulary knowledge that influences text comprehension includes knowing what each word represents and understanding the concepts connected with that word (Stahl & Murray, 1994; Stahl & Nagy, 2006). This deeper knowledge of word meanings provides an important base on which knowledge of new words can be built (Hirsch, 2003).

Students need robust receptive vocabulary knowledge to be successful in learning to read with comprehension (National Institute for Literacy, 2009; Neuman, 2006). Students can work toward this robust vocabulary knowledge when they 1) are actively engaged in learning new words (Dole, Sloan, & Trathen, 1995), 2) repeatedly encounter new words across multiple contexts, and 3) participate in instruction that employs multiple methods (National Institute for Child Health and Development [NICHD], 2000). This chapter describes specific ways to accomplish this type of receptive vocabulary development and ways that instruction then supports the use of this improved vocabulary knowledge in text comprehension.

> One argument for using real words instead of nonsense words in literacy instruction is that beginning readers are making crucial connections between the print and the words that are already part of their receptive vocabulary.

GETTING OFF TO A GOOD START: MAXIMIZING MOTIVATION AND ENGAGEMENT

In the first part of this book, we describe interventions for students who are emergent readers and writers. It is generally obvious to teachers and teams that they should not teach conventional decoding to students who do not have alphabet knowledge; however, it seems to be less obvious that it is not appropriate to teach reading comprehension to students who are not interested and engaged during reading or listening. Chapter 4 describes an approach to shared reading intended to maximize interaction and engagement with the text for these disinterested or unengaged students. Although no specific criteria exist regarding the amount or quality of interaction and engagement required before you make a shift away from shared reading, teaching students to comprehend text requires some level of self-motivated interest in constructing understandings. If you are still working hard to recruit and sustain student attention during shared reading, or you are using rewards or first-then approaches to get students to complete reading-related tasks, then your efforts to teach comprehension are unlikely to be successful.

In short, motivation and engagement are crucial to reading comprehension instruction. Given their importance, the approaches described in this chapter incorporate research-based principles for increasing motivation to actively engage in reading (Guthrie & Davis, 2003). For example, the comprehension lesson structures emphasize setting purposes for reading that focus on interesting content that is systematically related to concrete experiences and prior knowledge—and doing this for each student. The lesson structures also emphasize working with small groups of students to encourage them to engage socially with one another about the text and the specific reading purposes, and they emphasize selecting texts that are interesting, age respectful, and ability appropriate.

> Students' motivation and engagement are at the heart of reading comprehension instruction. Efforts to teach comprehension are unlikely to be successful without some level of self-motivated interest in constructing understandings.

Yet, none of these approaches will compensate for a student who is disinterested or disengaged during reading-related tasks. In that case, stick with the shared reading strategies described in Chapter 4 until the student is engaged enough during shared reading that the active work of reading with comprehension becomes possible.

VOCABULARY INSTRUCTION

Students at all ability levels can acquire new vocabulary when provided with rich opportunities (Chapman, Seung, Schwartz, & Bird, 1998; Romski & Sevcik, 1996). Accomplishing this requires vocabulary instruction that meets several different criteria:

- It focuses on the connections between new and known words (Beck, McKeown, & Kucan, 2002).

- It includes direct instruction of vocabulary words specific to the texts we want students to read (Anderson & Nagy, 1991).

- It provides students with repeated opportunities to encounter words in a variety of contexts (Stahl, 2005).

- It focuses on the words that students are most likely to encounter across texts and contexts (Beck et al., 2002).

- It helps students understand the definition of words and how words function in different contexts (Nash & Snowling, 2006; Stahl & Kapinus, 2001).

- It integrates a variety of approaches (NICHD, 2000).

This combination supports students with significant disabilities in developing the strong knowledge of words that provides the base on which new words can be learned (Hirsch, 2003). Several approaches to supporting vocabulary learning are described in the following sections.

Build Curiosity About Words

In their work on teaching vocabulary, Beck, McKeown, and Kucan (2013) discovered that a critical part of effective vocabulary instruction is getting students interested in and aware of words they encounter. We have to help them recognize when they encounter unknown words and increase their interest in learning about the meaning of those new words and how they relate to known words. This requires us to make instruction interesting and engaging and to find ways for students to seek out new words outside of the classroom.

Try encouraging students to look for new words in and out of school. Find ways to celebrate, record, and/or display the new words they find. One teacher we worked with built a massive web of words in her classroom. Others have bulletin boards devoted to new words, and still others have students add words to personal and class dictionaries. Just as some families collect quarters each time someone uses a word deemed inappropriate, some teachers put counters in a jar each time students use a novel word or recognize that they have encountered one during reading and listening. They have a word celebration when the jar is full, and they play games, read books with interesting vocabulary (e.g., Lemony Snicket), and write independently or as a group using many of the new and interesting words they learned while introducing new words as appropriate. (Possibilities include a Jeopardy-style game during which the teacher displays newly learned words and students earn points by responding with questions such as, "What is . . .")

Engage in Interactive Read-Alouds

One reason many students with significant disabilities struggle with vocabulary is that they have had limited access to text for reading and listening. School-age students without disabilities learn about 3,000 new words each year (Miller & Gildea, 1987; Nagy & Herman, 1987; Nagy, Herman, & Anderson, 1985). By third grade, most of those new words are acquired through reading (Nagy, 1988; Nagy & Herman, 1987). This access to new words is not possible when students are still learning to read independently. Therefore, we need to read aloud to students to give them access to the vocabulary they might otherwise never encounter.

More important, speech is not a substitute for reading or listening to text because speech does not have the lexical diversity of written language (Stanovich et al., 1996). Consider what happens when you are writing versus telling a story. When you tell the story in oral language, it is completely acceptable to report on a conversation between two people repeating, "He said . . . and then she said . . . and then he said!" But you learned as a very young writer to vary the words you use. Instead of he said, she said, you might write that he said and she replied and he added.

Reading aloud to students provides an important route through which we can begin to close the word gap for students with significant disabilities. Although we have to take care to select books within the range of the students' listening comprehension abilities, reading diverse text types aloud to students while they learn to independently read with comprehension will help to maximize vocabulary development (Gardner, 2004).

When you are reading aloud and encounter words that are unknown or unfamiliar to the students, briefly explain the words and continue reading. If you feel the words need more explanation or want to include them in more explicit vocabulary instruction, then talk about them when you are finished reading (Beck et al., 2013). Beyond taking a moment to briefly explain unfamiliar words, the research suggests that students learn the most from read-alouds when they are encouraged to interact and talk about the book (e.g., Biemiller & Boote, 2006; Brabham & Lynch-Brown, 2002; Coyne, McCoach, & Kapp, 2007; Spycher, 2009). This is really an extension of the shared reading described in Chapter 4, with an emphasis on the vocabulary.

As students develop their skills and are increasingly successful reading with comprehension, you can further extend their access to vocabulary learning by encouraging them to engage in wide reading of text. Self-directed reading serves multiple purposes, but this increased access to diverse vocabulary is one very important reason to support it (see Chapter 8).

Focus on Connections

As students begin to learn new words, they connect those words to other words they know and experiences they have had (Perfetti, 2007; Reichle & Perfetti, 2003; Wolf, 2007). The more connections a student can make with a new word, the easier it is to learn and the more likely the student is to build a deep, conceptual representation of the word (Beck et al., 2013). These deep, conceptual representations of words are helpful because they are also flexible, which helps the reader consider the possible meanings of a word when it is encountered in a new context (Perfetti, 2007).

The teacher we mentioned who built a massive word web in her classroom focused on the connections between words. Each time students encountered a new word, they wrote it on a small paper plate and worked alone, with peers, or the teacher to determine how the new word could be connected to the web. When the new word was somehow similar in meaning to another word in the web, it was connected with a strand of black yarn. When the connection reflected an antonym or less obvious connection, they used a strand of red yarn. Finally, the explanation for the connection was written on an index card, which was posted on the yarn connecting the words. As new words were added, existing words were reviewed. The web grew, covering the walls and much of the ceiling by the end of the year.

Word chaining is a much less elaborate version of this attention to connections between words. In word chaining, teachers introduce new words and ask students to determine other words they know that are connected to the target word. A favorite example occurred in an inclusive fourth-grade classroom where the teacher was introducing a unit on habitats, beginning with the desert. After briefly explaining the concept of a desert, she asked the group to contribute words that related to the word *desert.* The students with the richest vocabulary immediately offered words such as *cactus, sand,* and *hot.* With some encouragement, the students kept going and offered connections such as "the mall" and "Saturday morning." After getting those interesting responses, the teacher stopped and asked the students to chain their connections back to desert. The boy who offered the mall said, "I go to eat at the mall with my mom. There are these big pots with cactuses in front. Cactuses grow in the desert, and I see them at the mall." The girl who offered Saturday morning explained that she watched cartoons on Saturday morning with her dad and her dad's favorite character is the Road Runner. The Road Runner is in the desert, and she watches it on Saturday morning. These were not the deep connections to the idea of the desert as a habitat that the teacher had hoped to address. Nevertheless, they helped the teacher gain insight into the connections the students already had and gave her important places to start.

You can also focus on the connections between words, starting with words that are familiar to the students. For example, you can present two known words (e.g., *silo* and *warehouse*) and ask students to determine how they are related (e.g., they store things). Alternatively, you can present students with a set of words and ask them to find pairs that are related in some way and then explain the relationship. New words can be introduced when students are increasingly successful in determining the connections between the known words.

Select Vocabulary to Teach

Determining which words to teach is going to depend on students' existing vocabulary skills. Some students with significant disabilities acquire relatively small vocabularies (Beukelman et al., 1984; Cameto et al., 2010). Others develop much more robust vocabularies (van der Schuit, Segers, van Balkom, & Verhoeven, 2011), and our experience tells us we can help more students increase their vocabulary knowledge when we take a comprehensive approach to instruction that includes a focus on vocabulary. We simply cannot take for granted that the students with significant disabilities we teach have the same vocabulary base as their peers without disabilities.

As we select vocabulary to teach, we want to focus on high-utility words that are likely to appear across a variety of academic domains and contexts, which will allow us to teach them directly and ensure that students will encounter them across contexts. At the same time, we want to focus on words that are not already well known and understood by the student. There are many different approaches to selecting vocabulary (e.g., Biemiller, 2001, 2005; Hiebert, 2005; Nation, 2001; Stahl & Nagy, 2006), but none specifically addresses students with significant disabilities. As a result, we cannot rely on the few approaches that identify specific words to teach (e.g., Biemiller, 2001, 2005; Hiebert, 2005). Instead, we look to Beck and colleagues (Beck et al., 2002, 2013; Beck, McKeown, & Kucan, 2008) and their criteria for choosing the words to teach. They proposed that we consider three tiers of vocabulary:

- *Tier 1:* This tier includes the common, everyday words that most students know by the time they are in second or third grade. The approximately 8,000 words in Tier 1 include the core vocabulary words that are often the focus of AAC and several thousand additional words. We cannot take for granted that students with significant disabilities understand these words.

- *Tier 2:* This tier includes about 7,000 additional words that are less frequent but still appear across the content domains in school. These words are important for students to learn in order to read a wide range of text with comprehension. Many of the process words that appear in directions at school (e.g., *describe, determine*) are found in this tier.

- *Tier 3:* The hundreds of thousands of words in this tier are low frequency and content specific. These are the words that appear in bold in textbooks and other domain-specific texts. They are important in the context of specific units and lessons, but they often do not have application across domains. We rarely choose to teach these directly, but we use them in meaningful contexts as appropriate.

> Unless students are still acquiring Tier 1 words, the largest portion of vocabulary words we teach will be Tier 2 words—high-utility words that appear across many academic domains and contexts.

The words we choose to teach students with significant disabilities come largely from Tier 2, unless we know that the students are still acquiring Tier 1 words. Table 7.2 provides examples of the kinds of words that are found in each tier.

Table 7.2. Example words in each tier of vocabulary

Tier 1	Tier 2	Tier 3
man	distinguish	circumference
woman	fortunate	monsoon
orange	establish	stalagmite
large	category	chromosome
different	description	atmosphere
anybody	performed	carbohydrate
everything	maintain	viscosity

Tailor Vocabulary Instruction for Students Who Use Augmentative and Alternative Communication

One challenge we face in planning vocabulary instruction for students with significant disabilities is that as many as half of the students cannot say the words we are teaching (Erickson & Geist, 2016). These students are likely to use AAC systems. Until we teach them to spell and write, their expressive communication is restricted to the words we represent on their communication systems. Even with the most robust, high-tech SGDs, it is not possible to provide students with meaningful access to the approximately 8,000 words in Tier 1, let alone the additional 7,000 in Tier 2. Yet, not teaching those words puts these students at a great disadvantage.

Although the gap between expressive and receptive vocabulary is especially obvious among students with significant disabilities and complex communication needs, it exists for all students. Across the board, students understand many more words than they actually use expressively (Beck & McKeown, 1991). Nonetheless, students who use speech to communicate have the benefit of being able to say the words we are teaching them to understand, which improves their ability to learn the words (Beck et al., 2013). When students are unable to say words aloud using speech, we ask them to say the words to themselves (i.e., in their heads). We also teach them to use the words they do have available on the communication systems to talk about the new words they are learning.

Many years ago, a student named Jordan helped us to learn this lesson. Each week his mom programmed a set of words on his communication device. Jordan then spent the week learning to select the words that matched the definitions his teacher sent home. The words were primarily Tier 3 words, and Jordan rarely used the words in any context other than during the quiz at the end of the week. It was not until the word *escarpment* appeared on his device that we all realized there was a problem. It suddenly became clear to us that we were actually restricting the development of Jordan's receptive vocabulary to the words that we could program onto his device.

As an alternative, the team started teaching Jordan to use the words that were already on his SGD to talk about the new words he was learning. For example, instead of selecting the single word, *escarpment,* the team helped Jordan learn that he could express an understanding of escarpment by using the words, *big, tall, hill, close, water.* Learning to talk about words in this way helped Jordan demonstrate that he understood new words as he learned them. It also helped him incorporate the new words into his existing receptive vocabulary without complicating his communication system with new words that he would seldom use.

As you select words to teach students with significant disabilities who use AAC systems, take time to identify the words that the student has available and describe these words conceptually. As you teach the target words, also demonstrate how the student can use the words you identified to talk about the new word. While you are building students' receptive vocabulary via this approach, be sure to focus time each day on improving students' spelling and writing skills so that one day the students will be able to say whatever words they want using spelling.

COMPREHENSION INSTRUCTION

All of this focus on vocabulary supports oral language comprehension, which directly supports the development of reading comprehension ability (NICHD Early Child Care Research Network, 2005). Yet, teaching students to comprehend written language (i.e., text) requires instruction that goes beyond vocabulary. Effective reading comprehension instruction provides ongoing opportunities for engagement and interaction with text (Trabasso & Bouchard, 2002) and also involves

- Clearly stated purposes for reading that are systematically related to concrete experiences and students' prior knowledge

- Groups of students interacting with one another about the text and the preestablished purpose for reading

- Texts that are interesting and varied (Guthrie & Davis, 2003)

The basic framework we use to deliver reading comprehension instruction that reflects the research base is called *Anchor-Read-Apply*. The Anchor portion of the lesson is used to activate relevant student background knowledge and set the purpose for reading. The Read portion consumes the majority of the available time and focuses on extending the amount of text students can read or listen to, remember, and process in order to accomplish the purpose. The Apply portion features a brief task that provides students with an opportunity to demonstrate whether they were successful with the purpose and teaches them to go back to the text to confirm their responses or correct them as needed. Before the lesson, the teacher thoughtfully chooses the text to be read, and afterward, the teacher provides students with informative feedback. Each portion of the Anchor-Read-Apply structure is described in more detail next.

Choosing Texts for Lessons

Selecting texts is an important aspect of an Anchor-Read-Apply lesson. When we select texts, we must consider whether the content and style or genre will allow us to address important purposes, and we must consider the complexity. If we select texts that are too complex, then students are unable to engage meaningfully with the text. They might be able to read to identify a detail or find the answer to a question, but they will not be able to engage with the text in order to accomplish purposes that require them to focus attention on the lesson, construct more accurate inferences or main ideas, or process the entire text. Although there may be reasons outside of reading comprehension instruction to help students learn how to search for information in difficult text, the goal during Anchor-Read-Apply lessons is to select texts that are easy enough that the students can read or listen while they engage in constructing understandings relative to the purpose (see Chapter 8 for more information regarding text complexity).

Before Reading: Anchor Activities and Purposes

Successful silent reading comprehension involves knowledge of the world and knowledge of text structures (Cunningham, 1993; Erickson, Koppenhaver, Cunningham, 2017). We address both in the Anchor portion of an Anchor-Read-Apply lesson. We begin by activating or building students' knowledge of the world and then help them understand the structure of the text they are about to read. When possible, our preference is to activate the knowledge students already have. Helping them activate and learn to use existing knowledge helps them make connections between what they already know and what they are reading (Roberts, Torgesen, Boardman, &

Scammacca, 2008). It is also a strategy they can use when we are not around. If we begin every lesson by teaching students what they need to know to understand the text, then they will not be able to read successfully when we are not there to build knowledge prior to reading.

Activate Background Knowledge

Activating background knowledge can take many forms. Knowledge of a particular topic and knowledge of particular thinking skills are two types of knowledge to activate. For example, you might ask students to brainstorm a list of vocabulary related to a topic or preselect vocabulary from the text and ask the students to identify, define, or provide examples of each word. You might have students recall their own experiences related to the topic at hand or provide a direct experience (e.g., experiments, simulations, videos) to ensure that experiential limitations are not the cause of a student's difficulty with a particular text. You might ask students to sort photographs of items that are and are not related to the topic. Each of these activates student knowledge of the topic addressed in the text.

The Anchor activity often focuses on activating the thinking skills required for the lesson. For example, if we want students to read to sequence the events in a story, then we could activate their background knowledge about sequencing by reviewing the daily schedule. If we want students to read to compare and contrast characters, then we might ask them to compare and contrast people in their lives. This type of Anchor activity draws on everyday thinking skills and experiences to help students know how they will need to think while reading.

Build Knowledge of Text Structures

Other Anchor activities focus on helping students build an increasingly complex understanding of the structures of written language (Duke et al., 2011; Mesmer et al., 2012). This is often narrowly interpreted as being able to label parts of story grammar (e.g., character, setting) and other text-related jargon. Yet, students need to know how information is organized in different types of fiction and nonfiction texts to read with comprehension, which goes well beyond labeling and identifying parts of a story or types of transitions and text features.

Knowledge of text structures can be strengthened during an Anchor activity by helping students recall and discuss other texts they have read that were like the one they are about to read. Previewing the text and searching for specific text features is another effective strategy for building knowledge of text structure while focusing the readers' attention and enabling them to anticipate text events or content. Teachers might begin by helping students distinguish between narrative and information texts and then focus more specifically on the differences within those two main types of text. For example, when the lesson focuses on a story, teachers could help students learn to identify structures such as setting, characters, conflict, plot, and resolution. They might also help students learn to distinguish text structures in stories, other types of literature, and information texts that signal sequence, comparison, cause and effect, description, and problem solution (Simonsen, 1996).

For example, one middle school teacher was getting ready to read *Hercules: The Twelve Labors* (Storrie, 2007) with her students. She was fairly certain that her students did not have much experience with myths, but they had just completed a unit on legends. That gave her a way to anchor this new text with something that was known.

She began by comparing legends (i.e., stories that combine real events or life stories with exaggerated, heroic actions) with myths (i.e., stories that give reasons for real events or explain why people do things). She drew attention to the fact that both have parts that are real and parts that are not real. Next, she showed a two-minute clip of the Disney animated movie of *Hercules* (which most of the students had already seen) and asked the students to watch for parts that were real. Then she told the students that the purpose for reading today was to remember the parts of the first chapter that were real and not real as she drew a T chart on the white board with the headers, "real" and "not real."

Overly complex texts may make it impossible for students to meaningfully engage with the text. Select texts for Anchor-Read-Apply lessons that are easy enough so that students can read or listen while engaging in constructing understandings relative to the purpose.

Modifying an Activity for Students Who Use Augmentative and Alternative Communication

If this classroom had included a student who used AAC, then the teacher might have created a list of the real and pretend elements in the movie clip. The students could read the first chapter to determine whether any of these elements were also in the chapter. If the student did not have access to sufficient vocabulary to name elements from the video, then the teacher might have shown the clip in real time and played it again at a slower speed. (YouTube clips allow the viewer to change the playback speed by selecting the Settings icon and then the Speed selector.) While reviewing the video at a slower speed, the teacher might ask students to indicate when something real or pretend appears, stop the video, and create the list. The point of creating the list is to provide response options students can use during the Apply step when we want them focused on remembering their response to the purpose, rather than navigating through their communication system to construct a response or selecting from a teacher-made array of answer options.

Besides giving attention to background knowledge and knowledge of text structures during the Anchor portion, we set a clear purpose for reading.

Set Purposes for Reading   The final part of the Anchor activity involves clearly stating a purpose for reading. Some educators argue that they cannot always give students a purpose because they believe students have to learn to set their own. We agree that students need to be able to set their own purposes, but that only happens when we teach them how. Giving students a purpose before they read is what focuses or anchors the lesson on one or a few of the structural elements or aspects of the text. This allows the teacher to focus on different aspects of comprehension that are most relevant to each text. Without a purpose, the teacher really is not teaching the student how to comprehend better.

We continue to set purposes for reading for our students in our undergraduate and graduate courses. These students are quite capable of setting their own purposes for reading; however, we are selecting texts with specific instructional objectives in mind. Communicating these purposes to our students focuses them on reading in ways that match those objectives. Students are essentially left to one of two difficult tasks without the purpose of reading—reading to remember everything or reading to guess what the teacher will ask them (to do) after reading. If we know why we have selected a particular text, then we can support student learning by stating that as clearly as possible before texts are read. If we want to deliver a focused lesson to teach students how to do better with a particular aspect of text comprehension, then providing a useful purpose for reading is our main tool for focusing the lesson.

Effective purposes can be quite varied, but they share three important characteristics:

1. They help readers focus their attention on what is relevant to the day's lesson.

2. They lead readers to construct more accurate inferences or main ideas.

3. They require processing of (nearly) the entire text, at least on the initial reading.

A single text can, and perhaps should, be read on multiple occasions for different purposes, and the chapters or sections of longer texts should each be read for different purposes. Through repeated experiences with a single text, and focused experiences with the parts of longer texts, readers gain increased understanding of text structure and vocabulary and are better able to apply their relevant language-based knowledge to improve their reading comprehension.

Teachers in the United States can turn to their state standards in English language arts (ELA) to identify purposes for reading that are embedded in the standards. Depending on the grade level, students might need to learn to read to determine what the text is all about (i.e., main idea), decide how the characters are the same or different (i.e., compare/contrast), or explain why the author wrote the text (i.e., author's purpose). We literally look at the grade level standards, identify the comprehension skills addressed, and restate them in terms that students understand, starting with, "Read so that you can . . ." Figure 7.1 provides examples of Anchor activities and reading purposes that align with a selection of Dynamic Learning Maps Essential Elements that align with grade level standards in ELA. (To access the Dynamic Learning Maps Essential Elements for English Language Arts online, visit http://dynamiclearningmaps.org/sites /default/files/documents/ELA_EEs/DLM_Essential_Elements_ELA_(2013)_v4.pdf.)

The state standards offer one source of potential purposes for reading. In addition, teachers can select a text and then determine appropriate purposes based on understandings of what readers do while constructing meaning from text. Examples of these more general purposes for reading are listed in Table 7.3. These purposes can be applied across many kinds of texts and align directly with many of the purposes that are embedded in state standards in ELA.

During Reading (or Listening): Read With Purpose

Reading or listening should take the largest segment of time in a reading comprehension lesson. The Anchor and Apply steps are important, but the amount of time spent reading texts is a stronger predictor of reading gains than time spent talking about the text (Allington, 2014; Anderson, Wilson, & Fielding, 1988; Cipielewski & Stanovich, 1992; Foorman et al., 2006).

EE.RL.3.5 Determine the beginning, middle, and end of a familiar story with a logical order.	
Anchor activity	Purpose
Identify the things that happen at the beginning of the school day (using the schedule as needed).	Read to identify what happens in the beginning of the story (from a list of three story events).

EE.RI.4.2 Identify the main idea of a text when it is explicitly stated.	
Anchor activity	Purpose
Work with students to tell what a favorite activity is about in 10 words or less.	Read to tell what a text is all about in 10 words or less.

EE.RL.5.5 Identify story element that undergoes change from beginning to end.	
Anchor activity	Purpose
Work with students to generate a list of ways they have changed as they have grown up.	Determine how the story element changes from the beginning to the end of the story.

EE.RL.7.3 Determine how two or more story elements are related.	
Anchor activity	Purpose
Generate a list of people with associated actions or events that are familiar to the students. Work with them to decide how the people are related to the actions or events.	Read to determine how these characters, actions, events, and places are related in the story.

EE.RL.9-10.5 Identify where a text deviates from a chronological presentation of events.	
Anchor activity	Purpose
Write a series of sentences that tell the story of something that is familiar to the students (could be a school day). Intentionally put one of the events out of order. Read the sentences with the students and ask them to figure out which sentence is not where it belongs.	Read to identify the part of the story that the author tells out of order.

Figure 7.1.   Example Anchor activities and purposes for reading aligned with grade level Dynamic Learning Maps Essential Elements in English Language Arts. (From Dynamic Learning Maps Consortium. [2013]. *Dynamic learning maps essential elements for English language arts*. Lawrence, KS: University of Kansas.)

Table 7.3.   Example general purposes for reading

Purpose	Explanation
Calling up and connecting	Read to remember (call up) what you already know and connect it with the new information in the text.
Predicting or anticipating	Before reading, draw on background knowledge to make an educated guess regarding what is likely to happen or what is required as a next step.
Organizing	Read in order to sequence, categorize, prioritize, or otherwise organize the information.
Summarizing or concluding	Read to tell in a few words what the text is all about or identify the lesson to be learned.
Applying	Read to apply what you learned from the text to another situation.

Comprehension can be improved whether students read texts themselves or listen to others read them aloud. If we want to assist students in reaching the goal of independent reading, however, they must have regular and frequent opportunities to read texts themselves. Teachers can use two primary strategies to help students read successfully during Anchor-Read-Apply lessons—guiding student application of the purpose that has been set and selecting texts for reading at a level that the student can understand.

Guiding student application of the purpose during reading is most easily accomplished through two means—Anchor activities that help students successfully call up background knowledge, combined with clearly stated purposes. We can also guide application by reminding students of the purpose once or twice during reading. We reduce interruptions during reading, however, and avoid stopping to talk about the text or relevant points that might help students complete the purpose. The goal is to set purposes that require students to read or listen to texts of increasing length and complexity while holding information in their heads and integrating it with existing knowledge. If we read, stop, discuss, and record information as it is encountered, then we keep students from developing this critical ability. When students struggle, we respond by selecting easier purposes and easier texts to start and then increase the complexity of both as students' skills increase.

> To make gains in reading, students need to spend time doing it. Reading or listening should take the largest segment of time in a reading comprehension lesson.

After Reading: Apply What You Read

After students read a text for a given purpose, the Apply task allows them to demonstrate their understanding (or misunderstanding). A good Apply task enables students to check their understanding and allows educators to intervene as necessary to support learning. The challenge is generating an Apply task that matches the purpose for reading. Keep the following three principles in mind as you determine what you will ask students to do to demonstrate their understanding:

1. Focus on the specific purpose.

2. Make the task no more complex than needed for the students to demonstrate understandings.

3. Use selection and other identification tasks that level the playing field for students who do not have the ability to easily discuss what they read.

Also remember to follow a specific order when planning an Anchor-Read-Apply task. First, select the text. Then determine the purpose for reading. After the task and purpose are selected, appropriate Anchor activities and Apply tasks can be generated. Table 7.4 provides examples of Anchor activities, purposes, and Apply tasks that could be used with a wide variety of texts.

> During and after reading, focus instruction on the reading purpose established earlier.

Table 7.4.   Anchor activities, purposes, and Apply tasks

Anchor activity	Purpose	Apply task
The teacher must make sure the student can successfully sequence events–not a skill most students learn without instruction. Teach sequencing by using content that is very familiar to the student, such as days of the week, meals in the day, or the schedule students follow at school. Use examples of events that are correctly and incorrectly sequenced to ensure that students have the required background knowledge.	"Read so that you can put the story events in order."	The teacher writes the events on sentence strips, and the student points to put them in the correct order after reading.
If the student uses AAC, then ask the student to generate words that could be used to describe a person, place, event, or whatever is appropriate given the exact purpose you have set. Take any describing words the student can generate and write them on index cards. If the student does not have a comprehensive system, then prepare examples and nonexamples on index cards ahead of time and ask the student to indicate whether the word fits the purpose. Use any inaccurate responses as teaching opportunities, but do not simply correct the error.	"Read so that you can show me which of the five words I have written on index cards best describe the main character, setting, climax, problem, or resolution." (The teacher selects only one and returns to the text on another day if it seems important to find the words that best describe another feature of the text.)	The student selects from the words that are written on index cards (either generated by the student or selected by the student from the choices provided by the teacher).
Begin by making sure the student understands a Venn diagram. Create one with the student comparing and contrasting two very familiar people (e.g., mom and teacher). Once the Venn diagram structure is understood, ask the student to either generate descriptive words or select from the examples and nonexamples you have prepared.	"Read so that you can compare and contrast the two main characters in the story."	Students place, or guide placement of, the descriptive words in the right location on the Venn diagram.

Providing Informative Feedback

Providing informative feedback is the final step in a successful reading comprehension lesson. Building cognitive clarity is the primary purpose of such feedback; that is, helping students understand what they did that led to success or what might be done differently next time to increase success. Informative feedback is different from reinforcement or correction. Informative feedback focuses on helping students understand what they did; how information was found, remembered, or processed; and how the strategy or strategies employed would work with other texts. Nearly always, we return to the text to compare and contrast student responses with the text sources.

KWL, DR-TA, and Other Anchor-Read-Apply Formats

The general elements of Anchor-Read-Apply lessons exist in other approaches described in the literature. KWL (Ogle, 1986) is one such approach that most teachers

Turtle Facts

Know	**W**ant to know	**L**earned
Green Water Slow Shell Checkered Shell Pond, lake Long neck Hide in shell	Are there different kinds? Do they live in water? What do they eat? Can they leave their shell?	Some eat only vegetables Some eat only meat Some eat meat and vegetables Some live in water Some live on land Cannot leave shell

Figure 7.2. KWL graphic organizer. (*Source:* Dynamic Learning Maps Consortium [2013].)

learned about at some point in their teacher education programs. It is described here for use in comprehension lessons with information texts, but it can also be used as part of a thematic unit rather than a single text.

KWL is an acronym. K stands for what the students think they *know* about a topic, W stands for what they *want* to know, and L stands for what they *learned.* Asking students to share what they think they know about a topic is one way of activating their background knowledge. Their knowledge may be accurate, but asking them what they think they know gets students working to recall information and experiences related to the topic. Students then generate their own purposes for reading as they work in the W part of the lesson to determine what they want to know about the topic. They then read for the purpose of finding answers to their questions, and, after reading, the Apply task is to tell what they learned relative to their questions. Teachers usually use a graphic organizer to organize a KWL lesson (see Figure 7.2).

The Directed Reading-Thinking Activity (DR-TA; Stauffer, 1975) is another instructional approach that has an Anchor-Read-Apply format. DR-TA is used to guide students in making predictions based on their background knowledge during the Anchor step. They read for the purpose of confirming, refuting, or changing those predictions based on what they learn from the text. Students compare their predictions with what actually happens in the text during the Apply step. This strategy helps students become active and thoughtful readers who combine existing background knowledge with information the text provides.

To start the lesson, show students the title and the first few illustrations in the story. Then ask students to make a prediction and help them connect their predictions to create a sequence of events. The goal is to go beyond naming characters and single events and actually predict the series of events that will unfold. We usually support this by writing down what students predict and asking, "And then what?" After this Anchor activity, teachers clearly state the purpose, saying something such as, "Let's read to see how well our predictions match what happens in the story."

Whether the students then read or listen to the text, the teacher selects one or two predetermined stopping places and works with students to review their predictions and confirm, refute, or change them each time they stop reading. After finishing the text, the Apply task involves the teacher working with the students to identify the parts of their predictions that did and did not match the story. Finally, the teacher and students go back to the text to check their responses.

DR-TA works with stories or narrative texts that have a series of events. We use a slightly different "yes or no" approach with information texts. First, the teacher identifies an appropriate text, previews it, and generates a list of statements that do and do not match the text. Second, the teacher uses an Anchor activity that requires students to use their background knowledge to determine whether each statement is true (yes) or false (no). The teacher keeps a tally for the group, and students who have the necessary communication skills are asked to indicate why they selected yes or no. Sometimes students will indicate, "I don't know." In this case, we ask students, "What do you think you know?" Then we work them through gaining access to relevant background knowledge to make an informed guess. After responding to each statement, the teacher provides the purpose for reading: "Let's read to see if we are right." Next, students read the text from beginning to end. After reading, the Apply task requires students to revisit the statements and their responses. Finally, the teacher guides students back through the text to check their responses.

These are just three examples of comprehension lessons that have an Anchor-Read-Apply structure. There are many others. In fact, as students move beyond reading beginning level text for increasingly complex purposes and start focusing on reading comprehension strategies, most effective approaches to strategy instruction also have an Anchor-Read-Apply structure. This structure helps students draw on what they know and read while applying an appropriate strategy.

A FINAL NOTE: KEEPING AN EYE ON THE PRIZE

Reading with comprehension is a complex process. It requires the integration of knowledge of the world, knowledge of text structures, word reading, and a myriad of other skills that help readers actively construct understandings while reading. Improving reading comprehension requires targeted instruction that helps students learn to use their knowledge of the world and knowledge of text structures to construct understandings of text. Asking students to read and answer questions, on a literal or inferential level, does little more than assess how well the students understood the text. Even then, you only really assess how well the students understood the text if you do not allow them to look back at the text to find the answers. Looking back to find answers provides insight into students' verbal problem-solving skills but does little to provide information regarding text comprehension. Furthermore, answering questions does not help students improve their ability to comprehend text that they read or hear others read to them (NICHD, 2000). That means we must replace reading packets and endless questions with instruction that systematically anchors each reading, focuses students' attention through clearly stated purposes, and requires students to complete quick tasks to demonstrate their understandings before returning to the text to confirm responses with evidence from the text. At the same time, we have to attend to the complexity of the texts we ask students to read while building their oral language skills with specific attention to vocabulary. Ultimately, we have to keep our eyes on the prize and remember that everything we do in the name of reading instruction should serve to help students independently read a broader range of texts for increasingly complex purposes.

RECOMMENDED READINGS AND RESOURCES

The following readings and resources will deepen readers' understanding of how to provide effective instruction in reading comprehension and vocabulary for students with significant disabilities.

Dynamic Learning Maps Professional Development web site (http://dlmpd.com). See the following modules: Teaching Text Comprehension: Anchor-Read-Apply and DR-TA and Other Text Comprehension Approaches.

Erickson, K. (2003, June 24). Reading comprehension in AAC. *The ASHA Leader,* *8*(12), 6–9. Retrieved from https://leader.pubs.asha.org/doi/10.1044/leader.FTR1 .08122003.6

CHAPTER 8

Self-Directed Reading

Supporting Motivation and Fluency

Two boys taught us the importance of reading motivation, a topic nearly absent in the research addressing literacy in students with significant disabilities. Micah was a 9-year-old identified with significant learning disabilities and ADHD by his school. He told us he loved playing with dinosaurs, toy soldiers, cars and trucks, all sorts of blocks, and more. When asked about reading interests, however, he was silent. His mother explained that he read only school assignments, and then only if he were allowed to burn or shred the reading material when he finished the assignment. Our informal reading assessment revealed that he could read first-grade level texts silently with good comprehension and understand texts above grade level if they were read aloud to him, and his primary difficulty was decoding words of two or more syllables.

Brent was a 13-year-old with significant communication and physical impairments due to a rare neurological condition. He, too, had many interests, including traveling, watching documentaries, and spending time with his family. When asked about his reading interests, he said he preferred nonfiction, specifically the American Revolution, and really enjoyed two book series, The Magic School Bus *by Joanna Cole and Bruce Degen (https://scholastic.com/kids/books/the-magic-school-bus) and* Magic Treehouse *by Mary Pope Osborne (https://magictreehouse.com/books). An informal reading assessment showed that Brent could not read text at even the easiest levels of the reading inventory but could understand texts read aloud to him up to a third-grade level.*

Ability to read did not explain the difference in the two boys' motivation to read. Micah, though younger than Brent, was actually a higher-level reader. Disability did not explain the differences either. Brent had significant and complex disabilities, but Micah's impairments were undetectable in our interactions and the reading tasks we asked of him. The principal difference was that Brent was surrounded both at home and school by people who inquired about his interests, helped him find books on those personal interests, and read aloud with him daily. Micah's school focused on his reading difficulties and sought to remediate them with published and widely available strategies and materials. Most of the reading aloud that occurred at home or school was done by Micah, either to verify that he was completing his assignments or so his word identification or reading fluency could be assessed. His mother read aloud his assignments to help him complete them more efficiently and with less distress.

More than one person has suggested to us that some kids are just going to hate reading no matter what. Our experiences and the research suggest otherwise. In fact, every student we have met who hates reading has had some really good reasons. So, too, has every student who loves reading. In this chapter, you will learn how to teach in ways that encourage

> Every student we have met who hates—or loves—reading has had some really good reasons to do so.

students to choose to read or explore texts even when they do not have to and improve their reading skills in the process. You will learn principles for developing an environment that encourages interest in reading and helps students succeed when they choose to read.

RESEARCH BRIEF: WHY WE TEACH SELF-DIRECTED READING

Students who read widely in school (Organisation for Economic Co-operation and Development, 2010a) or out of school (Anderson et al., 1988; Krashen, 2004; Sullivan & Brown, 2013) become better readers (Wang & Guthrie, 2004). Their wide, independent reading contributes specifically to growth in reading fluency (Kuhn, 2005), vocabulary knowledge (Gardner, 2004), understanding of grammar and syntax (Muter, Hulme, Snowling, & Stevenson, 2004), inferential comprehension (Osana, Lacroix, Tucker, Idan, & Jabbour, 2007), and listening comprehension (Hedrick & Cunningham, 1995). More important, they obtain these benefits regardless of reading or cognitive abilities (Cunningham, 2005; Cunningham & Stanovich, 1998) as long as they are given the opportunity to read texts they can comprehend (Nagy, Anderson, & Herman, 1987). These benefits also have lasting impact and contribute to social well-being, employment, and economic success once students complete school (Organisation for Economic Co-operation and Development, 2010b).

Motivation is critical to students' reading achievement. Students who develop intrinsic motivation for reading find it an enjoyable and interesting experience, whereas those who are extrinsically motivated view reading as a way to acquire praise, recognition, or other incentives (Schaffner & Schiefele, 2016). Intrinsic motivation results in students who choose to read more during free time at school or at home, whereas extrinsic motivation has the opposite effect (Becker, McElvany, & Kortenbruck, 2010). Intrinsic motivation results from feelings of self-determination, which is the product of autonomy, or choice; a sense of belonging to a community; and feelings of competence (Ryan & Deci, 2000).

At the same time, research suggests that students with significant disabilities may be provided with extremely limited opportunities for independent reading in school (Kliewer & Biklen, 2001; Koppenhaver & Yoder, 1993; Mike, 1995; Ruppar, 2015). The reasons have not been studied but may be attributable to such causes as these:

- The very real difficulties of addressing the complex array of student needs in this population

- The time required to make materials accessible for independent reading

- Beliefs that students with significant disabilities cannot learn to read or do not require independent reading time until they can read independently at higher levels or master prerequisite skills

- A greater emphasis on direct instruction than reading experience

The encouraging news, however, is that when students with significant disabilities are provided with opportunities for wide reading in age- and ability-appropriate materials of interest, both emergent and beginning readers demonstrate measurable gains in reading achievement (Hatch & Erickson, 2018). Emergent readers demonstrated growth in concepts of print, writing, alphabet identification, rhyming, and phoneme blending as assessed with the Universally Accessible Emergent Literacy Battery (Erickson et al., 2005). Conventional readers demonstrated growth in vocabulary knowledge and reading comprehension as measured by the Gates-MacGinitie Reading Test–Fourth Edition (MacGinitie, MacGinitie, Maria, Dreyer, & Hughes, 2000), an accessible standardized reading test (Hatch & Erickson, 2018).

> If children have enough opportunity to read texts they can comprehend, then the benefits of wide independent reading, such as improved fluency, vocabulary, and inferential and listening comprehension, are obtained regardless of reading or cognitive abilities.

BUILDING A CLASSROOM LIBRARY

To implement an effective self-directed reading program in your classroom or home, you need materials that all students either can read and want to read or can understand and enjoy when listening to others read them aloud. One of your first tasks is to build an interesting and accessible collection of reading materials. Notice, we use the term *reading materials,* not *books.* Traditionally, schools have privileged books as the only acceptable form of reading. Even now some teachers overemphasize books and overlook the educational value of reading in other formats. Books are wonderful, with nearly infinite varieties from which to choose. Yet, ignoring other forms of reading denies the reality of reading in the real world and the increasing array of print presentations that attract different readers—magazines and newspapers, music and rap lyrics, tablet computers and reading apps, interactive web sites and digital read-alouds, and peer compositions and digital correspondence.

The Value of a Diverse Collection

The key is to build a collection that all students can read and want to read. A few students are interested in anything and everything, others only in fantasy or adventure, mystery or informational text. Some prefer magazine articles, others chapter books. Some want traditional paper reading materials, others digital reading. Some like reading comic books or graphic novels, others like sports programs or trading cards. See the "Possibilities for Your Classroom Library" textbox for a sampling of the range of reading materials you should make available to students in your classroom or home library. Make sure that whatever you incorporate into your collection enables students to see the text clearly, particularly when using digital materials, which sometimes are turned into visual experiences minus the print.

Possibilities for Your Classroom Library

An array of different print and digital texts can be part of your classroom library; the following list is just a sampling.

- Books (alphabet, book series, diaries, anthologies, wordless picture books)
- Directions (maps, recipes, Google maps, manuals, atlases)
- Reference books (dictionaries, encyclopedias)
- Comics, manga, and graphic novels
- Trading cards (baseball, television shows, musicians, super heroes, Star Wars)
- Newspapers and a wide array of magazines
- Travel brochures
- Sports programs
- Materials written by students
- Books on CD, DVD, or even audiotapes still found in some schools
- Books read aloud online (storylineonline.net, storyplace.org, BookFlix)
- Digital libraries (watchknowlearn.org, http://en.childrenslibrary.org)
- Digital resources like (micro-)blogs, wikis, e-mail, text messages, informational web sites (National Geographic for Kids Stories)
- Social media (Twitter, Facebook, Instagram)
- Accessible online book collections (tarheelreader.org, bookshare.org, accessible-bookcollection.org, https://tumblebooks.com)
- E-book apps (Scholastic Storia, A Story Before Bed, Tales2Go)
- Texts created through authoring apps (Book Creator, Storykit, Tikatok, Kid in Story)
- Sing-alongs and song lyrics (kididdles.com, NIEHS Kids' Sing-Alongs, YouTube music videos with lyrics)

Some students do not have any idea what they might be interested in because of limited life experiences or reading opportunities. We have known more than one child who did not particularly enjoy reading but would read a single text initially—a favorite book from previous experience, the weather forecast in the newspaper, the local train schedule, or a catalogue. Once that choice was honored with a place in the classroom or home library, teachers and parents could build on it with additional genres, topics, and experiences. See the textbox for a sampling of the range of genres to include in your classroom or home collection over time.

A Sampling of the Range of Genres to Include in Your Classroom or Home Collection

- Picture books such as *Different* (Evans, 2018)

- Picture storybooks such as *All Are Welcome* (Penfold, 2018)

- Realistic fiction such as *Giraffes Can't Dance* (Andreae, 2012)

- Historical fiction such as *The Giraffe That Walked to Paris* (Milton, 2013)

- Science fiction such as *Ricky Ricotta's Mighty Robot vs. The Uranium Unicorns From Uranus* (Pilkey, 2015)

- Biography and autobiography such as *The Girl Who Thought in Pictures: The Story of Dr. Temple Grandin* (Finley Mosca, 2017)

- Fantasy such as *Angela's Airplane* (Munsch, 2018)

- Folktales such as *The Enormous Potato* (Davis, 1999)

- Fairy tales such as *Once Upon a Slime* (Maxwell, 2018)

- Fables such as *Squids Will Be Squids: Fresh Morals, Beastly Fables* (Scieszka, 2003)

- Legends such as *Tomie dePaola's Big Book of Favorite Legends* (dePaola, 2007)

- Mysteries such as *Minnie and Moo: The Case of the Missing Jelly Donut* (Cazet, 2006)

- Mythology such as *Zeus and the Thunderbolt of Doom (Heroes in Training)* (Holub & Williams, 2012)

- Nonfiction such as *Otis and Will Discover the Deep: The Record-Setting Dive of the Bathysphere* (Rosenstock, 2018)

- Alphabet books such as *J is for Jazz* (Ingalls, 2014)

- Poetry such as *Once I Laughed My Socks Off: Poems for Kids* (Attewell, 2012)

- Joke books such as *Just Joking: 300 Hilarious Jokes, Tricky Tongue Twisters, and Ridiculous Riddles* (National Geographic Kids, 2012)

- Directions such as cookbooks, craft projects, or LEGO construction such as *Cookies!: An Interactive Recipe Book (Cook in a Book)* (Nieminen, 2018)

- Series books such as *Nate the Great* (Sharmat, 1977)

Children's literature that respectfully portrays disability is an additional category of books to consider. Texts with rich storylines in which disability is a part of the character's identity but not the central defining feature enable readers to identify with the character and view disability as just one more aspect of human life. *King for a Day* (Khan, 2014) is a perfect example. The central character, Malik, uses a wheelchair, but the story is about kite battles in Pakistan. A list of other similar texts can be found at Goodreads (https://goodreads.com/review/list/36555428-inclusive -literature?shelf=read). Criteria for identifying or creating other such texts can be found in Pennell et al. (2017).

The main reason for maintaining a diverse collection is to maximize the opportunity for all students to find something to read that connects with their topical interests and text preferences, which change over time and with experience. A text has no use if a child will not read it. The same holds true if a child cannot read it. This means your classroom collection also must include texts spanning a wide range of difficulty levels, particularly books that are easy to read relative to your students' abilities. Easier materials include wordless picture books, predictable texts, texts with repeated lines, simple texts matching the illustrations on each page, and texts with two to three words per page. A classroom collection should also range up to books that may be above grade level for your more confident and experienced readers. At home, families can fine-tune their children's book collection more specifically to what they can and want to read.

There is no magic number of books for a classroom or personal library, but evidence suggests that more is better, and teachers should continue to expand their classroom collection month by month and year by year. Parents should do the same at home. We met a special educator in Florida who had more than 600 books in his students' classroom library and an SLP in Minnesota who built her student collection to more than 10,000 books during her career. We met a mother and daughter in Arizona who could not afford a television, but they visited the public library twice weekly and estimated that they each read more than 300 books a year.

Students more readily engage in independent reading, despite significant disabilities, in settings where they have more choices, and they more eagerly interact with others about their reading. Exemplary teachers of typically developing first graders average 1,500 books in their in-class libraries (Allington, 2011), a reasonable long-range target for teachers of students with significant disabilities, who typically read at beginning levels. In addition, research from 42 countries found that the number of books in the home strongly predicted students' success in school (Evans, Kelley, & Sikora, 2014).

> To help readers view disability as just one aspect of life, choose texts that respectfully portray disability as part of the character's identity but not the central defining feature.

Tips for Building a Classroom Library on a Budget

Teachers spend an average of $600 per year of their own money on basic classroom supplies (Ness, 2017). We are not suggesting you spend any of your own money. Here are a variety of ways that teachers have expanded their in-class libraries without incurring out-of-pocket expenses.

Use Available Local Resources to Obtain Books
Fellow teachers, school librarians, children's librarians, and families should be your first contacts in acquiring books for your students. Retiring teachers are renowned for their generosity to colleagues, particularly those new to the profession. Perhaps they will donate some or all of their own children's book collection to you. Other teachers band together to share their collections, particularly in impoverished schools. If, for example, you and five other teachers each have 30 books you are willing to exchange monthly, then all of you have a collection of 180 books instantly. Similarly, librarians can be an invaluable

resource in helping you locate particular kinds of texts for particular kinds of readers, for problem-solving access for your students, and for helping you expand your collection. They may be able to direct you to sites such as Tar Heel Reader's Switch Interface page (https://tarheelreader.org/accessing-tar-heel-reader/switch-interface -devices) or Paths to Literacy's Accessible Books page (http://pathstoliteracy.org /accessible-books). They know books and how to search for information, and they are eager to help. Their professional organization, the American Library Association, has a page of information about and links to organizations that donate books (http:// libguides.ala.org/book-donations/seeking-books).

Families are a potentially overlooked resource in acquiring books for classroom collections. Families receive annual requests from schools for disinfectant wipes, packaged snacks, paper, and other classroom supplies. Teachers might also request book donations in lieu of Christmas or thank-you gifts, in honor of students on their birthdays, or simply as a way that families can share books no longer in use in home collections. Parents who can afford it may be willing to contribute more so that every class member is recognized by a book donation.

Teachers can help families by sending books home nightly with students. When working with families of students with complex communication needs, basic communication supports like those found at Project Core (http://project-core.com) can also be sent home to support parents and children in communicating about the books they are reading. One teacher we know in rural North Carolina has recorded read-alouds of the books in her collection and makes them available through her school wiki to parents who are unable to read aloud with their child or are simply too busy when their child wants to listen to a story. Others use a variety of apps and QR code generators to make read-alouds available to their students in school and at home.

Write Mini-Grants to Fund Your Classroom Library   DonorsChoose (http:// donorschoose.org) is an online charity that was founded in 2000 to support K–12 schools across the United States. Teachers can solicit charitable donations for educational projects, and site users choose projects or causes to contribute toward. We know teachers who have used DonorsChoose to fund reading technology, library expansions, a reading garden, book sets, and genre additions. DonorsChoose provides clear guidance on how to compose and submit a request at their site. Once your proposal is reviewed and accepted, it is posted on the organization's web site, and the requested materials are shipped to you when the project is funded. If you fund your classroom library through DonorsChoose, then be sure to photograph your students reading the books and have them write thank-you letters.

Use Free, Online Reading Resources   Tar Heel Reader (http://tarheelreader .org) is a collection of thousands of free, easy-to-read, accessible books on a wide range of topics. Each book can be speech enabled and accessed in multiple ways, including eye gaze, touch screens, and up to three switches. The books can be read online, on tablets, or on smartphones or downloaded and printed. Many public libraries provide free access to Tumble Books (http://tumblebooks.com), a subscription service of hundreds of high-quality, digital children's books on multiple grade levels that can be listened to or read silently. Take a field trip to your public library, make sure everyone gets a library card, and then help them (and their families) put Tumble Books (and the rest of the library's resources) to good use.

Find Books at Goodwill, Salvation Army, Habitat ReStores, Yard Sales, and Similar Places That Sell New and Gently Used Items   Such organizations and events often have books that they are trying to sell cheaply, sometimes more than they can get rid of. They periodically have deep discounts when they want to clear inventory, particularly at the end of the day or the end of a sales event. One teacher we know regularly visits these places in her community and talks about her students' needs and how much they would benefit from more books. More often than not she leaves with as many books as she can carry, usually at no cost.

Ask for Help From Clubs, Community Foundations, Church Groups, and Boy and Girl Scout Troops   Service organizations are always looking for a worthy cause. If you provide these organizations with specific guidelines as to the kinds of books you need, then you may be able to help them help your students. One teacher we know conducted an evening workshop for a local fraternity on how to create books using Microsoft PowerPoint. She gave them a list of her students' interests and had received more than 200 new digital books by the end of the semester. Community foundations want to help their communities. If you can show them how your classroom and students match their priorities, then your students may be supported.

It is crucial to provide students with a wide range of texts spanning different interests, materials, and genres, regardless of how you go about the task. Variety alone, however, is not enough to guarantee they make use of your classroom library. It is also critical to engage inexperienced readers by finding or making texts that are sufficiently easy for them to read.

PROVIDING TEXTS EASY ENOUGH TO ENGAGE STUDENTS

Challenge is the buzzword in much of schooling. Teachers are directed to push their students to read texts at their peak capability and beyond in order to maximize growth. We would suggest that *engagement* is a better metaphor. The best readers at each grade level, who by definition can understand more complex texts than their classmates, are the students who rarely, if ever, are challenged by the texts they read. As a consequence, because most of the texts they encounter are not difficult relative to their abilities, they read them easily and with greater understanding, apply the strategies they are being taught more successfully, and appreciate the value of reading more fully. They read more words more successfully and become highly efficient self-teaching readers, and they choose to read more on their own because it is enjoyable.

Students with significant disabilities have lives filled with challenges. They do not need to be challenged further by difficult reading materials. Rather, they need and deserve interesting, engaging, and easy reading experiences to build a strong foundation for lifelong reading. When choosing reading materials for your classroom, try to remember that texts can easily be too hard, but they can hardly be too easy. Five strategies for ensuring that inexperienced readers get to read texts easy enough to engage them include

1. Using simplified or wordless texts

2. Using predictable texts

3. Teaching students "a different rule of thumb" for gauging text difficulty

4. Facilitating students' reading of "just right" books

5. Conducting read-alouds

Texts can easily be too hard but can hardly be too easy.

These strategies are discussed in detail in the following sections.

Use Simplified or Wordless Texts

If students cannot yet read, then be prepared to support their exploration of texts with easily understandable texts. Teachers can decrease the complexity of texts for beginners in a number of ways. One of the easiest is to provide access to simplified texts, the most basic of which are wordless picture books. Students can look at, talk about, or retell the story based on their understanding of the illustrations. You can find many examples of these texts for all age groups by asking a bookseller or librarian or by entering terms such as *wordless picture books, wordless picture books for teens, or wordless picture books about* [topic; e.g., animals] into a search engine.

Teachers may need to make page-by-page connections from the book to students' real-world experiences to engage students with the most significant intellectual disabilities or extremely limited experiences with books. Web sites such as Tar Heel Reader (http://tarheelreader.org) and apps such as Book Creator (https://bookcreator.com), Pictello (http://assistiveware.com/product/pictello), or Kid in Story (http://enuma.com/products-kidinstory) make it possible to take photographs of students engaged in real-world experiences, import those photographs, and add text and speech in order to create highly personalized texts. Teachers recently have begun creating books employing only the most frequently occurring vocabulary words. These core words are the words we use most frequently when communicating across purposes, partners, and contexts, and they are among the most frequently occurring words in written English (Dennis, Erickson, & Hatch, 2013). A list of 40 of these words is provided in Table 8.1. Because these books include only a handful of unique words, and Tar Heel Reader has a read-aloud option, students with limited reading and symbolic communication experience can experience successful and engaging reading from the beginning that may also enhance acquisition of expressive vocabulary. As an example, see *Like, Not Like* (http://tarheelreader.org/2014/06/03/like-not-like).

Table 8.1. The Dynamic Learning Maps first 40 core vocabulary words

all	help	more	that
are	here	need	this
can	I	not	turn
different	in	on	up
do	is	open	want
don't	it	over	what
finished	like	put	when
get	look	she	where
go	make	some	who
he	me	stop	you

Text can also be simplified by reducing the number and complexity of words on each page. Alphabet label books do this fairly directly (e.g., *A:* apple, *B:* boy). Teachers creating language experience texts script narratives based on students' personal experiences, written in their own words, and supported by photographs. Other texts accomplish this by increasing the predictability of the narrative (e.g., repeated line or repeated pattern books). A wide range of such books is available in your local bookstore and online. Some of our favorites include Arthur Geisert's (1991) one-word book, *Oink,* and Jez Alborough's (2001) one-word book, *Hug,* Emily Gravett's (2006) four-word book, *Orange Pear Apple Bear,* and Reed A. Booke's three-homophone text, *Alphabet Play* (http://tarheelreader.org/2010/08/19/alphabet-play).

Many teachers assist students in composing familiar texts with familiar content and repeated lines. One preschool teacher we know had a parent volunteer take photographs during a field trip to the zoo. When the class returned to school, the teacher then helped the children compose a text entitled *At the Zoo* with a repeated pattern: "[Name of child] saw a [name of animal, prompted by photograph] at the zoo." The story ended with "We had fun at the zoo." Three of the 3- to 5-year-olds with ASDs were successfully reading the repeated line pages after the teacher had read aloud through the text just once.

Use Predictable Texts

A variety of common, predictable text structures can be used to support the emergent and beginning readers in your classes. Question and answer books, cumulative sequence texts, texts with predictable patterns, question and answer texts with implied questions, and repeated line texts work well across age groups. Some specific examples are described in Table 8.2.

The value of predictable texts such as these is that students often more rapidly make sense of them. They gain sensitivity to text structure, acquire vocabulary, and participate more readily and successfully in independent reading or interactions with others about the text. A 5-year-old we met with Rett syndrome, who had never used a switch before, began taking a turn with the repeated line, "Are you my mommy?" after just three pages of shared reading in Cara Dijs's (1990) book of that title.

A Word on Developmental Appropriateness

More than a few well-intentioned teachers and schools forbid the use of reading materials that are viewed as childish. For example, one teacher would not allow her high school students to read materials based on the *Barney and Friends* television show because it is geared toward preschool students. The problem with such rules is that they limit students' choices, which may limit growth in reading motivation. Such rules also tell students that school does not value their interests.

Other teachers act in more constructive ways. Instead of restricting choices, they allow students to read whatever they are interested in as long as it is not offensive to others in the classroom, school, or community. Then they investigate the source of interest and build on it. Do students like to read Barney because the text is understandable? Because they like fantasy? Dinosaurs? Books about television shows? Because their younger siblings read it to them at home? Answers to questions such as these help teachers know how to expand on, rather than restrict, student interests.

Table 8.2.   Examples of predictable text structures

Text type	Example	Description
Question and answer books	*Story of the Little Mole Who Went in Search of Whodunit* by Werner Holzwarth and Wolf Erlbruch (2007)	On each page, the mole asks a different animal if it is the one who did its business on his head. Each animal provides the same negative response and a demonstration of its business with sound effects.
Cumulative sequence texts	*Here is the Coral Reef* by Madeline Dunphy (2006)	On each page, an additional nugget is added and previous information repeated.
Predictable patterns	*Black? White! Day? Night!* by Laura Vaccaro Seeger (2016)	In this flap book of opposites, each page contains a single-word question, and when the flap is lifted, the single word opposite is exclaimed.
Question and answer texts with an implied question	*Tools* by Taro Miura (2006)	This text presents two pages of basic illustrations of tools of different trades, replicated to scale, with one- or two-word labels. Although there is no explicit question, the implied question as readers examine the tools is, "What worker uses these tools?" The next two pages present the answer—an illustration of the worker and single word label.
Pattern texts	*Duck! Rabbit!* by Amy Krouse Rosenthal and Tom Lichtenheld (2009)	This text is conducted as a dialogic argument between two people looking at what could be either a duck or a rabbit, depending on the viewer's perspective. An excellent YouTube video version features a young girl and young boy carrying on the book's dialogue with the text clearly visible (http://tinyurl.com/ocg4mxk).
Repeated line texts	*Not a Box* by Antoinette Portis (2011)	An unimaginative adult repeatedly asks a young rabbit what it is doing with a box. The young rabbit repeatedly denies that it is a box, and illustrations reveal the imaginary play. An excellent YouTube video animates the text as it is read aloud (http://tinyurl.com/p6zhuoa).

Teach a Different Rule of Thumb

As students become better readers, we often teach them independent strategies for identifying when an interesting book is sufficiently easy. We have observed some students counting on their fingers as they read, having been told that a book is appropriate if they find no more than five words on the page that they cannot read. Some call this the *five finger test;* others, the *rule of thumb.*

Apply this test to your own reading. Suppose you pick up a book and find four unknown words by the time you reach the bottom of the first page. You keep reading and find six or seven unknown words by the time you finish the second page; perhaps you find nine or 10 after finishing the third page. You have repeatedly been unable to apply cross-checking strategies, use of context, or decoding strategies. Your comprehension of the text is plummeting because there are so many confusing words and lost information. In the unusual event that you bother to look up the meaning of the words you do not know, your comprehension still deteriorates because you have to hold your partial text understanding in memory for long periods of time while you find the word, read through various definitions, and decide which one fits. You are well under the five errors per page guideline, and yet you are probably feeling frustrated by the difficulty of this book. In all likelihood, you seek an easier book if you have a choice.

Teach your students a different rule of thumb in which they stick up their thumb when they encounter a word they do not know. If they find the need to stick up any other fingers, then teach them that they may want to find an easier book. If they only find one word on the page that they do not know, then they have found a book they can read with greater comprehension and enjoyment.

Reconceptualize "Just Right" Books

Ever since Emmett Betts first conceptualized and quantified independent, instructional, and frustration level reading in his classic, *Foundations of Reading* (1946), schools have sought to match students to texts of appropriate difficulty in order to maximize their learning opportunities. Unfortunately, schools have overextended a reasonable reading instruction goal into independent reading, where it may reduce student choice and motivation. We know a third grader who was reduced to tears by a school librarian who would not let her read *Black Beauty* (Sewell, 1986) because it was a sixth-grade book. We visited a school where students could only read Accelerated Reader books that were within a year of their STAR test score. We regularly see teachers tell their students to pick Goldilocks books, books that are not too easy and not too hard but just right.

The fundamental problem is that all of these systems legislate and restrict students' choices. Reading level should be considered by teachers in planning reading lessons, choosing read-aloud materials, expanding in-class book collections, and encouraging students to explore new authors, topics, and genres. Reading levels should never be used to limit personal reading choices.

Instead of the Goldilocks guideline, we much prefer Richard McKenna's (1972) description of a "just right" book. He wrote that

> any book, however trashy and ephemeral, is good for children if they find pleasure in reading it. Any book that helps children form a habit of reading, that helps to make reading one of their deep and continuing needs, is good for them. (p. 26)

We teach students to try on books by looking at the front and back cover, skimming through the pages, and reading a page or two. We tell them to see if the book seems interesting to them and does not seem too difficult. We never tell them they cannot read it if it is too easy or too difficult. We just tell them that it will probably be more enjoyable if they do not have to struggle to figure out what the words say or mean.

We visited a small library in the Bronx once where there were no children's or adult sections, just a topical arrangement. The librarian organized the books in each section by typical height of the likely readers. That is, older readers were likely to be able to read more complex and lengthier books and be taller than the younger readers, so more difficult books were on the top shelf. Easier books were on the lowest shelf and approximate difficulty found by shelf height in between the bottom and the top. Readers could begin searching by referencing the shelf levels.

This shelving organization provides a metaphor for thinking about reading level as it pertains to reading motivation. We want students to learn to choose books they can and want to read. If we think of level as a single bookshelf, a narrow band around a test score, then we restrict student choices too severely to allow reading interests to be pursued and motivation to grow. If, instead, we think of reading level being the bookshelf containing the maximum level a student can read with understanding, and all the shelves beneath it, then we give students wide latitude in finding materials they may enjoy and read successfully.

> Never use reading levels to limit students' personal reading choices.

Conduct Read-Alouds

Another way to simplify texts is to read them aloud to students, either with a reading partner or a wide variety of technologies, including

- Books on CD, DVD, or even audiotape still found in many schools

- Digital screen readers such as Snap&Read (http://donjohnston.com)

- Video books recorded with tools such as Screencast-o-matic (http://www .screencast-o-matic.com)

- Books recorded and uploaded to the Internet by others (e.g., Daniel Pinkwater's (2010) *I am the Dog* at https://youtube.com/watch?v=vhllQyy7ipY)

- Text-to-speech read-aloud options at free web sites such as Tar Heel Reader (http://tarheelreader.org)

When students listen to texts as a way of temporarily bypassing or supporting developing reading skills, carefully consider the listening comprehension demands of the text relative to students' abilities. Gauge this informally by observing the students as they listen. Do they remain engaged? Do they react as you would expect to text content? Can they discuss the text in some fashion with others? Do they demonstrate an interest in listening to the text again?

The benefits of reading aloud to students from a wide variety of genres and reading material types extend beyond easing beginners into print. Students experience your delight in reading and experience fluent reading vicariously. They become aware of new materials, learn about the world, and acquire new vocabulary. They learn how to think about text, anticipate content or action, relate text to their own experiences, and discuss their understanding and questions.

When reading aloud to conventional readers, it is useful to structure the read-aloud with an Anchor-Listen-Discuss framework parallel to the Anchor-Read-Apply format described in Chapter 7. (Read-aloud interactions to use with emergent readers are found in Chapter 4.) Before reading a text aloud, begin by anchoring students' thinking in something familiar. Give them a purpose to focus their attention to the reading. After reading, discuss their thinking about the text purpose and other thoughts. Here is a short description of a teacher who is introducing his middle grades students to Lane Smith's (2010) *It's a Book* and then reading it aloud to them.

Anchor   The teacher asks the students to talk about characters. He asks them to name the character in the text he read aloud to them yesterday, *Charlie Parker Played Be Bop* (Raschka, 1997). Next, he tells them that he has a new book with two characters—a talking monkey and a talking donkey. He shows them the first 25 seconds of a video book trailer (https://youtube.com/watch?v=x4BK_2VULCU) and asks them to try to figure out what the donkey thinks a book is. When the class finishes discussing this question, the teacher moves to the next step in the lesson, reading aloud the text to the class.

Listen   The teacher reads the book aloud to the class, encouraging them to figure out who the third character is and whether he insults the donkey.

Discuss   After listening to the story, which the class enjoys greatly because of the word play, the class identifies the mouse as the third character and discusses whether the mouse is insulting the donkey. They use a dictionary to look up the word *insulting*.

Depending on your purpose, do not feel compelled to finish reading aloud a text in a single sitting or at all. If a text does not seem to be working for the group, then put it down, talk about it, and decide whether to proceed with the same text or start a new one. If a text is wonderful, then that is even more reason to stop, at least once in a while. One teacher who works in a facility for adjudicated youth makes it a regular practice to read aloud at the end of language arts time and to strategically run out of time before finishing. She often leaves the classroom to a chorus of entreaties, "Come on, Miss A. Don't do us like that. Please, Miss A, what happens next?" Sometimes she will pass out multiple copies of the book for the students to finish reading on their own. Other times she will use the stopping place as the beginning of a conversation the following day. Sometimes she will explain that there is no time to finish the book, but if they would like to "check out" the book from her, then they can finish reading it. She has also been known to begin reading aloud a few minutes early, tell the students they need to wrap up, and then continue reading when they beg her to continue. She is a masterful motivator.

Likewise, do not feel compelled to read from the beginning to the end of a text without stopping. You can pause to help students make connections to other texts they have read, other experiences they have had, or other content they have been learning. The better that students comprehend a text, and the more personal connections they can make, the more likely they are to be engaged in the experience and motivated to read themselves.

> Reading is not an arduous task for most students if we do not make it so.

Strategies to Reduce or Eliminate During Self-Directed Reading

We conclude this section with tips on what not to do when trying to engage students in successful independent reading. Two common strategies are the use of sound and animation and the use of symbolated text. The first should be used sparingly and the second eliminated. Sound effects and computer animation can sometimes attract the attention of students who have yet to learn to engage with text. They draw eyes to the page (screen). Their use should be limited, however, and reduced and eliminated once attention is gained because, ultimately, sound effects and animation do not focus the student's eyes on print.

The use of symbolated text (i.e., text presented with dual lines of matching picture symbols) is another widely used strategy and is based on the belief that symbols are easier to understand than text. For beginners, symbolated text clutters the page and complicates the process of learning to attend to print. For developing readers, research suggests that it does not aid either word identification or reading comprehension (see Erickson, Hanser, Hatch, & Sanders, 2009). Clinical evidence, as well as emerging research with young girls with Rett syndrome (Erickson & Koppenhaver, 2018), suggests that students' attention can be drawn to the page more effectively through print-referencing strategies during reading (i.e., pointing to text while talking about it in various ways). For example, parents or teachers can point and explain briefly, "That's a *T* like your name, Tamika," or "'He ran up and down.' See? Up. And down."

CREATING AN INVITING READING ENVIRONMENT

If you are like most adults, then you like to read in bed, on your couch, next to the fire, in the bathtub, under a shade tree, on a beach blanket, or in other comfortable locations. You may like to sip a cup of hot tea while you read. You might snack on popcorn or cheese crackers. Soft music may be playing in the background. You probably read because you find it enjoyable or informative or just plain relaxing. You may love to hop on the Goodreads web site (http://goodreads.com) and reflect when you finish a good book, message your best friend, or wake your spouse to share your thoughts.

You are a real reader. You do what real readers do. You probably do not love to read while sitting in a molded plastic chair at a hard, wooden desk. You probably do not read only from 9 a.m. to 9:15 a.m. Monday through Friday or consider fluorescent lights your reading light of choice. You probably do not relish being quizzed on your independent reading or seek extrinsic rewards each time you finish a book. If real readers do not seek such reading conditions, then why do we regularly place them in front of students with significant disabilities? Reading is not an arduous task for most students if we do not make it so.

If you want your students to learn to be successful, independent readers, then you can help them identify their own reading preferences and try to make reading in the classroom more like reading in the real world. Many teachers have addressed these goals in creative ways. Here are a few examples:

- *Dip into reading:* A special educator in Florida put a small wading pool in the back of his room filled with pillows. Four students a day are scheduled to dip into reading. Occasionally on Fridays, the class takes the pool outside, fills it with a few inches of water, dips their feet in the water, and reads on beach blankets.

- *Chill out with reading:* A teacher in Virginia worked with her students with significant cognitive disabilities to build an igloo out of gallon milk jugs. Two students at a time get to visit the igloo to chill out with reading each day.

- *"In-tents" reading:* A teacher in Illinois throws blankets over the tables on Fridays, passes out flashlights, and lets her students with significant cognitive disabilities have an "in-tents" reading experience.

- *Sock monkeys:* A special educator in Arizona found her students more willing readers when she let them hold sock monkeys.

- *Build reading into everyday routines:* A teacher of students with multiple disabilities in North Carolina put a music stand in her class bathroom. She placed a two-shelf bookcase outside the bathroom door, with the books on the top shelf facing outward so students could see the covers. When students were waiting to use the bathroom, they could point to a book and a classroom aide would place the book on their lap tray and turn the pages whenever they vocalized. When students were in the bathroom, the book was placed on the music stand and read aloud by the teacher or aide.

Students gradually develop a reading habit of mind when a large and varied reading collection is accompanied by daily time for reading, the possibility of snacks or drinks, comfortable seating, enjoyable experiences, choices, and an occasional surprise. That is, reading ceases to be an assignment or a duty and becomes one more activity of daily life.

> Creating an inviting reading environment helps make reading a routine part of life, not a chore.

GETTING SELF-DIRECTED READING UP AND RUNNING

No matter how large or small your classroom or home library, you will want to get students engaged in self-directed reading from the very beginning. Several strategies and principles have proven helpful for students with significant disabilities engaged in self-directed reading.

Use Time Wisely

Many students who cannot read well, and some who legitimately cannot decide on one book, turn scheduled independent reading time into an extended examination of different books without reading any of them. You can avoid this problem with a little planning. As a regular part of an opening routine—such as hanging up coats, turning in homework, or indicating a preference for hot lunch/cold lunch—ask students to also choose three books for independent reading time. If they finish one text, then they can immediately start another. If they do not like one book, then they can switch to another without restarting the search process.

If students have access difficulties or just prefer digital reading and have Internet access at home, then teachers or families can help set up a favorites page in Tar Heel Reader (http://tinyurl.com/p2zem6b). Then the student can manage digitally and with assistive technologies what others may do by hand.

Some teachers prefer the use of book baskets for students who sit in groups of four to six at a table. Students collect three to five books apiece on Monday morning and place them in the basket. The basket remains in the center of the table, along with other school supplies such as paper, writing tools, and rulers. Students take a book from the basket and read when it is independent reading time or when they finish a task before their peers.

Help Develop Reading Stamina

Many students with significant disabilities do not have a history of successful and enjoyable independent reading experiences on which to draw. They may be unable to read very well, be easily distracted, have few books at home, or have much more experience with worksheets than sustained reading. You cannot expect them to sit quietly and read for 30 minutes when you begin. You must help them build up to the 10–30 minutes you ultimately seek.

One middle school teacher gathered as many interesting and readable materials as he could and told his students that they were going to have 1 minute of silent reading. Then he picked up a kitchen timer, set it for 1 minute, picked up a book, and appeared to read. Actually, he was looking over the top of his book at the students. When they did not start reading, he repeated, "We're going to have 1 minute of silent reading. I'm going to reset the timer." This time most of the students began reading, so he stopped and said directly to one student, "Earl, it's not time to look out the window. It's silent reading time. I'm going to reset the timer." Eventually all of the students had their noses in books or magazines for 1 minute.

The next day, the teacher repeated the directions and reset the timer each time one or more students did not look like they were reading. Over the course of a few weeks, they gradually learned that it was easier to look like they were reading than to have the time extended every time they were not looking at texts. One student asked, "How do you know we're reading?" The teacher replied, "I don't. But I know that if you aren't looking at your books, you can't be reading. So, every time that happens, we will reset the timer."

After 3 weeks, the teacher announced, "It's silent reading time." He increased the time to 2 minutes without telling the students. There were no complaints. The class was reading for 10 minutes a day by December, and the timer hardly had to be reset. The class read silently for 15 minutes daily from February to the end of the school year.

Talk About Reading

Three kinds of discussions are critical during self-directed reading—teacher–student one-to-one conferences, teacher book talks, and student sharing with one another. Procedures for each are described next.

One-to-One Conferences   Each day, teachers confer with one student during a portion of independent reading time, discussing two to three questions from a list such as this:

- What are you reading? How do you like it? Does it feel good when you read it? Is it hard to read? Have you thought about what you want to read next?

- Can you read a part/page you liked out loud to me? Tell me about a part you liked? Tell me something you learned?

- What kinds of texts do you like to read? You may need to provide examples and yes/no response possibilities.

- Who else do you think might like to read this book? Have you recommended this text to anyone else in class?

The answers to questions like these help teachers guide students to more of the materials they like and can read easily and less of what they do not like or cannot read well. Student responses help teachers determine mini-lesson needs, problems they may need to resolve, and conversations to have with peers, librarians, or family members.

Here's what this exchange might look like for a student with complex communication needs using core vocabulary:

Teacher: What are you reading?

Student: *[Eye-points to book on lap tray.]*

Teacher: Do you like it?

Student: *[Eye-pointing to communication board.]* LIKE.

Teacher: I'm going to turn through the pages. Stop me when you see a part you liked. *[Teacher turns each page and looks at the student for a response.]*

Student:	*[Eye-pointing.]* STOP.
Teacher:	Tell me about this.
Student:	*[Eye-pointing.]* HE GO.
Teacher:	He is going. That pigeon is driving the bus. He's going to school. Do you want to tell me more?
Student:	*[Eye-pointing.]* FINISHED.
Teacher:	Okay. Who would like to read this book?
Student:	*[Eye-points toward classmate.]* SHE.
Teacher:	Do you mean Tanisha?
Student:	*[Smiles.]*
Teacher:	Tanisha, come here. Jake wants to tell you something.
Student:	*[Eye-pointing.]* YOU LIKE THIS.
Tanisha:	Thanks, Jake. Can I take it to read tomorrow? I want to finish reading *Whose Toes Are Those?* and *Rain Feet* today.
Student:	*[Eye-pointing.]* I WANT.
Tanisha:	You want my books when I'm done?
Student:	*[Smiles.]*
Tanisha:	I'll trade you tomorrow morning.
Student:	*[Smiles.]*
Teacher:	I guess I don't need to ask what you're going to read next. All right, keep reading.

Some teachers have turned this conferencing about reading interests into a much more tightly structured assessment by conducting running records, counting oral reading errors, checking the text reading level against the student's reading assessments, and conducting progress monitoring. Other teachers feel the need to assess independent reading in other ways, requiring response journals, book reports, book projects, and other products after students finish a text. All of those practices, well intentioned and occasionally useful, are more appropriately employed at other times in the day. Yet, if conducted during independent reading time, then each tells students that reading achievement or documented proof of reading are your primary concerns, and you really do not care about the students' interests.

Other teachers find student conferencing exhausting. If you teach a typical self-contained class, then you probably have 10 or fewer students. If you conference with one of them a day, then you will meet with all of them every 2 weeks. If you teach in a class of 20 or more students, then you may want to increase your student conferences to two a day. More than that and you will find independent reading time much more difficult to monitor and lose out on important informal observation and interaction opportunities.

Teacher Book Talks   A teacher book talk, or "book blessing" (Marinak, Gambrell, & Mazzoni, 2012, pp. 3–4), is a second type of talk that supports independent reading.

Gather half a dozen texts of various types (e.g., narrative and information books, joke books, magazines, newspapers), lengths, and difficulty appropriate to the range in your class. We often limit it to three texts with beginning or emergent readers with significant disabilities. Hold up the first book and begin. Here is an example geared toward generating students' interest in books about snakes.

Do you like to learn about snakes? I found three great snake books. The first one is called Snakes Slither and Hiss. *Did you know that there is a snake that can fly? Look, it shows it right here on page 26. If you want to learn about pit vipers, cobras, and sea snakes, then you have got to read this book!*

The second book is called Slinky, Scaly Snakes. *Did you know that snakes can shed their skin? It says, right here on p. 8: "Snakes grow quickly, but their skin doesn't stretch. When a snake's skin gets too tight, the snake has to shed it. This is called molting. The snake rubs its head on something rough like a log. After a few minutes the skin begins to peel." Look at this picture. You can see the snake's skin peeling away from its head. This is a great book to learn all about what snakes eat and do during the day and even how they smell with their tongues!*

This third book is called Reptiles. *Snakes are a kind of reptile. This book is a little harder to read than the other two, but look at all these great photographs of snakes, lizards, and crocodiles! You could read this with your sixth-grade book buddy or in our digital read-aloud collection. There's information about what reptiles eat and how they kill their prey. There are even dragons in this book!*

I've bookmarked all of these books on our Pinterest e-books site. Just click on the book cover and it will take you to the book you want.

Book blessings work well as a periodic mini-lesson or as a short activity before or after teacher read-alouds. Be sure to make the books available to students after the book talk. You may need a sign-up sheet for popular materials.

Student Sharing   Student sharing is the final kind of talk that is integral to supporting independent reading habits and building your classroom reading community. Immediately following independent reading time, take 5 minutes and have students share their answers to questions such as the following with one another, in pairs, threesomes, foursomes, or as a whole class:

- What did you read today? What did you (not) like about it?

- Do you think anyone else in your group might like to read this text? Tell them why.

- What are you taking home to read tonight? Why?

- How did you find this book? Where was it? Did anyone recommend it to you? Share your thoughts with the person who recommended it.

Provide Mini-Lesson Instruction

You will need to teach your students a variety of important strategies to increase their interest and ability to participate in independent reading. The key here is to remember these are mini-lessons. Have one important conversation or teach one important strategy per day. You will have had the opportunity to teach 180 important understandings and skills by the end of the school year. These mini-lessons generally can be divided into four categories:

1. Procedural mini-lessons that help students learn how the classroom and school library work

2. Searching mini-lessons that help students learn how to find materials they can, and want, to read

3. Reading mini-lessons that help students learn how to read successfully on their own

4. Sharing mini-lessons that help students learn how talk about books with others and be a good audience when someone is sharing a book with them.

Table 8.3 lists just a few examples of each.

Facilitate Self-Directed Reading for Older Students

At present, most students with significant disabilities read at emergent or beginning levels well into high school and beyond (Erickson & Geist, 2016; Towles-Reeves et al., 2009, 2012). Middle school and high school classrooms, however, may not provide the kinds of materials or experiences suggested in this chapter (Ruppar, 2015). They are no less necessary, and, in fact, may be more so. Beyond the strategies and structures suggested so far are a few additional ideas particularly appropriate for older students.

An English teacher in Minnesota who teaches in an inclusive high school integrates self-directed reading with her curriculum and instructional goals. Students in her class are free to choose whatever they want to read as long as it fits the designated genre. One student was obsessed with all things military. During the informational text unit, he chose *B is for Battle Cry* (Bauer, 2009); during the poetry unit, he read *Inside Out and Back Again* (Lai, 2013); during the novels unit, he read *Christmas in the Trenches* (McCutcheon, 2006), and so forth. Although written well below

Table 8.3.   Four categories of mini-lessons and sample lesson topics

Mini-lesson type	Sample topics
Procedural	Getting three texts to read first thing each morning.
	Being a good listener when classmates are sharing.
	Reading quietly with a partner.
Text search	Where your favorites are located.
	How to sample a page or two to see if you might like a book.
	How to make recommendations to classmates.
Reading	Monitoring comprehension (Does this make sense?).
	Making predictions while reading.
	Figuring out words you do not know.
Sharing	How to give a reason you (do not) like a book.
	How to ask classmates questions about books they (do not) like.
	How to take turns in sharing.

ninth-grade level, all of these texts fit the genre requirement and were understandable to the student.

A middle school we know decided to attack schoolwide student reading difficulties by integrating more self-selected reading in each class. One science teacher did so by allocating 10 minutes at the beginning of his Monday, Wednesday, and Friday classes for self-selected reading and discussion related to the instructional content. He used a small grant to acquire a few sets of the *Time for Kids* Nonfiction Readers and National Geographic Kids Readers and some tablets that enabled students to access web sites such as Newsela (https://newsela.com), Time for Kids (https://timeforkids.com), National Geographic for Kids (https://kids.nationalgeographic.com), and NASA Space Place (https://spaceplace.nasa.gov). He created collections of science books in Tar Heel Reader (https://tarheelreader.org/2013/02/06/help-favorites-and-collections) for his students with the most significant reading challenges. He found the 10 minutes so successful in increasing student interest in the instructional units, building their background knowledge, and increasing their out-of-school reading, that he changed it to 5 days a week after the Christmas break.

Book club groups are gaining popularity. They offer a welcome relief to the prevalent teacher-assigned reading and follow-up testing. They make excellent in-school or after-school classes or clubs (http://tinyurl.com/y7myb25j). Choral reading, open discussions focused on personal connections, and student choice over reading selections can increase student success in the experience and motivate further reading. Next Chapter Book Club (https://nextchapterbookclub.org) offers information and a structure for getting started in communities, all of which are even easier in school settings.

Tablets and e-readers are one final set of tools particularly useful for older readers who read significantly below grade level. Such technologies allow students the freedom to read what they wish without peers knowing what they are reading or that it is below grade level. Students tend to select what they can read rather than making sure their choices look like the chapter books and novels many of their classmates may be reading.

A FINAL NOTE: REPLACE REWARDS WITH CELEBRATIONS

Eliminating rewards programs in your classroom is our final suggestion for increasing your students' interest in reading. Reading rewards are a bad solution to a problem created by restrictive and artificial independent reading programs. Because students will not read for 30 minutes, we introduce a reward for doing so. Because students will not read during silent reading time, we introduce a reward if they do. Because students will not read the genre we demand, or the level we restrict them to, or the number of books we require? Reward, reward, reward.

Extrinsic rewards introduce difficulties. Students who read for points or prizes or to please teachers and parents are often less likely to read when there are no points and fewer restrictions in activity choices. Students who read anything because we coerce it instead of finding ways to encourage it are unlikely to read when the reward is removed. Most damaging, extrinsic rewards have been shown to negatively affect reading achievement over time (Becker et al., 2010).

Replace your reward systems with the activities and suggestions in this chapter. Grow your in-class library, read aloud to your students from a wide variety of texts, start small and gradually increase silent reading time, and listen carefully to your students during conferences and peer sharing. Introduce celebrations that neither reward champion readers nor exclude developing readers. If you can round up sufficient free books, service club donations, or mini-grant funds, then give all of the students a book of their own at these celebrations. There is a power in ownership not granted by borrowing or renting. Do the same each month with poetry, history, science, digital books, wordless picture books, newspapers, and anything else that you and your students are reading, have read, or should be aware of as a reading possibility.

> Relying on rewards to motivate reading makes students unlikely to read without those rewards. Instead of using rewards, encourage and celebrate reading.

As you teach your students how to read throughout the rest of your instructional program, always remember how important it is to also teach them why.

RECOMMENDED READINGS

The following readings will deepen readers' understanding of how to support students' fluency and motivation during self-directed reading.

Gambrell, L. B. (2011). Seven rules of engagement: What's most important to know about motivation. *Reading Teacher, 65,* 172–178. doi:10.1002/TRTR.01024

Miller, D., & Moss, B. (2013). *No more independent reading without support.* Portsmouth, NH: Heinemann.

Trelease, J. (2013). *The read-aloud handbook* (7th ed.). New York, NY: Penguin Books.

CHAPTER 9

Writing

Writing is "a process of constructing texts in traditional orthography, either print or Braille, that communicate experiences, thoughts, feelings, and understandings for diverse audiences and purposes" (Koppenhaver & Erickson, 2013, p. 1). This description represents a significant shift away from many prevalent writing instructional practices for students with significant disabilities. Over the years, we have observed classrooms where these students spend substantial amounts of time tracing or copying letters and words, choosing words or pictures to complete fill-in-the-blank sentences, reordering letters to spell words or words to make sentences, composing texts by selecting and arranging choices from word banks or picture symbol arrays, and memorizing lists of words for spelling tests. None of these practices teaches typically developing students or students with disabilities how to use traditional orthography to communicate their own thoughts independently to different audiences for a variety of purposes.

Instead of this traditional view of writing readiness, we believe that pencil, paper, time, and, sometimes, encouragement are the prerequisites for communicative writing. *Pencils* mean whatever writing tool and process a student employs to form or select letters in order to attempt to spell words. *Paper* refers to whatever medium the writing is composed in or on (e.g., white boards, word processing programs, apps). In Chapter 5, we addressed efficient and productive alternatives to get students with significant disabilities started writing. The assumptions underlying the ideas in this chapter are that you have found workable pencils and paper for your students, are providing them full access to the alphabet, and are able to answer "yes" to the four questions about whether conventional literacy instruction is appropriate to your students' current skills and understandings (see Chapter 1). If not, then continue to engage them in emergent literacy activities as described in Chapters 4 and 5 before you try the ideas to follow.

RESEARCH BRIEF: WHY AND HOW WE TEACH WRITING

Providing daily time for student writing, teaching strategies and processes for a variety of writing purposes, teaching writing skills that contribute to fluency, and creating a community of writers in the classroom are the most effective ways to foster growth in beginning writing (Graham, Kiuhara, McKeown, & Harris, 2012). Graham and colleagues also concluded that technology benefits writing outcomes and should be integrated into all aspects of instruction.

The evidence base involving a wide variety of students with significant disabilities draws similar conclusions. A review of studies of students with ASD determined that strategy instruction, modeling of processes and procedures for students, and the use of computers improved writing outcomes (Pennington & Delano, 2012).

The 15 studies reviewed included 29 instances of the use of mainstream instructional practices. A review of writing in individuals who use AAC found few instructional studies but did suggest that e-mail interactions motivated writing and provided a balanced opportunity for learning to communicate; modeling and direct instruction in letter sounds improved written communication; and word prediction software (see Chapter 11) increased spelling accuracy and more interpretable approximations (Koppenhaver & Williams, 2010).

Other reviews explored writing interventions for students with intellectual disabilities and students with significant disabilities. Joseph and Konrad (2009) concluded that students with intellectual disabilities improved in writing quantity and quality in response to writing instruction, and strategy instruction, in particular, was effective. Koppenhaver, Hendrix, and Williams (2007) noted that writing growth in students with severe and multiple disabilities was slow and uneven, composition rates were extremely slow, and best practices identified in teaching other populations had been experienced by literate adults with significant disabilities.

A growing number of studies suggest that an instructional strategy that works in mainstream classrooms is worth exploring in teaching students with significant disabilities. Successful outcomes have been obtained by employing models of writing processes and procedures, text structure instruction (e.g., persuasive writing), peer collaboration, print-rich environments, wide and purposeful writing, comprehensive instruction, instruction in planning and reviewing, and other best practices identified in mainstream classrooms (Blischak, 1995; Erickson et al., 1997; Hedrick, Katims, & Carr, 1999; Rousseau, Krantz, Poulson, Kitson, & McClannahan, 1994; Tefft Cousin et al., 1993; Williams, Koppenhaver, & Wollak, 2007). Many of these practices are described in this chapter.

Two studies provide classroom implementation models for practitioners. Bedrosian, Lasker, Speidel, and Politsch (2003) described a problem-solving model. Drawing on writing research in speech and language, peer interactions in AAC, and evidence-based practice guidelines, they created a beginning writing program for a student with complex communication needs and ASD. They provided explicit instruction in story grammar, planning, and peer and teacher modeling. They demonstrated how to document student growth in planning and translation, overall writing quality, and affective response to instruction.

Wollak and Koppenhaver (2011) described a different method of problem solving using existing models of writing (Flower & Hayes, 1981; van Kraayenoord, Moni, Jobling, Koppenhaver, & Elkins, 2004) to guide technology-supported writing instruction for young teenagers with a variety of disabilities. The authors noted that students who require assistive writing technologies must direct conscious attention to the tools they use, unlike typically developing peers. As a result, parents and educators must be more aware of the challenges that production (i.e., the tools of writing) may introduce into the writing process. For example, students who use scanning to gain access to their keyboard must hold their intended message in mind while also remembering to activate the scanning and time their selections to get the correct rows, blocks, or keys, not to mention the additional load of correcting mis-hits. In addition, Wollak and Koppenhaver addressed motivation and social context in their approach. They recognized that technology, student interactions with peers and teachers, and writing audiences influence student engagement in writing. Their multicomponent model guided selection, design, and delivery of writing instruction and assistive technologies.

GETTING OFF TO A GOOD START: ENCOURAGING BEGINNERS

The foundation of writing instruction is writing experience. Your students require time each day for putting their thoughts to paper using the alphabet, and they need you and other readers to understand that these first drafts require only sincere interest and feedback about the content. The instructional goal is to reduce, and ultimately eliminate, fears that you are going to find fault with their thinking and writing. You want all your students to write increasingly more words and do so more easily and fluently. Once they are translating their thoughts, feelings, experiences, and understandings into words, then you can teach them how to do so with increasing clarity. When we assist students too early with spelling guidance, editing checklists, sentence structure, and other aspects of form and convention, we make it too difficult for them to focus on communicating their thoughts.

> Work toward eliminating students' fears that you will find fault with their writing.

Try This Writing Experiment

Many years ago, Jim Cunningham, now Professor Emeritus of Literacy Studies at the University of North Carolina at Chapel Hill, introduced us to the following activity, which he described as handcuff writing. The experiment consists of writing under two conditions. Do not move on until you complete the first writing task (see Figure 9.1). You will need a timer with an audible signal of some kind so that you can write freely without the interruption of clock watching.

Writing task 1: Think of an activity you enjoy such as swimming, reading, camping, or visiting with friends. When you have an activity in mind, set the timer for 3 minutes and begin writing about the activity. Just describe the activity or how you feel about it. Write for the entire 3 minutes until the timer sounds. Now, take a short break, then read and complete the second writing activity.

Figure 9.1.   Writing experiment: Task 1.

Writing task 2: You are to continue the text you began during the first exercise. Now you must follow the five rules below. Once you have finished reading the rules, set your timer again and write for 3 more minutes while attempting to follow the five rules. You may keep the rules in front of you for reference. (Hint: Read each rule from right to left.)

> #deSu eB tSum eciOv evissaP •
> #elpiRt rO elgnIs reveN ,seviTagen elBuod Esu Ot rebmemeR •
> nA dNa ,% A hTiw noitseUq A ,# A hTiw tnemetaTs A dNe syawlA •
> #@ nA hTiw noitamalcXe
> ,Drow tsRif eHt fO retTel tsrIf ,.e.I) sElur noitazilatiPaC rebmemEr esaelP •
> drOw A fI .Drow drIht eHt fO Rettel Driht ,Drow dnoCes eHt fO Rettel dNoces
> ehT tRatser ,rEttel etairpoRppa Eht ezilatipAc oT sretTel tneiciffusNi saH
> #droW That hTiw ssecoRp
> #tfEl oT thGir moRf etirW •
> A sA meHt esU Nac uOy oS ,seLur eHt nI dewollOf erA seLur eHt fO lLa :etoN
> #gnltirw Ruoy Rof ledOm

Figure 9.2.   Writing experiment: Task 2.

After you finish the second writing task (see Figure 9.2), count the number of words in each of your two writing samples. Compare the totals. Ask yourself which form of writing was easier. Which made it easier to translate the ideas in your head into words on the page? Nearly everyone who completes this exercise composes more words in the free-writing condition (i.e., writing without worrying about grammar, spelling, punctuation, or formatting rules). Following just five simple rules challenges you in ways that your students are challenged every time they are told to follow an editing checklist while drafting or are interrupted while writing by teachers pointing out missing punctuation, misspelled words, the need for the student's name at the top of the paper, and so forth. Each of these suggestions makes it more difficult for students to focus on what they want to communicate in print. Spelling, grammar, and formatting issues are best addressed in instructional mini-lessons or later drafts in direct instruction after students have transferred thoughts and experiences from their heads to their papers. See the "Value and Encourage: Responding to Writing" section for more about responding effectively to student writing.

Support Topic Choice

When given time to write and no guidance, developing writers often tell you by words or inaction, "I can't think of anything to write about," and you scramble to suggest possibilities. To avoid this problem, many teachers assign writing topics to students and, with the advent of the Internet, do so with incredible ease. Time saving? You bet. Helpful for developing writers? Not much. Prompt-dependent writers do not gain independence or learn important components of the writing process such as generating and organizing their own topics for audiences they choose. Six strategies that are more productive are described next—using photo collections and categories, having students draw before writing, using "Gimme 5" to generate topic lists, "can't-stop-writing" time, class experience lists, and regular daily writing.

> Assigning topics may save time but does not help developing writers become more independent and learn to fully engage in the writing process.

Photo Collections and Categories   Give students inexpensive digital cameras and take a photo expedition around the school. Ask students to take pictures of what interests them, not what you think they should like. For example, you would expect that students would take pictures of animals at the zoo, but Maggie took pictures of boys. Eli, a student with ASD, took dozens of pictures of feet in all sorts of places. When you return to the classroom, transfer the pictures, whether expected or unexpected, to computers or iPads or print them to save in student writing folders.

Many inexpensive and sturdy cameras are available for less than $30 online or at discount stores for students who are physically able to use them. If students have significant physical impairments, then numerous switch-adapted cameras are available from R. J. Cooper (http://tinyurl.com/lhpmbk2), Adaptive Tech Solutions (http://tinyurl.com/lap3ddy), ORCCA Technologies (http://tinyurl.com/mzuecbb), Apple (an iPad with switch control; https://support.apple.com/en-us/HT201370), and others. Many families have smart phones or iPads in protective cases and will allow their children to take pictures over the weekend for school use if requested.

Another easy option is to use public domain photo collections such as Flickr (https://flickr.com/creativecommons) and others (http://tinyurl.com/otlsa6x). These sites provide access to high-quality photos and describe the conditions for free use.

Drawing   Students often draw pictures to accompany their writing, especially if that writing is to be published in some form. If you direct students to draw before writing, then you provide them with an opportunity not only to generate their own topics but also to organize their thinking about the topic (Sidelnick & Svoboda, 2000). Artistic quality is not an issue; rather, the purpose is to provide time for thinking while drawing. You can enhance this planning process by engaging students in conversation about their drawing before they begin writing, as in exchanges like this one:

Teacher: Tell me about your drawing.

Student: Big snake.

Teacher: Tell me more.

Student: Teeth.

Teacher: What else?

Student: Scare Mom.

Teacher: I can't wait to read about that when you're finished. Start writing!

Gimme 5   Ask students to list their thoughts in response to such topics as "5 Things That Make Me Happy," "5 Places I'd Like to Visit," "5 Things I'd Like to Do This Weekend," "5 Things I Don't Like About School," and so forth. Next, ask them to share their list with a partner or small group of classmates. This sharing process helps budding writers become more aware of audience and shared interests, and the lists often expand during sharing. If students do not have the writing skills to create their own lists, then dictation is a reasonable alternative. This activity makes a great writing mini-lesson early in the school year. It gets student writing off to a personal start, and it is a helpful get-acquainted strategy as students share their ideas. Save the lists in writing folders, and, if students struggle to find a writing topic, then direct them to revisit their lists.

Can't-Stop-Writing   Have students write for a short period of time, 2–3 minutes. Direct them to write repeatedly, whenever they have no ideas, "I can't think of anything to write," until they think of something. One middle school student with significant learning and behavior disabilities wrote:

you suck I hate school I hate school I hate school I hate school and the teachers I hate school and the teachers I hate school and the teachers

When he shared the text aloud, the teacher said it sounded like he did not like school much and he might want to elaborate his ideas during writing time. Then she asked everyone to put their can't-stop-writing texts in their writing folders. She repeated the exercise periodically through the year. On the last day of school, he wrote:

Oneday I am going to come the school when we start again. I am going to say bad words at all the teacher in the school. Because they make me made. Giving me all this work and the detention. Just wait too with start school again. I am going to surprise you with the bad words Iam going to say. I am going to say all kind of language that you problem have not heard before. it is going to be ___ ___ ___ ___ ___ you mother ___ ___ . It is going to be more than 7 words I am going to say. Do belivie what I wrote up there, you know Iam not going to say that.

Such writing is uncommon in most students, but we have encountered it more than a few times in students with behavior disorders or ASD. In the former case, it is usually intended to test teachers. In the latter, it often demonstrates a lack of awareness of social appropriateness and audience. By engaging in regular can't-stop-writing exercises, not overreacting to student attempts to escape writing activities and the classroom, having students share their writing, and modeling and teaching the writing process, you can help students share ideas they care about with increasing clarity and, in some cases, humor and voice.

Class Experience Lists   At the end of the day, help students reflect on what they have been seeing or doing. Keep a list of these experiences on chart paper in the classroom. Ask open-ended questions such as, "Anybody want to share anything today?" or "What's one thing we did today that you enjoyed?" Then ask students if they want to add the topic to the chart. When it is time for writing, read aloud several items on the list to remind students of possible topics of interest. Over time, students will reference these lists with increasing independence.

Just Do It   Nike's advertising slogan, "Just Do It," was a massively successful sales tool. Your students also need to "just do it"—do what real writers do and write daily. Students respond increasingly well when writing becomes a habit and not a surprise or occasional interruption. Help students find their own topics and they will have more to say, become more willing to write, and increasingly write more independently.

Use Models and Writing Demonstrations

Some students cannot or will not write, or write very little, despite our use of strategies such as those previously described. The following three strategies provide even more support through interaction and by demonstrating writing practices: "now you see it, now you don't," "tell me more" with dialogic writing, and the use of mentor texts to teach structure.

Now You See It, Now You Don't   Jayden was a student with multiple disabilities in an inclusive third-grade classroom. Every day he shared a prerecorded message about what he had done at home or something he was eagerly anticipating, but he did so with a single keystroke. When it was time for daily journaling, Jayden would touch the key and his message would be turned into his writing for the day. Even though his communication device provided access to letters, words, and phrases, he seldom added anything to the prestored message.

Jayden's one-to-one aide understood that this process was not helping Jayden learn to write more independently and effectively and came up with a strategy. One day, when Jayden chose the message from home, she read it aloud with him, "My dad is coming to eat lunch with me at school today. I'm looking forward to seeing him. He's a teacher, so he doesn't usually eat lunch with me." Then she said, "Oh, that sounds like fun. I'm going to write about someone I know at school."

Sitting beside him, she wrote letter by letter and read aloud each word as she spelled it, "Cathy is at Moore Street School today. She takes our lunch money." She then pointed to each word as she read it aloud a second time and said, "That's what I wrote. I can't wait to see what you write." She then removed his message and put her text away. Jayden wrote, using a combination of letter-by-letter spelling and whole-word selection, "Dad and Mom eat lunch with Jayden. Dad teaches PE." By treating Jayden's whole message selection as a topic and modeling the thinking and composition process in a short, related text, the paraprofessional was able get him started writing generatively during the daily journaling period.

Tell Me More With Dialogic Writing Another approach is to engage students in dialogic writing with an adult. Robbie was a 10-year-old boy with cerebral palsy and complex communication needs who typed with his left forefinger. He rarely wrote when encouraged to do so. His teacher knew that he watched a popular television program, so one day she printed a picture from the show and taped it above the computer monitor. Robbie smiled.

"Do you like this?" she asked. Robbie nodded, and she typed, "Robbie likes Ninja Turtles." Robbie could not read the text, but he knew how to get the computer to read it aloud and bounced in his chair as he listened.

"What do you like about them?" his teacher asked. He punched the air. "They fight? You like that they fight?" Robbie smiled and nodded. "Write that," she said, pointing at the keyboard.

He typed, "Fit." When the computer read it aloud, he cocked his head, looked at the word, and added an –*e*: "Fite."

The teacher added, "Ninja Turtles are green." After listening, Robbie, now very excited, typed without further prompting, "Turtles TV. On. Wach [watch]."

For several weeks, the teacher engaged Robbie with pictures of his interests, conversation about them, and encouragement for him to add to his text whatever he communicated. Over time, Robbie learned to select his own picture and write independently about it.

Mentor Texts to Teach Text Structure Teachers share mentor texts with students to provide a model of how to communicate their own ideas in increasingly more structured ways. Tacy was an 8-year-old with Down syndrome whose third-grade teacher welcomed her into an inclusive classroom but was unsure how to get Tacy to write more elaborated texts until she found a copy of *Wishes, Lies, and Dreams* (Koch, 1970) filled with short mentor poems for children. The following day, she introduced her class to a basic, nonrhyming poetry structure using colors and the students' five senses. She began the lesson by asking the students to name their five senses. She wrote these on the white board. Then she told the students that her favorite color was black. She wrote that on the board and then listed one example for each sense: "my father's hair" for *see*, "burnt toast" for *smell*, and so forth. She asked the students to take a piece of paper, write their favorite color at the top of the page, list their five senses, and then list and describe as many things as they could think of linking each of their five senses to that color.

As the students began brainstorming, the teacher took out a bag of yellow objects, Tacy's favorite color. She and Tacy explored and discussed each object—a pack of gum, a dish scraper, a jar of mustard, and other items. When the noise level in the room indicated that the class was done brainstorming, she directed the students to share their lists with one another, and she continued to explore and discuss *yellow* with Tacy.

Next, the teacher introduced Tacy and the students to the five-line color sense poem structure: [color] tastes like, smells like, feels like, sounds like, looks like. She explained that they could order these stems as they wished but should be sure to use specific descriptions such as, "Black looks like my father's tightly curled locks." She helped Tacy with structure as she wrote:

Yellow tastes like set apples [sweet].

Yellow sels like gam [smells like gum].

Yellow fels like prakle skrapr [feels like prickly scraper].

Yellow sunds like jekle kande [sounds like jiggly candy].

Yellow likes like spisse mustard [spicy].

Many other such structures have proven their value in supporting students as they compose meaningful and motivating texts. Madelyn was a 16-year-old with Down syndrome who read like a beginner and wrote little until her teacher shared riddles with her. Madelyn proceeded to write riddle after riddle about a favorite camp experience, including this one:

I have Smorea (S'mores)

I smell fire

I have llsherys (Hershey's)

Where am I?

campfire

Knock knock jokes, two lies and a truth, short and informational texts, picture books, and other basic texts provide useful models for students learning how to organize their thoughts on paper.

Value and Encourage: Responding to Writing

Guiding error correction is not the best approach for beginning writers, no matter how numerous the errors. You can have a more powerful and positive impact on your students' thinking and writing by responding in meaningful ways to the writing content. This can be particularly challenging with the nonconventional texts of beginning writers with significant disabilities. For example, after writing this text, the student author was unable to read it aloud:

Elvis so hod dog

Srr oy vjtde

Look it big part

I found st

The teacher knew, however, that the last sentence read, "I found the star," because it was a favorite activity of the student. The teacher told the student she was glad the student had found the star and that she should write more about it because it was such a special event.

Teachers have two goals in responding to first drafts. First, make sure students know that you value their writing. Encourage students who speak and those who use talking word processors to read aloud what they have written, responding positively to a specific aspect of the writing such as topic choice or an interesting element. Second, encourage students to add to their text, no matter how much or how little they write. If students write two letters, two words, or two pages, then value their writing and encourage them to tell you more. Table 9.1 shows samples of some helpful responses intended to demonstrate sincere interest or encourage further writing in first drafts and some less helpful examples.

Create Accepting and Responsive Writing Environments

You and your teaching assistants understand the importance of freeing students from fear of error, and you have many ways of responding to the content of students' writing with encouragement. Expect to have to educate other listeners and readers, such as classmates, family members, and classroom visitors.

Guide Responses From Classmates   We teach students three simple statements for responding to one another's working drafts (i.e., every draft prior to publication):

The best thing about your writing is ____.

One question I have is ____.

One way you can make this even better is ____.

Here is what that process looked like in a group of adolescents with significant disabilities using core vocabulary and gestures:

> Andre used the text-to-speech option on the computer to read his draft aloud: "I fel on mi hed." Each of his classmates had an index card near them with the response stems. When they pointed to the stem, the teacher would read it aloud to remind them what they were doing.

> Zander: *[Points to response stem on index card]* The best thing about your writing is ... *[points to core vocabulary]* not good.

> Alice: *[Points to response stem]* The best thing about your writing is ... *[points to vocabulary]* like.

Table 9.1.   Helpful and unhelpful responses to student drafts

Helpful responses	Unhelpful responses
"Read your text aloud to me, please."	"Good writing."
"I like that you wrote about . . ."	"Good job."
"That's really interesting. What else could you add about (the topic)?"	"You wrote a lot (of words)."
"Go read this to (classmate). He (or she) likes (topic), too."	"That's not how you spell ____. Let me show you how."
"Tell us more about (the topic)."	"Proofread your draft now and clean up the mistakes."
"You should consider working on this for our class wiki."	"You need to write more than that."

Teacher: So one of you thinks it's not good that Andre fell down and one of you likes his story so far?

Students: *[Nod and smile]*.

Teacher: Okay. Questions?

Zander: *[Points to response stem]* One question I have is . . . *[points to vocabulary]* who help?

Alice: *[Points to response stem]* One question I have is . . . *[points to vocabulary]* why?

Teacher: Those are good questions. You want to know whether someone helped him and why he fell down?

Students: *[Nod, smile, and vocalize]*.

Teacher: Okay, let's help Andre with some suggestions.

Zander: *[Points to response stem]* One way you can make this even better is . . . *[points to vocabulary]* more.

Alice: *[Points to response stem]* One way you can make this even better is . . . *[points to vocabulary]* yes *[nodding her head]*.

Teacher: So, Andre, Zander wants you to write more about what happened. And, Alice, I think you agree with Zander? You want to hear more, too?

Alice: *[Vocalizes excitedly]*.

The teacher then summarized the conversation for the group and handed Andre the notes for his revision. Over time, students will take over more of the process as they are able.

Guide Responses From Families and Visitors   Most of us can remember one or more teachers who soaked our papers in a sea of red ink and made us feel bad about our writing (in)abilities. You now understand firsthand the risk of such practices in handcuffing future writing engagement and effort. It is important to orient families and other classroom visitors to the ways you would like them to respond when they listen to a student read aloud or when they read a student's writing. Explain that you, and they, must have a tolerance for error so that all of us can see what students need to learn. If we do not correct student errors, then we keep students engaged as writers, and we know what to focus on in our instruction. Make sure visitors say something positive and encourage further writing (e.g., "I like cats, too." "Can't wait to see what you write about next." "That sounds like fun"). Ask classroom visitors to avoid going overboard in their comments (e.g., responding to "go str" with "Oh my, you want to go to your store! That's amazing! What a fantastic story! You are the greatest writer ever!"). Specific comments about, and interest in, the existing text are sufficient (e.g., "I like to go the store, too. Write some more about going to the store").

HELPING STUDENTS TRANSITION TO GENERATIVE WRITING

A common problem in programs serving students with significant disabilities is that some students will only copy words they find in the environment when they are given the opportunity and encouragement to write. Some do so to reduce anxiety.

Others have spent so much time on copying tasks that they do not understand the generative nature of writing. Strategies teachers have used to transition such students from copying to composing meaning include modeling and demonstrations, having students work in print-poor environments, and providing written dialogue and cloze statements for students to complete.

Modeling and Demonstrations   The "now you see it, now you don't" strategy that helped Jayden begin writing also works well for some students who think writing is a copying task. Teachers or parents think aloud while writing a brief text, read it aloud, remove it from view, and then say, "I can't wait to see what you write," and wait expectantly. This process helps some students begin to understand that writing involves thinking and communicating.

Purposefully Print-Poor Environments   Although we prefer the learning opportunities print-rich environments provide, sometimes we must remove print from the writing area when students confuse copying with generative writing. Some students begin to generate their own ideas with teacher modeling and encouragement and no opportunity to copy. For example, Nicholas was a 9-year-old boy with ASD and significant intellectual disabilities. His teachers regularly presented him with worksheets to help him learn to identify environmental print such as *women, men, stop,* and *exit.* Nicholas would identify the sign and copy the word on his worksheet. One day his language arts teacher created a worksheet exactly like the environmental print sheets he was familiar with, but inserted color photographs with no print. With a familiar activity but no opportunity to copy, Nicholas wrote *ball* while looking at a photograph of a football game and *book* and *rocks* in response to a father reading to a young child in a hammock.

Written Dialogue and Cloze Statements   Cloze structures can be used to cue some students to add their own ideas to text. Alan was a 10-year-old boy with Williams syndrome whose writing usually consisted of copied text with his name and a list of favorite television characters. One day, his mother wrote, "My name is Denise." Alan copied verbatim, and Denise wrote, "My name is ____." She pointed and explained, "My name is Denise. Your name isn't Denise. Write your name." Alan wrote his name in the blank. Next she wrote, "I like TV," which Alan copied. Then, "I like to watch ____." Alan immediately wrote in the blank "Ben 10." "I like Godzilla," she wrote next, and Alan copied the words verbatim. She wrote, "Godzilla is ____." Alan added, "ugly." Within a few weeks, Alan began to write short generative texts about his interests.

Students tend to copy less as they gain a clearer understanding of what writing is and how it is used to communicate their thoughts, participate daily in composing activities, and engage in the kinds of experiences previously described. Reading and listening to a wide variety of texts, learning to spell new words based on the sounds they hear, and the other instructional activities described in in this book contribute to increased abilities to compose personal ideas. Like Rome, copying was not built in a day, and it takes time to unlearn.

Teach Composition Skills Meaningfully

We visited a kindergarten class years ago to observe a student teacher. When we arrived, students were busily writing in journals. We looked over their shoulders and realized they were actually engaged in a handwriting exercise, repeatedly copying a capital letter *R*. When we asked why, one little boy explained that it was "R day." The journal writing did not involve meaningful composition.

Handwriting can contribute to composition if skills are contextualized (Graham, 2009–2010). The class could have been learning the letter *R* as they wrote to Ruby or Rob. They could have been writing about dinosaurs that RRRRoar or truck engines that RRRRRRRumble or dozens of other objects and actions that kindergarteners understand. Instead, writing was reduced to a physical act lacking cognitive, linguistic, or social purpose and context.

Teachers of students who have significant disabilities have found that important skills such as handwriting, keyboarding, using grammar, or planning are best taught in mini-lessons lasting 5–10 minutes a day. Then students write about topics of personal interest for 20 or more minutes. In this way, students gradually learn skills, always have a chance to apply skills immediately in real writing, and do not lose sight of the primary purpose of writing (i.e., communicating). Following are tips for integrating skills instruction with meaningful composition activities.

Spelling   We do not teach spelling while students are composing texts. We do not want to interrupt their train of thought. Instead, we help them begin to apply strategies they are being taught. For example, students can be guided in comparing and contrasting words they know with words they are trying to spell in a text (e.g., use *cat* to help spell *flat*) or using readily available resources such as the word wall or spelling prediction software to support their spelling in context. We try not to spell words for beginning writers, and we refrain from teaching them to use spellchecking programs or dictionaries to find words they do not know how to spell. Think about how frustrated poor Tacy would be trying to find the correct spelling of *candy* when she wrote *kande*. Spellcheck, spelling dictionaries, dictionaries, and the like are more useful supports for students who spell reasonably well, whose misspellings are almost right, and who are self-aware when they are unsure how to spell a word.

Teachers find combining one strategy and one technology more productive for students with significant disabilities. The strategy is simple: "When you are not sure how to spell a word, spell it the way you think it sounds." That strategy increases independence and, over time, with instruction and experience, increases awareness of letter–sound relationships throughout a word. Spelling, or word prediction, software is the most useful technology. Teaching students to use this software saves keystrokes and supports more conventional spelling through sophisticated prediction systems. See Chapter 11 for a discussion of this software.

Editing, Not Grammar Instruction   For many years, scientific reviews of grammar instruction consistently found that it is unwise for teachers to devote extensive instructional focus to it (e.g., Graham & Perin, 2007; Hillocks, 1987). Of course, conforming to a common set of rules about word use clarifies communication. It is equally clear, however, that learning to apply the rules is more useful than identifying or memorizing them. For that reason, teachers use mini-lessons to teach students to edit their own writing drafts by asking themselves questions about their writing. Teachers begin with one or a few writing conventions and begin to increase the number as students use them more consistently in their first drafts. They determine which conventions to teach by observing student difficulties and listening to student questions about writing. The following list is often a starting place for beginners:

- Use of a capital letter at the beginning of sentences
- Use of periods at the end of sentences
- Use of spaces between words
- Correct spelling of word wall words

Many other conventions can be added to this list as students gain comfort and consistency with what you have taught, including indenting paragraphs, using commas, and capitalizing proper nouns. The four conventions, however, will go a long way toward improving the appearance and readability of your students' writing. Students can be taught to self-monitor for conventions by reading their texts aloud to themselves or using talking word processors (i.e., text-to-speech software) and asking themselves, "Does that sound like what I meant to write?"

Handwriting   Handwriting is not a viable option for many students with significant disabilities, but it is important to teach handwriting to those who can use pencils. Students who find it difficult to write legibly and fluently also find it difficult to translate their thoughts and experiences into written language (Graham, 2009–2010; Santangelo & Graham, 2016). Handwriting instruction is best initiated after students have learned most of the letter names and understand that writing is a process of communicating their thoughts in written language. The abstract shapes of letters need to be anchored in the more meaningful experience of communicating thoughts. Research in handwriting instruction suggests that it should be taught because it influences writing fluency, quality, and length (Santangelo & Graham, 2016). It should be taught in primary grades, not be overemphasized (i.e., 10–15 minutes a day for instruction), and begin with manuscript letters, which are more easily mastered and more widely employed in reading (Graham, 2009–2010; Graham, Kiuhara, McKeown, & Harris, 2012). A free, research-based handwriting curriculum (Graham, 2009–2010) is available from the Center for Accelerated Learning at Vanderbilt University (https://peabody.vanderbilt.edu/docs/pdf/sped/CASL%20Handwriting%20Program.pdf). Skill practice should always be immediately followed by communicative writing experiences.

> Always follow skill practice with communicative writing experiences.

Teach Writing Through Revision

Two approaches to writing have traditionally been prevalent in classrooms. In the first, students are assigned a prompt (e.g., The biggest thing I ever saw . . .). Students write a lot or do not and turn in their first drafts to the teacher. Teachers grade these papers and return them with mistakes circled and comments in the margins. In the second, students are assigned a prompt, write a draft, and turn it in to the teacher. The teacher returns these drafts with mistakes circled and comments in the margins. Students are expected to respond to the feedback and turn the paper back in for a grade.

As noted earlier, writing prompts are not equally successful with all students and prevent them from identifying their own topics. The problem introduced by evaluating either first or second drafts is that both represent early thinking on a topic for most writers, not polished products. Evaluation of this sort also restricts the audience to a single individual, the teacher, who judges quality and marks errors. Both kinds of instruction remind writers how they should have written rather than teach them how they could write better and more independently.

Writing is thought written down. Ultimately, we want students to think clearly and well, communicate those thoughts to a variety of audiences, and do so independently. They need to learn to do so free of teachers' comments such as, "Need a more active verb" or "Don't forget word order." So, once students have gained some independence in identifying their own topics and audiences and are writing daily, we teach them to evaluate their own writing and revise independently. If you follow the earlier recommendation to always encourage students to add to their initial drafts, no matter how much, how little, or how conventionally they have written, then you have begun to teach them one of four early revision strategies that they can apply independently as they gain experience (i.e., addition). The others are subtraction (i.e., removing unwanted or unneeded text), replacement (i.e., removing unwanted or unneeded text and replacing it with other text that enhances the text), and reordering (i.e., rearranging the existing text to better convey the ideas) (Cunningham & Cunningham, 2009).

Evan, a third grader with ASD, and his one-to-one aide showed us the value of the addition strategy. Evan's teacher had provided the class with a series of line drawings, which they initially arranged in a logical sequence. The students discussed what was happening in each picture, and then the teacher asked them each to write a summary of what the pictures were all about. Evan's one-to-one aide encouraged him as he wrote with a label maker, the only writing tool that interested him at that time. Evan used the word *print* to mean, "I think I am done. Can I cut the label and stick it on the page?" His composition process was supported as follows.

Evan *[looking at picture]*:	Wind.
Aide:	Wind what?
Evan:	Wind.
Aide:	Just wind?
Evan:	Blow.
Aide:	Oh.
Evan *[types and says]*:	BLOW.
Aide:	Blow what?
Evan:	Blow house in.
Aide:	Okay.
Evan *[types and says]*:	BLOW ... IN ... HOUSE ... IN.

This process continued across six illustrations until Evan's first draft finally read:

WINDOW

BIRDS MAD

BOYS RUNING BIRDS

BLOW IN HOUSE IN

BIRDS OWIE HERTS

BIRD DINNER EATING BOY

It is a text substantially longer than most Evan had written to that point. Evan would have provided a single word per page without the aide's questioning. The next day, she and Evan returned to his first draft and repeated the process. Evan's second draft read:

p. 1   WINDOW OUT SIDE

p. 2   THE BIRD HOUSE

       BIRDS MAD

       TREE

p. 3   BOYS RUNING BIRDS

       SUN HAPPY

p. 4   BLOW IN HOUSE IN

       WHO KELDD COCK ROBIN

p. 5   BIRDS OWIE HERTS

       ARROW IN THE BIRD

       BOY IS SADE

       XSNDINT

       AMBULINS

p. 6   BIRD DINNER EATING BOY

       BIRDS EATING WERMS

Evan's aide did not confuse editing (i.e., fixing mistakes) with revision (i.e., improving the clarity of communication). Evan's second draft still requires work, but the ideas are his. The writing is an honest representation of his thinking about this six-picture event.

Teach Independent Revision

Donald Murray (1991) argued that "writing is revising" (p. 2). If students with significant disabilities are to become independent writers, then they must learn strategies for independent revision. Revision is a process of examining a text, seeing it in a new way (revisioning), and rewriting it to improve on the original for the intended purpose and audience. We want students to freely express their ideas in first drafts, but we want them to learn how to improve the clarity of those ideas in revision.

Teach underlying habits of mind (i.e., thinking in particular ways without conscious effort or attention) when teaching effective revision. If students are to be taught to revise their texts, and, ultimately to do so independently, then they must learn to think like writers. They must be able to identify ideas and experiences they want to share, become increasingly attuned to their audience, and consider what makes a piece of writing interesting and effective. Habits of mind require time and experience. As in all writing instruction, you will teach through mini-lessons, provide guided practice opportunities, and maintain a tolerance for error. If you keep specific observational notes of students' writing behaviors and interactions, then you will find subtle and incremental changes (e.g., revising more independently, editing more willingly, writing for longer periods of time) over the course of a few weeks, months, and school year. Revision can involve several techniques and habits of mind:

- Rereading one's own writing

- Understanding and buying into the reasons writers revise

- Writing for immediate audiences

- Reading and evaluating others' writing to identify characteristics of "wow" writing

- Seeing revision as a source of new possibility

Each of these is discussed next. Here are some of the mini-lessons teachers employ to encourage students to think like writers.

Mini-Lesson 1: (Re)Read What You Write   Students have to become readers of their own writing before they can revise effectively. Teachers begin by talking about rereading as a part of the writing process. They model writing a sentence (e.g., "I love basketball") and read it aloud. Next, they give themselves feedback (e.g., "I need to explain that I love playing basketball. I don't love big, orange, rubber balls!"), and then make a change in the original text. They draw a line through the original text or cut it apart to provide space for the new ideas so students can compare the first and second writing attempts. After they modify the text, they reread the change and approve it (e.g., "Yeah, that's what I meant to say").

Students with significant disabilities initially may be confused by encouragement to reread and assume they have made a mistake because that is why they usually have had to do something again. Stan and Blaine demonstrated this confusion. In their first draft Blaine had written *Hes has a efst (He has friends)* under a picture of white, black, and brown horses in a pasture. Their teacher wanted them to notice they had an extra word in the sentence and asked them to read the text to see if it sounded like what they wanted. They read what they thought, not the actual words on the page, and so they added *white*, *brown*, and *black* to the description of the horse's friends. The boys never did understand the problem, however—what they said and what they wrote were two different texts.

Students like Stan and Blaine will catch on with additional experience and a few modifications. For example, the teacher might point to each word as the boys read the words aloud. If that did not work, then she might turn on word-by-word highlighting and have the boys listen as the computer reads aloud what they had written. Additional mini-lessons can focus on helping students internalize questions such as, "Does what I wrote sound right?" "Do I need to add anything?" or "Did I write what I was thinking?"

Mini-Lesson 2: Buy Into Revision   Habits of mind supporting revision ultimately develop when students clearly understand why writers revise, and they are motivated to do so by a topic and an audience they value. Zak was a high school student with intellectual disabilities whose teacher periodically had the students jot down ideas about different topics of interest for their writing folders. Zak wrote the sentences shown in Figure 9.3 in response to a camping trip that he obviously had not enjoyed: *It was bad and cold. It was rotten.*

He wrote the sample shown in Figure 9.4 following a school dance: *Tina. It was fun. It was cool.* Zak followed up on his list during writing time and created the first

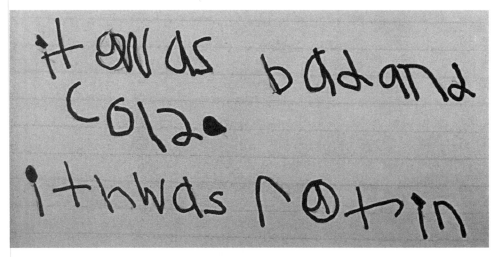

Figure 9.3. High school student Zak's writing about a camping trip. *(It was bad and cold. It was rotten.)*

draft shown in Figure 9.5: *Dear Tina, I love you. Love, Zak P.S. See you.* The teacher recognized a teachable moment and asked him what he liked most about Tina and suggested he make a list. He generated the additional brainstormed list shown in Figure 9.6: *She is adorable. She is a nice lady. Nice dancing.* He wanted help spelling *adorable,* but the teacher suggested he spell it the way it sounded, and every time he sought confirmation, the teacher just repeated, "You're doing great. Finish the word." Zak wrote *adahorbr.* She then guided him in rereading his brainstormed lists and love letter and suggested that Tina might like the letter even more with some added detail. She wondered aloud if Zak would like to revise his letter. He responded, "I can try my best." They laid out the two lists and the original letter so Zak could refer to them.

He wrote, *Dear Tina* and *You are a nice dancer* and then asked, "What should I write next?"

"Use your lists," the teacher replied.

He looked at each list and then said politely, "I might need some advice first."

"Well, okay," the teacher answered. "Let's read your letter so far. 'Dear Tina, You are a nice dancer.' Let's read your list of ideas. You've got two other things. You said you thought she was adorable, and you thought she was nice. What do you want to write next?"

His teacher expected him to write either that she was adorable or that she was nice. Instead, the brainstormed list gave him another idea, and he wrote *You are sweet.*

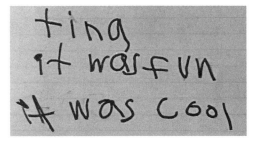

Figure 9.4. Zak's writing about a school dance. *(Tina. It was fun. It was cool.)*

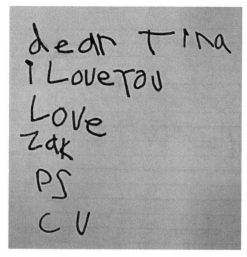

Figure 9.5. Zak's draft of a love letter to his friend Tina. *(Dear Tina, I love you. Love, Zak P.S. See you.)*

The teacher again guided him in rereading his letter and said, "So what next?"

This time he added *You have nice shoes.* Again, the brainstormed lists prompted an idea not found on any of the lists or previous draft.

"Do you want to add anything?" the teacher again prompted when he finished the sentence and paused.

"I love you?" he asked.

"That's very sweet," the teacher answered, and he concluded his revision, shown in Figure 9.7: *Dear Tina, You are a nice dancer. You are sweet. You have nice shoes. I love you, Zak.*

Zak delivered his love letter at lunchtime. Real writing experiences such as these help students understand why they should revise more than any formal mini-lesson, and they enable teachers to assist students in becoming more independent in the process. Students can revise lists for Santa Claus; letters to favorite athletes, musicians, or actors; or Valentine's Day poems for boyfriends or girlfriends. What seems to work best is writing for a known audience of one or a few classmate(s), a student need or interest to share, and response from that target audience.

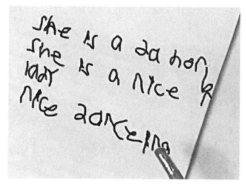

Figure 9.6. Zak's brainstormed list of ideas to add to his letter to Tina. *(She is adorable. She is a nice lady. Nice dancing.)*

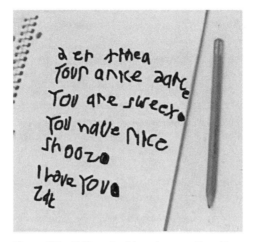

Figure 9.7. Zak's revised love letter to Tina. *(Dear Tina, You are a nice dancer. You are sweet. You have nice shoes. I love you, Zak.)*

Mini-Lesson 3: Write for Immediate Audiences   It is difficult for students with significant disabilities to understand audience in the abstract before they understand immediate audiences. Writing to an audience who writes back is one of the best ways for inexperienced writers to begin to understand audience. A wide variety of technologies expand the possibilities of structuring such writing experiences in motivating ways. Text messaging via Skype or Facebook, Twitter posts, blogging and commenting, and other online tools offer ideal opportunities for repeated exchanges and motivated revision in order to clarify communication (Williams et al., 2007).

We described the following motivated use of e-mail in the Writing: Text Types and Purposes Dynamic Learning Maps module (see https://unc.az1.qualtrics.com/jfe /form/SV_87E9nVilbi9ULsx?Q_JFE=qdg). Two high school students, Anna, who has significant language and learning disabilities, and Carie, who has Down syndrome, were troubled to find ants in the cabin where they were learning to read and write. They were encouraged by their teacher to write an e-mail to see if something might be done about this problem. The girls' teacher listened in as the two negotiated what to write and provided the accompanying translation. Figure 9.8 shows Anna and Carie's original text on the left and the teacher's text translation on the right.

Dr Dave,	Dear Dave,
Thebgs very w	The bugs are everywhere.
Not bit me	Don't bite me.
Bug are a	Bugs are everywhere.
I hate biges	I hate bugs.
Likedonatbus	I don't like bugs.
I not lake bigs	I don't like bugs.
Saponbug	Step on bug.
Not cut me	Don't cut me.
saddor	Seal the door.
ANNA CARIE	Anna Carie

Figure 9.8. A draft of an e-mail that two high school students, Anna and Carie, planned to send their camp leader, Dave, about bugs in their cabin. The students' original text appears on the left, with the teacher's translation of their text on the right.

Daer dave	Dear Dave,
Wearefan	You are funny.
We are tik about bigs inside	We are talking about bugs inside.
Wearetingthebugonsad	You are talking about bugs outside.
pLs ylld bigs for as	Please kill bugs for us.
tisihrdforsatrak	It is hard for us to work.
ANNA CARIE	Anna Carie

Figure 9.9. Anna and Carie's second message to their camp leader, rewritten to clarify what they meant. The students' original text appears on the left, with the teacher's translation on the right.

The camp leader, like Zak's teacher in the previous example, recognized a teachable moment and e-mailed a reply immediately.

> *I agree with you. I don't like bugs either. Did you bring bug spray to camp? You should always use it before you go outside. Maybe it is just that the bugs think you are sweet.*

This time the girls revised their initial message and tried to clarify the meaning of their previous request. The new message and teacher's translation text are shown in Figure 9.9.

The camp leader responded again, continuing to feign misunderstanding.

> *You have bugs inside! You should take medicine. That will kill the bugs. Then you will be healthy.*

This led the young writers to a second, and much clearer, revision, shown in Figure 9.10.

The girls drafted their note three times. Because they were motivated to share a message that mattered to them, they behaved as writers and worked to clarify their intent in each draft.

Revision accomplishes many important instructional goals. It leads students to compose their thoughts more clearly. It boosts reading volume as they read and reread their drafts. It raises student awareness of audience and the communicative purpose of writing as they receive and review the target audience's feedback. It enhances motivation to write through communicative purposes. Finally, it improves the quality of student writing over time as students try to share their ideas clearly with their intended audiences.

Mini-Lesson 4: Establish "Wow" Writing Criteria   Novice writers lack experience to judge what makes writing effective. Mini-lessons focused on evaluating and reasoning can lead to such understanding over time. Tar Heel Reader (http://tarheel

Dr devr	Dear Dave,
Yaer wall wall fennny	You're really, really funny.
We aresak	We aren't sick.
The begs are in yar room	The bugs are in our room.
They arebugar	There are bugs everywhere.
Yelld him	Kill them.
You so fennny	You're so funny.
ANNA CARIE	Anna and Carie

Figure 9.10. Anna and Carie's third message to their camp leader, rewritten to further clarify their meaning. The students' original text appears on the left, with the teacher's translation on the right.

reader.org) is ideal for this purpose. Following the last page of each text in Tar Heel Reader, guide your student(s) to rate the book by using the built-in three-star system. After each student has rated the text, discuss their decisions. Students initially give responses related to the topic ("It's about wrestling"), a feeling ("It's funny"), the illustrations ("I like the balloon pictures"), or text features ("It has easy words to read"). These become the initial "wow" writing criteria that are posted in the classroom.

As in all literacy instruction with these students, teachers accept all responses, clarify when needed, and build on them over time. The next mini-lesson involves an application of the "wow" writing list. This time teachers read two Tar Heel Reader texts aloud to the group and ask which one is better. Then they apply the "wow" writing" criteria, which usually do not fit very well. The book they chose is about fishing and not wrestling, it is informative but not funny, and there are no balloon pictures, but it does have easy words to read. "Maybe we need to modify our "wow" writing list," the teacher will suggest. "What shall we do about 'the topic is wrestling?'"

"Wrestling or fishing," says the wrestling fan. The teacher edits the first item.

The edited rules are often not better than the original. Yet, as teachers accumulate specific items, they soon have enough that mini-lessons can focus on what all the examples in item 1 have in common. Then a new, more general "wow" writing characteristic can replace all the specific examples, such as, "The topics are really exciting or interesting." Across time, students develop increasing sophistication in their understanding of good writing that is based on personal experience with text and repeated consideration of what they like to read. This is more effective than providing them with some generic, and ultimately arbitrary, list of rules that they cannot anchor in their own experience.

Mini-Lesson 5: See Revision as Possibility   For this series of mini-lessons, begin with an adapted form of an exercise that Hillocks (1995) designed to teach older students to revise through inquiry. First, identify a text for revision—a draft from a student you no longer teach, a sample from the Internet, or a draft you compose like one of your current students but with all details changed to prevent any students from feeling like they are on the spot. The following text is one such example: *The girl is blind. She has a dog.*

Next, generate ideas for the group to think about in relation to the text. For example, they could list as many ideas as possible for the following categories—all the places the person might go with the dog, things the dog might see, things the person might do for the dog, thoughts the person might have while going somewhere with the dog, or thoughts the dog might have while traveling with the person.

Next, meet with small groups of students and assist them in these conversations. They might suggest ideas such as these:

Places they are going: circus, school, library, mall, football game

What the dog sees: cat, cars, crack in the sidewalk, other dogs

What the girl does: feeds dog, hugs him, gives him warm bed

The girl's thoughts: Slow down, dog. Quit stopping and sniffing.

Dog's thoughts: My collar is too tight. Let's go sniff that tree.

Once you help the group brainstorm, work with students to include some of the information from their lists in the original text. One group wrote collectively:

> Once upon a time a person who is blind and his dog went to the circus. The dog saw a cat. He chased the cat. The person fell down.

Finally, compare the two drafts and talk about new ideas that were added, which draft is more interesting, and where the new ideas originated. Our goal in these conversations is to help students gradually internalize more sophisticated understandings of how and why to revise.

Use Student Interests to Motivate Writing

Growth in writing depends on a good deal of experience supplemented with effective instruction. Students are likely to write most about what they know best and find most engaging. For Cole, a high school student with intellectual disabilities, it was writing and illustrating his own superhero comic book. For Ashley, a middle school student with ASD, it was writing a personalized horror story. For Felicity, it was advocating for a friend, and for Erin, writing *Magic School Bus*-style texts. For Jay, it was writing about penguins and zoos; for Jessie, about horseback riding; for Cody, about *Tom and Jerry;* and for Taylor, about boa constrictors. You can motivate beginning writers by helping and encouraging students to identify their interests, write about those interests, expand on those interests with experience, and share texts with real audiences.

A FINAL NOTE: WRITING IMPROVES THROUGH EXPERIENCE

Few students with significant disabilities have much experience in composing their own thoughts in print, and still fewer have opportunities to revise those thoughts in order to improve the quality of their texts. Nearly all are novice writers who find composing a slow and difficult process, do not understand the purpose of spelling or grammar instruction, and write short, incomplete texts. As they accumulate the experiences, behaviors, and understandings described in this chapter, they can become more independent writers who can communicate their thoughts more clearly and conventionally for wider audiences and increasingly diverse purposes.

RECOMMENDED READINGS AND RESOURCES

The following readings and resources will deepen readers' understanding of how to teach students with significant disabilities to communicate through traditional writing.

Cunningham, P. M., & Cunningham, J. W. (2009). *What really matters in writing: Research-based practices across the curriculum.* New York, NY: Pearson.

Dynamic Learning Maps Professional Development web site (http://dlmpd.com). See the following modules: Writing: Text Types and Purposes; Writing: Production and Distribution; Writing: Research and Range of Writing; Writing Information and Explanation Texts; Writing: Getting Started With Narrative Writing; and Writing: Getting Started in Writing Arguments.

Graham, S., Bollinger, A., Olsen, C. B., D'Aoust, C., MacArthur, C., McCutchen, D., & Olinghouse, N. (2012). *Teaching elementary school students to be effective writers.* Retrieved from http://ies.ed.gov/ncee/wwc/PracticeGuide.aspx?sid=17

CHAPTER 10

Decoding,
Word Identification, and Spelling

As a classroom teacher in the late 1980s and early 90s, one of the authors, Karen, decorated word boxes for each of her students and displayed them proudly on the window sill in her classroom. Inside the boxes were index cards organized in two sections: Words I Know and Words I Am Learning. Each day, students reviewed known words and were taught new words via instruction that featured repeated trials (i.e., repetitions of each word until mastery) and a system of least-to-most prompting (i.e., expectant pauses before verbal reminders, visual demonstrations of the desired response). Some of the students had 100 or more cards in the word boxes, whereas other students had as few as three. Still others consistently had 8-10 words in the Words I Know section, but they seemed to forget one word they already knew each time they learned a new word. Consistent with the research literature (e.g., Spector, 2011), there was little evidence that even the students who were learning the words could use them to read connected text with comprehension.

In spite of the evidence that the approach was not working for all of the students, it was the only approach Karen knew. After all, every textbook and article she read while working toward her license to teach students with significant disabilities told her (erroneously) that students with significant disabilities could not learn to read phoneti-cally. Karen has clear memories of writing an individualized education program (IEP) for one student. The statement of present level of performance read something such as this: Stevie is a whole-word learner. He can read 12 words from the Dolch sight word list, but he is unable to use phonics to read words. *Then, the goals emphasized teaching Stevie to recognize and remember whole words. Within a few years, Karen began to recognize that an honest present level of performance statement would have read something such as this:* Stevie's teacher has no idea how to teach a child with autism who is nonspeaking how to read and spell words using phonics or de-coding. As a result, Stevie can recognize 12 words from the Dolch sight word list and is unable to use phonics or other strategies to decode words.

Unfortunately, Karen was not alone in her belief that students with significant dis-abilities could not learn to read and spell words using knowledge of letter–sound (grapheme–phoneme) correspondences. The research literature regarding reading instruction for these students is dominated by research focused on sight word instruc-tion (e.g., Browder et al., 2006; Spector, 2011), and programs that focus on teaching sight words, such as the Edmark Reading Program (2011) and PCI Reading (Haugen-McLane et al., 2007), continue to be widely used today. Unfortunately, the results of a meta-analysis completed by Browder and Xin (1998) continue to ring true today. That is, the research consistently provides "strong demonstrations of teaching students to name words, but falls short of demonstrating that students understand these words or apply them to their daily routines" (Browder & Xin, 1998, p. 130). Perhaps more important, there is little evidence that learning to read words in this way contributes to later success with independent reading (Browder et al., 2006; Spector, 2011).

Students with significant disabilities are not the only students who struggle to apply the sight words they learn. Children without disabilities often learn some words very early in their development via the whole-word (also called *prealphabetic* or *logographic*) approach often used with students with significant disabilities (Ehri, 2005). As Ehri explained, these early readers learn to recognize the visual shape of the whole word and match it with a pronunciation without processing the individual letters or letter–sound relationships in the words. Then, in contrast to students with significant disabilities, they quickly move on to partial or full alphabetic approaches to word reading because the nonalphabetic approach is so limited (Ehri, 2014). Without at least partial alphabetic connections to the letters in words, all readers find it difficult to remember the words they learn and then read them in other contexts (Ehri, 2014). We should not be surprised when students with significant disabilities struggle to learn and remember words that we teach as whole words without attention to the letters and sounds in those words. The use of prealphabet approaches to sight word instruction (e.g., massed trials such as flash cards, repeated practice naming or selecting words) may matter as much as the nature of their disability in explaining the challenges many students experience with learning to read.

It is important to distinguish this type of early, prealphabetic word identification and the kind of automatic sight word reading proficient readers do when they read with fluency and understanding. It is true that proficient readers identify most words without consciously processing the individual letters or sounds; however, that ability to read most words by sight is a result of using alphabetic strategies to learn the word in the first place (see, e.g., Ehri, 2005; Perfetti, 2007). Proficient readers do not learn new words using the kind of prealphabetic, logographic, visual strategies that are promoted for use with students with significant disabilities (Browder et al., 2009). They learn the words using strategies to successfully gain access to the pronunciation and/or meaning with enough success, enough times, that they can recognize them as sight words (Ehri, 2014).

The goal of this chapter is to describe an alphabetic approach to teaching students with significant disabilities a range of skills and strategies that will help them read and spell words—not only in isolation, but also while

> Prealphabetic, logographic, and visual strategies teach students to identify words, but this is not the same as automatic sight word reading done by fluent readers. Readers need to learn words through alphabetic strategies and apply those strategies to read words with enough success, enough times, that they recognize them as sight words.

reading text with comprehension or writing to communicate with others. The approach will help students develop a relatively large set of words they can recognize on sight so that, like other readers, they can focus their attention on comprehending the text rather than reading the words. At the same time, it will help them learn skills that allow them to determine how to read and spell words they have not been directly taught.

WHY WE TEACH DECODING, SPELLING, AND WORD IDENTIFICATION

The ability to identify words, including unfamiliar words, is one critical component of successful silent reading comprehension (see, e.g., NICHD, 2000). Efficiently identifying words in text allows readers to allocate more of their cognitive resources to making meaning (Ehri, 2005); however, efficiently identifying words requires readers to have a variety of strategies and skills that help them gain access to the pronunciation and meaning of unfamiliar words (Ehri, 2014). Similarly, spelling is one critical component of successful writing, but spelling also supports word identification (Graham & Hebert, 2011) and general reading ability (Graham & Santangelo, 2014). Students are unable to focus on ideas and the overall purpose of their writing when they struggle to spell words efficiently (Graham, Harris, & Fink-Chorzempa, 2002). This struggle with spelling often leads them to restrict the words they write to those they can confidently spell (Sumner, Connelly, & Barnett, 2014).

Spelling is required for students who use AAC if they are ever going to achieve independent and autonomous communication. The alphabet is the only symbol set flexible enough to allow them to communicate whatever they want, whenever they want, where they want, and with whomever they want (Koppenhaver, 2000). Any other symbol set is restricted in some way. For example, graphic symbols can play an important role in helping students who use AAC to get started with communication while they are learning to read and write, and once they learn, graphic symbols can help to enhance efficiency. Spelling, however, is required to support true independent, autonomous, and precise communication across topics, purposes, partners, and contexts.

In summary, we teach decoding, spelling, and word identification because they are critical to success in reading, writing, and communicating. Conventional literacy cannot be achieved without them; however, teaching reading, writing, and communication to students with significant disabilities requires a comprehensive, integrated approach that builds on research-based practices. It requires that we go beyond what we have always done (i.e., teaching sight words) and understand what is involved in successfully reading, spelling, and identifying words.

THE PROCESSOR MODEL OF WORD READING

It is clear that word reading requires more than learning to name words that have been repeatedly presented. Adams' (1990, 2004) processor model of word reading helps explain the complexities of word reading. As such, it provides the theoretical basis for an integrated, comprehensive approach to word reading instruction.

The model features the integration of four different processors involved in successful word identification—phonological, orthographic, meaning, and context (see Figure 10.1). Readers use their phonological processors to determine the sounds

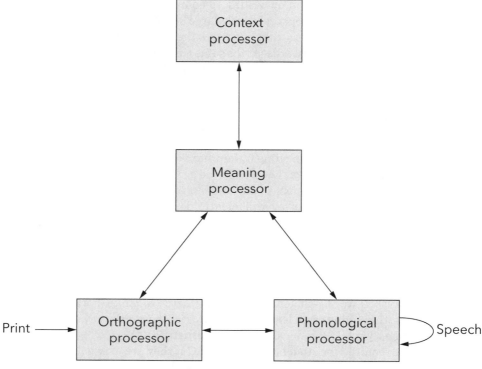

Figure 10.1.   A model of word reading (Adams, 1990, 2004).

associated with letters in words they are attempting to read and use that knowledge
to either retrieve or construct a potential pronunciation for a word. At the same time,
readers use their orthographic processor to recognize printed words and the spelling
strings and patterns that compose them. As the orthographic processor is strengthened, readers use their recognition of all of the letters in words (i.e., the entire spelling
string) to efficiently access pronunciations for words without processing each letter
individually. Although the orthographic and phonological processors are involved in
gaining access to the print (orthographic) and sounds (phonological) of words, the
meaning processor is involved in gaining access to possible meanings for words as
they are read. For example, when a reader encounters the word *wind*, the orthographic
processor recognizes that it is a real word with a familiar string of letters, *-ind*. At
the same time, the phonological processor is used to apply knowledge of letters and
sounds using a letter-by-letter ($w + i + n + d$) or onset-rime strategy ($w + ind$) or by
gaining access to a pronunciation automatically. The meaning processor is important
because it helps the reader assign potential meanings and pronunciations to the word
wind. This is when the context processor is engaged to use the surrounding context to
determine if the appropriate pronunciation is *wind* as in *The wind blew*, or *wind,* as in
He helped to wind the ball of yarn.

    It is important to choose methods that engage all four processors when teach-
ing students with significant disabilities to read words. Methods that focus on only
one make it challenging, if not impossible, for many students with significant disabilities to learn decoding strategies they can apply independently when reading text.

For example, we cannot teach students to read using nonsense words because nonsense words only engage the phonological processor and make it impossible to engage the other three. Similarly, we cannot rely solely on sight word instruction because that only engages the orthographic processor and keeps students from learning to integrate all of the processes to successfully read words in text.

Most important, nothing about Adams' model (1990, 2004) requires students to learn rules (e.g., a vowel is usually short when it is followed by one consonant), speak individual sounds or words, or approach reading by identifying sounds, remembering them, and blending them together (e.g., d-aw-g, dog). Each of these present challenges for students with significant disabilities (Flores et al., 2004). Efforts to teach these students using these approaches have not helped students develop the ability to decode untaught words with high levels of success (e.g., Cohen, Heller, Alberto, & Fredrick, 2008; Conners, Rosenquist, Sligh, Atwell, & Kiser, 2006; Fallon et al., 2004; Light, McNaughton, Weyer, & Karg, 2008).

GETTING OFF TO A GOOD START: ADDRESSING STUDENT NEEDS THOUGHTFULLY

The following sections describe a comprehensive, integrated approach to instruction in decoding, spelling, and word identification. This approach addresses the numerous challenges faced by students with significant disabilities, challenges that require us to be thoughtful as we address word reading and spelling needs (Flores et al., 2004). Specifically, the comprehensive, integrated approach addresses the fact that many students with significant disabilities have restricted receptive vocabulary and expressive communication skills (Erickson & Geist, 2016). Both challenges necessitate an approach that meets two criteria: 1) it emphasizes real words, rather than sounds in isolation or nonsense words, and 2) it does not require students to produce sounds orally or blend and segment the sounds in words orally. We describe a research-based approach (Ehri, Satlow, & Gaskins, 2009) that combines a spelling-based instructional routine (e.g., Cunningham & Cunningham, 1992; Cunningham & Hall, 1994, 2008) with onset-rime, analogy-based, keyword instruction (Gaskins et al., 1988).

MAKING WORDS: A SPELLING-BASED APPROACH TO DECODING

Making Words (Cunningham & Hall, 1994, 2008) is an activity designed to teach students to look for and use common spelling patterns to read and spell words. Originally designed as a multilevel, whole-class instructional activity, Making Words engages individual students by having them manipulate their own set of letters. As students select and arrange the letters to make words, teachers gain insight regarding the students' understandings and misunderstandings. The fact that Making Words does not require students to say individual letters, sounds, or words makes it accessible to a broad range of students with significant disabilities, including those with the most complex, multiple disabilities (Erickson & Koppenhaver, 1998; Hanser & Erickson, 2007).

Whole-Class Lessons

The basic, whole-class approach to Making Words is a multicomponent approach that helps students learn to blend and segment sounds in words, recognize spelling patterns in words, and apply what they have been taught to read and spell untaught words. The three components of a Making Words lesson are as follows:

1. Students use letters to build target words with adult guidance, checking/correcting spelling after each attempted word.

2. Students sort word cards to identify spelling patterns.

3. Students transfer learning by using the words they have made to spell new words with similar patterns.

To begin the activity, students are given access to letters that can be unscrambled to make a single word (e.g., *a, b, l, s, t* [*blast*]). At first, the letters include only a single vowel, but a second vowel is added as soon as students learn to put the vowel in the right place when making words. During the lesson, students are guided in using the letters to spell words of varying lengths, beginning with one- or two-letter words and progressing to words that use all of the letters. In planning the lesson, the adult sequences the target words so that minimal changes are made as the students progress from one word to the next. This not only increases student success but also enables students to recognize and understand within-word spelling patterns more efficiently. Examples of letter sets and words to make are provided in Table 10.1.

At each point in the lesson, the students first attempt to use the letters to make a word that the adult has indicated. After the attempt has been made, the adult shows the students the correctly spelled word written on an index card, piece of paper, or digital equivalent. Each student's spelling is then compared with the correct spelling, letter by letter. The students either confirm their correct spelling or make corrections as needed before the teacher moves on to the next word.

Each word is used in a sentence that is meaningful to the student during the word building part of the lesson. The focus is not to teach the meaning of the words, however, but rather, the letters, sounds, spelling patterns, and similarities and differences

Table 10.1. Sample Making Words letter sets and sequences

Letters	Words to make
a, b, m, n, t	a, an, at, bat, mat, man, ban, tan
a, d, n, s, t	a, at, an, tan, ant, sat, sad, sand, and
a, l, n, p, s	a, as, an, pan, nap, sap, lap, laps, naps
i, f, n, s, t	I, in, is, if, it, sit, fit, fin, fins, fits
b, i, g, n, t	I, it, in, pin, pig, pig, bit, big, bin
i, d, n, r, p, s	I, is, in, tin, tip, rip, nip, sip, dip, dips
e, g, n, p, t, s	set, pet, pen, ten, tens, pens, pets, gets
e, g, h, j, m, n, t	hem, hen, ten, men, met, jet, get, net
e, b, d, g, l, p, t	let, leg, beg, peg, pet, bet, bed, led
o, g, h, l, p, t	go, got, pot, lot, hot, hop, hog, log
o, b, j, l, r, s	so, sob, lob, job, rob, robs, lobs, jobs
o, c, d, n, s, t	no, on, ton, son, sod, cod, cot, cots
u, b, n, r, s	us, bus, bun, sun, sub, rub, run, runs, buns
u, b, g, n, r, t	nut, rut, rub, run, bun, bug, tug, rug
u, b, c, h, r, s, t	cut, cub, hub, hut, rut, rub, rubs, cubs

between each of the words the student makes. The purpose of the sentence is to engage the meaning and context processors described earlier in Adams' model (1990, 2004).

After all of the words have been made (i.e., spelled), students are guided in sorting the word cards. This sorting encourages students to explore the spelling patterns within each word. The adult initially suggests the pattern for sorting (e.g., number of letters, same first letter, same vowel, same ending), but gradually students are encouraged to identify and sort by their own rules. Finally, the students are directed to use the words they have made to try to spell additional words using letters not available in the lesson. For example, students who made the words *take, make,* and *sake* might be asked to spell *fake* and *rake* during this transfer step.

Small-Group or Individual Lessons

We make a few simple adjustments to the basic procedures when we are using Making Words with an individual or small group of students with significant disabilities who are all learning to read and spell words at beginning levels. First, we have to determine how the students will gain access to the letters. Students in general education classrooms typically have laminated squares (1- or 2-inch squares) with one letter printed on each. The uppercase letter is printed on one side and the lowercase on the other. Teachers make sets of letters that they store alphabetically in baggies, pocket organizers, boxes, or envelopes. At the beginning of the lesson, teachers distribute the letters that are needed.

Depending on students' specific needs, our modifications might be as simple as preparing the letter sets ahead of time so our lesson begins by handing each student an envelope or baggie with the letters they will need. For some students, we display the letters on a Lucite eye-gaze frame, and they select letters by looking. Other students will move magnetic letters on a cookie sheet to prevent the letters from constantly falling on the floor. Still other students will select the letters via partner-assisted scanning (i.e., the partner presents the letters to the learner one letter at a time, the student indicates when the partner presents a desired letter, and the partner moves the learner's selection). If students are gaining access to the letters via technology, then we take time to prepare a setup with just the letters that will be used in the lesson. No one solution works for all students, but every solution should provide students with access to the set of letters that will be used in the lesson rather than the full alphabet.

After figuring out how our students will select or move the letters, we have to determine the complexity of the lesson, which involves examining the students' spelling skills to determine the maximum length of the words students will be asked to make in the lesson. Our target is to ask students to spell words no more than two letters longer than the words they can spell independently. For example, a student who successfully spells two- and three-letter words will be asked to make words up to five letters long. Other adjustments include adding more reasons to sort the words students have made and adding more transfer activities at the end of the lesson. These minor adjustments—truncating the word building step, increasing the number of patterns to seek during word sorts, and including more words in the transfer step—focus the lesson on the specific needs of beginning readers and writers rather than the diverse needs of an entire class.

Remember that all three steps of the lesson are important. First, guide students through making the words. Then, ask students to sort the words based on a variety of features. Finally, ask students to use the words they made to spell new words in the transfer step. An example of a complete Making Words lesson is provided in the textbox. (A downloadable and photocopiable version of this sample lesson is available with the downloadable materials for this book.)

Sample Making Words Lesson

Letters

a, m, n, t, s

Words

am, as, an, at, sat, mat, man, tan, tans

Name Letters and Their Common Sounds

Before beginning to make words, have the students hold up or point to each letter, name it, and say its common sound. Show and name the lower- and uppercase forms of the letters. For students who cannot say the sounds, ask them to "think the sound" and then say each aloud for them.

Make Words

Have the students make each word. After students attempt a word, show them the correct spelling. Work with them to compare and contrast their effort with the correctly spelled word. Check letter by letter and fix as needed before moving to the next word.

1. Take two letters and make **am.** I **am** proud of you.

2. Take the **m** away and add a different letter to make **as.** He is **as** big **as** a bear.

3. Take the **s** away and add a different letter to spell **an.** I have **an** idea.

4. Take the **n** away and add a different letter to make **at.** We are **at** school.

5. Add a letter to make **sat.** He **sat** at his desk.

6. Take the **s** away and add a letter to spell **mat.** We have a **mat** at our door.

7. Now take the **t** away and add another letter to spell **man.** I like that **man.**

8. Take the **m** away and add another letter to spell **tan.** We have a **tan** rug.

9. Now add one more letter to make a four-letter word. Add one letter to **tan** and you can spell **tans.** Let's all say **tans** and listen for the letter we need to add. She **tans** easily in the summer.

Sort

Collect the letters, then read all the words in the pocket chart with the students.

1. Have the students sort the words into columns according to their first letter. Use partner-assisted scanning with students who cannot physically move the words.

2. Sort words into columns according to the number of letters in each.

3. Find all of the words that end with the –**an** spelling pattern.

Transfer

Ask students to use the words they made to spell other words using the tools (i.e., pens, pencils, keyboards, alternate pencils) they use for writing. Look at **at, sat, mat.** Use them to help you spell **fat.**

1. Look at **at, sat, mat,** and the word you just wrote, **fat.** Use them to spell **pat.**

2. Use them to spell **rat** and **cat.**

3. Look at **an, man, tan.** Use them to help you spell **can.**

4. Look at **an, man, tan,** and the word you just wrote, **can.** Use them to spell **fan.**

5. Now use them to spell **van** and **pan.**

Making Words, a spelling-based approach to decoding instruction, is the first half of our comprehensive, integrated approach to teaching students decoding, spelling, and word identification. During the word building step, we are focused on helping students build the phonological processor as described by Adams (1990, 2004). During the word sort step, we are focused on building the orthographic processor, and during the transfer step, we are helping students integrate their orthographic and phonological processors. Throughout the lessons, students are hearing the words they are making in meaningful sentences, which helps develop their meaning and context processors (Adams, 1990, 2004). Our goal is to complete a full Making Words lesson each day.

ONSET-RIME: AN ANALOGY-BASED APPROACH TO DECODING

The second half of the comprehensive, integrated approach to teaching students decoding, spelling, and word identification is analogy based. This approach helps students learn to use known words (called *keywords*) and word parts to read and spell other words. One major advantage is that students can learn this approach as beginning readers and writers and continue to use it even when they reach the point of reading and spelling complex, polysyllabic words. Combining this analogy-based approach to decoding with the letter-by-letter approach in Making Words provides students with the information they need about individual letters and the way they work in words. It also helps them learn to attend to important spelling patterns within words.

Onset-rime, keyword instruction teaches students to use known words to decode and spell unknown words by attending to spelling patterns, especially the rime, which is the part of the word that begins with the first vowel and extends to the end of each syllable (e.g., *-at* is the rime in the word *bat*). The onsets are the consonants that appear before the rime in the syllable (e.g., *b-* is the onset in the word *bat*; *str-* is the onset and *-eet* is the rime in the word *street*). Spelling patterns like this are the focus of this half of our comprehensive, integrated approach. Another benefit of this approach is that rimes are taught in the context of real words or keywords that serve as a point of reference for the student (Gaskins et al., 1988; Greaney, Tunmer, & Chapman, 1997).

Teaching Spelling Patterns: Rounding Up the Rhymes

We can use an activity called *Rounding Up the Rhymes* to help students become aware of spelling patterns during shared reading lessons. The teacher uses a book, passage, poem or other text that contains many rhyming words. While the teacher reads, the students are encouraged to chime in whenever they hear any words that rhyme. After reading, the teacher goes back to the beginning, reviews the rhyming pairs the students identified, and writes each on an index card. The words are placed in rhyming pairs in a pocket chart or on the board. The teacher reminds students that rhyming words usually have the same spelling pattern, and, together, they underline the spelling patterns in the displayed pairs. They determine which word pairs have the same spelling patterns, and then the teacher discards pairs that do not share a spelling pattern so he or she can help students focus on the words that do share a spelling pattern. The teacher then reviews each pair before leading the students in a transfer step. During this final step, students are asked to match new words to rhyming pairs that have the same spelling pattern. After the new words have been placed, the students read each set of rhyming words, and the teacher says a few other words that the students are asked to spell with the help of the words on the chart. An example of this structure using part of a poem is provided in Figure 10.2.

Keywords are introduced once students begin to understand that words that sound like they have the same ending often have the same spelling pattern. These keywords represent the 37 most common rimes in written English (Wylie & Durrell, 1970; see Table 10.2), which appear in hundreds of words that begin with just single consonants. There is no predetermined set of keywords; instead, the teacher or team selects one keyword to represent each of the 37 rimes. The keywords should already be a part of the students' receptive vocabulary and should be useful in the students' expressive communication, whether they use speech, signs, or other forms of AAC.

Step 1: Read the poem (or other text), and ask students to indicate when they hear words that rhyme.

Be Glad Your Nose Is on Your Face[1]
   (Prelutsky, 1984)
Be glad your nose is on your face,
not pasted on some other place,
for if it were where it is not,
you might dislike your nose a lot.

Imagine if your precious nose
Were sandwiched in between your toes,
that clearly would not be a treat,
for you'd be forced to smell your feet.

Step 2: Review the rhyming pairs students indicated and write them on index cards.

Step 3: Arrange cards in pairs and compare/contrast the patterns.

face	place	not	lot
nose	toes	treat	feet
f**ace**	n**ose**	n**ot**	tr**eat**
pl**ace**	t**oes**	l**ot**	f**eet**

Step 4. Remove pairs that do not share spelling patterns, and ask students to match new words to the remaining rhyming pairs.

face	place	Add **race**, **lace**, **pace**
not	lot	Add **pot**, **hot**, **spot**,

Step 5: Ask students to spell words using the sets of rhyming words to help.

face, place, race, lace, pace	Spell **brace** and **space**
not, lot, pot, hot, spot	Spell **cot** and **rot**

---

[1] https://www.poets.org/poetsorg/poem/be-glad-your-nose-your-face

Figure 10.2.   Sample Rounding Up the Rhymes lesson.

Table 10.2.   Thirty-seven most common rimes in written English

-ack	-ail	-ain	-ake	-ale	-ame	-an
-ank	-ap	-ash	-at	-ate	-aw	-ay
-eat	-ell	-est	-ice	-ick	-ide	-ight
-ill	-in	-ine	-ing	-ink	-ip	-it
-ock	-oke	-op	-ore	-ot	-uck	-ug
-ump	-unk					

From Wylie, R., & Durrell, D. (1970). Teaching Vowels Through Phonograms. Elementary English, 47(6), 787–791. Copyright 1970 by the National Council of Teachers of English. Used with permission.

Teachers and teams also pay attention to using as many of the consonants as possible when creating the keywords.

Once the keywords are identified, students are taught to read and spell them. As they begin to learn the keywords, students are explicitly taught to use the keywords to read and spell other words that share spelling patterns with the keywords. We use teacher-created texts, predictable chart writing, and a word wall to teach students to read and spell the keywords. Then, we use word sorts and compare/contrast activities to explicitly teach students how to use the keywords to read and spell other words.

Teacher-Created Texts and Predictable Charts

Chapter 4 discussed using Tar Heel Reader (http://tarheelreader.org) and other tools to create texts. Teachers can use the same tools to create texts that include keywords. Reading the words in meaningful texts will help students learn them in ways that they can apply in other contexts. Teachers can also use these text-creation tools to create stems for predictable chart writing (see Chapter 5) that include the keywords. For example, suppose you selected the word *name* as the keyword to represent the -*ame* rime. You could use the stem, *My name is* _____ in a predictable chart writing activity. Students would be very familiar with the word *name* by the time they finished 1) creating all of the sentences, 2) rereading them, 3) cutting them apart and rebuilding them, 4) being the sentence, and 5) creating a book. Most important, you would have a book for them to read repeatedly that included the keyword you were teaching.

Ensuring that students encounter the keywords in the books you are reading and the charts you are making together will help students begin to recognize the keywords in text. In addition to these text-based uses of the keywords, we teach the keywords explicitly, but not as isolated words.

Word Wall

At the core of the word reading intervention approach described in this chapter is a specific application of a word wall (see Cunningham, 2016, for a comprehensive description). The word wall is a large display to which words are added slowly and systematically during a school year or intervention period. Words added to the wall should be words the student is expected to read with automaticity and spell with accuracy at the end of the intervention period, typically a school year. For these two reasons, no more than five new words are added each week. Successful word walls are always available to students and easy to see. The words on them are practiced every day through a variety of activities, and students are expected to spell every word on the wall correctly in all of their writing.

Setting Up the Display   Creating a word wall requires some initial problem solving. The display must have each of the 26 letters of the alphabet as headers and room to add words printed large enough for the students to easily see from everywhere in the room. All of the letters and words must be on a single display, rather than separated on pages of a notebook, programmed on separate pages in a communication device, or otherwise presented in a dictionary-type alphabetical format. The displays in general education classrooms are quite literally posted on a classroom wall. Word walls created for individual students might be displayed on an open file folder, a trifold science display, or a large piece of chart paper. The key is to select a format that will accommodate approximately 90 words that will be added during the year, in a size the student can easily read.

A note about word walls and AAC: We used to recommend that word walls be programmed in students' AAC devices to facilitate communication about the words during word wall lessons. Our experience and a wise SLP, Cindy Kavanaugh, helped us understand that we negated the potential added benefits of our instruction in face-to-face communication when we did not expect students to gain access to word wall words from the logical arrangement of vocabulary already in their AAC systems. In other words, we want students either to spell the word wall words during instruction or use them by finding them in the places where they exist naturally in their AAC systems. In this way, they are more likely to use the words across reading, writing, and communication contexts and purposes.

Selecting Words for the Wall   For all beginning readers, the words that go on a word wall come from two primary sources: 1) the keyword list created by the teacher or team (e.g., *hat, sit, rain, make*) and 2) high-frequency words that appear across texts (e.g., *I, the, every*). A handful might be words that have great utility in the students' lives (e.g., name of school, favorite television show) and are likely to be encountered regularly in the texts the students read and write. Word wall words do not come from content-area vocabulary lists (e.g., *porpoise, myth, settlers*) because these words have only temporary utility during a particular unit of instruction. Such words, however, might be displayed on a bulletin board or thematic vocabulary wall during the unit. Word walls also do not include student names because these names rarely support reading of other words and rarely appear in written texts. In primary-grade classrooms, however, such words might be placed on a name wall to support students' attempts to write and communicate with one another. In general, the guideline to remember is that each word displayed on the word wall should be one that you expect the students to read with automaticity and spell with accuracy by the end of the school year.

Teaching the New Words   As five new words are added to the wall each week, teachers teach the word meanings or use and then use the words in complete sentences. Students are then guided in saying the words and clapping and chanting or cheering for the words while saying each letter (e.g., *b-i-n, bin*). Finally, each of the five new words is spelled, letter by letter, using a keyboard or other complete alphabet display if writing with a pencil is not possible. It is critical that students actually spell the words letter by letter at this point. If students merely select a whole word from a display or word bank, then a key to this powerful learning opportunity is lost.

Students who use AAC are guided in spelling each of the words by repeating each letter subvocally, or "in your head." While students are clapping and cheering for words, students with significant motor impairments might rock, tap their trays, vocalize, or participate in another clapping alternative. When it comes time to write the words, students with significant motor impairments use the alternate pencils or keyboards they use to write at other times.

New words added to the wall remain there for the duration of the school year. During the ensuing weeks, students are guided in practicing both new and previously learned words during brief lessons each day. The goal is not mastery of the words the first week they are posted. In fact, we do not wait for students to master the words before we add more. The goal is for students to learn to read and spell all of the words and learn how to use them to read and write other words over time. This means that teachers must plan and implement daily lessons that explicitly teach the words on the word wall. A simple Internet search will reveal thousands of word wall lessons. They can be as simple as calling words that students must first find on the wall, clap and chant or cheer for, and then write. Lessons can be as involved as a bingo variation in which students begin by filling their grid with words the teacher calls—which the students find on the wall, clap and chant or cheer for, and then write—and then cover the words as the teacher calls them in random order once again. Select activities that are engaging for your students and vary them from day to day. If the word wall begins to get repetitive, then conduct a new search and find some new lesson formats.

Reinforcing Learned Words   Finally, in addition to explicitly teaching the words on the wall each day, adults should refer students to the wall to support their reading and writing attempts across the day. For example, an adult directs students to use the word wall when they look for help reading an unfamiliar word encountered in a text. The conversation might go as follows:

Student: *[Looks up at the adult and vocalizes while gesturing for help and pointing to the word* might.*]*

Adult: You need help with that word?

Student: *[Indicates* yes *by looking up.]*

Adult: Okay. There is a word on your word wall that might help. Did you look?

Student: *[Indicates* yes *by looking up, then looks down for* no.*]*

Adult: You looked but couldn't find one. Okay, look under the letter *N.* Can you find the word?

Student: *[Looks at word wall and the words under the letter* N. *After a few seconds, the student sits upright and smiles.]*

Teacher: You found it? Say that word in your head. Now, look at this one. How is it the same, and how is it different? Is the beginning the same?

Student: *[Looks down to indicate* no.*]*

Teacher: You're right. The beginning is different. Say the sound in your head that this word begins with *[pointing to* might*]* and then use that word from your word wall to help you. Can you do it?

Student: *[Looks intently at the word, vocalizes some, and then looks up at the teacher, smiling.]*

The word wall is a powerful approach when combined with other strategies that support students in learning to use known words to read and spell unfamiliar words. The word wall also serves a primary role in helping students learn to read and spell high-frequency words when combined with daily opportunities for self-directed reading and writing.

Compare/Contrast Lessons

A compare/contrast activity is one way to help students learn to use their keywords to read and spell other words. A set of known keywords are displayed on index cards or the digital equivalent (e.g., *name, best, pink*). The adult reviews the words briefly with the students and then writes a sentence with one word underlined (e.g., *Is there something in that nest?*). The underlined word shares a spelling pattern with one of the known keywords. The adult reads the sentence aloud without saying the underlined word. The students are then asked to select the word that will "help them read the underlined word." Once all of the students have made a selection, the adult guides them in comparing and contrasting the selected word with the underlined word. The sequence for a compare/contrast lesson is shown in the textbox. (A downloadable and photocopiable version of this lesson plan is available with the downloadable materials for this book.)

A Compare/Contrast Lesson Plan

1. Introduce the keywords saying something such as, "We are going to work on using keywords to read other words that have the same spelling pattern. The words we'll use are *in* and *not*."

2. Write the keywords, saying each letter and letter sound.

3. Write one sentence that includes one word that shares a spelling pattern with one of the keywords. Underline the word that has the same spelling pattern as one of the keywords. You might say something such as, "Next, I am going to write a sentence with one word underlined. The underlined word will have the same spelling pattern as one of the two keywords: *in, not*. You tell or show me which keyword has the same spelling pattern as the underlined word. Then we'll use the keyword to help you read the underlined word."

4. Read the sentence, skipping the underlined word, "I can spin the dial."

5. Ask the students to indicate which keyword has the same spelling pattern as the underlined word.

6. Compare and contrast the keywords students select with the underlined word by pointing to and naming the letters in each and saying something such as, "Let's compare the spelling patterns. Are they the same?"

7. If they are the same, then tell the students, "Yes! They are the same." Name the letters that match while pointing to them. If the students selected the wrong keyword, then show and tell them why by comparing the letters.

Word Sorts

As students are learning to read and spell the keywords, we recommend alternating between the compare/contrast activity and word sorts. Many kinds of word sorts are used in classrooms around the United States. These word sort activities are focused on the common spelling patterns that appear in keywords. The goal is to help students learn their value and begin to recognize and use them when reading and writing. Teachers can begin with visual word sorts and progress to auditory and spelling word sorts.

Visual Word Sorts   If students are not familiar with sorting activities, then teachers might start with visual word sorts. A visual word sort involves selecting two keywords as column headers and then asking students to sort words to put them with the keyword that has the same spelling pattern. Begin the lesson by reviewing the keywords and clapping and chanting for them as is done during word wall activities. Then present the students with other words that have the same spelling patterns as the two keywords. Work with students to sort the new words into the column under the keyword with the matching spelling pattern. Move on to auditory sorts as soon as students understand the sorting concept.

Auditory Word Sorts Lesson Sequence   Auditory word sort lessons require students to go beyond visual matching. Auditory word sorts begin with the same introduction, clapping, chanting, and cheering for the keywords that will be the column headers. Then the teacher says a word that shares a spelling pattern with one of the keywords. The students must identify the matching keyword based on the sound of the word. Then the teacher shows the word so the students can compare and contrast to confirm the selection or make a new selection as appropriate. The general steps in an auditory word sort lesson are provided next. (A downloadable and photocopiable version of these steps is available with the downloadable materials for this book.)

1. Introduce the keywords. Say something such as, "We are going to sort some words. The words we'll use are *in, not.*"

2. Write each word while saying the name of each letter. Write the words on the top of two columns on the white board, chart paper, or other display.

3. Say a word that shares a spelling pattern with one of the keywords. Do not show students the new words. Say something such as, "Which one of your keywords ends like the word *shot?*"

4. After the students have indicated the keyword they think ends like the new word, show them the new word on an index card or write it on the white board, chart paper, or other display.

5. Guide students in comparing and contrasting the new word with the keyword they selected. Move the other word to compare with the correct keyword as needed.

If students really struggle to understand the task in these auditory sorts, then return to the visual word sort words until they understand the task, and then try the auditory sorts again.

Spelling Word Sorts   Start to incorporate spelling word sorts when students successfully identify the keyword that shares the spelling pattern when they hear the word (before they see it). The keywords are reviewed in this approach, and students clap and chant or cheer for them. Then the teacher says a new word that shares a spelling pattern with one of the keywords. The students are first asked to indicate which keyword ends the same as the new word. After they have indicated the correct keyword, the teacher asks the students to use the keyword to try to spell the new word. After the students attempt to spell the new word, the adult shows the correct spelling and guides the students in comparing and contrasting their attempts with the model. If there are errors, then the students identify the errors and fix them rather than starting over and copying the model. The sequence for a spelling-based word sort lesson is provided in the textbox. (A downloadable and photocopiable version of this lesson sequence is available with the downloadable materials for this book.)

Spelling-Based Word Sort Lesson Sequence

Spelling-based word sort lessons require students to use their keywords to try to spell other words that share the same spelling pattern. As in auditory word sort lessons, the teacher introduces the keywords and then says a word that shares a spelling pattern with one of the keywords. Students are asked to identify the keyword that has the same ending sounds or spelling pattern as the new word. After identifying the keyword, students are asked to use the keyword to spell the new word. Finally, the teacher shows students the new word and works with them to compare and contrast their effort with the model, fixing the errors as needed. The general steps in a spelling word sort lesson are as follows:

1. Introduce the keywords. Say something such as, "We are going to spell some new words using some keywords. The keywords we'll use are *not, day, best.*"

2. Write each word at the top of a column. As you write the words, say each letter.

3. Say a word that shares a spelling pattern with one of the key words. Say something such as, "I am going to say a word that has the same spelling pattern as one of these three words—*not, day,* or *best.* The first step is for you to tell me which keyword has the same ending as the word I say. The first word is *rot.*"

4. Ask students to identify the keyword that has the same ending sound or spelling pattern as the new word. Say something such as, "Which word—*not, day,* or *best*— has the same spelling pattern as *rot?* Show me."

5. Work with students to correct their selections as necessary by repeating the new word with each of the three keywords. Say something such as, "Which words end the same? *Rot-not; rot-day;* or *rot-best?*"

6. After the correct keyword is identified, ask students to use the selected keyword to spell the new word. Say something such as, "Now, use the word *not* to help you spell *rot.*"

7. Students attempt to spell *rot* using *not* as a model.

8. Show the word *rot* and compare and contrast it with the students' spelling efforts fixing errors as needed. Say something such as, "Let's see how you did. Here is the word *rot.* What part did you get right? Is there anything you need to fix?"

The three types of word sort activities (i.e., visual, auditory, spelling) serve different purposes. Generally, we only use visual sorts to help students understand that they are trying to put words in columns with keywords that have the same spelling patterns; however, students with hearing loss may need to stick with visual word sorts because they are unable to hear the similarities in the words as required for auditory word sorts. We try to move students who can hear on to spelling-based sorts as soon as they are successful with auditory sorts. Spelling sorts include the extra step of trying to spell each word using the keyword, which helps students in reading and writing. Students who use partner-assisted scanning with alternate pencils (i.e., an adult partner presents the alphabet one letter at a time, and the student indicates when the partner has presented a desired letter), however, may only do spelling-based sorts on rare occasions because of the time it takes them to select the letters required to spell each word in the lesson. Although you will have to decide which type of sort best addresses the needs of your students, we recommend doing word sorts of some kind on the days that you do not do compare/contrast activities.

Cross-Checking: A Self-Correction Strategy

As students learn to decode words using the letter-by-letter information they gain in Making Words and the spelling patterns they recognize from keywords, we teach them to cross check their decoding efforts with the meaning of those words in context. The lesson helps students learn to ask themselves, "Does that sound right?" and "Does that make sense?" Without explicit instruction in a strategy such as cross-checking, we find students do not always monitor themselves when reading.

A cross-checking lesson uses meaningful sentences. The teacher writes a sentence on the board, leaving a blank where the target word should be. The teacher reads the sentence to the class, skipping the missing word. The students are then asked to suggest words that would make sense in the blank. The teacher writes the words as students make suggestions. When students are out of suggestions, the teacher goes back through the list and rereads the sentence with each potential word. Together the group decides if each would make sense in the sentence. The teacher writes the onset (i.e., all of the consonants before the first vowel in the word). The teacher then leads the students in checking each of the words they suggested to see which would still be possible given the onset that has been revealed. The students then make additional suggestions ensuring that the new words start with the revealed onset. When the students are done, the teacher again reviews each word, reads it in the sentence, and works with the students to decide if the words make sense. When all of the words that fit both the meaning of the sentence and the onset have been determined, the teacher writes the rest of the word. The group then checks to see if they had the correct word in their list.

PROVIDING PRACTICE IN CONTEXT

This chapter presents an integrated, comprehensive approach for teaching decoding, word identification, and spelling skills to students with significant disabilities. As students are learning these skills, they need regular opportunities to apply them in two contexts—independent reading and writing.

Wide Reading to Build Automaticity

Students with significant disabilities often have extremely limited opportunities for independent reading in school (Kliewer & Biklen, 2001; Koppenhaver & Yoder, 1993; Mike, 1995; Ruppar, 2015); yet, independent reading is a critical part of any effort to teach students to read and spell words. Without extensive reading experiences, students cannot develop the level of word reading automaticity required for fluent reading with comprehension. Chapter 8 deals exclusively with self-directed reading. Those details do not have to be repeated here. It is worth noting, however, that going to all of the effort described in this chapter to teach students to read words is pointless if they are not given daily opportunities to use their word reading skills while reading texts they choose. Furthermore, we should encourage students to read texts that are not difficult relative to their abilities. The goal here is maximizing the number of words students read easily, with understanding, in connected text. The more they encounter books they can successfully read, the more likely they are to choose to read more on their own, and the more progress they will make in decoding and identifying the words they encounter.

Spelling Words in Meaningful Writing Contexts

In the same way that students must practice reading to become fluent in the application of their increasing decoding and word identification skills, they must write to gain fluency in the application of their spelling skills. Chapter 9 discusses writing instruction in great detail and points out that we do not teach spelling when students are composing texts because we do not want to interrupt their train of thought. Yet, we do teach mini-lessons to help them apply strategies they are being taught during word study, such as comparing and contrasting words they know with words they are trying to spell in a text (e.g., use *cat* to help spell *flat*) or using readily available resources such as the word wall while writing. In this way, we help students understand that they are learning to spell words so that they can communicate their ideas more effectively.

> Students need regular opportunities to apply decoding, word identification, and spelling skills by reading self-selected texts and by writing about self-selected topics.

A FINAL NOTE: USING OTHER PROGRAMS

Many commercially available reading programs teach parts of the integrated, comprehensive approach to decoding, word identification, and spelling instruction described in this chapter. If you use one of them, then it is important to consider what aspects of this comprehensive approach are addressed and whether the program leaves you adequate time to address the other skills and understandings students need to become effective word readers and spellers. Consider whether the program addresses each of the four processors in Adams' model (1990, 2004). Avoid programs that teach rules (e.g., *i* before *e* except after *c*) and a language (e.g., *diphthong, diagram*) about the language system. Students with significant disabilities struggle enough with language; it is important that we teach them in ways that do not require them

to learn meta-language (i.e., rules) about the language they are struggling to understand. Although some students successfully learn rules that help them decode words,
our experience is that these students have strong receptive language skills and can
listen with comprehension at or above their grade level. Students who struggle with
receptive language in general, or listening comprehension in particular, struggle to
learn to decode using approaches that require them to learn and apply rules. Even
when they are successful applying rules to read words in isolation, we find that the
cognitive resources required interfere with their ability to read connected text with
comprehension.

The combination of Making Words and the keyword approach described in
this chapter teaches students both letter-by-letter and analogy-based approaches
to decoding and spelling that help them learn to read and spell. Students with significant disabilities can become very successful, conventional readers and writers
when these approaches are taught in the combined way described in this chapter,
supported by the attention to high-frequency sight words on the word wall and then
promoted with daily opportunities to apply the skills in self-directed reading and
writing.

RECOMMENDED READINGS AND RESOURCES

Cunningham, P. M. (2011). *What really matters in spelling: Research-based strategies
and activities.* Boston, MA: Pearson.

Cunningham, P. M. (2016). *Phonics they use: Words for reading and spelling* (7th ed.).
Boston, MA: Pearson.

Iowa Department of Education and PBS Learning Media video of English language
arts strategies for students with significant cognitive disabilities (https://unctv
.pbslearningmedia.org/collection/reading) and video on crossing-checking uti-
lizing a cloze activity to promote decoding (https://unctv.pbslearningmedia.org
/resource/8be648a8-c900-48dd-8ed3-e488ce9ea5fd/delit_comclip24_utilizing
-a-cloze-activity-to-promote-decoding)

SECTION IV

Implementation

CHAPTER 11

Using Assistive Technology Effectively to Support Literacy

AT includes devices and services as noted in the Individuals with Disabilities Education Improvement Act (IDEA) of 2004 (PL 108-446). An AT device includes "any item, piece of equipment, or product system, whether acquired commercially off the shelf, modified, or customized, that is used to increase, maintain, or improve functional capabilities of individuals with disabilities." AT services "directly assist a child with a disability in the selection, acquisition, or use of an assistive technology device" (§300.5). Appropriate and ongoing provision of AT services focused on the implementation of carefully selected AT devices can minimize the numerous challenges faced by students with significant disabilities as they attempt to learn and use literacy across life domains. Although students with significant disabilities may use AT across life domains to support independence and functioning (e.g., wheelchairs for mobility, specialized feeding equipment), AT in this chapter focuses specifically on AT devices that support access to information, communication, and learning.

RESEARCH BRIEF: ASSISTIVE TECHNOLOGY

AT was initially guaranteed for Americans with disabilities in the Technology-Related Assistance for Individuals with Disabilities Act of 1988 (PL 100-407) (the Tech Act). The Tech Act made the distinction between AT devices and AT services, and these definitions appeared in the Individuals with Disabilities Act (IDEA) of 1990 (PL 101-476) and IDEA 2004 with little change. This distinction between AT devices and services is important for all students with disabilities as it was intended to ensure that students have access to the necessary devices as well as the supports they require to learn and use those devices. The combination is especially important for students with significant disabilities who typically require explicit instruction to learn to use AT devices once they are made available.

Although AT has been guaranteed for students with disabilities for nearly three decades in the United States, the use of AT to support students with significant disabilities is not well understood (Erickson, Hatch, & Clendon, 2010). It is clear, however, that students with significant cognitive disabilities have limited access to AT, despite the aforementioned guarantee (Bouck & Flanagan, 2016; Erickson & Geist, 2016). A meta-analysis of the research regarding the use of AT to support communication and learning among young children with disabilities suggests that it leads to strong, positive outcomes that increase as the severity of disability increases (Dunst, Trivette, Hamby, & Simkus, 2013), but similar information is not available with respect to school-age children with significant disabilities. Although the research is limited in scope, it does provide evidence for the assertion that many students with significant disabilities will fail to gain access to information and successfully engage as learners without appropriate AT devices and services.

Rose and Meyer (2002) were the first to make the distinction between AT to support access to information and AT to support access to learning. They did so to help educators understand that sometimes maximizing access to information undermines learning. For example, if the student's goal is to learn to read with comprehension, then providing digitized text that a computer reads to the student is counterproductive; listening to the text bypasses the need to learn to read with comprehension. AT can circumvent challenges imposed by a variety of disabilities; however, access to content without instruction focused on the specific needs of the student is inadequate (Boone & Higgins, 2007).

In every case, decisions regarding AT must match the instructional goal or context and the needs of the individual user. As such, students may use different AT in different contexts for different purposes. For example, students with significant disabilities may use picture symbols to support their communication across the day, but those same symbols will do little to support them in learning to decode words or understand text. The use of symbol-supported text has become a widespread solution for students with significant disabilities since the early 2000s; yet, it may actually impede a student's ability to learn to read (Erickson et al., 2010).

Symbol-supported text involves pairing or replacing individual words in text with picture symbols (Downing, 2005). Software programs such as PixWriter (Slater Software, 2008) and Writing With Symbols 2000 (Widgit Software, 2002) automatically or easily produce text that has symbols paired with words. This practice is intended to provide access to text that a student could not otherwise read, but evidence suggests that the presence of the picture symbols makes it more difficult for the student to learn to read and spell words (Erickson et al., 2010; Pufpaff, Blischak, & Lloyd, 2000; Rose & Furr, 1984; Saunder & Solman, 1984).

For multiple reasons, pairing symbols with words may make it more difficult for students to learn to read words. For example, it is possible that the symbols are confusing, especially when they represent abstract concepts, have multiple meanings, or serve more than one grammatical function (Erickson et al., 2010). This is particularly true when words are not easily represented by symbols, as is the case with verbs such as *do* or *is*. Because these words do not have picture referents, they must be represented by abstract, arbitrary symbols (see Figure 11.1). Although the

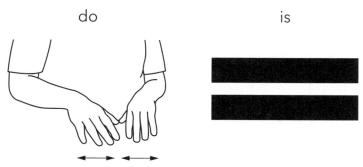

Figure 11.1. Boardmaker picture communication symbols for the verbs *do* and *is* (Mayer-Johnson, 2006).

orthographic (print) representation of these words is also abstract, printed words appear much more frequently and are more broadly understood than abstract picture symbols. As a result, students learning to read the words rather than recognize the abstract picture symbols have more opportunities to encounter the words and interact with others who understand them.

Symbols may also make learning to read more challenging when they represent multiple-meaning words such as *can* or *turn*. These words have consistent spellings across their multiple meanings, and their spellings do not conjure a particular visual image that is more closely related to one meaning than another. In contrast, symbols representing these words offer visual representations of a single meaning. For example, the word *can* has a single spelling for its use as a noun and verb and would require numerous symbols to represent each of the different meanings. Yet, just the noun form of the word requires numerous representations to capture (e.g., a *can* of soda, a trash *can*). Although the option to select specific symbols for each use exists with today's software, words such as *can* and *turn* would require students to learn several different symbolic representations with varying degrees of abstractness. The danger in using an inappropriate symbolic representation is that the meaning of the text is altered as a result of the meaning conveyed by the symbol.

Beyond potentially introducing confusion, pairing symbols with words makes it more difficult for students to learn to read the words. Investigations of the impact of symbols and pictures on the development of word identification began with children of all ages without disabilities more than five decades ago. In the earliest of these studies (Samuels, 1967), first-grade students did well during training when pictures were paired with words, but the advantage of pictures disappeared when the students were asked to read the words without the pictures. The pictures made these students appear to be learning more successfully during instruction, but in the end, they were more successful reading the words they learned without the benefit of pictures. In a follow-up study, other first-grade students receiving reading instruction that included pictures paired with words also learned more slowly than did peers who never had pictures.

In yet another study (Singer, Samuels, & Spiroff, 1973–1974), more than 160 first- and second-grade students were randomly assigned to one of four intervention groups: picture + word; no picture + word; picture + sentence; and no picture + sentence. All of the students received instruction until they could identify the words without pictures present. In the word-only conditions (no picture + word; no picture + sentence), students had more correct responses during the training and learned words in fewer trials than they did in the conditions that included pictures. These findings later were replicated in kindergarten nonreaders without disabilities (Blischak & McDaniel, 1995).

Research involving children and adults with intellectual disabilities has supported the findings of these studies involving students without disabilities in the primary grades. For example, Singh and Solman (1990) investigated the impact of picture/word pairs on the word reading skills of eight students with intellectual disabilities. All of the students read the fewest number of words correctly when those words were learned paired with pictures. Similarly, the adults with intellectual disabilities in Pufpaff et al. (2000) learned to read printed words more easily than they learned to read words paired with pictures or words printed in enhanced ways with the picture embedded in the printed word.

Symbols are an important part of the educational program of most students with significant disabilities. Many students require them to support face-to-face communication, and some find they support transitions and schedules. Like all AT, symbols have their place, however, and the instructional goals and contexts must be considered before using them. Given the evidence that suggests pairing symbols with words makes it more difficult to learn to read the words, educators must be very clear regarding their goals when they choose to produce symbol-supported text and should avoid symbol-supported text when the goals are related to reading.

Symbol-supported text provides one specific example of the kind of decisions teachers and teams must make when selecting AT to support their students. Symbols themselves are examples of AT supports that are highly effective in some contexts (e.g., communication) and not in others (e.g., learning to read), and they serve to remind teachers and teams that AT decisions are not universal and must be considered on a day-by-day basis. The following example illustrates what this looks like in practice.

> Decisions about AT must match the instructional goal or context and the user's needs. Because evidence suggests that pairing symbols with words makes it more difficult to learn to read the words, educators should avoid symbol-supported text for reading-related instructional goals.

MAKING THOUGHTFUL TEAM DECISIONS ABOUT ASSISTIVE TECHNOLOGY

Considering the instructional goals and contexts, as well as the needs of the learner, is critical to successful implementation of AT to support literacy learning and use. For Tess, it requires her team to map out the entire school day and identify when different forms of AT will best support her in gaining access to content and learning to read and write. Currently, Tess is 12 years old and in seventh grade, but Tess could be any age and her team would have to work in the same way they do now to successfully plan for and implement AT.

Tess uses a power chair that she drives using her head, with a special set of sensors called a head array. *She uses a dynamic display augmentative communication device that she accesses using eye gaze, but she also uses two switches with scanning when she is fatigued. At other times, she uses her eyes to point to words, symbols, and objects, presented in groups of four on a Plexiglas eye-gaze frame, or she makes selections using partner-assisted scanning. Tess writes using the alphabet display and word prediction available in her communication device, and she uses the eye-gaze interface to access the Internet and other software on the computer. She also uses the alphabet to communicate whenever she is out of her wheelchair and unable to use her communication device. In these cases, familiar communication partners ask Tess, "First half, second half?" meaning the letters a to m, and the letters n to z. Tess looks up to say "yes" to the desired half. Then the partner asks one more division (i.e., "a to f, g to m?") before naming the individual letters within the set. Each of these forms of AT has a role at different times in Tess's day.*

Tess's team meets regularly to map out her AT device and service needs. They look carefully at the demands of the instructional environment and the tasks Tess must complete across each day. They also carefully consider the AT devices Tess has available to her and the devices they may eventually need to acquire to support her. For example, each time Tess is asked to write, the team has a plan in place to match the AT device with the demands of the task. Tess uses her communication device when she is planning or generating ideas. She uses the keyboard and word prediction in her communication device when she is composing or revising. She also uses her communication device to communicate ideas, ask questions, and interact with the peers and adults throughout the writing process.

When tasks require reading, the team uses its knowledge of Tess's reading and listening comprehension skills to guide decisions regarding the use of AT. Tess can listen with comprehension much more effectively than she can read with comprehension, but both skills are well below grade level. The team works to provide her with daily access to materials she can read in order to build her independent reading comprehension skills. They also provide her with digitized text that she accesses by listening with the text reader on a laptop. Finally, they identify the materials that she cannot understand through reading or listening, and they teach her that content separately.

ASSISTIVE TECHNOLOGY TO SUPPORT LITERACY

Although AT in the broader context includes AT to support mobility and community access, most AT intended to support learning in school settings is classified into three categories—communication, productivity, and participation. It is sometimes difficult to classify individual solutions because carefully selected AT devices combined with effective services tend to result in benefits across two or more categories. For example, technologies that effectively support communication or increase productivity have clear potential to support participation in the classroom and beyond. Several types of AT support literacy learning and use because they address communication, productivity, and/or access to instructional materials. This section describes a few.

Assistive Technology to Support Communication

Communication development is a goal of emergent literacy instruction and contributes to increased success in conventional literacy. Given that fact, AT to support communication is especially important. AT to support communication is more commonly called *aided AAC* and includes a full range of solutions, including

- Symbols that have been printed on paper and laminated

- Software and apps on commercial technologies such as mobile phones and tablets

- Dedicated devices built specifically to support communication

Robust Communication Solutions   In general, the aim of any aided AAC solution is to support communication across partners, contexts, and purposes. Approaches that are only understood by one or two partners (e.g., idiosyncratic gestures), work only in specific contexts (e.g., activity- or text-specific communication symbols), or focus on teaching a single communication purpose (e.g., requesting) are insufficient to support the diverse and robust communication required during literacy learning.

Instead of these restrictive approaches, we must provide students with access to well-organized AAC solutions they can use across contexts, including many of the commercially available solutions available on dedicated communication devices or apps that work on tablets. Although they differ in their approach to organizing and representing the vocabulary, there are myriad robust solutions to AAC that students can learn to use while they are learning to read and write.

Core Vocabulary   Almost all robust AAC solutions offer students access to a set of words known as *core vocabulary words*. These words are the conceptual words used most frequently in oral and written English (Banajee et al., 2003; Dennis et al., 2013). Core vocabulary words are mostly pronouns, verbs, prepositions, and adjectives. Most important, very few are nouns. The biggest advantage of core words is that they can be used to communicate for a broad range of purposes, from basic requesting of desired items to building social relationships, sharing opinions, and exchanging information (Brady et al., 2016; Snodgrass, Stoner, & Angell, 2013; Van Tatenhove, 2009). This is important in literacy because students need flexible ways to communicate while learning to read and write. They need to be able to comment, ask questions, share opinions, express understanding, and engage in varied interactions with teachers and peers. These communication purposes can all be accomplished using core vocabulary words.

Providing Access to Augmentative and Alternative Communication   In supporting students with significant disabilities in communicating with AAC, the standard is to work with an AAC specialist or team to conduct a comprehensive assessment. This assessment is used to determine the best system for the student to use today and continue learning over time to meet even more needs tomorrow. When education teams, including families, have access to AAC specialists and teams, we recommend that they follow this path. It will result in a carefully selected solution that best meets the student's current and future needs.

Unfortunately, many students with significant disabilities in U.S. public schools do not have access to these specialists and teams. Others find themselves on waiting lists for months. Still others have been evaluated by these teams, but the resulting recommendation has been to work on aspects of AAC that are insufficient to support communication and interaction during literacy learning. Whatever the cause, there are at least 165,000 students with significant disabilities in U.S. public schools who cannot meet their face-to-face communication needs using speech, signs, or aided AAC (e.g., picture symbols on a device with speech output), and this is preventing them from making progress in many domains, including literacy (Erickson & Geist, 2016; National Center for Educational Statistics, 2017).

The Universal Core Vocabulary   The Center for Literacy and Disability Studies has been working to address this enormous need by creating a universal approach to AAC. Education teams and families can use this approach as a starting place to support robust communication for students who do not already have robust communication solutions. An example of the core vocabulary board we use as a starting place is shown in Figure 11.2.

We teach students to use core vocabulary to communicate by pointing to graphic symbols that represent words we are saying to students (Sennott, Light, & McNaughton, 2016). This pointing while talking is called *augmented input*. While we

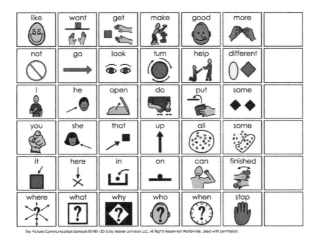

Figure 11.2. The Universal Core vocabulary from Project Core (From The Picture Communication Symbols © 1981-2015 by Mayer-Johnson, LLC. All Rights Reserved Worldwide. Used with permission.)

cannot point to a symbol that represents every word we say, pointing to symbols that represent at least some of our spoken words provides AAC users with some of the modeling that children without disabilities get when they hear others talking. In the context of literacy instruction, we use the core vocabulary to talk with students as we are engaged in activities, and we encourage their comments, questions, and interactions. We try to avoid using the core vocabulary or any form of AAC for the sole purposes of asking students to respond to our questions or show us what they know. Visit http://project-core.com to download the Universal Core vocabulary. The modules, materials, and supports available at this site can also help teachers and families learn more about supporting students with significant disabilities who do not have a flexible means of communicating across partners, purposes, and environments.

> To support the communication required for literacy learning, students need AAC solutions that they can use across multiple contexts, with multiple communication partners, and for a variety of purposes.

Assistive Technology to Support Access to Materials and Productivity

Teachers and students can use AT in several ways to support productivity in reading and writing tasks. For example, students whose disabilities include physical impairments need tools to allow them to gain independent access to books and turn pages as effortlessly as possible. When writing, they also need tools that minimize the demands of selecting letters and spelling words. Students whose disabilities include visual impairments need access to features such as large print, contrast, and, if the visual impairments are significant, text that is read aloud and/or presented in braille. Although AT is often seen as a way to bypass the demands of reading and writing for students with disabilities, we see AT as a means of supporting productivity so that students can learn to read and write better.

Assistive Technology to Support Access to Reading   It is now possible for students with significant disabilities to use technology to gain access to anything they are asked to read. For example, Bookshare (http://bookshare.org) offers access to hundreds of thousands of books in digitized formats to individuals with significant learning, visual, and/or physical disabilities. Sites such as Tar Heel Reader (http://tarheelreader.org) offer tens of thousands of books for emergent and beginning readers of all ages. If the text is not already available in a digitized form, then apps on smart phones and tablets can now capture and convert any text. All of these texts can be read using a variety of online and offline tools that offer switch access, text highlighting, read-aloud, and options for changing font size, color, and contrast.

All of this access to digitized text, together with an increasing number of reading tools, enables students with significant disabilities to listen to and/or read a wide range of text, and this is advantageous. Yet, when using these tools, we still must consider the goal of our instruction and the student's individual profile. For example, if our goal is to help students improve their reading fluency and comprehension, then we must give them text that they can read successfully—listening to text read aloud will not improve their ability to read text independently with fluency and comprehension. Furthermore, we cannot assume that listening to a text makes it more accessible. In our work with students with a range of significant disabilities, we repeatedly find that their ability to listen with comprehension is much lower than their teams think. They can understand anything we explain to them, but when listening to extended text, they struggle to comprehend it. Listening to a text read aloud may be the best solution when the goal of our instruction is to support students in gaining access to information, but teams must first determine the text level at which students can listen and understand (Erickson, 2013). See Chapter 7 for more information.

Assistive Technology to Support Writing   Many students with significant disabilities need access to AT to support writing because the act of writing with a pen or pencil is too physically demanding. For some, the problem is solved with a standard keyboard and word processing software. For others, additional supports are needed. Identifying one or more ways that students can produce or gain access to letters of the alphabet is the first step in identifying AT to support writing. When students cannot use standard pens, pencils, and keyboards, we often start with low-tech alternate pencils that students use with partners. For example, a common solution is a print alphabet flip chart (see Figure 11.3), which allows the partner to point to and say each letter name, one at a time. The student with significant disabilities can use two switches, gestures, or other means to indicate, "go to the next one" and "write that one for me." Alternatively, the partner can present each letter and the student simply indicates, "write that one for me" using a single switch, gesture, or other means. The letters on this flip chart are in alphabetical order with a vowel in the first position in each set of letters (*a–d; e–h; i–m; o–t; u–z*). We present each letter, one at a time, when we first use the chart. We present the letters group by group as students get more skilled, and we move to letter by letter after the student selects the group. This and many other alternate pencils are available for free download from a variety of places, including the web site of the Center for Literacy and Disability Studies (http://med.unc.edu/ahs/clds/resources).

Figure 11.3.   Print alphabet flip chart.

Students who have the skills to interact directly with the computer can take advantage of software that may support their productivity in writing. For example, text-to-speech feedback in word processing software will provide students with letter-by-letter, word-by-word, or text-level speech feedback while they write. Word prediction software is another solution that is frequently supportive.

Word prediction software uses word frequency and grammar rules (and more recently, information about location provided by GPS technology) to produce a list of word choices as the student begins to type a word; the software revises the list as new letters are added, until the desired word is predicted. Word suggestions can appear before or after the student types the first letter. Some word prediction programs offer phonetic spelling supports, which allow students to represent the sounds they hear in words and then identify the correct spelling of the word from the list produced by the software. Word prediction supports students with motor impairments by reducing the number of letters they must type to spell an entire word. Although the specific features in each word prediction solution vary, they generally improve spelling accuracy, support syntax (grammar), which can ultimately improve writing quality. More important, word prediction helps at least some students write better even when they are asked to write without it (see, e.g., Anson et al., 2006).

We are often asked about the use of picture or word banks as alternatives to word prediction for students with significant disabilities. These supports might help students demonstrate understanding in content area instruction, but we do not recommend them as a means of supporting productivity in writing. Word and picture banks dramatically restrict opportunities for students to compose text that reflects their own thoughts and ideas. The product may look superior when students select words or pictures from a bank, but the process of creating it neither helps students learn to generate their own ideas for writing nor resembles the process of composing text.

The use of AAC devices to compose text is related to the use of word and picture banks. It is true that most highly literate AAC users compose text using a combination of spelling with word prediction and the symbols that are in their AAC system (e.g., Graham & Hill, 2007). Most important, these literate individuals can spell and use word prediction to compose text, but they use symbols to increase their productivity or communication rate. While students are learning to read and write, we encourage teams to focus on writing with spelling and word prediction instead of symbols. Our goal is to help students understand that they can use spelling to say whatever they want to say, whenever they want to say it, and to whomever they want to say it. Students who begin writing using the symbols in their device often struggle to make the transition to writing using a combination of spelling, word prediction, and symbols. As a result, they can produce a wide variety of texts, but those texts are limited by the vocabulary that someone else programmed into their communication device. We are willing to trade off early success in using symbols to create easily read products for lifelong literacy that allows students unrestricted access to their own ideas through spelling.

> The product may look superior when students select words or pictures from a bank, but the process of creating it neither helps students learn to generate their own ideas for writing nor resembles the process of composing text.

GETTING ASSISTIVE TECHNOLOGY UP AND RUNNING

Making decisions about AT devices and services requires at least some knowledge of what is available. Rapid changes in technology make it impossible to provide an exhaustive list of AT devices students with significant disabilities may require or benefit from when learning to read and write. Certain categories of technologies, however, are helpful to keep in mind. In the field of AT, these categories are often described as communication, productivity, and/or access to instructional materials. Some students with significant disabilities require AT in all three. For example, a recent survey of more than 38,000 students with significant cognitive disabilities suggests that nearly 40% would benefit from AT to augment the speech they have or as an alternative to the lack of speech (Erickson & Geist, 2016). The same survey also revealed that 45% of students with significant disabilities need AT devices or other supports to productively use computers (DeBarthe & Erickson, 2014). Almost all students with significant disabilities will require AT at some point to support their participation across academic and social contexts.

The SETT Framework

The SETT framework is one evidence-based approach to making informed decisions regarding AT devices and services (Zabala, 2005). SETT is an acronym for **S**tudent, **E**nvironments, **T**asks, and **T**ools that describes a framework used to organize and direct AT decision making. The SETT framework goes beyond matching the student's needs and abilities with the technology features to determining how well the technology matches the demands of the environment and the goals of the task. This approach is consistent with the view expressed throughout this chapter that decisions regarding AT must take into account the goals of each instructional activity if the technology is going to effectively support access to information and/or learning.

The Student   The SETT framework begins with the student. Teams, including parents and professionals, consider the student's specific profile. Two starting questions teams might ask are 1) What does the student need to do that he or she cannot do right now? 2) What abilities and disabilities are getting in the way? In the case of literacy learning, these questions should be asked in the context of the literacy learning opportunities and everyday interactions with print that promote literacy, language, and communication development for all students.

The Environment   The team also considers the environment as they begin to generate responses to these questions. Considering the demands and characteristics of the environment will affect decisions about AT, as well as the likelihood that the AT will be used effectively rather than abandoned. Some of the questions to ask include

- How many other students are in the environment with the target student?

- How much support is available for the student and the AT?

- What materials are the other students using?

- What are the attitudes and expectations of the adults and others in the environment regarding the student and AT?

The Task   Considering the demands of the specific tasks is also critical when making decisions regarding AT. As described earlier in this chapter, understanding whether a task is intended to help students communicate or learn to read would dramatically affect our decisions regarding the use of symbols. Likewise, if the task requires students to spell in order to demonstrate understandings of letter–sound relationships, as opposed to requiring students to write effectively for an external audience, then we would make a different decision about the use of supports such as word prediction.

The Tools   After considering the student, environment, and task, teams can then turn their attention to the available technologies or tools. People often want to start by thinking about the technology because they believe that the right technology will solve all kinds of problems. Unfortunately, the right technology cannot be determined without also considering the student, environment, and task. What might be the right technology for one student in one environment to complete certain types of tasks may fail miserably for the same student in other environments or with other tasks.

Considering the training, strategies, and supports that adults will require to support student use of tools is an important part of this final SETT stage. The tools may include technologies or specific services the student needs or other tools, training, strategies, or services that the team or teacher needs. All too often, this is forgotten, and an evaluation team recommends tools that are theoretically great solutions for the student but the value is not realized. This occurs because the adults who interact with the student each day do not have the required tools, training, strategies, and/or services to support the student's learning and use of the tool.

The SETT framework is described in far greater detail in a variety of published sources. The most accessible is the web site of Joy Zabala, the creator of the SETT framework (http://joyzabala.com).

Red Yellow Green

Red Yellow Green is one approach we use to support day-to-day implementation of AT decisions. The approach uses a stoplight analogy to help teams think about the relative demands of different aspects of the school day and the relative supportiveness of different AT devices. Some aspects of the school day or devices are classified as green because they have low demands or are highly supportive. Others are yellow because they present moderate demands or offer moderate levels of support. Still others are red because they are very demanding. This Red Yellow Green approach has been used most successfully to make sure that students with significant disabilities are not asked to work on academic tasks classified as red while using AT that is also classified as red.

To use this approach, start by listing all mobility or positioning AT the student must use throughout the day. (Enlist the support of occupational and physical therapists who serve the student.) This is easy for students without physical disabilities. The list might include things such as the chair at the table, the floor, the chair at a desk, and the bench at the lunch table. The list will be much longer for students with physical disabilities and include items such as wheelchair with all supports firmly in place, standing frame, corner chair for the floor, bean bag, and other adaptive seating. After the list is complete, each is classified as red, yellow, or green depending on the level of physical effort that is required to maintain attention, interact, and communicate while using the mobility or positioning AT. For example, the standing frame might be classified as red because it is physically taxing, whereas the wheelchair with all straps and belts firmly in place might be classified as green because of the support it offers.

Next, if the student uses any forms of AT to support communication, create a list of those technologies and approaches. This list might include gestures, yes/no, a laminated core vocabulary display, and/or a communication device with voice output. Once the list is created, each means of communication is categorized as red, yellow, or green based on the student's ability to use it to successfully communicate with others. For example, yes/no may be classified as green if the student can easily indicate yes and no. In contrast, the communication device with voice output might be classified as red if the student has to exert great effort or is just learning to use it to communicate effectively.

Finally, list the academic tasks across the day and classify them as red, yellow, or green based on the individual student. The classification of academic tasks may change daily or weekly as students learn and progress (as opposed to mobility and positioning AT and communication options, whose classification changes less frequently). For this reason, teachers often get into the habit of marking academic tasks as red, yellow, or green while they are writing their lesson plans. These decisions about red, yellow, or green will change as students gain skills and as demands change over time. For example, when planning for an emergent writer who is just learning to use an alternate pencil (see Chapter 5), the teacher might indicate that independent writing is a red academic task. With time and experience, it may become yellow or green for the same student. Similarly, when planning for a student who struggles to learn and remember letters, sounds, and words, the teacher may indicate that working with words (see Chapter 10) is a red activity; it may become yellow or green as the student learns the routines and strategies.

Although this chapter describes only three domains—physical position, communication means, and academic tasks—you could add others. For example, many

Communication	Positions	Academic
G BIGmack	**G** Wheelchair	**G** Morning meeting
G Four-location eye gaze	**Y** Bolster seat	**Y** Shared reading
G Two-hand choices	**R** Prone stander	**G** Shared writing
G Yes/no	**R** Side lying frame	**G** Independent reading
Y Communication notebook with partner assisted scanning	**R** Big red ball	**R** Independent writing
R Scanning on communication device	**Y** Rifton chair	**R** Math activity
		G Science experiment

Figure 11.4. Katie's Red Yellow Green chart.

students with significant disabilities need sensory breaks or input during the day. The options could be rated as red, yellow, or green based on their ability to help the student get regulated or otherwise prepared for learning. Whether you have two, three, four, or more domains marked, the team looks across the set and creates a plan for the day to ensure students are not faced with two red options at any one time. A red position cannot be paired with a red academic task. A red means of communication cannot be learned while simultaneously working on a red academic task or using positioning AT classified as red. Conversely, a student can work on building balance and strength in a demanding (red) physical position while engaged in green academic tasks. A student can also work on a demanding, new communication device while seated in a green position and working on a green or yellow academic task. Figure 11.4 shows what Katie's planning chart looked like after her team engaged in this process.

A FINAL NOTE: MAKING GOOD DECISIONS ABOUT ASSISTIVE TECHNOLOGY

Making decisions about AT use requires knowledge of the student, the environment, the task (including learning goals associated with it), and available technology. Teams must work together on a regular basis to ensure that they are using technology to provide students with access to information and learning. Teams must also remember that identifying the appropriate AT device is just one step in a process that almost always involves AT services to ensure that the student can use the device and it is maintained in good working order.

RECOMMENDED READINGS AND RESOURCES

The following readings and resources will deepen readers' understanding of how to use AT effectively in literacy instruction for students with significant disabilities.

Dell, A. G., Newton, D., & Petroff, J. G. (2011). *Assistive technology in the classroom: Enhancing the school experiences of students with disabilities* (2nd ed.). Boston, MA: Pearson/Merrill/Prentice Hall.

Dynamic Learning Maps Professional Development web site (http://dlmpd.com). See the following module: Writing With Alternate Pencils.

Robinson, A. (2014) *Using the SETT framework.* Video presented by the Oklahoma ABLE Tech organization. Available at https://youtube.com/watch?v=Dw5cfo-iCXc

Zabala, J. S. (n.d.). *Get SETT for successful inclusion and transition.* Available at http://ldonline.org/article/6399

CHAPTER 12

Organizing and Delivering Effective Instruction

Most students with significant disabilities present with complex needs that are best supported through the thoughtful work of an interprofessional team (Erickson, 2017). Such a team brings together professionals from different backgrounds who work with students and caregivers to deliver the highest quality of intervention (World Health Organization, 2010). Each team member plays an important role when it comes to delivering the kind of comprehensive literacy instruction featured in this book. For example, families bring critical knowledge of students' interests and experiences, SLPs bring expertise in the development of oral language, educators bring expertise in the development of reading and writing skills, and occupational therapists and AT specialists bring expertise in access to the tools required for literacy (see Chapter 11). The students themselves play an active role in choosing books to read, topics for writing, and ideas to share with others. Together, every member of the team collaborates in delivering high-quality literacy intervention, which increases the likelihood that students with significant disabilities will learn to read and write in ways that support and enrich their participation and success in school and beyond.

Yet, if you are just one teacher, therapist, or caregiver without access to a supportive, interprofessional team, do not be afraid to just get started. What we have learned through the years is that students with significant disabilities benefit when the adults in their lives are willing to jump in. One of the first studies published by the team at the Center for Literacy and Disability Studies (then known as the Carolina Literacy Center) involved a series of interviews of literate adults with significant disabilities (Koppenhaver, Evans, & Yoder, 1991). Eighteen of the 22 adults in that study reported that their mothers were very important in helping them learn to read and write. Nineteen recalled a single teacher who was very important in helping them learn to read and write. Most participants pointed to a single person who made the difference. They had clear memories of the person who single handedly put them on the path to literacy learning success. Be that person! Be the one teacher, therapist, mom, dad, aunt, uncle, grandmother, grandfather, brother, sister, peer, or other believer who puts the students in your life on the path to learning to read and write—or learning to read and write better.

GETTING STARTED: CREATING A COMPREHENSIVE LITERACY PROGRAM

We encourage you to create the most comprehensive program you can using the strategies described in this book. Comprehensive instruction delivered imperfectly is better than perfect instruction in just one area, and it is certainly better than no instruction at all.

When we began providing classroom- and school-based professional development and consulting support, we always started with one of the many components of comprehensive instruction and added components as teachers grew comfortable with those already introduced. Unfortunately, there are not enough consultants in the world with expertise in literacy, AT, AAC, and significant disabilities to support everyone through the component-by-

> Comprehensive instruction delivered imperfectly is better than perfect instruction in just one area, and it is certainly better than no instruction at all.

component implementation of comprehensive literacy instruction. If you have the luxury of access to someone with that expertise, then take advantage of it and methodically work through each component until you are comfortable. Otherwise, we encourage you to jump in. Many of the students we have met through the years struggle with reading and writing because they have not had access to comprehensive instruction that simultaneously builds new skills while ensuring they have time to apply those skills in their independent reading and writing. If you start with just one component, then your students may not benefit, and you may be tempted to quit before they have a chance to start down the literacy learning path.

Delivering Comprehensive Literacy Instruction

As you prepare to provide comprehensive literacy instruction with an individual student or group, the first step is determining whether the students are most likely to benefit from comprehensive emergent or conventional literacy instruction. As described in previous chapters, start this process by answering four simple questions (Erickson, Koppenhaver, & Cunningham, 2017):

1. Does the student identify most of the letters of the alphabet, most of the time?

2. Is the student interested and engaged during shared reading?

3. Does the student have a means of communication and interaction?

4. Does the student understand that print has meaning?

If you answered "no" to one or more questions, then the student is most likely to benefit from comprehensive emergent literacy instruction. If you responded "yes" to all four questions, then the student is likely to benefit from comprehensive conventional literacy instruction. Figure 12.1 illustrates the four questions and the combination of interventions that would result if a student required comprehensive emergent or conventional literacy instruction.

Planning for a Group   Deciding whether you should provide emergent literacy instruction only, conventional instruction only, or a combination is the next step when planning instruction for a group of students. If all of the students have at least one "no" for the questions in Figure 12.1, then start with the emergent interventions. If you responded "yes" to all of the questions for all students, then start with the conventional interventions. If you have a mix of some students—some with all "yes" responses and some with one or more "no" responses—then we recommend combining the interventions in the way described next. We suggest this because it is not possible (or even desirable)

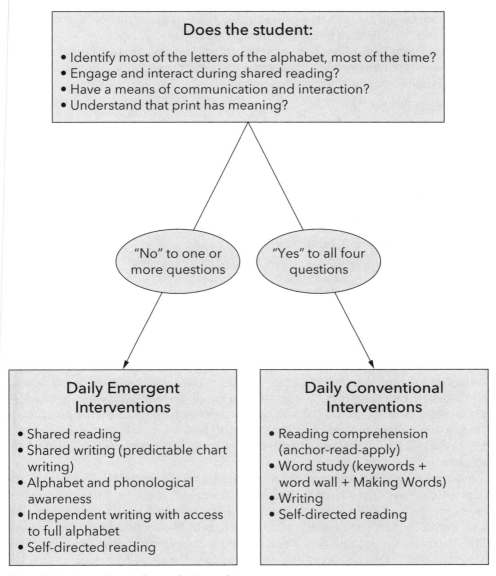

Figure 12.1. Comprehensive literacy decision making.

to run two completely separate literacy programs in one classroom. Instruction delivered to students in small groups yields great benefits (Connor, Morrison, & Slominsky, 2006; Elbaum, Vaughn, Hughes, & Moody, 1999; Wasik, 2008), and we want to maximize the amount of time students spend interacting with the teacher. Each division of the instructional time to create more individualized solutions reduces that student–teacher interaction time. For example, teachers were teaching literacy for 2 hours each day in one middle school where we did some work; unfortunately, each student received no more than 15 minutes of literacy instruction. The teachers had so individualized the instruction that they worked with only one or two students at a time. Students who were not with the teachers were completing structured tasks independently so as not to interrupt the teacher. Our goal is to shift the balance so that each student gets 90–120 minutes of focused literacy instruction each day.

We combine approaches to accomplish this in classrooms where some students require emergent literacy instruction and some require conventional literacy instruction. This involves doing the following each day:

- Shared reading (Chapter 4)

- Reading comprehension (Chapter 7)

- Decoding, spelling, and word identification (Chapter 10) with an emphasis on alphabet and phonological awareness (Chapter 3)

- Predictable chart writing (Chapter 5)

- Self-directed reading (Chapters 4 and 8)

- Independent writing (Chapters 5 and 9)

- Writing instruction (Chapter 9)

Details about these instructional components are provided next.

Shared Reading With a Mixed Group   Include all students in shared reading when teaching mixed groups. The students with more skills and understanding serve as great models for their peers who are learning to comment and interact during shared reading. Teachers may often have to work to keep students with more skills from dominating, but they can use any number of classroom management strategies to limit their turns (e.g., raise your hand, pass a talking stick, keep a simple tally for each interaction) or encourage them to make sure their peers have a chance to comment and interact. Working with the whole group, the teacher follows the guidance offered in Chapter 4 during a shared reading interaction early in the school day.

Later in the school day, a teaching assistant, therapist, or other adult who supports instruction repeats the shared reading with the smaller group of students working on emergent literacy. At the same time, the teacher conducts a reading comprehension lesson with the group of students who would benefit from conventional instruction. The students who need emergent literacy instruction benefit in many ways. First, they have the benefit of participating in shared reading with peers who are more skilled at interacting and engaging. Second, they get to revisit the same book, in the same day, and repeated reading often increases interaction and engagement (Fleury & Hugh, 2018; McGee & Schickedanz, 2007). Finally, getting this second reading without their conventionally literate peers may leave more opportunity for the emergent readers to take the lead in commenting and interacting with the reader. Meanwhile, teachers have carved out the time they need to work on reading comprehension with students working on conventional reading and writing.

Reading Comprehension With a Mixed Group   Include only the students working on conventional literacy in reading comprehension instruction. The kinds of supports needed to keep emerging readers and writers engaged during reading can interfere with the thinking teachers want to promote in students receiving conventional instruction. For example, students who are emerging readers need to stop and talk about or otherwise interact with the text in order to maintain their attention.

In contrast, students working on conventional reading comprehension need to learn to sustain their own attention and remember the text without stopping and talking about it page by page. Therefore, only the students receiving conventional reading and writing instruction participate in the reading comprehension lessons.

Decoding, Spelling, and Word Identification, Emphasizing Alphabet and Phonological Awareness, With a Mixed Group   It is relatively easy to focus on letter names and sounds and their relationships to words during all of the decoding, spelling, and word identification lessons described in Chapter 10. While students working on conventional reading and writing skills attempt to decode, spell, and identify the words throughout the lessons, students working on emergent literacy are focused on the letters and sounds within the words. For example, while some students make words using a small set of letters, the emergent readers identify the letters one at a time as a peer or adult names them or provides the sounds. Teachers might ask a student who successfully spelled the word to call out the letters needed to make the word while students working at the emergent level identify them. In word sort activities, students who are working on emergent literacy skills might name the letters in the words that others are sorting or sort words that contain a target letter. There are many ways to differentiate the instruction to have a dual focus. Just keep in mind that the students working on emergent literacy are working on alphabet and phonological awareness, while their classmates working on conventional literacy skills are focused on decoding, spelling, and word identification.

Predictable Chart Writing With a Mixed Group   Although predictable chart writing is primarily focused on building concepts about print and other emergent literacy skills and understandings, this activity can help students working on conventional literacy skills focus on sentence structure (syntax), punctuation, capitalization, and spelling. Try following the procedures described in Chapter 5 and including the students working at a conventional level in creating the chart. Consider the conventional skills you would like to address (e.g., include a word your conventionally literate students are struggling to spell, focus on punctuation with dialogue) as you select the sentence stem for the chart. As you teach the lesson, ask the students working at the conventional level to help spell the words that complete each sentence. Ask them to guide you through each step of capitalization and punctuation. Ask them to lead others in reading and rereading the chart. You may ask them to engage in self-directed reading or writing while you work with the emergent students on cutting up and reassembling the sentences, working as a group to "be" the sentence, and creating the book; however, encourage the students working at a conventional level to join in as you read the book that results from the chart. Give them a copy to add to their personal collection of books to read for pleasure.

Self-Directed Reading With Mixed Groups   Self-directed reading is a part of comprehensive emergent and conventional literacy instruction. It can be easier in mixed groups, however, than with groups that only include students receiving the former. In mixed groups, the students working at conventional levels provide excellent models for those students who are not yet readers. They may also sustain their interest in reading more easily than their peers who are emerging in their understandings. This makes it easier to support and engage all students as they work to develop the habit of reading and apply the skills they are acquiring through your instruction.

Independent Writing in Mixed Groups   Like self-directed reading, independent writing is a part of comprehensive emergent and conventional literacy instruction. As described in Chapters 5 and 9, our expectations for writers are different when they are emergent versus conventional, but the ways we engage and encourage them to self-select and write about topics are the same. As with self-directed reading, students who are working on writing at the conventional level provide an excellent model for those students who are emerging in their understandings. The students working on writing at a conventional level likely find it easier to engage in writing for longer periods of time, which can support all of the students in engaging longer. Take care to respond to and celebrate all writing equally because some students will be producing texts that are much easier to read and more conventional than others.

Writing Instruction in Mixed Groups   Writing instruction as described in Chapter 9 is reserved only for the students working on conventional literacy. Although all students should engage in writing each day, the mini-lessons and structures described are for students who already have command of the letters of the alphabet, are interested and engaged in literacy activities, have a means of communication and interaction, and understand concepts about print (see the four questions from earlier in this chapter). It is not impossible to effectively differentiate the instruction to support students working on emergent literacy skills. Those students, however, may benefit more from engaging in self-directed reading or writing while the teacher focuses on writing instruction with those students who are conventional readers and writers.

Scheduling Time to Teach   After deciding what to teach, the next step involves identifying at least 90 minutes in your schedule—and ideally, 120 or more—to devote to literacy instruction. This does not need to be a single block, but be sure to identify segments of time throughout the day to address each component of comprehensive instruction. Figure 12.2 provides estimates of the time most teachers find they need for each component of emergent and conventional literacy instruction when delivered separately or in combination. Obviously, the times will vary depending on the complexity of student needs; students who use communication devices and students with physical disabilities often need considerably more time to meaningfully engage in each component.

In summary, we divided this book into sections to focus separately on emergent and conventional literacy and clearly describe comprehensive instruction in each. Any individual student will require instruction that focuses on one or the other because we stick with comprehensive emergent literacy instruction until we confidently respond "yes" to the four questions in Figure 12.1. Then we move on to comprehensive conventional instruction. However, when trying to deliver instruction to the diverse groups of students found in most classrooms, teachers may need to make adjustments and combine the components to systematically address all students' needs. Teaching comprehensive literacy requires a significant amount of time each day, regardless of the focus of instruction.

Comprehensive Instruction Across Settings

The emergent and conventional literacy instruction described in this book can be delivered in any number of environments. Many general education teachers will find that the approaches are familiar and closely aligned with much of what they do with their students without disabilities, which will allow these teachers to more effectively include students with significant disabilities in their classrooms. We hope special

	Emergent	Conventional	Combined
Shared reading	Two times for 10–15 minutes		10–15 minutes combined + (10–15 minutes emergent only)
Predictable chart writing	20–30 minutes		10–15 minutes combined to create the chart + (20–30 minutes emergent only for remaining steps)
Alphabet and phonological awareness	20–30 minutes		20–30 minutes emergent only (during word study)
Writing	20–30 minutes	30 minutes	30 minutes
Self-directed reading	10–15 minutes	30 minutes	30 minutes
Reading comprehension (anchor-read-apply)		30 minutes	30 minutes (conventional only)
Word study (keywords, word wall, Making Words)		30 minutes	30 minutes
Total	90–135 minutes	120 minutes	130 minutes + 10–15 minutes once per week for creating predictable chart

Figure 12.2.   Time estimates for components of emergent, conventional, and combined literacy instruction.

education teachers find that the comprehensive approaches in this book help them provide their students with universal access to quality, comprehensive instruction, which teachers can supplement with specialized instruction as detailed on their students' IEPs. Outside of the classroom, SLPs are likely to find new approaches that will allow them to more effectively address their clients' literacy, language, and communication skills in their clinics and in classrooms. Parents should find a guide that allows them to fill in the gaps of their child's school program or take the lead in helping their child learn to read and write while sitting around the kitchen table, sharing stories at bedtime, and interacting with the print they encounter throughout their lives. Delivering comprehensive instruction in any setting takes knowledge of the specifics of the environment and all of its demands and resources. Here we describe a few common settings that present their own unique challenges.

Teaching Emergent Readers and Writers in General Education Settings Focused on Conventional Literacy
The skill gap between many students with significant disabilities who are emerging readers and writers and their peers without disabilities is often quite obvious, but that should not keep students with significant disabilities

from being successfully included in general education. Across the grade levels, general education classrooms are full of naturally occurring opportunities to work on each component of emergent literacy. For example, students without disabilities write for many reasons every day. Each time they write, the emerging writer could also write, but the expectations for the product would shift accordingly (see Chapter 5). Elementary school teachers address decoding and spelling on a regular, if not daily, basis. Each of these lessons provides an opportunity to focus on alphabet knowledge and phonological awareness (see Chapter 3). There tends to be less emphasis on decoding and spelling in middle school and high school, but vocabulary and other word-focused instruction offers a similar opportunity to address alphabet knowledge and phonological awareness. Shared reading (see Chapter 4) can be supported in many ways across the grades. We often turn to teacher- and peer-created books aligned with the content being taught in the class. That way emerging readers are working to engage and interact with books that are ability appropriate, age respectful, and aligned with the grade-level content. We can also include strategies such as predictable chart writing in general education settings all the way through high school. One high school teacher created a predictable chart (see Chapter 5) each time she reviewed vocabulary with the students in her class. She used sentence stems that highlighted the words students are learning (e.g., *A flagellum is like a* _____.). The students working at grade level got to review the vocabulary while the teacher created the chart (Step 1 of predictable chart writing). The student with significant disabilities completed the remaining steps of predictable chart writing with various peers and the teaching assistant when other students were doing independent or partner work throughout the rest of the week. The book that resulted at the end of the week provided one more text for shared reading in weeks to come. It takes a little creativity, but emergent readers and writers can receive the comprehensive instruction they require while remaining meaningfully included in general education classrooms.

Teaching Comprehensive Literacy in Separate Special Education Settings

Approximately 3% of students with significant disabilities are educated in general education settings across the United States, while an additional 15% spend at least some of their time (40%–80%) in general education settings (Erickson & Geist, 2016). The rest are educated in separate settings, spending less than 20% of their school day with peers without disabilities. This means that teachers in separate special education settings must take responsibility for delivering the comprehensive literacy instruction their students require. As previously described, this means devoting 90–120 minutes a day to literacy instruction and making a big shift away from focusing exclusively on IEP goals and one-to-one instruction.

Too many students with significant disabilities only receive instruction that targets the few goals in their IEPs or other narrowly defined skills that relate to literacy in some way (Ruppar, 2015). Because we have never seen (nor do we recommend) an IEP with enough goals to capture all areas of comprehensive emergent or conventional literacy instruction, any program focused exclusively on IEP goals is insufficient to result in meaningful reading and writing improvements. Instead of focusing solely on IEP goals, teachers might use the decision-making process described in this chapter to determine whether they will implement comprehensive emergent literacy instruction, comprehensive conventional literacy instruction, or a combination of the two. Next, the teacher could consider the standards each student is supposed to achieve in any given school year, along with each student's present levels of academic achievement and functional performance relative to those standards and the components of the comprehensive instruction to be delivered. The gaps between each student's present levels, the standards, and the planned instructional program become the focus of the specialized instruction the student requires, which is then reflected in IEP goals. The students will still require specialized instruction targeting their IEP goals, but that is provided in addition to, or as part of, the comprehensive instruction all students require.

A lack of instructional time is a common challenge among many teachers of students with significant disabilities in separate settings, especially when all of the students have significant physical support needs. Precious few minutes remain for instruction by the time students get the related services supports they need, participate in important specials (i.e., art, music, physical education), receive services from itinerant teachers of the students with visual or hearing impairments, and take the time they need to function as independently as possible throughout the school day. Add to this the fact that many students require one-to-one or even two-to-one supports to manage personal care needs, and instructional time is in short supply. For example, students in some high school classrooms require two people to help them get changed at least twice each school day and someone to feed them at snack and lunchtime. Hours disappear quickly when the eight or 10 students in the class all have this level of support need. In one class we know, students arrive at 8:00 a.m.; it is 9:45 a.m. by the time everyone has something to eat and is changed, and every adult in the classroom is in a full sweat. It is hard work and the adults are efficiently working to get the day started. When they do this one more time in the afternoon, their 6-hour school day is reduced to 2 1/2 hours. Now insert one special each day, and the teacher is down to 1 3/4 hours for instruction. You get the idea, and many teachers reading this book live with this reality every day.

Cycle through the components that are appropriate for your students when you simply do not have 90–120 minutes per day to devote to instruction, let alone literacy instruction. Identify the times when you can do one or two components each day and work to protect them so that instruction really does happen. Then, during those times, complete a lesson that addresses the next component on your list. For example, on Monday, do shared reading and the first step of predictable chart writing. On Tuesday, try to get to a lesson focused on alphabet and phonological awareness and get your students writing. On Wednesday, have the students first spend some time doing independent reading and then do the next step of a predictable chart writing lesson before returning to the beginning of the cycle with shared reading. In this way, your students get every component of comprehensive emergent literacy instruction before you repeat one. At a minimum, aim to complete at least two cycles each week. Over time, you might increase it to three or four, and you will see increased rates of learning among your students as you increase the number of cycles.

Delivering Comprehensive Instruction Across Multiple Settings   If you cannot offer comprehensive instruction because you work with students for just a brief period each day or each week, then consider the students' profiles and the kinds of instruction they are receiving across their school day. If the students' literacy instruction addresses only sight words, then focus on teaching decoding, spelling, reading comprehension, and writing. If the students have parents who read with them at

bedtime each day, then focus on helping the student develop alphabetic and phonological awareness and engage in shared writing such as predictable chart writing. (Other examples of parental support are described next.) The key is to look at all of the components and identify those areas of instruction that are receiving the least attention in other settings. Then focus on those components.

HOW PARENTS CAN HELP PROVIDE COMPREHENSIVE INSTRUCTION

Aaron's mom played a significant role in helping ensure that he had access to comprehensive literacy instruction throughout his school career. Aaron's mom paid careful attention to the type of instruction he received at school, and then she focused on what was not addressed there. In the primary grades, that meant she spent time encouraging and supporting Aaron in writing for topics he selected. When he reached the upper elementary grades and there was little time for self-directed reading at school, she built a library of books and encouraged Aaron to spend more time reading at home. As Aaron continued into middle and high school, reading comprehension instruction became a focus at home because school spent less time teaching reading and more time directing students to read to gain access to information independently.

Regardless of the specific setting in which comprehensive literacy instruction is implemented, it will be most effective when it is delivered in the same integrated, engaging, and interactive way it is delivered to students without disabilities in general education settings (McSheehan et al., 2006; Ryndak et al., 1999). Most students with significant disabilities never receive this type of instruction. Instead, they are taught narrowly defined skills via massed trials in one-to-one instructional contexts (Ruppar, 2015). Task analysis has traditionally been used in planning instruction for students with significant disabilities (i.e., breaking down complex tasks into component skills that are taught to mastery, often via forward or backward chaining). This ongoing tradition might help students acquire literacy-related skills, but it fails to help them apply those skills in meaningful reading and writing tasks outside of the context where they are taught (e.g., Baker, Rivera, & Mason, 2019; Spooner, Rivera, Browder, Baker, & Salas, 2009). Ultimately, we cannot guarantee that all students with significant disabilities will become conventional readers and writers. We can guarantee that most will not—unless we make significant shifts away from the way we have taught in the past toward the types of comprehensive instruction described throughout this book.

COMMON QUESTIONS

We close this chapter by addressing questions we commonly encounter when we work with groups of teachers, therapists, and/or parents and caregivers who are working to organize and implement comprehensive literacy instruction. As we prepared this list, we also reached out to many of our colleagues and friends who work to help others learn about and implement this instruction. Many questions they shared addressed specific components discussed in one or more chapters elsewhere in the book (e.g., How can I gain access to enough texts, especially for older students who are beginning readers?). Here, we address questions that focus on pulling all the components together.

How do I provide comprehensive instruction when I am required to use a specific curriculum? First, determine which components of emergent and conventional literacy the required curriculum addresses. Does the program teach sight words only? Does it teach many different literacy skills but none with the depth described in this book? Is it actually a literacy instructional program, or does it simply use text to present information? After determining what the curriculum addresses, use the chart in Figure 12.1 to figure out what else to add to create a comprehensive program for your students. After you have identified what is missing and start teaching in a more comprehensive way, take videos, keep work samples, and keep track of the ways that your more comprehensive approach is more effective than the required curriculum. If you take the time to document the effectiveness of a comprehensive approach, then you may have more control over the ways you teach your students in the future.

We have been at this a long time without much success. When is it time to give up? Is it too late to get started? Our experience says it is never time to give up. We know many individuals with significant disabilities who did not learn to read and write until their late teens, early 20s, and beyond. When students make little to no progress after months or even years of instruction, we usually find that their instruction has not been comprehensive, integrated, engaging, or interactive. Before you give up, reflect, regroup, and restart the clock as you begin anew with a different, more comprehensive approach.

How do I get started when my students have intense behaviors? We had the great fortune of working with a teacher at one of our intensive summer camps who showed us the power of literacy as a mediator of intense behaviors. The camper she was working with was an emerging reader, writer, and communicator who initially expressed very little interest in anything other than the YouTube videos he preferred to watch repeatedly. The teacher kept track of the videos he selected during their first day working together. She attempted to interact with him while he watched the video by making the same types of comments she would typically make during shared reading while also demonstrating how he might use a picture-based communication system to make comments. The teacher introduced a game on the second day. She showed the camper the first letter that matched the name of the songs he had been listening to on YouTube. She then encouraged (but did not require) the camper to select the letter for the song he wanted and then ran with him across the room to watch the video on the interactive white board. She continued to follow his lead and interests throughout the week, creating new ways to engage him in reading and writing tasks. As his engagement increased, his intense behaviors decreased. He continued to be boisterous and active, but he was no longer difficult to manage. Now suppose that this teacher was given a year to continue to follow his lead, support his communication, and keep him engaged and interacting. The 6-foot-tall boy with intense behaviors would be an entirely different young man who was rapidly moving toward conventional reading, writing, and communication. We have always asserted that engaging the minds of students is one way to reduce challenging behaviors. This teacher and camper reinforced that assertion.

Why should I focus on literacy instead of more functional skills? You should teach literacy because it is the most important functional skill your students can acquire. Literacy opens doors to employment (Wood, 2010), autonomous communication (Erickson, 2017), and even brain development (Skeide et al., 2017). Learning to read and write will make it easier for your students to learn any other skills they need, and it gives them the power to seek support (and direct the delivery of that support) when they do not have the skills they need. The distinction between literacy and functional skills is false and likely made by people who did not know how to teach literacy to students with significant disabilities. Literacy is so highly related to postschool success that schools should continue to make comprehensive literacy instruction a priority in students' programs until the day they graduate or otherwise complete their schooling. Too often, students reach adolescence and the focus turns entirely away from literacy learning to experiences in the community, at their jobs, and so forth. These experiences, however, can be used to continue literacy development. Students can write about the myriad transition and work experiences they are having. Teachers can plan word study lessons around the words that students need to read and write in the various community experiences they will encounter. Tar Heel Reader provides a very easy way to create books that can be used during reading comprehension lessons to help students learn the sequence of steps in a new job, the differences between the roles of their coworkers, or the intentions of a boss who may seem a little too harsh on the surface. No line needs to be drawn between so-called functional skills and literacy. Literacy is functional, and literacy instruction can help students learn all of those skills that have traditionally been placed on the other side of the imaginary line.

How do I know my students are learning? You will know that your comprehensive instruction is working when you see students reading and writing more successfully, more often, and with greater interest and engagement. More specifically, it is working for the emergent reader and writer you are teaching when the student is

- More interested and engaged during instruction

- More aware of print in the environment

- Successful in identifying letters of the alphabet

- More aware of print concepts (e.g., one-to-one relationship between spoken and written word; left-to-right, top-to-bottom directionality)

You will also know it is working when the student has four "yes" responses to our questions (Figure 12.1). It is working for conventional readers and writers you are teaching when they

- Moan and groan when you tell them they have to stop reading and writing to go somewhere or do something else

- Start relating things learned during reading comprehension lessons to other aspects of life and vice versa

- More accurately spell or represent the sounds in words they want to write and more accurately decode unfamiliar words in text

- Use reading and writing to accomplish personal goals beyond instructional time

- Engage more actively in instruction

These are just a few of the differences that will let you know that your instruction is working. You can track some of these by tallying the number of student-initiated comments during shared reading, recording the letters students identify and produce across the day, and noting when the student demonstrates understandings of various print concepts by accurately cutting apart the individual words in the sentences created in predictable chart writing or pointing to the words while you read the chart. For conventional readers and writers, you can track progress in reading using cloze or maze passages and other tasks. (See the Intervention Central web site at https://interventioncentral.org/teacher-resources/test-of-reading-comprehension for a maze passage generator.) You can track progress in spelling untaught words during writing. You can note when students successfully communicate multiple ideas to others after reading a text or when writing.

One day we might feel compelled to write the book about approaches to assessment in comprehensive literacy instruction for students with significant disabilities, but that is unlikely to happen until we see significant changes in opportunities to learn. For too long, we have put the proverbial cart before the horse and worried too much about assessing progress without doing what students need to make progress in the first place. Just get started. Then reflect regularly on your practice and focus on instruction that is comprehension, integrated, engaging, and intensive. Then you will not wonder if it is working because your students will show you it is working each and every day through their improved abilities to read, write, communicate, and interact meaningfully with others.

A FINAL NOTE

Throughout this book, we have emphasized methods and principles of instruction to guide your efforts to teach all students with significant disabilities to read and write. We have emphasized instruction over assessment, and we have provided specific guidance regarding ways to highly contextualize that instruction to move beyond skill mastery to meaningful application and use of skills across purposes, places, texts, and audiences.

In Chapter 2, we introduced the Literacy Bill of Rights (Yoder, 2000). We close here by reminding you that students with significant disabilities require others in their lives to work with them to ensure those rights. Very few students with significant disabilities will learn to read and write without teachers, therapists, parents, caregivers, and others who are willing to tackle the complex work of teaching literacy. It is not always easy to determine what to teach, where to teach it, and how to find the time to give it the attention it deserves, but the payoff is worth the effort. Students with significant disabilities have everything to gain from increased efforts to teach them to read and write in meaningful ways. We owe it to them to dive in!

References

Acheson, D. J., & MacDonald, M. C. (2011). The rhymes that the reader perused confused the meaning: Phonological effects during on-line sentence comprehension. *Journal of Memory and Language, 65*(2), 193–207. doi:10.1016/j.jml.2011.04.006

Adams, M. J. (1990). *Beginning to read: Thinking and learning about print.* Cambridge, MA: The MIT Press.

Adams, M. J. (2004). Modeling the connections between word recognition and reading. In N. J. Unrau & R. B. Ruddell (Eds.), *Theoretical models and processes of reading* (5th ed., pp. 1202–1227). Newark, DE: International Reading Association.

Adams, M. J. (2011). From alphabetic basics to reading. In S. J. Samuels & A. E. Farstrup (Eds.), *What research has to say about reading instruction* (4th ed., pp. 4–24). Newark: DE: International Reading Association.

Adlof, S. M., Klusek, J., Hoffmann, A., Chitwood, K. L., Brazendale, A., Riley, K., . . . Roberts, J. E. (2018). Reading in children with fragile X syndrome: Phonological awareness and feasibility of intervention. *American Journal on Intellectual and Developmental Disabilities, 123,* 193–211. doi:10.1352/1944-7558-123.3.193

Ahlgrim-Delzell, L., Browder, D., & Wood, L. (2014). Effects of systematic instruction and an augmentative communication device on phonics skills acquisition for students with moderate intellectual disability who are nonverbal. *Education and Training in Autism and Developmental Disabilities, 49,* 517–532. http://daddcec.org/Publications/ETADD Journal.aspx

Ahlgrim-Delzell, L., Browder, D. M., Wood, L., Stanger, C., Preston, A. I., & Kemp-Inman, A. (2016). Systematic instruction of phonics skills using an iPad for students with developmental disabilities who are AAC users. *Journal of Special Education, 50,* 86–97. doi:10.1177 /0022466915622140

Al Otaiba, S., Lake, V. E., Greulich, L., Folsom, J. S., & Guidry, L. (2012). Preparing beginning reading teachers: An experimental comparison of initial early literacy field experiences. *Reading and Writing, 25*(1), 109–129. doi:10.1007/s11145-010-9250-2

Al Otaiba, S., Lewis, S., Whalon, K., Drylund, A., & McKenzie, A. R. (2009). Home literacy environments of young children with Down syndrome: Findings from a web-based survey. *Remedial and Special Education, 30*(2), 96–107. doi:10.1177/0741932508315050

Alborough, J. (2001). *Hug.* Somerville, MA: Candlewick Press.

Allen, R. V. (1976). *Language experiences in communication.* Boston, MA: Houghton-Mifflin.

Allington, R. L. (2011). *What really matters for struggling readers: Designing research-based programs* (3rd ed.). Boston, MA: Pearson.

Allington, R. L. (2013). What really matters when working with struggling readers. The *Reading Teacher, 66,* 520–530. doi:10.1002/TRTR.1154

Allington, R. L. (2014). How volume reading affects both reading fluency and reading achievement. *International Electronic Journal of Elementary Education, 7,* 13–25.

Allor, J., Mathes, P., Roberts, J., Cheatham, J., & Al Otaiba, S. (2014). Is scientifically based reading instruction effective for students with below-average IQs? *Exceptional Children, 80*(3), 287–306. doi:10.1177/0014402914522208

Allor, J. H., Mathes, P. G., Roberts, J. K., Cheatham, J. P., & Champlin, T. M. (2010). Comprehensive reading instruction for students with intellectual disabilities: Findings from the first three years of a longitudinal study. *Psychology in the Schools, 47*(5), 445–466. doi:10.1002 /pits.20482

Allor, J. H., Mathes, P. G., Roberts, J. K., Jones, F. G., & Champlin, T. M. (2010). Teaching students with moderate intellectual disabilities to read: An experimental examination of a comprehensive reading intervention. *Education and Training in Autism and Developmental Disabilities, 45*(1), 3–22. http://daddcec.org/Publications/ETADDJournal.aspx

Anderson, R., & Nagy, W. (1991). Word meanings. In R. Barr, M. Kamil, P. Mosenthal, & P. D. Pearson (Eds.), *Handbook of reading research* (Vol. 2, pp. 690–724). New York, NY: Longman.

Anderson, R. C., Wilson, P. T., & Fielding, L. G. (1988). Growth in reading and how children spend their time outside of school. *Reading Research Quarterly, 23,* 285–303. doi:10.1598/RRQ.23.3.2

Andreae, G. (2012). *Giraffes can't dance.* New York, NY: Scholastic, Cartwheel Books.

Anson, D., Moist, P., Przywara, M., Wells, H., Saylor, H., & Maxine, H. (2006). The effects of word completion and word prediction on typing rates using on-screen keyboards. *Assistive Technology, 18*(2), 146–154. doi:10.1080/10400435.2006.10131913

Anthony, J. L., & Francis D. J. (2005). Development of phonological awareness. *Current Directions in Psychological Science, 14,* 255–259. doi:10.1111/j.0963-7214.2005.00376.x

Archer, A. L., & Hughes, C. A. (2011). *Explicit instruction. Effective and efficient teaching.* New York, NY: Guilford Press.

Attewell, S. (2012). *Once I laughed my socks off: Poems for Kids.* Scotts Valley, CA: CreateSpace Independent Publishing Platform.

Bailey, R. L., Angell, M. E., & Stoner, J. B. (2011). Improving literacy skills in students with complex communication needs who use augmentative/alternative communication systems. *Education and Training in Autism and Developmental Disabilities, 46*(3), 352–368. http://daddcec.org/Publications/ETADDJournal.aspx

Baker, J. N., Rivera, C., & Mason, L. (2019). Teaching emergent literacy skills to students with autism spectrum disorder. *Intervention in School and Clinic, 54*(3), 166–172. doi:10.1177/1053451218767907

Banajee, M., Dicarlo, C., & Stricklin, S. (2003). Core vocabulary determination for toddlers. *Augmentative and Alternative Communication, 19,* 67–73. doi:10.1080/0743461031000112034

Barker, R. M., Saunders, K. J., & Brady, N. C. (2012). Reading instruction for children who use AAC: Considerations in the pursuit of generalizable results. *Augmentative and Alternative Communication, 28*(3), 160–170. doi:10.3109/07434618.2012.704523

Bauer, P. (2009). *B is for battle cry: A civil war alphabet.* Ann Arbor, MI: Sleeping Bear Press.

Beck, I., & McKeown, M. (1991). Conditions of vocabulary acquisition. In R. Barr, M. L. Kamil, P. Mosenthal, & P. D. Pearson (Eds.), *Handbook of reading research* (Vol. 2, pp. 789–814). Mahwah, NJ: Lawrence Erlbaum Associates.

Beck, I. L., McKeown, M. G., & Kucan, L. (2002). *Bringing words to life.* New York, NY: Guilford Press.

Beck, I. L., McKeown, M. G., & Kucan, L. (2008). *Creating robust vocabulary: Frequently asked questions and extended examples.* New York, NY: Guilford Press.

Beck, I. L., McKeown, M. G., & Kucan, L. (2013). *Bringing words to life: Robust vocabulary instruction* (2nd ed.). New York, NY: Guilford Press.

Becker, M., McElvany, N., & Kortenbruck, M. (2010). Intrinsic and extrinsic reading motivation as predictors of reading literacy: A longitudinal study. *Journal of Educational Psychology, 102,* 773–785. doi:10.1037/a0020084

Bedrosian, J., Lasker, J., Speidel, K., & Politsch, A. (2003). Enhancing the written narrative skills of an AAC student with autism: Evidence-based research issues. *Topics in Language Disorders, 23,* 305–324. doi:10.1097/00011363-200310000-00006

Bellon, M. L., & Ogletree, B. T. (2000). Repeated storybook reading as an instructional method. *Intervention in School and Clinic, 36*(2), 75–81. doi:10.1177/105345120003600202

Bellon, M., Ogletree, B., & Harn, W. (2000). The application of scaffolding within repeated storybook reading as a language intervention for children with autism. *Focus on Autism and Other Developmental Disabilities, 15,* 52–58. doi:10.1177/108835760001500107

Bellon-Harn, M. L., & Harn, W. E. (2008). Scaffolding strategies during repeated storybook reading: An extension using a voice output communication aid. *Focus on Autism and Other Developmental Disabilities, 23,* 112–124. doi:10.1177/1088357608316606

Ben-Eliyahu, A., Moore, D., Dorph, R., & Schunn, C. D. (2018). Investigating the multidimensionality of engagement: Affective, behavioral, and cognitive engagement across science activities and contexts. *Contemporary Educational Psychology, 53,* 87–105. doi:10.1016/j.cedpsych.2018.01.002

Benjamin, R. G., Schwanenflugel, P. J., Meisinger, E. B., Groff, C., Kuhn, M. R., & Steiner, L. (2013). A spectrographically grounded scale for evaluating reading expressiveness. *Reading Research Quarterly, 48,* 105–133. doi:10.1002/rrq.43

Betts, E. A. (1946). *Foundations of reading instruction: With emphasis on differentiated guidance.* New York, NY: American Book Company.

Beukelman, D. R., Yorkston, K. M., Poblete, M., & Naranjo, C. (1984). Frequency of word occurrence in communication samples produced by adult communication aid users. *Journal of Speech and Hearing Disorders, 49,* 360–367. doi:10.1044/jshd.4904.360

Biemiller, A. (2001). Teaching vocabulary: Early, direct, and sequential. *American Educator, 25,* 24–28. Retrieved from https://www.aft.org/periodical/american-educator/spring-2001/teaching-vocabulary

Biemiller, A. (2005). Size and sequence in vocabulary development: Implications for choosing words for primary grade vocabulary instruction. In A. Hiebert, & M. Kamil (Eds.), *Teaching and learning vocabulary: Bringing research to practice* (pp. 223–242). Mahwah, NJ: Lawrence Erlbaum Associates.

Biemiller, A., & Boote, C. (2006). An effective method for building vocabulary in primary grades. *Journal of Educational Psychology, 98,* 44–62. doi:10.1037/0022-0663.98.1.44

Blischak, D. M. (1995). Thomas the writer: Case study of a child with severe physical, speech, and visual impairments. *Language, Speech, and Hearing Services in Schools, 26,* 11–20. doi:10.1044/0161-1461.2601.11

Blischak, D. M., & McDaniel, M. A. (1995). Effects of picture size and placement on memory for written words. *Journal of Speech and Hearing Research, 38,* 1356–1362. doi:10.1044/jshr.3806.1356

Boone, R., & Higgins, K. (2007). The role of instructional design in assistive technology research and development. *Reading Research Quarterly, 42,* 135–140. doi:10.1598/RRQ.42.1.5

Booth, R. W., & Weger, U. W. (2013). The function of regressions in reading: Backward eye movements allow rereading. *Memory and Cognition, 41,* 82–97. doi:10.3758/s13421-012-0244-y

Bouck, E. C., & Flanagan, S. M. (2016). Exploring assistive technology and post-school outcomes for students with severe disabilities. *Disability and Rehabilitation: Assistive Technology, 11,* 645–652. doi:10.3109/17483107.2015.1029537.

Bowman, M., & Treiman, R. (2004). Stepping stones to reading. *Theory Into Practice, 43,* 295–330. doi:10.1207/s15430421tip4304_8

Brabham, E. G., & Lynch-Brown, C. (2002). Effects of teachers' reading-aloud styles on vocabulary acquisition and comprehension of students in the early elementary grades. *Journal of Educational Psychology, 94,* 465–473. doi:10.1037/0022-0663.94.3.465

Brady, N. C., Bruce, S., Goldman, A., Erickson, K., Mineo, B., Ogletree, B. T., . . . Wilkinson, K. (2016). Communication supports and services for individuals with severe disabilities: Guidance for assessment and intervention. *American Journal on Intellectual and Developmental Disabilities, 121,* 121–138. doi:10.1352/1944-7558-121.2.121

Broadcast the Dream. (2014). *Broadcast: A man and his dream* [Web site]. Retrieved from http://broadcastthedream.com

Browder, D., Ahlgrim-Delzell, L., Courtade, G., Gibbs, S. L., & Flowers, C. (2008). Evaluation of the effectiveness of an early literacy program for students with significant developmental disabilities. *Exceptional Children, 75,* 33–52. doi:10.1177/001440290807500102

Browder, D., Ahlgrim-Delzell, L., Spooner, F., Mims, P. J., & Baker, J. N. (2009). Using time delay to teach literacy to students with severe developmental disabilities. *Exceptional Children, 75,* 343–364. doi:10.1177/001440290907500305

Browder, D. M., Mims, P. J., Spooner, F., Ahlgrim-Delzell, L., & Lee, A. (2008). Teaching elementary students with multiple disabilities to participate in shared stories. *Research and Practice for Persons with Severe Disabilities, 33,* 3–12. doi:10.2511/rpsd.33.1-2.3

Browder, D. M., & Spooner, F. (2011). *Teaching students with moderate and severe disabilities.* New York, NY: Guilford Press.

Browder, D. M., & Spooner, F. (2014). *More language arts, math, and science for students with severe disabilities.* Baltimore, MD: Paul H. Brookes Publishing Co.

Browder, D. M., Wakeman, S. Y., Spooner, F., Ahlgrim-Delzell, L., & Algozzine, B. (2006). Research on reading instruction for individuals with significant cognitive disabilities. *Exceptional Children, 72,* 392–408. doi:10.1177/001440290607200401

Browder, D. M., & Xin, Y. P. (1998). The meta-analysis and review of sight word research and its implications for teaching functional reading to individuals with moderate and severe disabilities. *Journal of Special Education, 32,* 130–153. doi:10.1177/002246699803200301

Brown, C. (1991). *My left foot.* London, England: Minerva Press.

Butler, D. (1980). *Cushla and her books.* Boston, MA: The Horn Book.

Byington, T. A., & Kim, Y. (2017). Promoting preschoolers' emergent writing. *Young Children, 72*(5), 74–82. https://www.jstor.org/stable/90015861

Cain, K., & Oakhill, J. (1999). Inference making ability and its relation to comprehension failure. *Reading and Writing, 11,* 489–503. doi:10.1023/A:1008084120205

Cameto, R., Bergland, F., Knokey, A.-M., Nagle, K. M., Sanford, C., Kalb, S. C., … Lauer, K. (2010). *Teacher perspectives of school-level implementation of alternate assessments for students with significant cognitive disabilities: A report from the National Study on Alternate Assessments.* Retrieved from https://ies.ed.gov/ncser/pubs/20103007/pdf/20103007.pdf

Carlson, N. (2003). *How about a hug?* New York, NY: Puffin Books.

Cazet, D. (2006). *Minnie and Moo: The case of the missing jelly donut.* New York, NY: HarperCollins.

Channell, M. M., Loveall, S. J., & Conners, F. A. (2013). Strengths and weaknesses in reading skills of youth with intellectual disabilities. *Research in Developmental Disabilities: A Multidisciplinary Journal, 34,* 776–787. doi:10.1016/j.ridd.2012.10.010

Chapman, R. S., Seung, H. K., Schwartz, S. E., & Bird, E. K. R. (1998). Language skills of children and adolescents with Down syndrome: Production deficits. *Journal of Speech, Language, and Hearing Research, 41,* 861–873. doi:10.1044/jslhr.4104.861

Cheek, A. E. (2016). *Effects of online module + ecoaching on comprehension instruction for students with significant intellectual disability* Retrieved from http://libres.uncg.edu/ir/uncg/clist.aspx?id=13570

Cheek, A. E., Harris, B. A., & Koppenhaver, D. A. (2019). *Technology-supported shared storybook reading for children with severe intellectual disabilities using augmentative and alternative communication.* Manuscript under review.

Cheng, K. H., & Tsai, C. C. (2014). Children and parents' reading of an augmented reality picture book: Analyses of behavioral patterns and cognitive attainment. *Computers and Education, 72,* 302–312. doi:10.1016/j.compedu.2013.12.003

Chiappe, P., Siegel, L. S., & Gottardo, A. (2002). Reading related skills of kindergartners from diverse linguistic backgrounds. *Applied Psycholinguistics, 23,* 95–116. doi:10.1017/S014271640200005X

Chiong, C., Ree, J., Tekeuchi, L., & Erickson, I. (2012). *Print books vs. e-books: Comparing parent-child co-reading on print, basic, and enhanced e-book platforms.* New York, NY: Joan Ganz Cooney Center.

Cipielewski, J., & Stanovich, K. E. (1992). Predicting growth in reading ability from children's exposure to print. *Journal of Experimental Child Psychology, 54,* 74–89. doi:10.1016/0022-0965(92)90018-2

Ciullo, S., Lembke, E. S., Carlisle, A., Thomas, C. N., Goodwin, M., & Judd, L. (2016). Implementation of evidence-based literacy practices in middle school response to intervention: An observation study. *Learning Disability Quarterly, 39,* 44–57. doi:10.1177/0731948714566120

Cochran-Smith, M., & Zeichner, K. M. (2005). *Studying teacher education: The report of the AERA panel on research and teacher education.* Mahwah, NJ: Lawrence Erlbaum Associates.

Cohen, E. T., Heller, K. W., Alberto, P., & Fredrick, L. D. (2008). Using a three-step decoding strategy with constant time delay to teach word reading to students with mild and moderate mental retardation. *Focus on Autism and Other Developmental Disabilities, 23,* 67–78. doi:10.1177/1088357608314899

Cole, K., Maddox, M., Lim, Y. S., & Notari-Syverson, A. (2002). *Language is the key: Talking and books, talking and play* [Resource guide]. Seattle, WA: Washington Research Institute.

Coleman, P. (1991). *Literacy lost: A qualitative analysis of the early literacy experiences of preschool children with severe speech and physical impairments.* Unpublished doctoral dissertation, University of North Carolina at Chapel Hill.

Coleman-Martin, M. B., Heller, K. W., Cihak, D. F., & Irvine, K. L. (2005). Using computer-assisted instruction and the nonverbal reading approach to teach word identification. *Focus on Autism and Other Developmental Disabilities, 20,* 80–90. doi:10.1177/10883576050200020401.

Collins, B. C. (2012). *Systematic instruction for students with moderate and severe disabilities.* Baltimore, MD: Paul H. Brookes Publishing Co.

Colozzo, P., McKeil, L., Petersen, J. M., & Szabo, A. (2016). An early literacy program for young children with Down syndrome: Changes observed over one year. *Journal of Policy and Practice in Intellectual Disabilities, 13*, 102–110. doi:10.1111/jppi.12160

Conners, F. A., Rosenquist, C. J., Sligh, A. C., Atwell, J. A., & Kiser, T. (2006). Phonological reading skills acquisition by children with mental retardation. *Research in Developmental Disabilities, 27*, 121–137. doi:10.1016/j.ridd.2004.11.015

Connor, C. M., Morrison, F. J., & Slominsky, L. (2006). Preschool instruction and children's emergent literacy growth. *Journal of Educational Psychology, 98*, 665–689. doi:10.1037 /0022-0663.98.4.665

Coyne, M. D., McCoach, D. B., & Kapp, S. (2007). Vocabulary intervention for kindergarten students: Comparing extended instruction to embedded instruction and incidental exposure. *Learning Disability Quarterly, 30*, 74–88. doi:10.2307/30035543

Craig, C. J. (1996). Family support of the emergent literacy of children with visual impairments. *Journal of Visual Impairment and Blindness, 90*, 194–200. https://journals.sagepub.com /home/jvba

Cunningham, A. (2005). Vocabulary growth through independent reading and reading aloud to children. In E. H. Hiebert & M. L. Kamil (Eds.), *Teaching and learning vocabulary: Bringing research to practice* (pp. 45–67). Mahwah, NJ: Lawrence Erlbaum Associates.

Cunningham, A. E., & Stanovich, K. E. (1997). Early reading acquisition and its relation to reading experience and ability 10 years later. *Developmental Psychology, 33*(6), 934–945. doi:10.1037/0012-1649.33.6.934

Cunningham, A. E., & Stanovich, K. E. (1998). What reading does for the mind. *American Educator, 22*(1–2), 8–15. https://www.aft.org/sites/default/files/periodicals/cunningham.pdf

Cunningham, A. E., Zibulsky, J., Stanovich, K. E., & Stanovich, P. J. (2009). How teachers would spend their time teaching language arts: The mismatch between self-reported and best practices. *Journal of Learning Disabilities, 42*(5), 418–430. doi:10.1177/0022219409 339063

Cunningham, J. W. (1993). Whole-to-part reading diagnosis. *Reading and Writing Quarterly, 9*, 31–49. doi:10.1080/1057356930090103

Cunningham, J. W. (2001). The National Reading Panel report. *Reading Research Quarterly, 36*, 326–335. doi:10.1598/RRQ.36.3.5

Cunningham, J. W., & Cunningham, P. M. (1992). Making Words: Enhancing the invented spelling-decoding connection. *The Reading Teacher, 46*, 106–115. https://www.jstor.org /journal/readingteacher

Cunningham, J. W., Koppenhaver, D. A., Erickson, K. A., & Spadorcia, S. A. (2004). Word identification and text characteristics. In J. V. Hoffman & D. L. Schallert (Eds.), *The texts in elementary classrooms* (pp. 21–37). Mahwah, NJ: Lawrence Erlbaum Associates.

Cunningham, P. M. (2016). *Phonics they use: Words for reading and spelling* (7th ed.). Boston, MA: Pearson.

Cunningham, P. M., & Allington, R. L. (2016). *Classrooms that work: They can all read and write* (6th ed.). New York, NY: Pearson.

Cunningham, P. M., & Cunningham, J. W. (2009). *What really matters in writing: Research based practices across the elementary curriculum*. New York, NY: Pearson.

Cunningham, P. M., & Hall, D. P. (1994). *Making Words: Multilevel, hands-on, developmentally appropriate spelling and phonics activities*. Greensboro, NC: Carson-Dellosa.

Cunningham, P. M., & Hall, D. P. (2008). *Making Words first grade: 100 hands-on lessons for phonemic awareness, phonics and spelling*. New York, NY: Pearson.

Cunningham, P. M., Hall, D. P., & Defee, M. (1991). Non-ability-grouped, multilevel instruction: A year in a first-grade classroom. *The Reading Teacher, 44*, 566–571.

Cunningham, P. M., Hall, D. P., & Defee, M. (1998). Nonability-grouped, multilevel instruction: Eight years later. *The Reading Teacher, 51*, 652–664.

Cuskelly, M., Povey, J., & Jobling, A. (2016). Trajectories of development of receptive vocabulary in individuals with Down syndrome. *Journal of Policy and Practice in Intellectual Disabilities, 13*, 111–119. doi:0.1111/jppi.12151

D'Agostino, S. R., Dueñas, A. D., & Plavnick, J. B. (2018). Increasing social initiations during shared book reading: An intervention for preschoolers with autism spectrum disorder. *Topics in Early Childhood Special Education*. doi:10.1177/0271121418816422

Dahl, R. (1998). *Charlie and the chocolate factory*. New York, NY: Puffin Books.

Darling-Hammond, L. (2000). Teacher quality and student achievement: A review of state policy evidence. *Education Policy Analysis Archives, 8,* 1–44. doi:10.14507/epaa.v8n1.2000

Davidson, M. M., Kaushanskaya, M., & Weismer, S. (2018). Reading comprehension in children with and without ASD: The role of word reading, oral language, and working memory. *Journal of Autism and Developmental Disorders, 48,* 3524–3541. doi:10.1007/s10803-018-3617-7.

Davie, J., & Kemp, C. (2002). A comparison of the expressive language opportunities provided by shared book reading and facilitated play for young children with mild to moderate intellectual disabilities. *Educational Psychology, 22,* 445–460. doi:10.1080/0144341022000003123

Davis, A. (1999). *The enormous potato.* Toronto, Canada: Kids Can Press.

Davis, J. B. (2013). *The burp book: Burp it, belch it, speak it, squeak it!* Scotts Valley, CA: CreateSpace Independent Publishing Platform.

De Jong, P. F., Bitter, D. L., Van Setten, M., & Marinus, E. (2009). Does phonological recoding occur during silent reading, and is it necessary for orthographic learning? *Journal of Experimental Child Psychology, 104,* 267–282. doi:10.1016/j.jecp.2009.06.002

DeBarthe, G., & Erickson, K. (2014). *The role of AT/AAC in the next generation assessment.* Paper presented at the Council for Exceptional Children, Philadelphia, PA. Retrieved from https://dynamiclearningmaps.org/sites/default/files/documents/publication/The_Role _of_AT_in_Next_Generation_Assessments_DeBarthe%26Erickson%2C2014.pdf

DeBruin-Parecki, A. (1999). *Assessing adult/child storybook reading practices.* Ann Arbor, MI: University of Michigan, Center for the Improvement of Early Reading Achievement.

dePaola, T. (2007). *Tomi dePaola's big book of favorite legends.* New York, NY: Putnam Juvenile.

Dennis, A. (2018). *Parent communication during shared reading with girls with Rett syndrome: The impact of print referencing.* Unpublished doctoral dissertation, University of North Carolina at Chapel Hill.

Dennis, A., Erickson, K., & Hatch, P. (2013). *The Dynamic Learning Maps core vocabulary: Overview* [Technical review]. Retrieved from https://www.med.unc.edu/ahs/clds/files /2018/09/vocabulary-overview.pdf

Dessemontet, R. S., & de Chambrier, A-F. (2015). The role of phonological awareness and letter–sound knowledge in the reading development of children with intellectual disabilities. *Research in Developmental Disabilities, 41–42,* 1–12. doi:10.1016/j.ridd.2015.04.001

Dessemontet, R. S., de Chambrier, A.-F., Martinet, C., Moser, U., & Bayer, N. (2017). Exploring phonological awareness skills in children with intellectual disability. *American Journal on Intellectual and Developmental Disabilities, 122,* 476–491. doi:10.1352/1944-7558-122.6.476

Dijs, C. (1990). *Are you my mommy?* New York, NY: Little Simon.

Dilorenzo, K., Carlotta, A., Bucholz, J., & Brady, M. (2011). Teaching letter–sound connections with picture mnemonics: Itchy's alphabet and early decoding. *Preventing School Failure, 55*(1), 28–34. doi:10.1080/10459880903286763

Dole, J. A., Sloan, C., & Trathen, W. (1995). Teaching vocabulary within the context of literature. *Journal of Reading, 38,* 452–460.

Don Johnston Human Learning Tools. (n.d.). *Building wings.* Retrieved from https://learning tools.donjohnston.com/building-wings

Donnellan, A. M. (1984). The criterion of the least dangerous assumption. *Behavioral Disorders, 9,* 141–150. doi:10.1177/019874298400900201

Downing, J. (1971). *The cognitive clarity theory of learning to read.* Paper presented at the Annual Conference of the United Kingdom Reading Association. Retrieved from https://files.eric.ed.gov/fulltext/ED095477.pdf

Downing, J. (1979). *Reading and reasoning.* New York, NY: Springer-Verlag.

Downing, J. E. (2005). *Teaching literacy to students with significant disabilities: Strategies for the K-12 inclusive classroom.* Thousand Oaks, CA: Corwin Press.

Dr. Seuss. (1960). *Green eggs and ham.* New York, NY: Random House.

Duke, N. K., Pearson, P. D., Strachan, S. L., & Billman, A. K. (2011). Essential elements of fostering and teaching reading comprehension. In S. J. Samuels & A. Farstrup (Eds.), *What research has to say about reading instruction* (4th ed., pp. 51–93). Newark, DE: International Reading Association.

Dunphy, M. (2006). *Here is the coral reef.* Berkeley, CA: Publishers Group West.

Dunst, C. J., Trivette, C. M., Hamby, D. W., & Simkus, A. (2013). *Systematic review of studies promoting the use of assistive technology devices by young children with disabilities.* Morganton, NC: Orelena Hawks Puckett Institute Retrieved from https://files.eric.ed.gov /fulltext/ED565254.pdf

Dynamic Learning Maps Consortium. (2013). *Dynamic Learning Maps Essential Elements for English language arts.* Lawrence, KS: University of Kansas

Earle, G. A., & Sayeski, K. L. (2017). Systematic instruction in phoneme–grapheme correspondence for students with reading disabilities. *Intervention in School and Clinic, 52*(5), 262–269. doi:10.1177/1053451216676798

Edmark Reading Program [Software]. (2011). Austin, TX: PRO-ED.

Edmister, E. (2007). *Repeated reading and augmentative and alternative communication.* (Unpublished dissertation). University of Kansas, Lawrence, KS.

Edmonds, B. C., & Spradlin, T. (2010). What does it take to become a high-performing special education planning district? A study of Indiana's special education delivery service system. *Remedial and Special Education, 31,* 320–329. doi:10.1177/0741932508327451

Ehri, L. (2005). Development of sight word reading: Phases and findings. In M. Snowling & C. Hulme (Eds.), *The science of reading: A handbook* (pp. 135–154). Malden, MA: Blackwell.

Ehri, L. (2014). Orthographic mapping in the acquisition of sight word reading, spelling memory, and vocabulary learning, *Scientific Studies of Reading, 18,* 5–21, doi:10.1080/10888438 .2013.819356

Ehri, L. C., Deffner, N. D., & Wilce, L. S. (1984). Pictorial mnemonics for phonics. *Journal of Educational Psychology, 76,* 880–893. doi:10.1037/0022-0663.76.5.880

Ehri, L. C., Nunes, S. R., Willows, D. M., Schuster, B. V., Yaghoub-Zadeh, Z., & Shanahan, T. (2001). Phonemic awareness instruction helps children learn to read: Evidence from the National Reading Panel's meta-analysis. *Reading Research Quarterly, 36,* 250–287. doi:10.1598/RRQ.36.3.2

Ehri, L. C., Satlow, E., & Gaskins, I. (2009). Grapho-phonemic enrichment strengthens keyword analogy instruction for struggling young readers. *Reading and Writing Quarterly, 25,* 162–191. doi:10.1080/10573560802683549

Eiter, B. M., & Inhoff, A. W. (2010). Visual word recognition during reading is followed by subvocal articulation. *Journal of Experimental Psychology: Learning, Memory, and Cognition, 36,* 457–470. doi:10.1037/a0018278

Elbaum, B., Vaughn, S., Hughes, M., & Moody, S. W. (1999). Grouping practices and reading outcomes for students with disabilities. *Exceptional Children, 65,* 399–415. doi:10.1177 /001440299906500309

Erickson, K. A. (2013, October). Reading and assistive technology: Why the reader's profile matters. *Perspectives on Language and Literacy, 39,* 11–14. https://www.questia.com/library /p164699/perspectives-on-language-and-literacy/i4244555/vol-39-no-4-fall

Erickson, K. A. (2017). Comprehensive literacy instruction, interprofessional collaborative practice, and students with severe disabilities. *American Journal of Speech-Language Pathology, 26,* 193–205. doi:10.1044/2017_AJSLP-15-0067

Erickson, K. A., Clendon, S., Abraham, L., Roy, V., & Van de Carr, H. (2005). Toward positive literacy outcomes for students with significant developmental disabilities. *Assistive Technology Outcomes and Benefits, 2*(1), 45–54. https://www.atia.org/wp-content/uploads/2015 /10/ATOBV2N1.pdf

Erickson, K. A., & Geist, L. A. (2016). The profiles of students with significant cognitive disabilities and complex communication needs. *Augmentative and Alternative Communication, 32*(3), 187–197. doi:10.1080/07434618.2016.1213312

Erickson, K. A., Hanser, G., Hatch, P., & Sanders, E. (2009). *Research-based practices for creating access to the general curriculum in reading and literacy for students with significant intellectual disabilities.* Chapel Hill, NC: Center for Literacy and Disability Studies, University of North Carolina.

Erickson, K. A., Hatch, P., & Clendon, S. A. (2010). Literacy, assistive technology, and students with significant disabilities. *Focus on Exceptional Children, 42,* 1–16. doi:10.17161 /fec.v42i5.6904

Erickson, K. A., & Koppenhaver, D. A. (1998). Using the "write talk-nology" with Patrik. *Teaching Exceptional Children, 31,* 58–64. doi:10.1177/004005999803100108

Erickson, K. A., & Koppenhaver, D. A. (2007). *Children with disabilities: Reading and writing the Four-Blocks way.* Greensboro, NC: Carson-Dellosa.

Erickson, K. A., & Koppenhaver, D. A. (2018). *Visual attention to digital print in young girls with Rett syndrome.* Manuscript in preparation.

Erickson, K. A., Koppenhaver, D. A., & Cunningham, J. W. (2006). Balanced reading intervention and assessment in augmentative communication. In R. J. McCauley & M. E. Fey (Eds.), *Treatment of language disorders in children* (pp. 309–345). Baltimore, MD: Paul H. Brookes Publishing Co.

Erickson, K. A., Koppenhaver, D. A., & Cunningham, J. W. (2017). Comprehensive reading intervention in augmentative communication. In R. J. McCauley, M. E. Fey, & R. B. Gillam (Eds.), *Treatment of language disorders in children* (2nd ed., pp. 275–308). Baltimore, MD: Paul H. Brookes Publishing Co.

Erickson, K. A., Koppenhaver, D. A., & Yoder, D. E. (Eds.). (2002). *Waves of words: Augmented communicators read and write.* Toronto, Ontario, Canada: ISAAC Press.

Erickson, K. A., Koppenhaver, D. A., Yoder, D. E., & Nance, J. (1997). Integrated communication and literacy instruction for a child with multiple disabilities. *Focus on Autism and Other Developmental Disabilities, 12*(3), 142–150. doi:10.1177/108835769701200302

Every Students Succeeds Act of 2015, PL 114-95, 20 U.S.C. §§ *1001 et seq.*

Evans, A. (2018). *Different.* Scotts Valley, CA: CreateSpace Independent Publishing Platform.

Evans, M. D. R., Kelley, J., & Sikora, J. (2014). Scholarly culture and academic performance in 42 nations. *Social Forces, 92,* 1573–1605. doi:10.1093/sf/sou030

Ezell, H. K., & Justice, L. M. (2005). *Shared storybook reading: Building young children's language and emergent literacy skills.* Baltimore, MD: Paul H. Brookes Publishing Co.

Fallon, K. A., Cappa, J., & Day, J. (2008, November). *The home literacy experiences of young children who require AAC.* Poster presented at the meeting of the American Speech-Language-Hearing Association, Chicago, IL. Retrieved from https://www.asha.org/Events/convention/handouts/2008/0925_Cappa_Jayme

Fallon, K. A., Light, J., McNaughton, D., Drager, K., & Hammer, C. (2004). The effects of direct instruction on the single-word reading skills of children who require augmentative and alternative communication. *Journal of Speech, Language, and Hearing Research, 47,* 1424–1439. doi:10.1044/1092-4388(2004/106)

Finley Mosca, J. (2017). *The girl who thought in pictures: The story of Dr. Temple Grandin.* Seattle, WA: The Innovation Press.

Finnegan, E. G. (2012). Two approaches to phonics instruction: Comparison of effects with children with significant cognitive disability. *Education and Training in Autism and Developmental Disabilities, 47,* 269–279. http://daddcec.org/Publications/ETADDJournal.aspx

Fleury, V. P., & Hugh, M. (2018). Exploring engagement in shared reading activities between children with autism spectrum disorder and their caregivers. *Journal of Autism and Developmental Disorders, 48,* 3596–3607. doi:10.1007/s10803-018-3632-8

Flores, M. M., Shippen, M. E., Alberto, P., & Crowe, L. (2004). Teaching letter sound correspondences to students with moderate intellectual disabilities. *Journal of Direct Instruction, 16,* 173–188. https://www.nifdi.org/research/journal-of-di

Flower, L. S., & Hayes, J. R. (1981). A cognitive process theory of writing. *College Composition and Communication, 32,* 365–387. doi:10.2307/356600

Flowerday, T., & Shell, D. F. (2015). Disentangling the effects of interest and choice on learning, engagement, and attitude. *Learning and Individual Differences, 40,* 134–140. doi:10.1016/j.lindif.2015.05.003

Foorman, B. R., Schatschneider, C., Eakins, M. N., Fletcher, J. M., Moats, L., & Francis, D. J. (2006). The impact of instructional practices in grades 1 and 2 on reading and spelling achievement in high poverty schools. *Contemporary Educational Psychology, 31*(1), 1–29. doi:10.1016/j.cedpsych.2004.11.003

Foulin, J. N. (2005). Why is letter-name knowledge such a good predictor of learning to read? *Reading and Writing Quarterly, 18,* 129–155. doi:10.1007/s11145-004-5892-2

Fuchs, L. S., Fuchs, D., & Compton, D. L. (2004). Monitoring early reading development in first grade: Word identification fluency and nonsense word fluency. *Exceptional Children, 71,* 7–21. doi:10.1177/001440290407100101

Gambrell, L. B., Malloy, J. A., Marinak, B. A., & Mazzoni, S. A. (2014). Evidence-based best practices for comprehensive literacy instruction in the age of Common Core Standards. In L. B. Gambrell & L. M. Morrow (Eds.), *Best practices in literacy instruction* (5th ed., pp. 11–36). New York, NY: Guilford Press.

Gamse, B., Jacob, R., Horst, M., Boulay, B., & Unlu, F. (2008). *Reading First impact study final report.* Washington, DC: National Center for Education Evaluation and Regional Assistance, Institute of Education Sciences, U.S. Department of Education.

Gardner, D. (2004). Vocabulary input through extensive reading: A comparison of words found in children's narrative and expository reading materials. *Applied Linguistics, 25,* 1–37. doi:10.1093/applin/25.1.1

Gardner, H. (1999). Multiple approaches to understanding. In C. M. Reigeluth (Ed.), *Instructional design theories and models: A new paradigm of instructional theory* (Vol. II, pp. 69–89). Mahwah, NJ: Lawrence Erlbaum Associates.

Gaskins, I., Downer, M., Anderson, R., Cunningham, P., Gaskins, R., & Schommer, M. (1988). A metacognitive approach to phonics: Using what you know to decode what you don't know. *Remedial and Special Education, 9,* 36–41. doi:10.1177/074193258800900107

Gates, A. I., & Bond, G. L. (1936). Reading readiness: A study of factors determining success and failure in beginning reading. *Teachers College Record, 37,* 679–685.

Geisert, A. (1991). *Oink.* Boston, MA: Houghton Mifflin.

Geist, L., Erickson, K. A., Hatch, P., Erwin-Davidson, L., & Dorney, K. (2017, November). *Classroom-wide core vocabulary instruction for students with significant cognitive disabilities: Year two insights and results.* Paper presented at the annual meeting of the American Speech-Language-Hearing Association, Los Angeles, CA.

Gettinger, M., & Stoiber, K. C. (2014). Increasing opportunities to respond to print during storybook reading: Effects of evocative print-referencing techniques. *Early Childhood Research Quarterly, 29,* 283–297. doi:10.1016/j.ecresq.2014.03.001

Gillon, G. (2017). *Phonological awareness: From research to practice.* New York, NY: Guilford Press.

Gillon, G. (with Clendon, S., Cupples, L., Flynn, M., Iacono, T., Schmidtkie, T., Yoder, D., & Young, A.). (2003). Phonological awareness development in children with physical, sensory, or intellectual impairment. In G. Gillon (Ed.), *Phonological awareness: From research to practice* (pp. 183–223). New York, NY: Guilford Press.

Gipe, J., Duffy, C. A., & Richards, J. C. (1993). Helping a non-speaking adult male with cerebral palsy achieve literacy. *Journal of Reading, 36,* 380–389.

Girolametto, L., & Weitzman, E. (2002). Responsiveness of child care providers in interactions with toddlers and preschoolers. *Language, Speech, and Hearing Services in Schools, 33,* 268–281. https://doi.org/10.1044/0161- 1461(2002/022)

Good, T. L., & Brophy, J. E. (2008). *Looking in classrooms* (10th ed.). New York, NY: Pearson.

Goodwin, B. (2018). *Student learning that works: How brain science informs a student learning model.* Denver, CO: McREL International.

Gough, P. B., & Tunmer, W. E. (1986). Decoding, reading, and reading disability. *Remedial and Special Education, 7,* 6–10. doi:10.1177/074193258600700104

Gould, S. J. (1996). *The mismeasure of man.* New York, NY: W. W. Norton.

Graham, S. (2009–2010). Want to improve children's writing? Don't neglect their handwriting. *American Educator, 33,* 20–40. Retrieved from https://www.aft.org/sites/default/files/periodicals/graham.pdf

Graham, S., Bollinger, A., Olsen, C. B., D'Aoust, C., MacArthur, C., McCutchen, D., & Olinghouse, N. (2012). *Teaching elementary school students to be effective writers.* Retrieved from http://ies.ed.gov/ncee/wwc/PracticeGuide.aspx?sid=17

Graham, S., Harris, K. R., & Fink-Chorzempa, B. F. (2002). Contribution of spelling instruction to the spelling, writing, and reading of poor spellers. *Journal of Educational Psychology, 94,* 669–686. doi:10.1037/0022-0663.94.4.669

Graham, S., & Hebert, M. (2011). Writing to read: A meta-analysis of the impact of writing and writing instruction on reading. *Harvard Educational Review, 81*(4), 710–744. doi:10.17763/haer.81.4.t2k0m13756113566

Graham, K. & Hill, K. (2007, September). *A pilot study comparing AAC vocabulary usage patterns based on user experience.* Poster presented at the 2007 Clinical AAC Research Conference, Lexington, KY. Retrieved from https://aacinstitute.org/legacy/CAAC/2007/Accepted Submissions/GrahamPoster.pdf

Graham, S., Kiuhara, S., McKeown, D., & Harris, K. R. (2012). A meta-analysis of writing instruction for students in the elementary grades. *Journal of Educational Psychology, 104,* 879–896. doi:10.1037/a0029185

Graham, S., & Perin, D. (2007). A meta-analysis of writing instruction for adolescent students. *Journal of Educational Psychology, 99,* 445–476. doi:10.1037/0022-0663.99.3.445

Graham, S., & Santangelo, T. (2014). Does spelling instruction make students better spellers, readers, and writers? A meta-analytic review. *Reading and Writing, 27,* 1703–1743. doi:10.1007/s11145-0 14-9517-0

Grandin, T. (1995). *Thinking in pictures.* New York, NY: Vintage Books.

Graves, D. H. (1995). *A fresh look at writing.* Portsmouth, NH: Heinemann.

Gravett, E. (2006). *Orange pear apple bear.* New York, NY: Simon & Schuster.

Gray, W. S. (1969). *The teaching of reading and writing* (2nd ed.). Glenview, IL: UNESCO/Scott, Foresman and Co.

Greaney, K., Tunmer, W., & Chapman, J. (1997). Effects of rime based orthographic analogy training on the word recognition skills of children. *Journal of Educational Psychology, 89,* 645–651. doi:10.1037/0022-0663.89A645

Greene, B. A., Miller, R. B., Crowson, H. M., Duke, B. L., & Akey, K. L. (2004). Predicting high school students' cognitive engagement and achievement: Contributions of classroom perceptions and motivation. *Contemporary Educational Psychology, 29,* 462–482. doi:10.1016/j.cedpsych.2004.01.006

Greer, C. W., & Erickson, K. A. (2018). A preliminary exploration of uppercase letter–name knowledge among students with significant cognitive disabilities. *Reading and Writing, 31,* 173–183. doi:10.1007/s11145-017-9780-y

Guthrie, J. T. (2004). Teaching for literacy engagement. *Journal of Literacy Research, 36,* 1–30. doi:10.1207/s15548430jlr3601_2

Guthrie, J. T., & Davis, M. H. (2003). Motivating struggling readers in middle school through an engagement model of classroom practice. *Reading and Writing Quarterly: Overcoming Learning Difficulties, 19,* 59–85. doi:10.1080/10573560308203

Guthrie, J. T., & Klauda, S. (2014). Effects of classroom practices on reading comprehension, engagement, and motivations for adolescents. *Reading Research Quarterly, 49,* 387–416. doi:10.1002/rrq.81

Guthrie, J. T., Wigfield, A., Metsala, J. L., & Cox, K. E. (1999). Motivational and cognitive predictors of text comprehension and reading amount. *Scientific Studies of Reading, 3,* 231–256. doi:10.1207/s1532799xssr0303_3

Guthrie, J. T., Wigfield, A., & You, W. (2012). Instructional contexts for engagement and achievement in reading. In S. L. Christenson, A. L. Reschly, & C. Wylie (Eds.), *Handbook of research on student engagement* (pp. 601–634). New York, NY: Springer Science.

Haebig, E., & Sterling, A. (2017). Investigating the receptive-expressive vocabulary profile in children with idiopathic ASD and comorbid ASD and fragile X syndrome. *Journal of Autism and Developmental Disorders, 47,* 260–274. doi:10.1007/s10803-016-2921-3

Hall, D. P., & Williams, E. (2001). *Predictable charts: Shared writing for kindergarten and 1st grade.* Greensboro, NC: Carson-Dellosa.

Hammett-Price, L. H., van Kleeck, A., & Huberty, C. J. (2009). Talk during book sharing between parents and preschool children: A comparison between storybook and expository book conditions. *Reading Research Quarterly, 44,* 171–194. doi:10.1598/RRQ.44.2.4

Hammill, D. D. (2004). What we know about correlates of reading. *Exceptional Children, 70,* 453–468. doi:10.1177/001440290407000405

Hansen, B. D., Wadsworth, J. P., Roberts, M. R., & Poole, T. N. (2014). Effects of naturalistic instruction on phonological awareness skills of children with intellectual and developmental disabilities. *Research in Developmental Disabilities, 35,* 2790–2801. doi:10.1016/j.ridd.2014.07.011

Hanser, G. (2006). Promoting emergent writing for students with significant disabilities. *OT Practice, 11,* CE-1–CE-7.

Hanser, G., & Erickson, K. A. (2007). Integrated word identification and communication instruction for students with complex communication needs: Preliminary results. *Focus on Autism and Developmental Disabilities, 22,* 268–278. doi:10.1177/10883576070220040901

Hatch, P., & Erickson, K. A. (2018). Teacher experience, text access, and adolescents with significant disabilities. *Assistive Technology Outcomes and Benefits, 12,* 56–72. https://www.atia.org/wp-content/uploads/2019/01/ATOB-V12_Iss1_Article4.pdf

Haugen-McLane, J., Hohlt, J., & Haney, J. L. (2007). *PCI reading program.* Austin, TX: PRO-ED.

Heath, S. B. (1983). *Ways with words: Language, life, and work in communities and classrooms.* Cambridge, England: Cambridge University Press.

Hedrick, W. B., & Cunningham, J. W. (1995). The relationship between wide reading and listening comprehension of written language. *Journal of Reading Behavior, 27,* 425–438. doi:10.1080/10862969509547890

Hedrick, W. B., Katims, D. S., & Carr, N. J. (1999). Implementing a multimethod, multilevel literacy program for students with mental retardation. *Focus on Autism and Other Developmental Disabilities, 14,* 231–239. doi:10.1177/108835769901400405

Herlihy, C., Kemple, J., Bloom, H., Zhu, P., & Berlin, G. (2009, June). *Understanding Reading First: What we know, what we don't, and what's next.* Washington, DC: MDRC.

Hiebert, E. H. (2005). In pursuit of an effective, efficient vocabulary curriculum for elementary students. In E. H. Hiebert & M. L. Kamil (Eds.), *Teaching and learning* (pp. 243–263). Mahwah, NJ: Lawrence Erlbaum Associates.

Hillocks, G., Jr. (1987). Synthesis of research on teaching writing. *Educational Leadership, 44,* 71–82. www.ascd.org/ASCD/pdf/journals/ed_lead/el_198705_hillocks.pdf

Hillocks, G., Jr. (1995). *Teaching writing as reflective practice.* New York, NY: Teachers College Press.

Himmelman, J. (2006). *Chickens to the rescue.* New York, NY: Henry Holt and Co.

Hindson, B., Byrne, B., Fielding-Barnsley, R., Newman, C., Hine, D., & Shankweiler, D. (2005). Assessment and early instruction of pre-school children at risk for reading disability. *Journal of Educational Psychology, 97,* 687–704. doi:10.1037/0022-0663.97.4.687

Hirsch, E. D. (2003). Reading comprehension requires knowledge—of words and the world. *American Educator, 27,* 10, 12–13, 16–22, 28–29, 44. https://www.aft.org/sites/default/files/periodicals/Hirsch.pdf

Hogan, N., & Wolf, L. (2002). "I am a writer": Literacy, strategic thinking and meta-cognitive awareness. In K. A. Erickson, D. A. Koppenhaver, & D. E. Yoder (Eds.), *Waves of words: Augmentative communicators read and write* (pp. 21–40). Toronto, Ontario, Canada: ISAAC Press.

Holub, J., & Williams, S. (2012). *Zeus and the thunderbolt of doom.* New York, NY: Aladdin Publishing.

Holdaway, D. (1984). *The foundations of literacy.* Portsmouth, NH: Heinemann.

Holzwarth, W., & Erlbruch, W. (2007). *Story of the little mole who went in search of whodunit.* New York, NY: Harry N. Abrams.

Hoover, W. A., & Gough, P. B. (1990). The simple view of reading. *Reading and Writing: An Interdisciplinary Journal, 2,* 127–160. doi:10.1007/BF00401799

Hoyer, K. M., & Sparks, D. (2017, February). *Instructional time for third- and eighth-graders in public and private schools: School year 2011-2012.* Washington, DC: U.S. Department of Education, National Center for Education Statistics.

Huang, F. L., Tortorelli, L. S., & Invernizzi, M. A. (2014). An investigation of factors associated with letter–sound knowledge at kindergarten entry. *Early Childhood Research Quarterly, 29,* 182–192. https://doi.org/10.1016/j.ecresq.2014.02.001

Hulme, C., Bowyer-Crane, C., Carroll, J., Duff, F., & Snowling, M. (2012). The causal role of phoneme awareness and letter–sound knowledge in learning to read: Combining intervention studies with mediation analyses. *Psychological Science, 23,* 572–577. doi:10.1177/0956797611435921

Individuals with Disabilities Education Act (IDEA) of 1990, PL 101-476, 20 U.S.C. 1400 §§ *et seq.*

Ingalls, A. (2014). *J is for jazz.* Chicago, IL: Bright Connections Media.

Institute of Education Sciences. (n.d.). *Repeated reading: Students with a specific learning disability.* Washington, DC: Author. Retrieved from https://ies.ed.gov/ncee/wwc/Evidence Snapshot/576

International Communication Project. (2014). *The opportunity to communicate is a basic human right.* Retrieved from https://internationalcommunicationproject.com

Jimenez, B. A., Browder, D., & Courtade, G. R. (2009). An exploratory study of self-directed science concept learning by students with moderate developmental disabilities. *Research and Practice for Persons with Severe Disabilities, 34,* 33–46. doi:10.2511/rpsd.34.2.33

Johnson, G. (1998). Principles of instruction for at-risk learners. *Preventing School Failure, 42,* 167–174. doi:10.1080/10459889809603733

Johnston, S. S., Buchanan, S., & Davenport, L. (2009). Comparison of fixed and gradual array when teaching sound-letter correspondence to two children with autism who use AAC. *Augmentative and Alternative Communication, 25*(2), 136–144. doi:10.1080/07434610902921516

Jones, C. D., Clark, S. K., & Reutzel, D. R. (2013). Enhancing alphabet knowledge instruction: Research implications and practical strategies for early childhood educators. *Early Childhood Education Journal, 41,* 81–89. doi:10.1007/s10643-012-0534-9

Jones, C. D., & Reutzel, D. R. (2012). Enhanced alphabet knowledge instruction: Exploring a change of frequency, focus, and distributed cycles of review. *Reading Psychology, 33,* 448–464. doi:10.1080/02702711.2010.545260

Joseph, L. M., & Konrad, M. (2009). Teaching students with intellectual or developmental disabilities to write: A review of the literature. *Research in Developmental Disabilities, 30,* 1–19. doi:10.1016/j.ridd.2008.01.001

Joshi, R. M., Binks, E., Graham, L., Ocker-Dean, E., Smith, D., & Boulware-Gooden, R. (2009a). Do textbooks used in university reading education courses conform to the instructional recommendations of the National Reading Panel? *Journal of Learning Disabilities, 42*(5), 458–463. doi:10.1177/0022219409338739

Joshi, R. M., Binks, E., Hougen, M., Dahlgren, M., Ocker-Dean, E., & Smith, D. (2009b). Why elementary teachers might be inadequately prepared to teach reading. *Journal of Learning Disabilities, 42*(5), 392–402. doi:10.1177/0022219409338736

Justice, L. M., Chow, S., Capellini, C., Flanigan, K., & Colton, S. (2003). Emergent literacy intervention for vulnerable preschoolers: Relative effects of two approaches. *American Journal of Speech-Language Pathology, 12,* 320–332. doi:10.1044/1058-0360(2003/078)

Justice, L. M., & Ezell, H. K. (2004). Print referencing: An emergent literacy enhancement strategy and its clinical applications. *Language, Speech, and Hearing Services in Schools, 35,* 185–193. doi:10.1044/0161-1461(2004/018)

Justice, L. M., & Kaderavek, J. N. (2003). Topic control during shared storybook reading: Mothers and their children with language impairments. *Topics in Early Childhood Special Education, 23*(3), 137–150. doi:10.1177/02711214030230030401

Justice, L. M., Kaderavek, J. N., Bowles, R., & Grimm, K. (2005). Language impairment, parent child shared reading, and phonological awareness: A feasibility study. *Topics in Early Childhood Special Education, 25*(3), 143–156. doi:10.1177/02711214050250030201

Justice, L. M., Kaderavek, J. N., Fan, X., Sofka, A., & Hunt, A. (2009). Accelerating preschoolers' early literacy development through teacher-child storybook reading. *Language, Speech, and Hearing Services in the Schools, 40,* 67–85. doi:10.1044/0161-1461(2008/07-0098)

Justice, L., Logan, J., Isitan, A., & Sackes, M. (2016). Home literacy environment of young children with disabilities. *Early Childhood Research Quarterly, 37,* 131–139. doi:10.1016/j.ecresq.2016.05.002

Justice, L. M., McGinty, A. S., Piasta, S. B., Kaderavek, J. N., & Fan, X. (2010). Print-focused read-alouds in preschool classrooms: Intervention effectiveness and moderators of child outcomes. *Language, Speech, and Hearing Services in the Schools, 41,* 504–520. doi:10.1044/0161-1461(2010/09-0056

Justice, L. M., Pence, K., Bowles, R. B., & Wiggins, A. (2006). An investigation of four hypotheses concerning the order by which 4-year-old children learn the alphabet letters. *Early Childhood Research Quarterly, 21,* 374–389. doi:10.1016/j.ecresq.2006.07.010.

Justice, L., & Redle, R. (2014). *Communication sciences and disorders: A clinical evidence-based approach* (3rd ed.). Boston, MA: Pearson.

Kamil, M. L. (2004). Vocabulary and comprehension instruction: Summary and implications of the National Reading Panel findings. In P. McCardle & V. Chhabra (Eds.), *The voice of evidence in reading research* (pp. 213–234). Baltimore, MD: Paul H. Brookes Publishing Co.

Katims, D. S. (1991). Emergent literacy in early childhood special education: Curriculum and instruction. *Topics in Early Childhood Special Education, 11,* 69–84. https://doi.org/10.1177/027112149101100108

Katims, D. S. (1994). Emergence of literacy in preschool children with disabilities. *Learning Disability Quarterly, 17,* 58–69. doi:10.2307/1511105

Katims, D. S. (2000). Literacy instruction for people with mental retardation: Historical highlights and contemporary analysis. *Education and Training in Mental Retardation and Developmental Disabilities, 35*(1), 3–15. http://daddcec.org/Publications/ETADDJournal.aspx

Kentner, G. (2012). Linguistic rhythm guides parsing decisions in written sentence comprehension. *Cognition, 123*(1), 1–20. doi:10.1016/j.cognition.2011.11.012

Khan, R. (2014). *King for a day.* New York, NY: Lee & Low Books.

Kim, J. S., Hemphill, L., Troyer, M., Thomson, J. M., Jones, S. M., LaRusso, M. D., & Donovan, S. (2016). Engaging struggling adolescent readers to improve reading skills. *Reading Research Quarterly, 52*(3), 357–382. doi:10.1002/rrq.171

Kintsch, W. (1998). *Comprehension: A paradigm for cognition.* Cambridge, United Kingdom: Cambridge University Press.

Kintsch, W. (2004). The construction-integration model of text comprehension and its implications for instruction. In R. B. Ruddell & N. J. Unrau (Eds.), *Theoretical models and processes of reading* (5th ed., pp. 1270–1328). Newark, DE: International Reading Association.

Kirk, E. W., & Clark, P. (2005). Beginning with names: Using children's names to facilitate early literacy learning. *Childhood Education, 81,* 139–144. doi:10.1080/00094056.2005.10522257

Kliewer, C. (2008). Joining the literacy flow: Fostering symbol and written language learning in young children with significant developmental disabilities through the four currents of literacy. *Research and Practice for Persons with Severe Disabilities, 33,* 103–121. doi:10.2511/rpsd.33.3.103

Kliewer, C., & Biklen, D. (2001). "School's not really a place for reading": A research synthesis of the literate lives of students with severe disabilities. *Research and Practice for Persons with Severe Disabilities, 26,* 1–12. doi:10.2511/rpsd.26.1.1

Kliewer, C., Fitzgerald, L. M., Meyer-Mork, J., Hartman, P., English-Sand, P., & Raschke, D. (2004). Citizenship for all in the literate community: An ethnography of young children with significant disabilities in inclusive early childhood settings. *Harvard Educational Review, 74*(4), 373–403. doi:10.17763/haer.74.4.p46171013714642x

Klingner, J. K., Urbach, J., Golos, D., Brownell, M., & Menon, S. (2010). Teaching reading in the 21st century: A glimpse at how special education teachers promote reading comprehension. *Learning Disability Quarterly, 33,* 59–74. doi:10.1177/073194871003300201

Koch, K. (1970). *Wishes, lies, and dreams: Teaching children to write poetry.* New York, NY: HarperCollins.

Koppenhaver, D. A. (2000). Literacy in AAC: What should be written on the envelope we push? *Augmentative and Alternative Communication, 16,* 270–279. doi:10.1080/07434610012331279124

Koppenhaver, D. A., Coleman, P. P., Kalman, S. L., & Yoder, D. E. (1991). The implications of emergent literacy research for children with developmental disabilities. *American Journal of Speech-Language Pathology, 1,* 38–44. doi:10.1044/1058-0360.0101.38

Koppenhaver D. A., & Erickson K. A. (2003). Natural emergent literacy supports for preschoolers with autism and severe communication impairments. *Topics in Language Disorders, 23,* 283–292. doi:10.1097/00011363-200310000-00004

Koppenhaver, D. A., & Erickson, K. A. (2013). *Writing: Text types and purposes video transcript.* Lawrence, KS: Dynamic Learning Maps Alternate Assessment Consortium, Kansas University.

Koppenhaver, D. A., Erickson, K. A., & Skotko, B. G. (2001). Supporting communication of girls with Rett syndrome and their mothers in storybook reading. *International Journal of Disability, Development, and Education, 48*(4), 395–410. doi:10.1080/10349120120094284

Koppenhaver, D. A., Evans, D. A., & Yoder, D. E. (1991). Childhood reading and writing experiences of literate adults with severe speech and motor impairments. *Augmentative and Alternative Communication, 7*(1), 20–33. doi:10.1080/07434619112331275653

Koppenhaver, D. A., Hendrix, M. P., & Williams, A. R. (2007). Toward evidence-based literacy interventions for children with severe and multiple disabilities. *Seminars in Speech and Language, 28,* 79–90. doi:10.1055/s-2007-967932

Koppenhaver, D. A., Milosh, C. L., & Cheek, A. E. (2019). *"Literacy used to be a folder": Emergent communication and literacy for children with significant disabilities.* Manuscript in preparation.

Koppenhaver, D. A., & Williams, A. (2010). A conceptual review of writing research in augmentative and alternative communication. *Augmentative and Alternative Communication, 26,* 158–176. doi:10.3109/07434618.2010.505608

Koppenhaver, D. A., & Yoder, D. E. (1992). Literacy issues in persons with severe physical disabilities. In R. Gaylord-Ross (Ed.), *Issues and research in special education* (Vol. 2, pp. 156–201). New York, NY: Teachers College Press.

Koppenhaver, D. A., & Yoder, D. E. (1993). Classroom literacy instruction for children with severe speech and physical impairments (SSPI): What is and what might be. *Topics in Language Disorders, 13*(2), 1–15. doi:10.1097/00011363-199302000-00003

Korat, O. (2009). The effects of CD-ROM storybook reading on children's early literacy as a function of age group and repeated reading. *Education and Information Technologies, 14,* 39–53. doi:10.1007/s10639-008-9063-y

Korat, O., & Shamir, A. (2007). Electronic books versus adult readers: Effects on children's emergent literacy as a function of social class. *Journal of Computer Assisted Learning, 23,* 248–259. doi:10.1111/j.1365-2729.2006.00213.x

Korat, O., & Shamir, A. (2008). The educational electronic book as a tool for supporting children's emergent literacy in low versus middle SES groups. *Computers and Education, 50,* 110–124. doi:10.1016/j.compedu.2006.04.002

Korat, O., Shamir, A., & Heibal, S. (2013). Expanding the boundaries of shared book reading: E-books and printed books in parent–child reading as support for children's language. *First Language, 33,* 504–523. doi:10.1177/0142723713503148

Krashen, S. (2004). *The power of reading: Insights from the research* (2nd ed.). Portsmouth, NH: Heinemann.

Kuhn, M. R. (2005). A comparative study of small group fluency instruction. *Reading Psychology, 26,* 127–146. doi:10.1080/02702710590930492

Lai, T. (2013). *Inside out and back again.* New York, NY: HarperCollins.

Langstaff, J., & Rojankovsky, F. (1973). *Over in the meadow.* Boston, MA: Houghton Mifflin Harcourt.

Lanter, E., Watson, L. R., Erickson, K. A., & Freeman, D. (2012). Emergent literacy in children with autism: An exploration of developmental and contextual dynamic processes. *Language, Speech, and Hearing Services in Schools, 43,* 308–324. doi:10.1044/0161-1461 (2012/10-0083)

Lau, K. L. (2009). Grade differences in reading motivation among Hong Kong primary and secondary students. *British Journal of Educational Psychology, 79*(4), 713–733. doi:10.1348 /000709909X460042

Leech, K. A., & Rowe, M. L. (2014). A comparison of preschool children's discussions with parents during picture book and chapter book reading. *First Language, 34*(3), 205–226. doi:10.1177/0142723714534220

Lemons, C. J., King, S. A., Davidson, K. A., Puranik, C. S., Fulmer, D., Mrachko, A. A., . . . Fidler, D. J. (2015). Adapting phonological awareness interventions for children with Down syndrome based on the behavioral phenotype: A promising approach? *Intellectual and Developmental Disabilities, 53,* 271–288. doi:10.1352/1934-9556-53.4.271

Lemons, C. J., Mrachko, A. A., Kostewicz, D. E., & Paterra, M. F. (2012). Effectiveness of decoding and phonological awareness interventions for children with Down syndrome. *Exceptional Children, 79,* 67–90. doi:10.1177/001440291207900104

Liboiron, N., & Soto, G. (2006). Shared storybook reading with a student who uses alternative and augmentative communication: A description of scaffolding practices. *Child Language Teaching and Therapy, 22,* 69–95. doi:10.1191/0265659006ct298oa

Lieber, J., Horn, E., Palmer, S., & Fleming, K. (2008). Access to the general education curriculum for preschoolers with disabilities: Children's school success. *Exceptionality, 16,* 18–32. doi:10.1080/09362830701796776

Light, J., & Kelford Smith, A. (1993). The home literacy experiences of preschoolers who use augmentative communication systems and of their nondisabled peers. *Augmentative and Alternative Communication, 10,* 255–268. doi:10.1080/07434619412331276960

Light, J., & McNaughton, D. (1993). Literacy and augmentative and alternative communication (AAC): The expectations and priorities of parents and teachers. *Topics in Language Disorders, 13,* 33–46. doi:10.1097/00011363-199302000-00005

Light, J., & McNaughton, D. (2009). *Accessible Literacy Learning (ALL): Evidence-based reading instruction for learners with autism, cerebral palsy, Down syndrome, and other disabilities.* Pittsburgh, PA: Mayer-Johnson.

Light, J., McNaughton, D., Weyer, M., & Karg, L. (2008). Evidence-based literacy instruction for individuals who require augmentative and alternative communication: A case study of a student with multiple disabilities. *Seminars in Speech and Language, 29,* 120–132. doi:10.1055/s-2008-1079126

Light, J., & Smith, A. K. (1993). Home literacy experiences of preschoolers who use AAC systems and of their nondisabled peers. *Augmentative and Alternative Communication, 9,* 10–25. doi:10.1080/07434619312331276371

Linebarger, D., Piotrowski, J., & Greenwood, C. R. (2010). On-screen print: The role of captions as a supplemental literacy tool. *Journal of Research in Reading, 33,* 148–167. doi:10.1111/j.1467-9817.2009.01407.x

Lipson, M. Y., & Wixson, K. K. (2013). *Assessment of reading and writing difficulties: An interactive approach* (5th ed.). Boston, MA: Pearson.

Lonigan, C. J., Burgess, S. R., & Anthony, J. L. (2000). Development of emergent literacy and early reading skills in preschool children: Evidence from a latent variable longitudinal study. *Developmental Psychology, 36,* 596–613. doi:10.1037/0012-1649.36.5.596

Lonigan, C. J., & Whitehurst, G. J. (1998). Relative efficacy of parent and teacher involvement in a shared-reading intervention for preschool children from low-income backgrounds. *Early Childhood Research Quarterly, 13,* 263–290. doi:10.1016/S0885-2006(99)80038-6

Loveall, S. J., Channell, M. M., Phillips, B. A., Abbeduto, L. J., & Conners, F. A. (2016). Receptive vocabulary analysis in Down syndrome. *Research in Developmental Disabilities, 55,* 161–172. doi:10.1016/j.ridd.2016.03.018

Luke, S. G., & Henderson, J. M. (2013). Oculomotor and cognitive control of eye movements in reading: Evidence from mindless reading. *Attention, Perception, and Psychophysics, 75,* 1230–1242. doi:10.3758/s13414-013-0482-5

MacGinitie, W., MacGinitie, R., Maria, K., Dreyer, L., & Hughes, K. (2000). *Gates-MacGinitie reading tests* (4th ed.). Rolling Meadows, IL: Riverside Publishing.

Marinak, B. A., Gambrell, L. B., & Mazzoni, S. A. (2012). *Maximizing motivation for literacy learning: Grades K-6.* New York, NY: Guilford Press.

Martin, A. J., & Dowson, M. (2009). Interpersonal relationships, motivation, engagement, and achievement: Yields for theory, current issues, and educational practice. *Review of Educational Research, 79,* 327–365. doi:10.3102/0034654308325583

Marvin, C. (1994). Home literacy experiences of preschool children with single and multiple disabilities. *Topics in Early Childhood Special Education, 14,* 436–454. doi:10.1177/027112149401400405

Marvin, C., & Mirenda, P. (1993). Home literacy experiences of preschoolers enrolled in Head Start and special education programs. *Journal of Early Intervention, 17,* 351–367. doi:10.1177/105381519301700402

Mason, J. M., & Stewart, J. P. (1990). Emergent literacy assessment for instructional use in kindergarten. In L. M. Morrow & J. K. Smith (Eds.), *Assessment for instruction in early literacy* (pp. 155–175). Upper Saddle River, NJ: Prentice-Hall.

Maxwell, A. (2018). *Once upon a slime.* Boston, MA: Hachette Book Group, Little, Brown Books for Young Readers.

May, L., Byers-Heinlein, K., Gervain, J., & Werker, J. F. (2011). Language and the newborn brain: Does prenatal language experience shape the neonate neural response to speech? *Frontiers in Psychology, 2*(Article 222), 1–9. doi:10.3389/fpsyg.2011.00222

McArthur, D., Adamson, L., & Deckner, D. F. (2005). As stories become familiar: Mother–child conversations during shared reading. *Merrill-Palmer Quarterly, 51,* 389–411. doi:10.1353/mpq.2005.0025

McCutcheon, J. (2006). *Christmas in the trenches.* Atlanta, GA: Peachtree Publishers.

McDonnell, A. P., Hawken, L. S., Johnston, S. S., Kidder, J. E., Lynes, M. J., & McDonnell, J. J. (2014). Emergent literacy practices and support for children with disabilities: A national survey. *Education and Treatment of Children, 37,* 495–530. doi:10.1353/etc.2014.0024

McGee, L. M., & Schickedanz, J. A. (2007). Repeated interactive read-alouds in preschool and kindergarten. *The Reading Teacher, 60,* 742–751. doi:10.1598/RT.60.8.4

McGraw, A., & Mason, M. (2017). Reading as an imaginative act: Strategies for reading. *Idiom, 53*(3), 50–56. https://idiomjournal.wordpress.com/

McKenna, R. (1972). *New eyes for old: Nonfiction writings.* Winston-Salem, NC: J. F. Blair.

McKenzie, A. R. (2009). Emergent literacy supports for students who are deaf-blind or have visual and multiple impairments: A multiple-case study. *Journal of Visual Impairment and Blindness, 103,* 291–302. doi:10.1177/0145482X0910300507

McSheehan, M., Sonnenmeier, R., Jorgensen, C., & Turner, K. (2006). Beyond communication access: Promoting learning of the general education curriculum by students with significant disabilities. *Topics in Language Disorders, 26,* 266–291. doi:10.1097/00011363-200607000-00008

Melby-Lervåg, M., Lyster, S. H. A., & Hulme, C. (2012). Phonological skills and their role in learning to read: A meta-analytic review. *Psychological Bulletin, 128,* 322–352. doi:10.1037/a0026744

Mesmer, H. A., Cunningham, J. W., & Hiebert, E. H. (2012). Toward a theoretical model of text complexity for the early grades: Learning from the past, anticipating the future. *Reading Research Quarterly, 47,* 235–258. doi:10.1002/rrq.019

Meyer, D. K., & Turner, J. C. (2002). Discovering emotion in classroom motivation research. *Educational Psychologist, 37,* 107–114. doi:10.1207/S15326985EP3702_5

Mike, D. G. (1995). Literacy and cerebral palsy: Factors influencing literacy learning in a self-contained setting. *Journal of Reading Behavior, 27,* 627–641. doi:10.1080/10862969509547902

Miller, G. A., & Gildea, P. M. (1987). How to misread a dictionary. *AILA Bulletin,* Pisa, 13–26.

Milton, N. (2013). *The giraffe that walked to Paris.* Cynthiana, KY: Purple House Press.

Mims, P., Browder, D., Baker, J., Lee, A., & Spooner, F. (2009). Increasing participation of students with significant cognitive disabilities and visual impairments during shared stories. *Education and Training in Developmental Disabilities, 44,* 409–420. http://daddcec.org/Publications/ETADDJournal.aspx

Mims, P. J., Hudson, M. E., & Browder, D. M. (2012). Using read-alouds of grade-level biographies and systematic prompting to promote comprehension for students with moderate and severe developmental disabilities. *Focus on Autism and Other Developmental Disabilities, 27,* 67-80. doi:10.1177/1088357612446859

Miura, T. (2006). *Tools.* San Francisco, CA: Chronicle Books.

Mol, S. E., & Bus, A. G. (2011). To read or not to read: A meta-analysis of print exposure from infancy to early adulthood. *Psychological Bulletin, 137,* 267–296. doi:10.1037/a0021890

Moon, C. (2017). Prenatal experience with the maternal voice. In M. Filippa, P. Kuhn, & B. Westrup (Eds.), *Early vocal contact and preterm infant brain development* (pp. 22–37). New York, NY: Springer. doi:10.1007/978-3-319-65077

Moon, C., Lagercrantz, H., & Kuhl, P. K. (2013). Language experienced in utero affects vowel perception after birth: A two-country study. *Acta Paediatrica, 102,* 156–160. doi:10.1111/apa.12098

Morgan, P. L., & Fuchs, D. (2007). Is there a bidirectional relationship between children's reading skills and reading motivation? *Exceptional Children, 73,* 165–183. doi:10.1177/001440290707300203

Morris, D., Bloodgood, J. W., Lomax, R. G., & Perney, J. (2003). Developmental steps in learning to read: A longitudinal study in kindergarten and first grade. *Reading Research Quarterly, 38,* 302–328. doi:10.1598/RRQ.38.3.1

Morris, D., Trathen, W., Gill, T., Schlagal, R., Ward, D., & Frye, E. M. (2017). Assessing reading rate in the primary grades (1–3). *Reading Psychology, 38,* 653–672. doi:10.1080/02702711.2017.1323057

Mucchetti, C. A. (2013). Adapted shared reading at school for minimally verbal students with autism. *Autism, 17,* 358–372. doi:10.1177/1362361312470495

Munsch, R. (2018). *Angela's airplane.* Toronto, Canada: Annick Press.

Murray, B. A., Stahl, S. A., & Ivey, M. G. (1996). Developing phoneme awareness through alphabet books. *Reading and Writing: An Interdisciplinary Journal, 8,* 307–322. doi:10.1007/BF00395111

Murray, D. (1991). *The craft of revision.* Austin, TX: Holt, Rinehart, and Winston.

Musselwhite, C. (2006). *Famous.* Volo, IL: Don Johnston.

Muter, V., Hulme, C., Snowling, M. J., & Stevenson, J. (2004). Phonemes, rimes, vocabulary, and grammatical skills as foundations of early reading development: Evidence from a longitudinal study. *Developmental Psychology, 40,* 665–681. doi:10.1037/0012-1649.40.5.665

Nagy, W. E. (1988). *Teaching vocabulary to improve reading comprehension.* Newark, DE: International Reading Association.

Nagy, W. E., Anderson, R. C., & Herman, P. A. (1987). Learning word meaning from context during normal reading. *American Educational Research Journal, 24,* 237–270. doi:10.3102/00028312024002237

Nagy, W. E., & Herman, P. A. (1987). Breadth and depth of vocabulary knowledge: Implications for acquisition and instruction. In M. G. McKeown & M. E. Curtis (Eds.), *The nature of vocabulary acquisition* (pp. 19–35). Mahwah, NJ: Lawrence Erlbaum Associates.

Nagy, W. E., Herman, P. A., & Anderson, R. (1985). Learning words from context. *Reading Research Quarterly, 20,* 233–253. doi:10.2307/747758

Nash, H., & Snowling, M. (2006). Teaching new words to children with poor existing vocabulary knowledge: A controlled evaluation of the definition and context methods. *International Journal of Language and Communication Disorders, 41,* 335–354. doi:10.1080/13682820600602295

Nation, I. S. P. (2001). *Learning vocabulary in another language.* Cambridge, United Kingdom: Cambridge University Press.

Nation, K. (2005). Children's reading comprehension difficulties. In M. Snowling & C. Hulme (Eds.), *The science of reading: A handbook* (pp. 248–265). Malden, MA: Blackwell Publishing.

Nation, K., & Norbury, C. F. (2005). Why reading comprehension fails: Insights from developmental disorders, *Topics in Language Disorders, 25,* 21–32. doi:10.1097/00011363-200501000-00004

Anderson, R. C., et al. (1985). *Becoming a nation of readers: The report of the Commission on Reading.* Washington, DC: National Academy of Education.

National Center for Educational Statistics. (2017). *Fast facts: Back to school statistics.* Retrieved from https://nces.ed.gov/fastfacts/display.asp?id=372

National Early Literacy Panel. (2008). *Developing early literacy: Report of the National Early Literacy Panel.* Washington, DC: National Institute for Literacy. Retrieved from https://lincs.ed.gov/publications/pdf/NELPReport09.pdf

National Geographic Kids (2012). *Just joking: 300 hilarious jokes, tricky tongue twisters, and ridiculous riddles.* Washington, DC: National Geographic Children's Books.

Eunice Kennedy Shriver National Institute of Child Health and Human Development. (2000). *Report of the National Reading Panel: Teaching children to read*: Reports of the subgroups (00-4754). Washington, DC: U.S. Government Printing Office. Retrieved from https://www.nichd.nih.gov/publications/pubs/nrp/smallbook

National Institute for Child Health and Development, Early Child Care Research Network (2005). *Child care and child development: Results from the NICHD study of early child care and youth development.* New York, NY: Guilford Press.

Ness, A. (2017, August 2). *Teachers spend hundreds of dollars a year on school supplies. That's a problem.* Retrieved from https://www.edweek.org/tm/articles/2017/08/02/teachers-spend-hundreds-of-dollars-a-year.html

Neuman, S. B. (2006). Speak up! How to help children build a robust vocabulary day by day. *Scholastic Early Childhood Today, 20*(4), 12-13.

Neuman, S. B., & Dwyer, J. (2009). Missing in action: Vocabulary instruction in PreK. *The Reading Teacher, 62,* 384–392. doi:10.1598/RT.62.5.2

Neumann, M. M., Finger, G., & Neumann, D. L. (2017). A conceptual framework for emergent digital literacy. *Early Childhood Education Journal, 45,* 471–479. doi.org:10.1007/s10643-016-0792-z

Nieminem, L. (2018). *Cookies!: An interactive recipe book (cook in a book).* New York, NY: Phaidon Press.

No Child Left Behind Act of 2001, PL 107-110, 115 Stat. 1425, 20 U.S.C. §§ 6301 *et seq.*

Noddings, N. (2013). *Caring: A relational approach to ethics and moral education* (2nd ed.). Berkeley, CA: University of California Press.

O'Brien, D., & Rogers, T. (2016). Sociocultural perspectives on literacy and learning. In L. Corno & E. M. Anderman (Eds.), *Handbook of educational psychology* (3rd ed., pp. 311–322). New York, NY: Routledge.

Ogle, D. M. (1986). K-W-L: A teaching model that develops active reading of expository text. *The Reading Teacher, 39,* 564–570. doi:10.1598/RT.39.6.11

Organisation for Economic Co-operation and Development. (2010a). *PISA 2009 results: What students know and can do–Student performance in reading, mathematics, and science* (Vol. 1). doi:10.1787/9789264091450-en

Organisation for Economic Co-operation and Development. (2010b). *The high cost of low educational performance: The long-run economic impact of improving PISA outcomes.* Paris, France: Author. doi:10.1787/9789264077485-en

Osana, H. P., Lacroix, G. L., Tucker, B. J., Idan, E., & Jabbour, G. W. (2007). The impact of print exposure quality and inference construction on syllogistic reasoning. *Journal of Educational Psychology, 99,* 888–902. doi:10.1037/0022-0663.99.4.888

Owocki, G., & Goodman, Y. (2002). *Kidwatching: Documenting children's literacy development.* Portsmouth, NH: Heinemann.

Palacios, N. (2017). Why all teachers matter: The relationship between long-term teacher and classroom quality and children's reading achievement. *Journal of Research in Childhood Education, 31,* 178–198. doi:10.1080/02568543.2016.1272509

Park, Y., Brownell, M. T., Benedict, A. E., & Bettini, E. F. (2019). Multiple dimensions of instructional effectiveness in reading: A review of classroom observation studies and implications for special education classrooms. *Exceptionality, 27,* 1–17. doi:10.1080/09362835.2017.1283628

Peeters, M., de Moor, J., & Verhoeven, L. (2011). Emergent literacy activities, instructional adaptations and school absence of children with cerebral palsy in special education. *Research in Developmental Disabilities, 32,* 659–668. doi:10.1016/j.ridd.2010.12.002

Penfold A. (2018). *All are welcome.* New York, NY: Knopf Books for Young Readers.

Pennell, A. E., Wollak, B., & Koppenhaver, D. A. (2017). Respectful representations of disability in picture books. *Reading Teacher, 71,* 411–419. doi:10.1002/trtr.1632

Pennington, R. C., & Delano, M. E. (2012). Writing instruction for students with autism spectrum disorders: A review of literature. *Focus on Autism and Other Developmental Disabilities, 27,* 158–167. doi:10.1177/1088357612451318

Perfetti, C. A. (2007). Reading ability: Lexical quality to comprehension. *Scientific Studies of Reading, 11,* 357–383. doi:10.1080/10888430701530730

Perkins, D., & Unger, C. (1999). Teaching and learning for understanding. In C. M. Reigeluth (Ed.), *Instructional design theories and models: A new paradigm of instructional theory* (Vol. II, pp. 91–114). Mahwah, NJ: Lawrence Erlbaum Associates.

Petursdottir, A., McMaster, K., McComas, J., Bradfield, T., Braganza, V., Koch-McDonald, J., & Scharf, H. (2009). Brief experimental analysis of early reading interventions. *Journal of School Psychology, 47,* 215–243. doi:10.1016/j.jsp.2009.02.003

Pew Research Center. (2012). *The rise of e-reading.* Washington, DC: Pew Research Center's Internet and American Life Project.

Phillips, B. M., Clancy-Manchetti, J., & Lonigan, C. J. (2008). Successful phonological awareness instruction with preschool children. *Topics in Early Childhood Special Education, 28,* 3–17. doi:10.1177/0271121407313813

Pianta, R. C. (1998). Applying the concept of resilience in schools: Cautions from a developmental systems perspective. *School Psychology Review, 27,* 407–428.

Piasta, S. B., Groom, L. J., Khan, K. S., Skibbe, L. E., & Bowles, R. P. (2018). Young children's narrative skill: Concurrent and predictive associations with emergent literacy and early word reading skills. *Reading and Writing, 31,* 1479–1498. doi:10.1007/s11145-018-9844-7

Piasta, S. B., Petscher, Y., & Justice, L. M. (2012). How many letters should children in public preschool programs know? The diagnostic efficiency of various preschool letter naming benchmarks for predicting first-grade literacy achievement. *Journal of Educational Psychology, 104,* 945–958. doi:10.1037/a0027757

Piasta, S. B., & Wagner, R. K. (2010a). Developing early literacy skills: A meta-analysis of alphabet learning and instruction. *Reading Research Quarterly, 45,* 8–38. doi:10.1598/RRQ.45.1.2

Piasta, S. B., & Wagner, R. K. (2010b). Learning letter names and sounds: Effects of instruction, letter type and phonological processing skill. *Journal of Experimental Child Psychology, 105,* 324–344. doi:10.1016/j.jecp.2009.12.008

Pilkey, D. (1994). *The dumb bunnies.* New York, NY: Scholastic.

Pilkey, D. (2015). *Ricky Ricotta's mighty robot vs. the uranium unicorns from Uranus.* New York, NY: Scholastic.

Pinkwater, D. (2010). *I am the dog.* New York, NY: HarperCollins.

Portis, A. (2011). *Not a box.* New York, NY: HarperFestival.

Prelutsky, J. (1984). *The new kid on the block.* New York, NY: Greenwillow Books.

Pressley, M., & Allington, R. (2014). *Reading instruction that works: The case for balanced teaching* (4th ed.). New York, NY: Guilford Press.

Pufpaff, L. A., Blischak, D. M., & Lloyd, L. L. (2000). Effects of modified orthography on the identification of printed words. *American Journal on Mental Retardation, 105*(1), 14–24. doi:10.1352/0895-8017(2000)105<0014:EOMOOT>2.0.CO;2

Raschka, C. (1997). *Charlie Parker played be bop.* New York, NY: Scholastic.

Rayner, K., & Pollatsek, A. (1989). *The psychology of reading.* Upper Saddle River, NJ: Prentice Hall.

Reichenberg, M. (2014). The importance of structured text talks for students' reading comprehension: An intervention study in special schools. *Journal of Special Education and Rehabilitation, 15,* 77–94. doi:10.2478/JSER-2014-0012

Reichle, E. D., & Perfetti, C. A. (2003). Morphology in word identification: A word-experience model that accounts for morpheme frequency effects. *Scientific Studies of Reading, 7,* 219–238. doi:10.1207/S1532799XSSR0703_2

Richards, B. A., & Frankland, P. W. (2017). The persistence and transience of memory. *Neuron, 94,* 1071–1081. doi:10.1016/j.neuron.2017.04.037

Ringgold, F. (1996). *Tar beach.* New York, NY: Penguin-Random House.

Roberts, L. (2002). *Dirty Bertie.* London, England: Little Tiger Press.

Roberts, C. A., Leko, M. M., & Wilkerson, K. L. (2013). New directions in reading instruction for adolescents with significant cognitive disabilities. *Remedial and Special Education, 34,* 305–317. doi:10.1177/0741932513485447

Roberts, G., Torgesen, T., Boardman, A., & Scammacca, N. (2008). Evidence-based strategies for reading instruction of older students with learning disabilities. *Learning Disability Research and Practice, 23,* 63–69. doi:10.1111/j.1540-5826.2008.00264.x

Roberts, T. A., Vadasy, P. F., & Sanders, E. A. (2018). Preschoolers' alphabet learning: Letter name and sound instruction, cognitive processes, and English proficiency. *Early Childhood Research Quarterly, 44,* 257–274. doi:10.1016/j.ecresq.2018.04.011

Rockoff, J. E. (2004). The impact of individual teachers on student achievement: Evidence from panel data. *American Economic Review, 94*(2), 247–252. doi:10.1257/0002828041302244

Romski, M. A., & Sevcik, R. A. (1996). *Breaking the speech barrier: Language development through augmented means.* Baltimore, MD: Paul H. Brookes Publishing Co.

Rose, D., & Meyer, A. (2002). *Teaching every student in the digital age: Universal design for learning.* Alexandria, VA: Association for Supervision and Curriculum Development.

Rose, T. L., & Furr, P. M. (1984). Negative effects of illustrations as word cues. *Journal of Learning Disabilities, 17*(6), 334–337. doi:10.1177/002221948401700605

Rosenstock, B. (2018). *Otis and Will discover the deep: The record-setting dive of the bathysphere.* Boston, MA: Hachette Book Group, Little, Brown Books for Young Readers.

Rosenthal, A. K., & Lichtenheld, T. (2009). *Duck! Rabbit!* San Francisco, CA: Chronicle Books.

Rousseau, M. K., Krantz, P. J., Poulson, C. L., Kitson, M. E., & McClannahan, L. E. (1994). Sentence combining as a technique for increasing adjective use in writing by students with autism. *Research in Developmental Disabilities, 15,* 19–37. doi:10.1016/0891-4222(94)90036-1

Ruppar, A. L. (2015). A preliminary study of the literacy experiences of adolescents with severe disabilities. *Remedial and Special Education, 36*(4), 235–245. doi:10.1177/0741932514558095

Ruppar, A., Fisher, K. W., Olson, A. J., & Orlando, A. (2018). Exposure to literacy for students eligible for the alternate assessment. *Education and Training in Autism and Developmental Disabilities, 52*(2), 192–208.

Rush, W. L. (1986). *Journey out of silence.* Swanley, England: Media Publishing.

Rvachew, S., Rees, K., Carolan, E., & Nadig, A. (2017). Improving emergent literacy with school-based shared reading: Paper versus e-books. *International Journal of Child-Computer Interaction.* doi:10.1016/j.ijcci.2017.01.002

Ryan, R. M., & Deci, E. L. (2000). Intrinsic and extrinsic motivations: Classic definitions and new directions. *Contemporary Educational Psychology, 25,* 54–67. doi:10.1006/ceps.1999.1020

Ryan, R. M., & Deci, E. L. (2009). Promoting self-determined school engagement: Motivation, learning, and well-being. In K. R. Wenzel & A. Wigfield (Eds.), *Handbook of motivation at school* (pp. 171–195). New York, NY: Routledge.

Ryndak, D., Morrison, A., & Sommerstein, L. (1999). Literacy prior to and after inclusion in general education settings. *Journal of The Association for Persons with Severe Handicaps, 24,* 5–22. doi:10.2511/rpsd.24.1.5

Samuels, J. (1967). *Attentional processes in reading: The effects of pictures on the acquisition of reading responses.* Minneapolis, MN: University of Minnesota.

Samuels, S. J., Ediger, K. M., Willcutt, J. R., & Palumbo, T. J. (2005). Role of automaticity in metacognition and literacy instruction. In S. E. Israel, C. Block, K. L. Bauserman, K. Kinnucan-Welsch (Eds.), *Metacognition in literacy learning: Theory, assessment, instruction, and professional development* (pp. 41–59). Mahwah, NJ: Lawrence Erlbaum Associates.

Santangelo, T., & Graham, S. (2016). A comprehensive meta-analysis of handwriting instruction. *Educational Psychology Review, 28,* 225–265. doi:10.1007/s10648-015-9335-1

Saunder, R. J., & Solman, R. T. (1984). The effect of pictures on the acquisition of a small vocabulary of similar sight-words. *British Journal of Educational Psychology, 54*(3), 265–275. doi:10.1111/j.2044-8279.1984.tb02590.x

Scarborough, H. S., & Brady, S. A. (2002). Toward a common terminology for talking about speech and reading: A glossary of the "phon" words and some related terms. *Journal of Literacy Research, 34*(3), 299–336. doi:10.1207/s15548430jlr3403_3

Schaffner, E., & Schiefele, U. (2016). The contributions of intrinsic and extrinsic reading motivation to the development of reading competence over summer vacation. *Reading Psychology, 37*, 917–941. doi:10.1080/02702711.2015.1133465

Scholastic. (2015a). *Kids and family reading report: 2015.* New York, NY: Author. Retrieved from https://www.scholastic.com/content/dam/KFRR/PastReports/KFRR2015_5th.pdf

Scholastic. (2015b). *Kids and family reading report: Australia, 2015.* NSW, Australia: Author. Retrieved from http://www.scholastic.com.au/schools/ReadingLeaders/KFRR/assets/pdf/KFRR_AUS.pdf

Scholastic (2015c). *Kids and family reading report: United Kingdom.* London, England: Author. Retrieved from https://d3ddkgxe55ca6c.cloudfront.net/assets/t1454587759/a/3f/36/kfrr-uk-fnl-11-1423200.pdf

Schuele, M., & Boudreau, D. (2008). Phonological awareness intervention: Beyond the basics. *Language Speech and Hearing Services in Schools, 39*, 3–20. doi:10.1044/0161-1461(2008/002)

Scieszka, J. (2003). *Squids will be squids: Fresh morals, beastly fables.* New York, NY: Puffin Books.

Seeger, L. V. (2016). *Black? White! Day? Night! A book of opposites.* New York, NY: Macmillan, Roaring Brook Press.

Segal-Drori, O., Korat, O., Shamir, A., & Klein, P. (2010). Reading electronic and printed books with and without adult instruction: Effects on emergent reading. *Reading and Writing, 23*, 913–930. doi:10.1007/s11145-009-9182-x

Sénéchal, M., LeFevre, J., Smith-Chant, B., & Colton, K. (2001). On refining theoretical models of emergent literacy: The role of empirical evidence. *Journal of School Psychology, 39*(5), 439–460. doi:10.1016/S0022-4405(01)00081-4

Sennott, S., Light, J., & McNaughton, D. (2016). AAC modeling intervention research review. *Research and Practice for Persons with Severe Disabilities, 41*, 101–115. doi:10.1177/1540796916638822

Sennott, S. C., & Mason, L. M. (2016). AAC modeling with the iPad during shared storybook reading pilot study. *Communication Disorders Quarterly, 37*(4) 242–254. doi:10.1177/1525740115601643

Seuss, Dr. (1960). *Green eggs and ham.* New York, NY: Random House, Beginner Books.

Sewell, A. (1986). *Black beauty.* New York, NY: Random House.

Shamir, A. (2009). Processes and outcomes of joint activity with e-books for promoting kindergarteners' emergent literacy. *Educational Media International, 46*(1), 81–96. doi:10.1080/09523980902781295

Shamir, A., & Korat, O. (2007). Developing educational e-book for fostering kindergarten children's emergent literacy. *Computers in the School, 24*, 125–143. doi:10.1300/J025v24n01_09

Share, D. L. (1999). Phonological recoding and orthographic learning: A direct test of the self-teaching hypothesis. *Journal of Experimental Child Psychology, 72*(2), 95–129. doi:10.1006/jecp.1998.2481

Sharmat, M. W. (1977). *Nate the great.* New York, NY: Yearling Books.

Sheehan, A. D., & Sheehan, C. M. (2000). Lost in a sea of ink: How I survived the storm. *Journal of Adolescent and Adult Literacy, 44*(1), 20–32.

Shmidman, A., & Ehri, L. (2010). Embedded picture mnemonics to learn letters. *Scientific Studies of Reading, 14*, 159–182. doi:10.1080/10888430903117492

Sidelnick, M. A., & Svoboda, M. L. (2000). The bridge between drawing and writing: Hannah's story. *Reading Teacher, 54*, 174–184. doi:10.1007/s10648-015-9335-1

Sienkiewicz-Mercer, R. (n.d.). *Things that ought to be on the Internet, but weren't: A speech by Ruth Sienkiewicz-Mercer.* Retrieved from http://text.oschene.com/rsm_speech.html

Sienkiewicz-Mercer, R., & Kaplan, S. B. (1989). *I raise my eyes to say yes.* Boston, MA: Houghton Mifflin Harcourt.

Simonsen, S. (1996). Identifying and teaching text structures in content area classrooms. In D. Lapp, J. Flood, & N. Farnan (Eds.), *Content area reading and learning: Instructional strategies* (2nd ed.). Boston, MA: Allyn & Bacon.

Singer, H., Samuels, S. J., & Spiroff, J. (1973–1974). The effect of pictures and contextual conditions on learning responses to printed words. *Reading Research Quarterly, 9*, 555–567. doi:10.2307/747002

Singh, N. N., & Solman, J. (1990). A stimulus control analysis of the picture-word problem in children who are mentally retarded: The blocking effect. *Journal of Applied Behavior Analysis, 23*, 525–532. doi:10.1901/jaba.1990.23-525

Skeide, M. A., Kumar, U., Mishra, R. K., Tripathi, V. N., Guleria, A., Singh, J. P., . . . Huettig, F. (2017). Learning to read alters cortico-subcortical cross-talk in the visual system of illiterates. *Neuroscience, 3*, e1602612. doi:10.1126/sciadv.1602612

Skibbe, L. E., Thompson, J. L., & Plavnick, J. B. (2018). Preschoolers' visual attention during electronic storybook reading as related to different types of textual supports. *Early Childhood Education Journal, 46*, 419-426. doi:10.1007/s10643-017-0876-4

Skinner, E. A., & Belmont, M. J. (1993). Motivation in the classroom: Reciprocal effects of teacher behavior and student engagement across the school year. *Journal of Educational Psychology, 85*, 571–581. doi:10.1037/0022-0663.85.4.571

Skotko, B., Koppenhaver, D., & Erickson, K. (2004). Parent reading behaviors and communication outcomes in girls with Rett syndrome. *Exceptional Children, 70*(4), 145–166. doi:10.1177/001440290407000202

Slater Software. (2008). *PixWriter*. Suffolk, VA: SunCastle Technology.

Smith, B. R., Spooner, F., Jimenez, B. A., & Browder, D. (2013). Using an early science curriculum to teach vocabulary and concepts to students with severe developmental disabilities. *Education and Treatment of Children, 36*(1), 1–31.

Smith, L. *It's a book*. New York, NY: Roaring Brook Press.

Snodgrass, M., Stoner, J., & Angell, M. (2013). Teaching conceptually referenced core vocabulary for initial augmentative and alternative communication. *Augmentative and Alternative Communication, 29*, 322–333. doi:10.3109/07434618.2013.848932

Snowling, M., & Hulme, C. (2005). Learning to read with a language impairment. In M. Snowling & C. Hulme (Eds.), *The science of reading: A handbook* (pp. 397–412). Malden, MA: Blackwell Publishing.

Spector, J. E. (2011). Sight word instruction for students with autism: An evaluation of the evidence base. *Journal of Autism and Developmental Disabilities, 41*, 1411–1422. doi:10.1007/s10803-010-1165-x

Spooner, F., Rivera, C. J., Browder, D. M., Baker, J. N., & Salas, S. (2009). Teaching emergent literacy skills using cultural contextual story-based lessons. *Research and Practice for Persons with Severe Disabilities, 34*, 102–112. doi:10.2511/rpsd.34.3-4.102

Spycher, P. (2009). Learning academic language through science in two linguistically diverse kindergarten classes. *Elementary School Journal, 109*, 359–379. doi:10.1086/593938

Stahl, S. (2005). Four problems with teaching word meanings (and what to do to make vocabulary an integral part of instruction). In E. H. Hiebert & M. L. Kamil (Eds.), *Teaching and learning vocabulary: Bringing research to practice* (pp. 95–114). Mahwah, NJ: Lawrence Erlbaum Associates.

Stahl, S. A., & Kapinus, B. (2001). *Word power: What every educator needs to know about teaching vocabulary*. Washington, DC: National Education Association.

Stahl, S. A., & Murray, B. A. (1994). Defining phonological awareness and its relationship to early reading. *Journal of Educational Psychology, 86*, 221–234. doi:10.1037/0022-0663.86.2.221

Stahl, S. A., & Nagy, W. E. (2006). *Teaching word meanings*. Mahwah, NJ: Lawrence Erlbaum Associates.

Stanovich, K. E. (1980). Toward an interactive-compensatory model of individual differences in the development of reading fluency. *Reading Research Quarterly, 16*, 32–71. doi:10.2307/747348

Stanovich, K. E. (2000). *Progress in understanding reading: Scientific foundations and new frontiers*. New York, NY: Guilford Press.

Stanovich, K. E., Cunningham, A. E., & Freeman, D. J. (1984). Intelligence, cognitive skills, and early reading progress. *Reading Research Quarterly, 19*, 278–303. doi:10.2307/747822

Stanovich, K. E., West, R. F., Cunningham, A. E., Cipielewski, J., & Siddiqui, S. (1996). The role of inadequate print exposure as a determinant of reading comprehension problems. In C. Cornoldi & J. Oakhill (Eds.), *Reading comprehension disabilities: Processes and intervention* (pp. 15–32). Mahwah, NJ: Lawrence Erlbaum Associates.

Staples, A., & Edmister, E. (2012). Evidence of two theoretical models observed in young children with disabilities who are beginning to learn to write. *Topics in Language Disorders, 32*(4), 319–334. doi:10.1097/TLD.0b013e3182724d29

Stauffer, R. (1975). *Directing the reading-thinking process.* New York, NY: Harper & Row.

Storrie, P. D. (2007). *Hercules: The twelve labors.* Minneapolis, MN: Lerner Publishing.

Strouse, G. A., & Ganea, P. A. (2017). A print book preference: Caregivers report higher child enjoyment and more adult–child interactions when reading print than electronic books. *International Journal of Child-Computer Interaction, 12,* 8–15. doi:10.1016/j.ijcci.2017.02.001

Sullivan, A., & Brown, M. (2013). *Social inequalities in cognitive scores at age 16: The role of reading.* London, England: Centre for Longitudinal Studies.

Sulzby, E. (1985). Kindergarteners as writers and readers. In M. Farr (Ed.), *Advances in writing research: Children's early writing development* (Vol. 1, pp. 127–199). Norwood, NJ: Ablex.

Sulzby, E. (1991). The development of the young child and the emergence of literacy. In J. Flood, J. Jensen, D. Lapp, & J. R. Squire (Eds.), *The handbook of research in the teaching of the English language arts* (pp. 273–285). New York, NY: Macmillan.

Sulzby, E., Branz, C. M., & Buhle, R. (1993). Repeated readings of literature and low socioeconomic status black kindergartners and first graders. *Reading and Writing Quarterly, 9,* 183–196. doi:10.1080/1057356930090205

Sumner, E., Connelly, V., & Barnett, A. L. (2014). The influence of spelling ability on vocabulary choices when writing for children with dyslexia. *Journal of Learning Disabilities, 49,* 293–304. doi:10.1177/0022219414552018

Sun, K. K., & Kemp, C. (2006). The acquisition of phonological awareness and its relationship to reading in individuals with intellectual disabilities. *Australasian Journal of Special Education, 30,* 86–99. doi:10.1080/10300110609409367

Swanson, E. A. (2008). Observing reading instruction for students with LD: A synthesis. *Learning Disability Quarterly, 31,* 1–19. doi:10.2307/25474643

Swanson, E. A., Solis, M., Ciullo, S., & McKenna, J. W. (2012). Special education teachers' perceptions and instructional practices in response to intervention implementation. *Learning Disability Quarterly, 35,* 115–126. doi:10.1177/0731948711432510

Taub, D., Apgar, J., Foster, M., Ryndak, D. L., Burdge, M. D., & Letson, S. (2019). Investigating the alignment between English language arts curricula developed for students with significant intellectual disability and the CCSS. *Remedial and Special Education.* doi:10.1177/0741932519843184

Teale, W. H., & Sulzby, E. (1986). *Emergent literacy: Writing and reading.* Norwood, NJ: Ablex Publishing Corp.

Technology-Related Assistance for Individuals with Disabilities Act of 1988, PL 100-407, 29 U.S.C. §§ 2201 *et seq.*

Tefft Cousin, P., Weekley, T., & Gerard, J. (1993). The functional uses of language and literacy by students with severe language and learning problems. *Language Arts, 70*(7), 548–556.

Towles-Reeves, E., Kearns, J., Flowers, C., Hart, L., Kerbel, A., Kleinert, H., & Thurlow, M. (2012). *Learner characteristics inventory project report.* Minneapolis, MN: University of Minnesota.

Towles-Reeves, E., Kearns, J., Kleinert, H., & Kleinert, J. (2009). An analysis of the learning characteristics of students taking alternate assessments based on alternate achievement standards. *Journal of Special Education, 42,* 241–254. doi:10.1177/0022466907313451

Trabasso, T., & Bouchard, E. (2002). Teaching readers how to comprehend text strategically. In C. Collins & M. Pressley (Eds.), *Comprehension instruction: Research-based best practices* (pp. 176–200). New York, NY: Guilford Press.

Travers, J. C., Higgins, K., Pierce, T., Boone, R., Miller, S., & Tandy, R. (2011). Emergent literacy skills of preschool students with autism: A comparison of teacher-led and computer-assisted instruction. *Education and Training in Autism and Developmental Disabilities, 46,* 326–338. http://daddcec.org/Publications/ETADDJournal.aspx

Treiman, R., Levin, I., & Kessler, B. (2007). Learning of letter names follows similar principles across languages: Evidence from Hebrew. *Journal of Experimental Child Psychology, 96,* 87–106. doi:10.1016/j.jecp.2006.08.002

Treiman, R., Pennington, B., Shriberg, L., & Boada, R. (2008). Which children benefit from letter names in learning letter sounds? *Cognition, 106,* 1322–1338. doi:10.1016/j.cognition .2007.06.006.

Treiman, R., & Rodriguez, K. (1999). Young children use letter names in learning to read words. *Psychological Science, 10,* 334–338. doi:10.1111/1467-9280.00164

Trenholm, B., & Mirenda, P. (2006). Home and community literacy experiences of individuals with Down syndrome. *The Down Syndrome Educational Trust, 10,* 30–40. doi:10.3104 /reports.303

Turnbull, K., Bowles, R. P., Skibbe, L. E., Justice, L. M., & Wiggins, A. K. (2010). Theoretical explanations for preschoolers' lowercase alphabet knowledge. *Journal of Speech, Language, and Hearing Research, 53,* 1757–1768. doi:10.1044/1092-4388(2010/09-0093.

U.S. Department of Education. (2010). *A blueprint for reform: The reauthorization of the Elementary and Secondary Education Act.* Washington, DC: Office of Planning. Retrieved from https://www2.ed.gov/policy/elsec/leg/blueprint/blueprint.pdf

U.S. Department of Education, Institute of Education Sciences, National Center for Education Statistics. (2015a, October 22). *The NAEP reading achievement levels by grade.* Retrieved from https://nces.ed.gov/nationsreportcard/reading/achieve.aspx

U.S. Department of Education, Institute of Education Sciences, National Center for Education Statistics. (2015b). *The nation's report card: 2015 mathematics and reading assessments.* Retrieved from https://www.nationsreportcard.gov/reading_math_2015 /#?grade=4

U.S. Department of Education, Institute of Education Sciences, What Works Clearinghouse. (2015, April). *Shared book reading.* Retrieved from https://files.eric.ed.gov/fulltext /ED555654.pdf

U.S. Department of Education, Institute of Education Sciences, National Center for Education Statistics, National Assessment of Educational Progress. (2017). *The nation's report card: 2017 NAEP reading report card.* Retrieved from https://www.nationsreportcard.gov/reading _2017/report-page?grade=4&nation=achievement-group

U.S. Society for Augmentative and Alternative Communication. (2016, Nov. 1). *Bylaws of the United States Society for Augmentative and Alternative Communication.* Retrieved from https://ussaac.org/wp-content/uploads/2018/07/bylaws.pdf

van der Schuit, M., Peeters, M., Segers, E., Van Balkom, H., & Verhoeven, L. (2009). Home literacy environment of pre-school children with intellectual disabilities. *Journal of Intellectual Disability Research, 53,* 1024–1037. doi: 10.1111/j.1365-2788.2009.01222.x

van der Schuit, M., Segers, E., van Balkom, H., & Verhoeven, L. (2011). How cognitive factors affect language development in children with intellectual disabilities. *Research in Developmental Disabilities, 32,* 1884–1894. doi:10.1016/j.ridd.2011.03.015

van Kraayenoord, C. E., Moni, K. B., Jobling, A., Koppenhaver D. A., & Elkins, J. (2004). Developing the writing of middle school students with developmental disabilities: The WriteIdeas model of writing. *Literacy Learning: The Middle Years, 12,* 36-46.

Van Tatenhove, G. M. (2009). Building language competence with students using AAC devices: Six challenges. *SIG 12 Perspectives on Augmentative and Alternative Communication, 18,* 38–47. doi:10.1044/aac18.2.38

van Wingerden, E., Segers, E., van Balkom, H., & Verhoeven, L. (2014). Cognitive and linguistic predictors of reading comprehension in children with intellectual disabilities. *Research in Developmental Disabilities, 35,* 3139–3147. doi:10.1016/j.ridd.2014.07.054

Verhallen, M. J. A. J., Bus, A. G., & de Jong, M. T. (2006). The promise of multimedia stories for kindergarten children at risk. *Journal of Educational Psychology, 98*(2), 410–419. doi:10.1037/0022-0663.98.2.410

Verucci, L., Menghini, D., & Vicari, S. (2006). Reading skills and phonological awareness acquisition in Down syndrome. *Journal of Intellectual Disability Research, 50,* 477–491. doi:10.1111/j.1365-2788.2006.00793.x

Wang, J. H., & Guthrie, J. T. (2004). Modeling the effects of intrinsic motivation, extrinsic motivation, amount of reading, and past reading achievement on text comprehension between U.S. and Chinese students. *Reading Research Quarterly, 39,* 162–186. doi:10.1598 /RRQ.39.2.2

Wasik, B. A. (2008). When fewer is more: Small groups in early childhood classrooms. *Early Childhood Education Journal, 35,* 515–521. doi:10.1007/s10643-008-0245-4

Waugh, R. E., Fredrick, L. D., & Alberto, P. A. (2009). Using simultaneous prompting to teach sounds and blending skills to students with moderate intellectual disabilities. *Research in Developmental Disabilities, 30,* 1435–1447. doi:10.1016/j.ridd.2009.07.004

Wendon, L., & Carter, S. (2014). *Phonics teacher's guide 2014: Teach all 44 sounds of the English language.* Baron, Cambridge, England: Letterland International.

Wentzel, K. R. (2009). Students' relationships with teachers as motivational contexts. In K. R. Wentzel & A. Wigfield (Eds.), *Handbook of motivation at school* (pp. 301–322). New York, NY: Routledge/Taylor & Francis Group.

Wershing, A., & Hughes, C. (2002). Just give me words. In K. Erickson, D. Koppenhaver, & D. Yoder (Eds.), *Waves of words: Augmentative communicators read and write* (pp. 45–56). Toronto, Ontario, Canada: ISAAC Press.

Whitehurst, G. J., & Lonigan, C. J. (1998). Child development and emergent literacy. *Child Development, 69,* 848–872. https://doi.org/10.1111/j.1467-8624.1998.tb06247.x

Widgit Software. (2002). *Writing with symbols 2000* (Version 2.6) [Computer software]. Warwickshire, United Kingdom: Author.

Wigfield, A., Eccles, J. S., Fredricks, J. A., Simpkins, S., Roeser, R. W., & Schiefele, U. (2015). Development of achievement motivation and engagement. In M. E. Lamb & R. M. Lerner (Eds.), *Handbook of child psychology and developmental science* (Vol. 3, 7th ed., pp. 657–700). New York, NY: Wiley.

Wigfield, A., & Guthrie, J. T. (1997). Motivation for reading: An overview. *Educational Psychologist, 32,* 57–58. doi: 10.1207/s15326985ep3202_1

Williams, A., Koppenhaver, D., & Wollak, B. (2007). Email interactions of preservice teachers and adolescents with special needs. *American Reading Forum: Yearbook, 27.* Retrieved from http://americanreadingforum.org/yearbook/yearbooks/07_yearbook/html/arf_07_Williams.htm)

Wolf, M. (2007). *Proust and the squid.* New York, NY: HarperCollins.

Wollak, B. A., & Koppenhaver, D. A. (2011). Developing technology-supported, evidence-based writing instruction for adolescents with significant writing disabilities. *Assistive Technology Outcomes and Benefits, 7,* 1–23. Retrieved from https://www.atia.org/wp-content/uploads/2015/10/ATOBV7N1.pdf

Wood, W. C. (2010). *Literacy and the entry-level workforce: The role of literacy and policy in labor market statistics.* Washington, DC: Employment Policies Institute.

World Health Organization (2010). *Framework for action on interprofessional education and collaborative Practice.* World Health Organization. Retrieved from http://whqlibdoc.who.int/hq/2010/WHO_HRH_HPN_10.3_eng.pdf?ua=1

Wylie, R., & Durrell, D. (1970). Teaching vowels through phonograms. *Elementary English, 47,* 787–791. https://www.jstor.org/journal/elemengl

Yoder, D. E. (2000). *Having my say.* Keynote presentation at the biennial meeting of the International Society for Augmentative and Alternative Communication (ISAAC), Washington, DC.

Yoder, D. E. (2001). Having my say. *Augmentative and Alternative Communication, 17,* 2–10. https://doi.org/10.1080/aac.17.1.2.10

Zabala, J. (2005). Ready, SETT, go! Getting started with the SETT framework. *Closing the Gap, 23*(6), 1–3. http://www.joyzabala.com/uploads/Zabala_CTG_Ready_SETT_.pdf

Zelinsky, P. O. (1990). *The wheels on the bus.* New York, NY: Dutton Books for Young Readers/Penguin Random House.

Index

NOTE: Page numbers followed by *f* indicate figures; *t* indicates tables.

AAC, *see* Augmentative and alternative communication
Alliteration, teaching of, 44, 44*t*
Alphabet awareness
   development of, 36–48
   explicit, targeted instruction, 36
Alphabet books, 45
Alphabet instruction, embedded, 45–47
Alphabet knowledge, 5*t*, 10–11, 33–35
   language, letters, and sounds, 48
Alphabet puzzles and games, 45–46
Alphabetic principle, 5*t*, 45
Alternate pencils, 5*t*
Anchor, 131–132
Anchor-Read-Apply structure
   anchor activities and purpose, 109–110, 113*f*, 115*f*
   apply what you read, 114, 115*f*
   choosing texts for lessons, 109
   KWL, DR-TA, and other formats, 115–117
   reading comprehension, 95
ASD, *see* Autism spectrum disorder
Assistive technology (AT), 185–198
   getting it up and running, 194–197
   making good decisions, 197
   Red Yellow Green, 196–197, 197*f*
   SETT framework, 194
   support of access to materials and productivity, 191–194
   support of communication, 189–191
   support of literacy, 189–194
   symbol-supported text and, 185–188, 186*f*
   team decisions about, 188–189
Auditory word sorts lesson sequence, 177
Augmentative and alternative communication (AAC), 3–4, 17
   modifying activity for, 111
   providing access to, 190–191
   vocabulary instruction tailored for, 108
Autism spectrum disorder (ASD), 6

Background knowledge, activation, 110
Big Paper, 71
Boy and Girl Scout Troops, help for classroom library, 126
Build knowledge of text structures, 110–111

Can't-stop writing, 145–146
Captioned movies and video clips, 61–62
Celebration of student writing, 71–72
Church groups, help for classroom library, 126
Class experience lists, 146
Classroom library, 121–126
   diverse collection, 121–122
   possibilities for, 122
   range of genres, 123–124
   tips for building on a budget, 124–126
Cognitive clarity, 20
Cognitive engagement, 19–20
Communication
   core vocabulary, 190
   robust solutions, 189–190
   assistive technology (AT) in support of, 189–191
Communications book, 4
Community help, for classroom library, 126
Compare/contrast lessons, 176
Composition skills, teaching of, 151–152
Comprehension, definition, 100–102
Comprehensive instruction, 24–25, 108–111
   activities of, 25*f*
   anchor activities and purpose, 109–110, 113*f*, 115*f*
   choosing texts for lessons, 109
   keeping an eye on the prize, 117
   providing informative feedback, 115
Comprehensive literacy-based instruction, 87–98, 88*t*
   creation of a program, 199–208
   how parents can help, 208
   how to know when it is working, 210
   organizing and delivering, 199–211
   origins of, 87–88
   planning for a group, 200–204, 201*f*
   scheduling time to teach, 204, 205*f*
   skills, comprehension, and composition, 98
   in a specific curriculum, 209
   specific definitions, 93–94
   teaching in general education settings, 205–206
   teaching in multiple settings, 207–208
   teaching in separate special education settings, 206–207

Comprehensive literacy-based instruction—
     continued
  why focus on literacy, 209–210
  why is it needed?, 92–93
Comprehensive literacy decision making, 201*f*
Computer program reading of text, 61
Computers and apps, 46
Concept of word, 5*t*
Conceptual knowledge, functions of print
     and self-perceptions, 6
Connection, focus on, 105–106
Core vocabulary, 3–4, 5*t*
  Augmentative and alternative
     communication solutions, 190
  high-frequency, 4
  universal, in Augmentative and alternative
     communication, 190–191, 191*f*
Core vocabulary words, 127–128, 127*t*
Cross-checking, self-correction strategy, 179
CROWD, 56–58, 58*f*

Day-to-day writing demonstrations, 76
Decoding, 163–181
  analogy-based approach to, 171–179
  with a mixed group, 203
  spelling-based approach to, 167–171
  why we teach, 165
Developmental appropriateness, 128
Dialogic reading, 56
Dialogic writing, 147
Directed Reading-Thinking Activity, 116–117
Discuss, 132
DR-TA, *see* Directed Reading-Thinking Activity
Drawing, 145

Editing, 152–153
Electronic books, 59–60
Embedded approaches to instruction, 44–48
Emergent literacy, 4–5
  beginnings of, 13–14
  theoretical models of, 6–7
Emergent literacy comprehensive
     instruction, 7–13
  alphabet knowledge and phonological
     awareness, 10–11
  independent reading, 11–12
  independent writing, 12–13
  shared reading, 8–9
  shared writing, 9–10
  time estimates for, 205*f*
Emergent readers, 49–51
  teaching in general education settings,
     205–206
Emergent reading, 49–62
  definition, 49
  encouragement of, 62

Emergent writers, teaching in general
     education settings, 205–206
Emergent writing, 63–84
  definition, 64
  fostering of, 83–84
  getting started, 69–75
  pair with pictures, 74
  pair with student read-alouds, 74–75
  progression over time, 65–69, 66*f*, 67*f*, 68*f*,
     69*f*, 70*f*
  supporting growth toward conventional
     writing, 75–83
  welcoming community, 72
Engagement, 103–104
  texts easy enough for, 126–133
Enhanced alphabet instruction, 37–38
Environmental print, 46
Explicit alphabet knowledge, 36–38
  instructional routine, 39
Explicit phonological awareness instruction,
     40–44

Familiarity of texts, 59
Five finger test, 129
Follow the CAR, 54–56, 55*f*, 58*f*
Following along as partner reads, 61

Gap-filling inferences, 101, 101*t*
General education settings, teaching
     comprehensive literacy in, 205–206
Generative writing
  helping students transition to, 150–162
  modeling and demonstrations, 151
  print-poor environments, 151
  teach through revision, 153–155
  teaching composition skills, 151–152
  written dialogue and cloze statements, 151
Gimme 5, 145

Handwriting, 153
High expectations, 26–27

Independent reading, 11–12, 60–62
Independent writing, 12–13
  with a mixed group, 204
Individuals with Disabilities Education
     Improvement Act (IDEA), assistive
     technology and, 185
Informative feedback, in reading
     comprehension, 115
Inside-out literacy processes and skills, 5*t*, 6
Intellectual disabilities, 3
Interactive read-alouds, 105
International Communication Project, 17

Just do it, 146

Key literacy terms, 5t
Keywords, 173t
Knowledgeable others, 16–17
KWL, 115–116, 116f

Language comprehension, 5t, 90
Learning. *see* Literacy learning
Letter form production, 39
Letter identification, 39
Letter knowledge, 6
Letter recognition in text, 39
Letter sound identification, 39
Listen, 132
Listen with purpose, 112
Listening comprehension, 88t
Literacy Bill of Rights, 28
Literacy learning
  cognitive engagement, 19–20
  cognitive clarity, 20
  communication and interaction, 17–18
  comprehensive instruction, 24–25
  conditions for success, 15–16
  encouragement of risk taking, 22–23
  environment for, 30
  high expectations, 26–27
  knowledgeable others, 16–17
  personal connection to curriculum, 21–22
  repetition with variety, 18–19
  significant time allocation, 26
Local resources for books, 124–125
Logographic approach, 164

Make and publish the book, 83, 83f
Making Words, 167–171
  sample lesson, 170–171
  small-group or individual lessons, 169–171
  whole-class lessons, 167–169, 168t
Means of communication and interaction, 17–18
Memory game, 43
Mentor texts, 147–148
Metalinguistic awareness, 5t
Metalinguistic skills, phonological and syntactic awareness, 6
Mini-grants, for classroom library, 125
Mini-lesson instruction, in self-directed reading, 137–138, 138t
Mixed group
  decoding, spelling and word identification for, 203
  independent writing, 204
  predictable chart writing, 203
  self-directed reading with, 203

shared reading with, 202
  writing instruction, 204
Mnemonics, 40
Morning message, 76
Motivation and engagement, 103–104
Motivation to read, 119–120

Nursery rhymes, raps, and poetry, 47

Older students, facilitation of self-directed reading for, 138–139
One-on-one conferences, in independent reading time, 135–136
Online books, viewing or reading, 61
Online reading resources, free, 125
Onset-Rime, analogy-based approach to decoding, 171–179
Opportunities to demonstrate writing, 78–79
Oral language knowledge and comprehension, 5t, 6
Outside-in literacy process and skills, 5t
Outside-in processes, 6

Partner-assisted pencils, 5t
PEER, 56
Personal connection to curriculum, 21–22
Phonemic awareness, 5t
  versus phonological awareness, 34
Phonemic awareness skills, 41
Phonetic spelling, 4
Phonics, 5t
Phonological awareness, 5t, 10–11, 35–36
  development of, 36–48
  embedded instruction, 47–48
  explicit, targeted instruction, 36
  language, letters, and sounds, 48
  with a mixed group, 203
  versus phonemic awareness, 34
Photo collections and categories, 144–145
Picture books (wordless), 127
Prealphabetic approach, 164
Predictable chart, 79–83, 82f, 83f, 173
  with a mixed group, 203
Predictable texts, 128, 129t
Print concepts, 5t, 6
Print functions, 5t, 6
Print referencing, 58
Procedural knowledge, letters, sounds, and words, 6
Processor model, word reading, 165–167, 166f
Project Core, 4
Providing practice in context, 179–180
Publish student writing, 73
Purposes for reading, 111–112, 113f, 115f

Read-alouds, 131
(Re)read what you write, 156
Read with purpose, 112
Reading, assistive technology to support
    access, 192
Reading comprehension, 5t, 94–95, 99–113
    with a mixed group, 202–203
Reading environment, creation of, 133
Reading materials (texts), selection of, 58–59
Reading stamina, development of, 134–135
Reconceptualize "just right" books, 130–131
Red Yellow Green, implementation of
    assistive technology decisions, 196–197,
    197f
Repetition with variety, 18–19
Responses from classmates, education for,
    149–150
Responses from families and visitors,
    education for, 150
Revision
    see as a possibility, 161–162
    independent, 155–156
    student understanding of, 156–159, 157f,
    158f, 159f
    teach writing through, 153–155
Reward programs, replace with celebrations,
    139–140
Rhyme awareness teaching, 42–44, 43f
Risk taking, encouragement of, 22–23
Rounding Up the Rhymes
    sample lesson, 172f
    teaching spelling patterns, 171–173
Rule of thumb, 129

Segmenting words into syllables, 41–42
Self-directed reading, 95–96, 119–140
    getting up and running, 134–139
    with a mixed group, 203
    for older students, 138–139
    strategies to reduce or eliminate, 132–133
    why we teach, 120–121
Sentence strips, 81–83, 82f
SETT framework, 194
    environment, 195
    student, 195
    task, 195
    tools, 195
Shared reading, 8–9, 47–48, 51–54
    with a mixed group, 202
    structured and unstructured approaches,
    53–54
Shared writing, 9–10
Sign in, up, or out, 77–78, 77t
Significant time allocation, 26
Silent reading comprehension, 88–89, 88t, 89f
Simplified (or wordless) texts, 127
Single-message voice output device, 3

Small-group or individual lessons, Making
    Words, 169–171
Sound knowledge, 6
Special education settings, teaching
    comprehensive literacy in, 206–207
Spelling, 152, 163–181
    with a mixed group, 203
    role in communication, 17
    why we teach, 165
    words in meaningful writing contexts, 180
Spelling-based approach, Making Words,
    167–171
Spelling-based word sort lesson sequence,
    178–179
Spelling patterns, Rounding Up the Rhymes,
    171–173
Spelling word sorts, 177–178
Splint, 3
Student behaviors, intense, how to get
    started, 209
Student interests, use to motivate writing,
    162
Student names, use in teaching, 46
Student needs, comprehensive, integrated
    approach to, 167
Student sharing, in self-directed reading, 137
Symbolic communications, 17–18
Syntactic awareness, 5t

Talk about reading, in self-directed reading,
    135
Teacher book talks, 136–137
Teacher created texts, predictable charts
    and, 79–83, 82f, 83f, 173
Topic choice, developing writers, 144–146

Universal core vocabulary, 190–191, 191f
Use of time in self-directed reading, 134
Used books, for classroom library, 126

Variability of student reading, 74
Visual strategy, 164
Visual word sorts, 177
Vocabulary, definition, 102–103
Vocabulary instruction, 99–113
    focus on connection, 105–106
    tailored for augmentative and alternative
    communication students, 108
    three tiers of, 107, 107t
    which words to teach, 106–107

Welcome to Our Classroom poster, 73
Whole-class lessons, Making Words, 167–169
Whole-text print processing, 90–91

Whole-to-part (WTP) model, silent reading
    comprehension, 88–89, 89*f*
Wide reading to build automaticity, 180
Word chaining, 105–106
Word curiosity, 104–105
Word identification, 88*t*, 89–90, 163–181
    with a mixed group, 203
    why we teach, 165
Word knowledge, 5*t*, 6
Word reading, processor model, 165–167, 166*f*
Word sorts, 177
Word study, 97
Word wall, 173–176
    reinforcing learned words, 175–176
    selecting words, 174
    setting up display, 174
    teaching new words, 174–175
WTP, *see* Whole-to-part model, silent
    reading comprehension
Write for immediate audiences, 159–160,
    160*f*, 161*f*

Writing, 141–162
    assistive technology to support access,
        192–194, 193*f*
    encouraging beginners, 143–150
    improvement through experience, 162
    judging effectiveness of, 160–161, 160*f*,
        161*f*
    responding to, 148–149, 149*t*
    teaching of, 141–142
Writing environments, accepting and
        responsive, 149–150
Writing experiment, 143–144, 143*f*
Writing instruction, 97
    with a mixed group, 204
Writing models and demonstrations,
        146–148
    mentor texts to teach text structure,
        147–148
    Now you see it, now you don't, 146–147
    tell me more with dialogic writing, 147
Writing tools and surfaces, 69–71, 71*t*